DATE DUE

DEMCO 38-296

BEYOND THE GREAT WALL

BEYOND THE GREAT WALL

*Urban Form and Transformation
on the Chinese Frontiers*

Piper Rae Gaubatz

STANFORD UNIVERSITY PRESS, STANFORD, CALIFORNIA, 1996

Stanford University Press
Stanford, California
© 1996 by the Board of Trustees of the
Leland Stanford Junior University

Printed in the United States of America

CIP data appear at the end of the book

Stanford University Press publications are distributed exclusively by
Stanford University Press within the United States, Canada, Mexico,
and Central America; they are distributed exclusively by Cambridge
University Press throughout the rest of the world.

Original printing 1996
Last figure below indicates year of this printing:
04   03   02   01   00   99   98   97   96   95

For James E. Vance, Jr.
and Hou Renzhi

Preface

The Great Wall is much more than the ancient series of defensive walls and fortifications that stretches along the traditional northern borders of the heartland of China. It is also a symbol of the persistence of Chinese culture over centuries and the historical divide between the Chinese people and their early homeland and the peoples and lands beyond. This book explores the foundation, development, and distinctive forms of Chinese outpost cities established in those lands over the past 21 centuries. It focuses on five cities. Hohhot, the capital of Inner Mongolia, Xining, the capital of Qinghai Province, and Urumqi, the capital of the Xinjiang Uygur Autonomous Region, all lay beyond the Great Wall. Lanzhou, the capital of Gansu Province, was during different periods either beyond the wall or just inside it. Kunming, the capital of Yunnan Province, is representative of the many cities the Chinese established on their southern and southwestern frontiers, a realm to which the Great Wall was never extended but that was equally geographically and culturally beyond the Chinese heartland. These Chinese frontier outposts, established in regions inhabited by Mongols, Tibetans, Uygur, and other peoples, have all survived to the present through centuries of the expansion and contraction of the Chinese empire across the vast expanses of the frontier. They serve as lasting monuments to the tenacity of Chinese culture in the sometimes perilous and resource-poor frontier regions. Yet they also demonstrate the flexibility of that culture in coexisting with local cultures and creating multicultural cities. In the following pages, I examine the beliefs, ideals, and practices that influenced the founders, administrators, and Chinese and non-Chinese residents of these cities, and the ways in which the interaction between those beliefs and the realities of frontier life shaped urban form, landscapes, and architecture. This book thus not only addresses the issue of frontier urbanization in multicultural settings, but also explores the nature and character of urbanization in the core area.

This book is a study of historical and contemporary urban geography. Like many geographical studies, it integrates perspectives from a number of different fields—in this case history, anthropology, architecture, and planning—with fieldwork. The research involved twelve months of urban fieldwork and extensive work with both Chinese and non-Chinese literature in these fields. I hope the resulting synthesis will be of interest to readers with a range of different backgrounds in Asian, urban, and frontier studies.

This project began, as perhaps most good geographies should, with a long look at a map and a journey. Studying maps of ethnicity in China in 1985, while a graduate student in geography at the University of California, Berkeley, I was intrigued by the border area between Qinghai and Gansu provinces, a region where Han Chinese, Tibetan, and Mongolian cultures meet. As an urban geographer with strong interests in both urban morphology and cultural geography, I wondered how cities would be shaped in such a cultural milieu. I traveled to the region in the summer of 1986 and found a fascinating blend of urban styles and traditions, which, although changing rapidly under China's post-1979 economic transformation, seemed to reflect centuries of interaction between the peoples of the region. When I returned to the United States, I formulated a dissertation proposal and applied for funding to explore the historical development of the multicultural city of Xining, Qinghai Province. In 1987, I was awarded dissertation research grants by the Committee on Scholarly Communication with the People's Republic of China (CSCPRC, now the Committee on Scholarly Communication with China) and the Fulbright Doctoral Dissertation Research Abroad (DDRA) program. Before beginning my research in China, I accompanied my colleague from the University of California at Berkeley, Stan Stevens, while he conducted dissertation field research in the Mount Everest region of Nepal. In discussing fieldwork approaches, we explored the idea of enlarging the regional context of my study and concluded that my project would be more effective as a more broad-based, comparative study, encompassing a wider range of Chinese frontier situations. I decided to broaden the project to the five cities that are the focus of this book: Xining, Lanzhou, Hohhot, Urumqi, and Kunming.

I conducted fieldwork in China from September 1987 to October 1988, during which time I was hosted by the Geography Department at

Beijing University as a "Senior Advanced Research Student." I was assigned three advisers: Hou Renzhi, Han Mukang, and Yu Xixian. These three proved remarkably effective not only in helping to guide my research, but in providing the recommendations and contacts necessary to carry out research in the far frontier regions of China. I am particularly grateful to Hou Renzhi for our many broad-ranging discussions of urban geography, to Yu Xixian for his insights into traditional urban form, and to Han Mukang for being one of the most effective facilitators I have ever met.

Upon my return to the United States in late 1988, I began to write the dissertation on which this book is based. In 1989, I received a one-year postdoctoral fellowship from the East-West Center in Honolulu, Hawaii, in order to transform the dissertation into a book manuscript. During my year in Hawaii, I conducted further research, which included a trip to the Toyo Bunko (East Asia Library) in Tokyo supported by the East-West Center, and substantially rewrote and reorganized the manuscript to such a degree that the book now bears only a superficial resemblance to the dissertation. I am grateful to the East-West Center for providing me with the support to carry out those revisions, and particularly to Elizabeth Buck, Tu Weiming, Gerard Finin, Huma Ghosh, Tom Maschio, Coralee Cooper, and Richard Smith for their input and companionship during that year.

There are a number of individuals and institutions I would like to thank for their kind assistance on this project. In China, in addition to Hou Renzhi, Han Mukang, and Yu Xixian at Beijing University, I would particularly like to acknowledge the assistance of Buyankuu, Institute of Mongolian History, Inner Mongolia University; Guo Laixi, Director, Institute of Geography, Chinese Academy of Sciences, Yunnan Province; Liu Man, Department of Chinese, Lanzhou University; Wang Cheng, Chief, China International Travel Service, Xining Branch; Xian Xiaowei, Department of Geography, Lanzhou University and Sichuan Normal University; Zhao Weicheng, Deputy Director, Institute of Geography, Chinese Academy of Sciences, Yunnan Province; and Zhu Liangwen, Cochairman, Department of Architecture, Yunnan Institute of Technology. I would also like to thank the many helpful staff members and graduate students I worked with during the course of my research from the Department of Geography, Beijing University; the Geography Institute of the Chinese Academy of Sciences, Beijing; the Qinghai Institute of Minorities, Xining; the Grasslands Research Institute, Xining; the Institute of Archaeological Research, Urumqi; the Architectural Preservation Office,

Urumqi; the Geography Department of Yunnan Normal University, Kunming; and the Geography Department of Lanzhou University. Special thanks to Ann Marie Grathwol, Eleanor Lavine, Dallas McCurley, and Jocelyn Tan for their friendship at Beijing University.

In the United States I would like to express my appreciation to James Vance of the Department of Geography, University of California at Berkeley, for his excellent work as the chair of my dissertation committee. I would also like to thank Robert Reed and Bernard Nietschmann of the same department and Thomas Gold of the Department of Sociology for their support through the course of this project. Thanks are also due to Roger Michener of the Department of Sociology, Princeton University, for recommending that I explore geography as a field of graduate study; to Carville Earle of the Department of Geography and Anthropology, Louisiana State University, for recommending that I publish the book with Stanford University Press; and to Dru Gladney of the East-West Center and Sen-dou Chang of the Department of Geography, University of Hawaii, for reading drafts of this manuscript and providing valuable suggestions.

I would also like to acknowledge the support of the Committee on Scholarly Communication with China, and particularly Kyna Rubin, in providing not only funding for the project but ongoing logistical support throughout the research period. I am also grateful to the Fulbright Doctoral Dissertation Research Abroad program for supporting my dissertation research.

I have benefited from the help of many staff members at a number of libraries and archival collections where I conducted research for this project. I would like to thank those who assisted me at the East Asian Collection and the Center for Chinese Studies library at the University of California, Berkeley; Green Library at Stanford University; the East Asian Collection at the Hoover Institution; the Map Collection at the University of Washington, Seattle; the Map Collection at the Library of Congress; the Photographic Collection at the National Archives; the East Asia Collection at the University of Hawaii; the library at Beijing University; the library at Yunnan Normal University; and the Toyo Bunko.

At Stanford University Press, I would like to express my appreciation to the many capable staff members who have contributed their skills to this project, specifically Muriel Bell, Jan Spauschus Johnson, Peter Kahn, Amy Klatzkin, and John Ziemer.

I owe a special vote of gratitude to all of my family, and especially to my parents, Don and Cathy Gaubatz, for their support throughout this project and for their many letters, which have always been a highlight of my trips to China. My uncle Larry Stitt was also very supportive in encouraging me to continue my education. Most of all, I would like to thank my husband, Stan Stevens, for his substantial contributions to this work. Whether accompanying me to drink tea with the imam of a mosque in Xinjiang or proofreading late into the night in California, his thoughtful insights and challenging questions have always inspired me to reach for new heights.

Finally, a brief word about conventions and style. With the exception of some place-names, such as Urumqi and Hohhot, and a few departures noted in the text, all Chinese terms are romanized in the Pinyin system. Proper names like Chinggis Khan are given in their conventional form. All maps are diagrammatic representations and not necessarily drawn to absolute scale. They were prepared by me using the Aldus Freehand program on both Macintosh and IBM-compatible computers. All photographs are mine unless otherwise noted.

P.R.G.

Contents

Photographs follow pages 182 and 288

Maps, Tables, and Figures

MAPS

TABLES

FIGURES

BEYOND THE GREAT WALL

Introduction

Over the course of more than two thousand years of history, the Chinese have established scores of cities in the broad expanse of continental frontier reaching from the grasslands of Mongolia to Central Asia, the Qinghai-Tibet plateau, and the rugged highlands on the borders of Southeast Asia. This study explores the patterns and processes of Chinese urban settlement on the frontiers from ancient times to the present day and focuses on five large cities in the western borderlands: Kunming, in the highlands of southwest China's Yunnan Province; Lanzhou, the first city on the Yellow River as it flows east toward China's heartland and the last Chinese city before the desert stretches of the westward Silk Routes;[1] Xining, on the northeasternmost reaches of the Tibetan plateau; Hohhot, at the edge of the Mongolian grasslands; and Urumqi, a Chinese outpost in Central Asia, in the shadows of the Tianshan range.

The popular Western view of China has been shaped by images of China's southeastern rice-growing regions: landscapes of stately tile-roofed pagodas, drooping willow trees, and barefoot peasants laboring in diked rice paddies. To many Westerners China is an essentially rural civilization, and a land that is peopled and shaped by a single culture of great antiquity. But China has a history of far greater diversity than this image allows. It is a land of urban as well as rural traditions, of heterogeneous regions of multicultural interaction as well as regions of considerable cultural homogeneity. This is true not only in the core areas of eastern China, but even more so on the frontiers, where a number of peoples have each contributed important cultural traditions and innovations in the shaping of urban places.

Although the People's Republic of China (PRC) classifies more than 90 percent of the population as Han Chinese, some regions are quite culturally diverse.[2] At the time of the 1949 revolution, the Han Chinese population occupied only about one-third of the land area. Until recent migrations of Han Chinese, the remainder of the land area was populated by majorities of non–Han Chinese peoples: Tibetans, Uygur, Mongolians, Hui, Bai, and many others.[3] Thirty-nine of the 55 non–Han Chinese peoples officially recognized by the PRC occupy China's western frontier regions.

In the regions beyond the Great Wall, the Chinese thus encountered and interacted with a number of other peoples as they established frontier forts, trading posts, and administrative centers. Most of these peoples were traditionally characterized by Chinese annalists as either nomadic peoples ranging across the untamed and uncivilized wilderness of the far western frontier or economically and culturally backward hill peoples inhabiting the southwestern frontier. In the Chinese perspective the encounter between Chinese and non-Chinese on the frontier thus became an encounter between a civilization characterized by ancient agricultural traditions and sophisticated urban settlements, and peoples so uncivilized as to warrant the label "barbarians." There were indeed nomadic peoples throughout many of the frontier regions, and some regions of the frontier were exclusively populated by nomads. But some parts of the frontier were inhabited by settled agricultural communities of non-Chinese peoples, and in some regions there were highly developed indigenous urban traditions characterized by a carefully regulated articulation of space and refined architectural practices. A wide range of settlement practices and subsistence patterns coexisted in the frontier regions and the lands beyond.

The Chinese preferred to build their own cities on the frontiers rather than to settle in existing settlements. The proto-urban settlements first established in the frontier regions were completely new constructions, though they were sometimes built near existing indigenous settlements or even on the abandoned sites of indigenous settlements. Although each of these settlements began as a small enclave for the Chinese, they became increasingly multicultural as non-Chinese people came to live in or near them during the course of their development.

Frontier cities accordingly developed distinctive styles, embodying multicultural elements not only in their sociocultural character but in their physical appearance as well. In cities where Chinese, Muslim, and Tibetan culture intersected, for example, landscapes were created that contained elements particular to each cultural tradition. Robert Ekvall, a missionary and self-trained ethnographer, captured an image of urban, multicultural China in his description, derived from later observations, of what

Daozhou, a city on the Gansu-Tibet frontier, must have looked like in 1895: "The great fortress-like, two-storied, flat-roofed houses owed their design to the Tibetan tradition of building for defense, and their timbers to the great Tibetan forests along the upper part of the Dao River. And above the flat roofs stretched the castellated line of the Chinese city wall and the pinnacled minaret of the Muslim prayer tower, together with the curving sweep of temple roofs that dominated the city skyline" (Ekvall 1938: 14–15).

This depiction might once have been used for a number of Chinese settlements along the Chinese-Tibetan borderlands of Gansu, Qinghai, and Sichuan in traditional times. Others more closely resembled the cities of eastern China, but even then elements of Tibetan, Hui, or Central/ Southwest Asian architectural tradition might characterize particular neighborhoods and sites. Though this cultural diversity is not always so visually striking as it was when Ekvall wrote, it persists to this day on the Chinese frontiers.

Yet a distinctive style of frontier urbanism developed through the Chinese establishment of cities within non-Chinese areas as Chinese urban traditions were joined with indigenous urban traditions. Common processes shaped both the creation and the modification of local urban forms and activities in widely different Chinese frontier areas. These common processes are most clearly evident in the contrasts between monumental and vernacular architecture and planning, in the establishment of Chinese "new towns" with clearly defined segregation between cultural groups, in trade relationships (both economic and spatial) between Chinese and non-Chinese peoples, in the adoption of Chinese cultural practices by non-Chinese peoples, and in the persistence of local cultures despite the Chinese influence. These features are not unique to the frontier cities of China, but they are much more pronounced there than they are in the cities of eastern China.

Yet while frontier cities are quite different from the cities of the east, they also conform rigidly in some key aspects to the ideals set out in the Chinese classics for all Chinese cities. In fact, as a group, they conform as much to these ideals, particularly in terms of city shape and the orientation of major buildings and thoroughfares, as their eastern counterparts, if not more. Thus cities on the frontiers in some ways are archetypical Chinese cities, as well as specialized frontier settlements. Frontier cities represent a considerable effort on the part of the Chinese empires throughout their histories to replicate both archetypical urban forms and, in miniature, the socio-spatial form of the empire itself.

Most discussions of frontiers, from the work of Frederick Jackson Turner and Owen Lattimore to the present day, are only tangentially concerned with cities. Frontier regions have commonly been portrayed as antithetical to urbanism. This perception reflects, in part, a view of the American frontier experience in which cities arrived late on the scene to mark the final taming and integration of frontier regions into national society (Billington 1956; Turner 1920). As John Reps has demonstrated, however, this view is a figment of romantic imagination, for cities in fact played an early and integral role in the settlement of the American frontier. The American frontier was settled as much through the establishment of towns as through the establishment of farms (Reps 1981: 2).

For more than two millennia, the Chinese frontiers have been urban across much of western China. In contrast to the American frontier, which today survives primarily in history books and late-night movies, this frontier remains very much alive today. It continues to be a region that is highly differentiated from the core area of China in every respect: politically, economically, socially, and culturally. Despite a veneer of national culture, these differences pose a challenge for standard analyses of Chinese urban form and provide an opportunity to test long-accepted hypotheses. Exploring and identifying specific aspects of Chinese urban forms that have endured on the frontier provides insight not only into frontier urbanism, but also into the nature of Chinese urbanism more generally.

The frontier also serves as a crucible for change and a region of intercultural diffusion of innovations. Urban styles and practices have clearly diffused between Chinese and non-Chinese peoples through the zone of frontier interaction, contributing to the development of unique forms. Patterns of diffusion and the adoption of urban and architectural ideas on the frontier reveal the value placed on these ideas.

The Chinese frontier regions afford unusual if not unique opportunities to study urban forms, for the daunting task of generalizing across a wide expanse of environments and culture regions is made possible by their shared political, economic, social, and cultural relations to the Chinese state. This shared experience contributes directly to a similarity of urban forms among otherwise quite different urban places, and thus provides a basis for comparison between the cities.

Research on Chinese Urban Development and Form

Research on Chinese urban development and form has been focused primarily on a few cities in the east of China, particularly former capitals and port cities.[4] Beijing is the most widely described city. Other eastern cities, Xi'an, Shanghai, and, to a lesser extent, Guangzhou, Tianjin, Nanjing, Wuhan, Suzhou, Hangzhou, Luoyang, Shenyang, Jinan, Chongqing, and Qingdao, also dominate the literature on Chinese urbanism. Models for Chinese urbanism have thus been derived mostly (though not exclusively) from one set of cities. Few studies make reference to, much less analyze, the cities of western China.

Of the major English-language studies of Chinese urbanism, the classic work by a geographer is Paul Wheatley's book *Pivot of the Four Quarters* (1971), which focuses primarily on archaeological evidence of early city forms in China. Other pioneering works in the field include several articles and a dissertation by Sen-dou Chang (1961; 1963; 1970), who identifies common forms of Chinese cities, maps their distribution, and discusses spatial and historical variations in form. The most broad-scale study to date is the 1989 book *Cities in China* by the German geographer Alfred Schinz, which provides both a brief overview of the history of urbanization in China and historical and geographic descriptions of more than 180 cities.

Three landmark studies on Chinese urbanism by nongeographers are G. William Skinner, ed., *The City in Late Imperial China* (1977), Mark Elvin and G. William Skinner, eds., *The Chinese City Between Two Worlds* (1974), and John W. Lewis, ed., *The City in Communist China* (1971), which survey aspects of late-imperial, early-twentieth-century, and mid-twentieth-century urbanization in eastern China. A recent monograph in English by the Chinese architectural historian Wu Liangyong (1986) provides a good overview of traditional Chinese city form. Nancy Schatzman Steinhardt's 1990 book, *Chinese Imperial City Planning*, provides a broad-ranging analysis of the form and development of imperial capitals. And there have been several substantial individual city studies published in recent years, including William Rowe's *Hankow: Commerce and Society in a Chinese City, 1796–1889* (1984) and *Hankow: Conflict and Community in a Chinese City, 1796–1895* (1989). These later works, along with David Buck's earlier *Urban Change in China: Politics and Development in Tsinan, Shantung, 1890–1949* (1978), offer an excellent historical treatment of urban economic, social, and political conditions in single cities.

Like their English counterparts, most standard Chinese works on Chinese urban form and development, such as *Zhongguo chengshi jianshe shi* (History of urban construction in China; 1982), do not address cities outside the Chinese core. However, in contrast to the English-language literature, several general works on architectural history published in recent years, including most notably Liu Dunzhen, *Zhongguo gudai jianzhushi* (History of ancient Chinese architecture; 1987) and Sun Dazhang, *Zhongguo gudai jianzhu shihua* (Historical narrative of ancient Chinese architecture; 1987), contain discussions of cities in frontier regions. Treatments of some urban issues on the frontiers are also to be found in recent issues of such Chinese scholarly journals as *Jianzhushi* (Architect) and *Chengshi guihua* (Urban planning).

Urban Geography, Urban Morphology

This book is a study of urban geography, or, more specifically, of urban morphology—the study of the evolution of urban form in both physical and social manifestations. Urban morphology focuses on the linkages between human culture, ideology, and economies and the built form of the city. The geographical analysis of urban morphology involves a synthesis of research techniques ranging from standard social science methodologies, such as interviewing and statistical analysis, to techniques of visual analysis more familiar to the humanities. Like professional analyses of architecture, urban morphological fieldwork involves trained observation and the analysis of physical phenomena—in this case, of urban landscapes and districts and the elements they embody. This research can be done only through extensive legwork, sketching, mapping, and photography. The research process is based on a dialogue between interviewing, written sources, and fieldwork as a groundcheck and guide to new lines of inquiry. These approaches can be used to examine historical change, as well as current conditions. Change can be analyzed at the scale of districts and even individual buildings through the use of historical photographs, maps, and plans, interviewing, and documentary sources. Most analyses of Chinese urban morphology to date have focused on the macro-scale of city location and the overall placement of walls and monumental architecture. In addition to such macro-scale analysis, this book will discuss the morphology of infrastructure elements, such as streets, markets, and neighborhoods, and micro-scale morphology at the level of architectural form and decoration of individual structures.

The study of Chinese frontier cities contributes to the continuing exploration of one of the primary themes of urban geography: the connections between overall urban morphology, the structural elements of the city and its cultural, social, and political conditions. The physical form of the city at once embodies these human factors and their historical relationships and influences them. The city is a symbol of both cultural beliefs and power relations. Beliefs, values, and power relations both shape and are reaffirmed by the structure of the city itself.

For this reason, the form of cities cannot be described in terms of the physical structure of the built environment alone. An analysis of urban form must include cultural, social, and economic structures, as well as physical structures at a range of scales, from overall form to vernacular architecture. Urban geography, in short, requires an integrative research approach.

The five main cities of this study—Kunming, Hohhot (Huhehaote), Lanzhou, Urumqi (Wulumuqi), and Xining (see Map 1), in which I conducted research during 15 months of fieldwork between 1986 and 1988—present an array of different geographical and cultural contexts and date

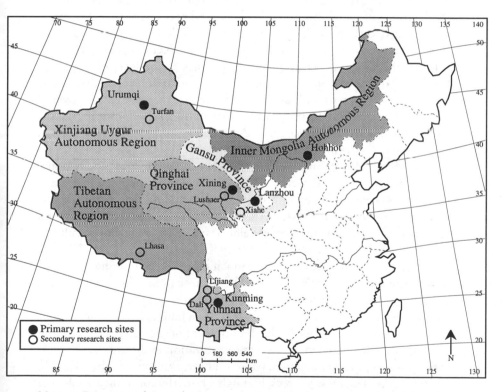

Map. 1. Primary and secondary research sites. (The base map used for this and Maps 2 and 12–15 is adapted from the map "China's Administrative Divisions" in China Handbook Editorial Committee, eds. 1983. *Geography*. Beijing: Foreign Languages Press.)

back to different eras of establishment, ranging from the Han dynasty (202 B.C.–A.D. 220) to the Ming dynasty (1368–1644). All have survived centuries of life on the frontier; all are large, with populations of over one million; and all are capitals of the ethnically diverse provinces or autonomous regions in which they are situated. In order to provide secondary examples of Chinese and non-Chinese inter-influences in urban environments and to illustrate indigenous urban traditions, I discuss the cities of Dali (Yunnan Province), Lushaer (Qinghai Province), Turfan (Xinjiang), Xiahe (Gansu Province), and Lhasa (Tibet). All these cities were originally established by non-Chinese peoples and continue to have substantial non-Chinese populations.

I analyze these cities in terms of the premise that cities and their shapers are at once agents of and the results of social and cultural processes, and that cities are cultural artifacts continually shaped and reshaped by the dynamics of social, cultural, economic, and political change. I examine not only broad facets of the city as a cultural landscape (city siting, urban symbolism, and urban morphology), but also urban cultural interaction between the Chinese and non-Chinese peoples at the level of neighborhoods, use districts, transportation patterns, and architectural detail. The ten cities are compared across five dimensions: (1) elements of overall form, such as city wall forms, cardinal orientation, street patterns, the siting of monumental buildings, and the location and nature of residence, commercial, governmental, military, ethnic, religious, place-origin, and class districts; (2) elements of economic form, including local and regional production strategies, as well as local, regional, and long-distance trade patterns; (3) elements of architectural form, including the relation of vernacular and monumental styles to local styles; (4) elements of social form, such as class structure and power relations; and (5) elements of cultural form, such as belief systems.

Given the premise set out above, much more is required than a simple look at the cities as they are today. The historical establishment and development of these frontier cities is the foundation of the research. Common processes emerge not only across far-reaching areas, but across different periods of time as well. The development of each city is traced from the first references in Chinese sources to habitation in the area to the present day. Contemporary analysis, based on both extensive fieldwork and a review of recent Chinese sources, highlights both the continuity of Chinese urban forms and the spatial, structural, and socioeconomic transformations of Chinese cities during the twentieth century. I analyze historical changes in morphology in conjunction with changing attitudes about the symbolism of cities, new living patterns, and the application of architectural models, as well as changes in the role of religion and other aspects of culture and regional identity. Recent urban development policies are also compared between frontier and core regions, with an emphasis on the differential application of policies and on issues unique to frontier regions.

This study is as much an analysis of people as of places. I approach the city as a cultural artifact, both as a whole and as the sum of numerous individual elements. The city is at once a physical object, an economic system, and a sociocultural concept. The tangible and intangible elements that combine to make it up are inseparable: neither is material for a coherent analysis on its own. In a broad sense, my research draws upon the fields of history, sociology, anthropology, economics, architecture, and urban planning.

Methodology

Fieldwork

I carried out the fieldwork for this study over the course of two trips to China: three months in 1986 and twelve months in 1987–88. In 1986 I spent time in nine different provinces and autonomous regions looking for research sites and making a preliminary reconnaissance. In 1987–88, I was affiliated with the department of geography at Beijing University as a senior advanced research student supported by grants from the Committee on Scholarly Communication with the People's Republic of China and the Fulbright Doctoral Dissertation Research Abroad program. I had three excellent advisers at Beijing University: Professor Hou Renzhi, Professor Yu Xixian, and Professor Han Mukang. I alternated four- to six-week stays in the cities I was studying with brief one- to two-week stays at Beijing University to discuss my work with my advisers there. In this manner I was able both to make repeat visits to my research sites and to benefit from consultations at Beijing University.

My fieldwork consisted of the analysis and mapping of development and change in the form, architectural styles, and districts of each city through extensive on-site observation, photography, documentation, and the preparation of sketch maps and measurements. These findings were cross-checked with local experts, such as academic researchers and community leaders. I focused my research on two levels: identifying and analyzing the evidence of past forms in the contemporary landscape, and identifying and analyzing contemporary processes of both change and continuity. This type of field analysis is crucial in investigations of the interface between Chinese and non-Chinese peoples because the Chinese literature tends to be limited to the perspective of Chinese accounts and analyses.

To cover each city as thoroughly as possible, I carried out fieldwork mostly on foot or by bicycle or bus. During these daily forays through the cities, I took notes, made sketches, and maintained a photographic record of architecture and city landscapes. In Kunming, Lanzhou, Xining, and Urumqi, graduate students and/or professors from local universities accompanied me on a few of these trips. Their assistance, primarily in answering on-the-spot questions and pointing out features they considered significant, was invaluable. For the most part, however, I carried out the fieldwork on my own. Virtually all the people I met and spoke with were quite open and friendly, if a bit baffled by my interest in what they considered ordinary and unremarkable.

In each city I set out first to locate and analyze remnants of the old city walls and any other pre-1949 structures still standing. This process involved comparing information from old maps and gazetteers with contemporary maps, then looking around and asking questions. Many of these structures are now contained within factories and other work units, and I am grateful to the numerous gatekeepers and managers who permitted me to enter their premises in the course of my investigations. If possible, I asked permission before photographing or entering potentially sensitive buildings, such as mosques and temples. One of the most important aspects of this initial stage of my research was to gain access to the upper floors of the tallest buildings in various neighborhoods so that I could get a bird's-eye view of the cities.

I also used a combination of field investigation and documents to establish the past and present locations of ethnic enclaves and areas of ethnic diversity within each city. During these preliminary investigations, I constructed spatial and chronological sequences of growth and change for each city. With this basic understanding of the spatial dimensions of each city, I continued my research by searching out finer levels of significance ranging from variations in architectural style to what types of goods were being sold in the markets, and systematically visited each city district to analyze its particular character.

Documentary Evidence

Recent Chinese scholarly publications, government documents, and local gazetteers and histories (*difangzhi*) were valuable not only as documentation of the cities' origins, development, and recent change, but also as a fieldwork tool. Historical maps and descriptions were critical in my efforts to identify and interpret past features and urban patterns in the contemporary landscape. Contemporary Chinese publications on urban planning and preservation theory proved particularly useful in interpreting contemporary landscapes and change, and identifying new directions in Chinese urban form. I found *Jianzhushi* the most useful contemporary theoretical journal for Chinese architecture and planning. Also useful, and less theoretical, were such journals as *Jianzhu xuebao* (Architectural journal), *Chengshi guihua* (City planning), *Jingji dili* (Economic geography),[5] and *Chengshi wenti* (Urban problems). In addition to these Chinese sources, I consulted archival materials during my postdoctoral year at the East-West Center in Honolulu, Hawaii (1990–91), during several research trips I made to Japan to use facilities such as the Toyo Bunko and other libraries in Tokyo, on later trips to China, and during additional research trips to the University of California (Berkeley), Stanford University, and the Hoover Institution.

During 1987–88 I was able to make use of university library collections in Kunming, Xining, Lanzhou, Hohhot, Urumqi, and Beijing, as well as materials supplied by Chinese scholars from their personal libraries. But by far the best sources turned out to be locally published works I found in the field. These publications, which are not available outside of China, and, in fact, are rarely available outside the city of publication, proved to be invaluable.

Nineteenth- and early-twentieth-century travelers' and scholars' accounts and historical photographs and maps were a source of information on pre-1949 landscapes. Chinese photographic records like Liu Zhiping's *Zhongguo yisilanjiao jianzhu* (Islamic architecture of China; 1985), which contains pre–Cultural Revolution photographs of 45 mosques throughout China, were of considerable use as well. I have also surveyed photographic and map collections at the Library of Congress, the National Archives, the University of Washington (Seattle), Stanford University, the University of Hawaii, and the University of California (Berkeley). The Library of Congress and the National Archives collections include U.S. Army photographs of Kunming and Yunnan Province in general during the Second World War, as well as numerous photographs from eastern China. The University of Washington has an excellent collection of Chinese city maps, many of which were made by the Japanese in the late 1930s during their occupation of China.

The Structure of the Book

The first three chapters set the geographical and historical background for the remainder of the book. Chapter One discusses the Chinese frontiers in the context of world frontiers and describes their human geography. Chapter Two traces the historical development of the five cities that are the focus of the study. And Chapter Three provides a broad-ranging discussion of the functions of the cities on the frontier, from defense and domination to transportation and trade.

Chapters Four–Six address broad-scale aspects of urban form. The Chinese tradition of city building is presented in Chapter Four. This is followed by a discussion of non-Chinese urban traditions in Chapter Five, including extended treatments of Islamic and Lamaist city forms. Chapter Six then surveys the fusion of these varying forms as they are articulated on the Chinese frontiers.

Chapters Seven and Eight shift the focus on urban form to a finer level of detail within the city. Chapter Seven is devoted to both Chinese and non-Chinese monumental architecture. Chapter Eight then looks at a number of manifestations of regionalism, including stylistic variations in both monumental architecture and vernacular architecture that often reflect traditions transplanted to the frontier by migrants from other regions.

In Chapters Nine and Ten I turn to contemporary issues in China's frontier cities: the first discusses the persistence of traditional forms in the contemporary city; the second looks at new types of frontier urban forms. The book concludes with a summary of the important themes and an analysis of the significance of the frontier cities for Chinese civilization.

The Chinese Frontiers

The Chinese are less a nation than a fusion of peoples united
by a common culture, and the history of China is the record of
an expanding culture.
—C. P. Fitzgerald, *China: A Short Cultural History*, 1965

Though the Chinese may well be a fusion of peoples united by a common
culture, as Fitzgerald would have it, the People's Republic of China, like
most of the regimes that preceded it, extends far beyond the limits of the
expansion of Chinese culture to control areas significantly different from
the core. The Chinese frontier that I explore in this study is not the politically defined border areas of China, but rather the internal zone of contact
between Chinese and non-Chinese peoples within the contemporary political boundaries. I have limited my discussion to the western Chinese
frontier, an arc of territory extending southward from Inner Mongolia,
through Gansu, Qinghai, the border regions of Tibet and Sichuan, and
Yunnan, and extending westward into Xinjiang and Tibet (see Map 1).[1]
The western frontier is much less well integrated with the core of China
than the northeastern frontier and has been less affected by the new industrial development planning that has been promoted for parts of the
southeastern frontier, such as Hainan Island. The western frontier remains a living frontier zone of interaction between peoples and cultures.[2]

World Frontiers and the Frontiers of China

Frontiers have captured the interest of geographers, historians, and
political scientists since the publication of Frederick Jackson Turner's late-
nineteenth-century writings on the American frontier. Turner viewed the
frontier in Darwinian terms, asserting that American culture grew out of
a set of social practices that were shaped by and able to survive the frontier
experience. Any practices that were not compatible with that experience

were either modified or abandoned. The surviving social forms he identified include many of the democratic ideals that have been considered fundamental to American society. Since Turner's time, numerous historians and social scientists have built on or rebutted his thesis about the U.S. frontier, and have applied his theories to other regions such as Australia and South Africa. In the context of these multidisciplinary frontier studies, the Chinese frontier has played a particularly important role. Owen Lattimore's studies of the Chinese frontier during the 1940s revolutionized the field, providing the inspiration for a new direction in frontier studies with a modification of Turner's approach that gave a more active role to the indigenous inhabitants of frontier regions.

Analyses of frontiers have often been bounded by three assumptions: first, that frontiers are nonurban phenomena; second, that frontiers should be analyzed primarily as political and economic phenomena; and third, that there is a linear "frontier process," in which a frontier rises only once and is then inevitably incorporated into the core region. These assumptions characterize many of the studies of frontiers in the Western world, and the first two have dominated discussions of the Chinese frontiers as well. I take a different approach to the frontier in China: I focus on frontier urbanism rather than the rural frontier (as Reps [1979, 1981] does for the United States); I see the frontier not only as a political and economic phenomenon, but as a unique arena for the expression of social and cultural relations; and I hold that there were successive cycles of growth and contraction of Chinese settlement on the frontiers, not a single rise and fall as in the linear model.[3]

For geographers, frontiers pose a particularly interesting and complex set of relationships. While regional geography usually identifies and analyzes regions defined by certain common characteristics, the frontier is the space between such regions. And yet many frontiers can be classed as regions in their own right, by virtue of shared environments and histories. The most common shared experience of frontier peoples is their relationship to the core areas. As such, the relationship to the core area is the frontier's key defining feature.

By referring to "Chinese" frontiers in this study, I emphasize the relationship between each of the areas I discuss and the successive Chinese empires. This relationship provides a common link and shared experience throughout these widely dispersed cities. Yet it is important to recognize that the vast reaches of China's inland frontiers are surrounded by other great core areas as well, so that the frontier has also been influenced by its relationship with the civilizations of India, Central Asia, and Russia. It is largely the combination of multiple influences from several core areas, in addition to the region's own unique features, that produces distinctive frontier cultures and societies.

Opinions on the character of the frontier vary significantly among those who analyze social relations in frontier regions. Some claim that the frontier is a lawless area: the venue of smugglers, outlaws and others who do not conform to social norms of the heartland (Bodley 1982; Broek 1941). Others contend that the frontier is not lawless, that instead it has its own rules, which may be different from those of the core area but are nonetheless quite rigid (Lattimore 1940; McNeill 1983). Still others see it as a crucible for the development of new cultural forms (Sauer 1930; Turner 1920; Webb 1951). Several case studies of current frontiers expose them as areas of conflict between indigenous cultural persistence and the efforts of the governments and peoples of the core area to encourage social, cultural, and economic change (Avedon 1984; Barsh 1984; Bodley 1982; Tapp 1986).

Among the many issues associated with the frontier, two are particularly important to an understanding of its relevance for urban development: the role played by the indigenous people (or nondominant group) who reside there and the nature of the frontier as a temporal or a spatial phenomenon. In the following pages I will review a few of the differing opinions on these topics and their relevance to the Chinese frontiers.

The Depiction of Frontier Peoples

There is a broad division in the literature between those who see the frontier as a virtually uncivilized, unclaimed, and even uninhabited area free for a settler group to occupy and civilize and those who see it as an area of contact and contest between two or more societies. Frederick Jackson Turner defined the first group. It was not that Turner did not recognize the presence of Native Americans. In fact, he was acutely aware of them. However, Turner portrayed the Native Americans as yet another of the many natural hazards to be faced and overcome in forcing the frontier farther west. In the *Atlantic Monthly* of September 1896, Turner wrote: "Militant qualities were favored by the annual expansion of the settled area in the face of hostile Indians and the stubborn wilderness" (Turner 1920: 213). The "hostile Indians," in Turner's view, required a similar response from the settlers as the "stubborn wilderness," though, in fact, settlers and their governments did often trade and make treaties and alliances with the Native Americans.

Several studies of frontiers in America, Canada, Australia, and South Africa echo Turner's implication that the indigenous peoples of the frontier are an obstacle to be overcome like the wilderness itself (e.g., Andrews 1966; Billington 1956; Gerhard 1959; Webb 1951; Wyman & Kroeber 1965). This viewpoint seems to derive from a belief that each of these cases involved a technologically superior group moving into a vast territory of relatively low population density in which land was available for the taking—which is to say, from the indigenous peoples. The common theme of these studies is that the hardships of the frontier experience, combined with the opportunity for land and expansion, led to the creation of new social forms, such as American democracy.

Although Turner's theses would hardly have been accepted in traditional China,[4] the Chinese too tended to regard their "hostile Indians" as more or less equivalent to the "stubborn wilderness." There were many different peoples on the frontiers, and the Chinese evaluated each of them differently, but in general all were regarded as lesser, uncivilized societies. As one sixteenth-century Chinese writer noted of the non-Chinese peoples in the south: "The barbarians are like wild deer. To institute direct civil service administration by Chinese magistrates would be like herding deer into the main hall of a house and attempting to tame them. . . . In a wilderness area, therefore, one should adjust one's methods to the character of the wilderness. . . . To leave these tribal chiefs to themselves . . . is like releasing deer into the wilderness" (quoted in Wiens 1954: 219). Although the Chinese granted titles to local elites, conducted trade with non-Chinese peoples, and fought (and sometimes lost) wars with them, they rarely treated them as equals (see Eberhard 1982: 100–104 for an interesting discussion of Chinese attitudes toward minorities). So narrow was the Chinese perspective, in fact, that even transactions with foreign governments were often handled through the Ministry of Rites, which managed tribute from lesser peoples, rather than through diplomatic channels that would have recognized them as equal sovereign states.[5] Yet the Chinese frontiers were at times occupied by vast empires rivaling the power of the Chinese empire itself. As Morris Rossabi implies in the title of his book *China Among Equals* (1983), China was not the only great empire on the continent.

In Western literature and academic writing, Carl Sauer made one of the first arguments for the recognition of indigenous societies on the frontier in his 1930 critique of American frontier studies, "Historical Geography and the Western Frontier." According to Sauer, "Actually, a very important frontier, or series of frontiers, lies behind the coming of the white man. The Indian was not the negligible factor in modifying the country that he is commonly considered to have been" (Sauer 1930: 280).

But China, not the United States, was the venue for the earliest major analysis to fully account for a frontier of exchange and contact between societies—Owen Lattimore's *Inner Asian Frontiers of China* (1940). Lattimore saw the Chinese-Mongolian interface as the *locus classicus* of all frontier history—a place where sedentary and nomadic cultures were in contact in spite of the irreconcilable natures of their economies (1940: 53–55).[6] In recognizing the advantages of both cultures, and the difficulties involved with any attempts to combine them or subsume one within another, Lattimore laid the grounds for frontiers as zones of contact between peoples, rather than wilderness areas to be overcome. He explains that this zone would contain the "least typical" marginal territories of each culture. Contact between the two cultures would affect both (Lattimore 1940: 249).

Thanks to the influence of Lattimore, subsequent studies of frontier situations in Asia by both Americans and Europeans tend to emphasize the interrelations and simultaneous influences of cultures upon each other, rather than the supplanting of one culture by another. This different style of analysis may also reflect the comparatively long period of history the scholar of Asia must cover, for though in principle scholars of Western civilization might study, say, the frontiers created and controlled by the Roman empire, in fact there is little analysis of Western frontiers as frontiers before the fifteenth century. The Western frontier era is usually framed in a time period of about 500 years, from the early Spanish conquests to the end of the nineteenth century.[7] Indeed, William McNeill boldly asserts that the kind of "open" (land for the taking) frontier that developed in North and South America, Australia, and South Africa after 1500 never arose in earlier times (McNeill 1983: 12). Most authors describe the process in terms of the opening and closing of the frontier zone (Lamar & Thompson 1981; McNeill 1983; Thompson 1981; Turner 1920; Webb 1951). In contrast, scholars of Asian frontiers tend to follow the history of frontier interactions at least from the Han dynasty. The history of Asian frontiers is an ancient tale of repeated conquests and repeated retreats, of domination and cultural exchange.

Owen Lattimore suggested that the main characteristics of the Chinese frontier were set by the end of the Han dynasty (Lattimore 1940: 20). He describes the Chinese Inner Asian frontier as "a constant factor in the history not only of China but of the deep steppe" (ibid., p. 511). He presents the frontier as a zone in which at least two different modes of subsistence, usually nomadic and sedentary, come into contact. This zone of contact is characterized by its own social and cultural norms, which he called "frontier feudalism." Moreover, he emphasizes that the frontier is important to the core cultures in terms of defining their own cultures and boundaries (Lattimore 1940, 1962).[8]

Owen Lattimore's concept of frontier feudalism offers a framework for political and economic relations on the frontier in which China's Inner Asian frontier was ruled by feudal chiefs who either sold their allegiance to the Chinese in return for titles and land or made alliances with the Chinese after conquering territory along the frontiers on their own. Under this system, the Chinese empire identified and co-opted local elites by granting them political, economic, and military support to maintain or expand its spheres of control. In return, the elites ensured that commerce and other Chinese ventures on the frontier would remain favorable to the Chinese. The establishment of this system served to break down the social organization of the frontier nomads and replace it with a patron-client relationship: the "feudal" lord, backed by the Chinese, taxed local people or conscripted their labor, and protected them in return. As a result, the elites were able to make political and economic use of local nomads or former nomads in the same way that a feudal lord might use sedentarized peasants (Lattimore 1940, 1962).

The ultimate expression of the subjugation of the frontier peoples, under Chinese frontier feudalism, was the transition from clan-based social hierarchies and organization to territorial organization. The increasing identification of leadership and control with place, rather than with family organization, gradually broke down the traditional systems of the frontier peoples and bound them into the Chinese system. This was nowhere more true than on the Mongolian frontier, where, during the Qing dynasty (1644–1911), the Manchu effectively broke down the Mongols' banner system by reorganizing it territorially, so that peoples from different banners were classed together in new banners, and peoples of the same banner were split and reclassified under other banners. Such measures were generally accomplished through deals made between the Chinese government and local leaders, in which local leaders agreed to defend a specific territory in return for concessions and titles from the Chinese (Lattimore 1962: 514–41).

Stephen Pastner extended Lattimore's idea of frontier feudalism to Baluchistan (Pakistan), Eastern Ethiopia, and Djibouti, and found that a form of frontier feudalism was present in all three areas. Like Lattimore, he saw this as a phenomenon imposed by the state as an efficient means of control and resource extraction (Pastner 1979). According to Lattimore, the frontier serves as a point of exchange between peoples with widely varying economic and political power. A class is formed that serves as mediators between the different cultures.[9] Further, in a situation in which economic and political relations on the frontier are maintained at an unequal level, with a dominant group steadily extracting resources in exchange for patronage, it is to the advantage of the dominant group to maintain the frontier as a marginal region, incorporated with the core only through honorary tithes and a flow of goods. Once a mediating class is formed between the groups, this power relationship could be perpetuated for some time.[10] The formation of an intermediate or comprador group might serve to control the extent of the diffusion of ideas in both directions, since it would be in the interest of the intermediaries to maintain the patron-client relationship between the core and the frontier.

Other researchers who have tested Lattimore's theories in Asia and abroad include Mary Ellen Alonso (1979), Ladis K. Kristof (1959), Alastair Lamb (1968), and more recently Richard Von Glahn (1987) and Thomas Barfield (1989). Von Glahn uses both Lattimore's work and the papers in Lamar and Thompson (1981) as his basic references for frontier theory in his study of Chinese agricultural settlement in Sichuan between 1000 and 1250.[11] He is concerned above all with the cultural, social, and spatial conflicts that arise in zones of frontier contact between indigenous and intrusive societies.

The Barfield study is a sweeping analysis of relations between the Chinese empire and the nomadic peoples of Central Asia and the northern frontier from the time of the Han dynasty to the mid-Qing. One of the author's basic assertions is that the frontier empires, with the notable exception of the Mongol empire, coalesced at times when it was possible to make economic linkages with the Chinese empire. Thus the Chinese preference for trade over direct conquest in the frontier zones, as exemplified by systems like "frontier feudalism," proved advantageous for the empires of the steppe (Barfield 1989: 9).

The Temporal Frontier and the Spatial Frontier

Many of the geographers, historians, political scientists, economists, and others who write about the frontier see it as a temporal phenomenon: a stage in a linear process of evolution from one type of society to another. Ladis Kristof, for example, asserts that "the state tends to view frontiers and frontiersmen as a temporary expedient; as appropriate to a period of transition. The ultimate goal is a boundary, not a frontier" (Kristof 1959: 280).[12] Walter Prescott Webb also emphasizes the limited life span of the frontier. The Great Frontier he describes in the New World was the instigator of and the product of a worldwide economic boom lasting from the fifteenth century to the beginning of the twentieth century (Webb 1951: 13). The boom and the frontier ended simultaneously. For Howard Lamar and Leonard Thompson, the frontier lasts only until the "intrusive" group gains the upper hand. Or as they put it, "the frontier 'opens' in a given zone when the first representatives of the intrusive society arrive; it 'closes' when a single political authority has established hegemony over the zone" (Lamar & Thompson 1981: 7). These perceptions all emphasize the frontier as a step in a political and economic process: the spatial dimension of the frontier is no more than a stage on which to play out the drama of the frontier process.

But China clearly does not lend itself to this model. There the frontier has persisted through many centuries of expansions *and* contractions of the state. The Chinese frontier is cyclic, becoming alternately more and less integrated with the core area.[13] Even during the relatively short time span of the Song dynasty, these areas did not remain "fully and irreversibly integrated into the Han world" (Von Glahn 1987: 7). The frontier has varied spatially and culturally with the empire's political vicissitudes and the migrations of different peoples. Yet there has also been a degree of geographic continuity. The regions that can be categorized as frontiers today have never been fully integrated into the national system and are nearly as much "frontier," in both cultural and economic terms, as they were during the Han dynasty. Thus, in China, the frontier has a strong, though constantly changing, spatial dimension as a region.

The fact that vast parts of the Chinese frontier, unlike many other world frontiers, were not primarily regions of agricultural settlement also makes the concept of the frontier as an opening agrarian phase in the developmental process inappropriate (for a similar view, see Skinner 1977: 18). In areas where the climate and topography were not well suited for Chinese-style agriculture, such as the steppes and deserts of the north and northwest, initial Chinese settlement was primarily military and administrative. The frontier of China was often, and in some cases remains, a frontier of control rather than a frontier of settlement.

The Chinese frontiers that are the subject of this study might be referred to as China's persistent frontiers. Once there were many other frontier regions in China, for what in the past centuries has been the "core" region of China was historically settled and politically integrated through a series of expansions into new areas. These expansions, particularly the Chinese expansion into the south (see Wiens 1954), were more or less typical of the "linear" frontier settlement process familiar from the past few centuries in the United States, Australia, Russia, and South Africa. This study is less concerned, however, with these historic frontiers, which have long since passed into the mainstream of Chinese culture, than with the persistent frontiers of the southwest, west, and northwest. It is these farther frontiers which continue to the present as areas with great cultural diversity and a substantial non-Chinese presence in spite of having had extended periods of contact with and settlement by the Chinese people.

Frontiers of Settlement and Frontiers of Control

In any examination of frontier urbanism, it is important to distinguish between "frontiers of settlement" and "frontiers of control." In the first instance settlers from the core area penetrate and increasingly occupy an area, residing not only in cities but in the rural areas as well. In such situations it is common for the settlers to displace, or at least disrupt, local settlement and subsistence. Frontiers of control, by contrast, are those in which settlers tend to cluster in cities or forts, making little attempt to expand into a hinterland perceived as either too marginal or too hostile to support rural settlement. The far frontier regions of China, particularly the northwestern frontiers in Qinghai and Xinjiang,[14] were frontiers of control, not settler frontiers. In these cases environmental constraints may have been the key factor discouraging extensive Chinese rural settlement until relatively recent years. Each region—the deserts of Xinjiang, the high-altitude Qinghai-Tibet plateau, and the grasslands of Inner Mongolia—favored nomadic subsistence strategies quite alien to Chinese ways of life. Settled agriculture was possible in the oases of Xinjiang, but many were already occupied by local peoples, and large-scale Chinese settlement would have required displacing them. The purpose of frontiers of control like these was to maintain buffer regions and trade routes, not to expand the core Chinese settlement area. Resources were extracted through trade with local peoples, not through direct Chinese resource extraction and production. As a result cities became the primary focus of Chinese activity within the vast reaches of these frontiers. Though often of humble size compared with the cities of the core area, these frontier centers nonetheless played an important role in national security and the economy.

China also had settler frontiers. The Yangzi valley and southern China were once settler frontiers, and so, too, was Sichuan, which was penetrated by Chinese agriculturalists as early as the Qin dynasty (221–206 B.C.) and was thoroughly settled by Chinese agriculturalists by the thirteenth century. Yunnan and Gansu had areas that were settler frontiers and other areas that functioned as frontiers of control. In both provinces some areas were settled by Chinese agriculturalists, while the majority of the land in the two provinces remained occupied and largely under the control of non-Chinese peoples until the twentieth century. Here, as in the true frontiers of control, the urban centers provided a link between the Chinese and the non-Chinese. But in these partially settled frontier regions, the cities fulfilled another function as well, linking both rural and urban frontier Chinese with the Chinese empire.

Diffusion Across the Frontiers

As Lattimore saw it:

The mixed culture (of the steppe frontier) was a bridge between the steppe and China, and over it passed influences in both directions; but it was only from half-way across the bridge that the two worlds appeared as if linked. At each head of the bridge it could be seen that they were still two different worlds. (Lattimore 1940: 549)

The portrayal of the frontier as a vast region of interaction between peoples suggests that cultural and social diffusion might well take place along the frontiers. Though in the Chinese case there has been cultural diffusion in both directions across the frontiers, the unique relationship between the Chinese empire and the border peoples has favored the diffusion of Chinese culture to the frontier peoples, with little movement in the other direction. In fact the Chinese on the whole have resisted any intimation that non-Chinese peoples contributed to the formation of their core area culture and society. Foreign researchers have to some extent reified this view by portraying the Chinese as members of an ancient, largely homogeneous, and static culture.

This view has been strengthened by centuries of strong central governance, with imperial rule reaching to and affecting all levels of society. The empire formalized and enforced Chinese high culture. Leo Moser provides a good discussion of the dichotomy between formal Chinese culture, with its emphasis on universalism and expectations of uniformity, and the diverse and locally variant forms of "informal" Chinese culture (Moser 1985: 1–9). As he observes, the Chinese have a strong "cultural resistance to systematic discussion of variety within the country" (ibid., p. 7). This reluctance to discuss diversity at any level has led to centuries of portrayals of China, by both Chinese annalists and outsiders, as a remarkably homogeneous place unified by a common culture of belief and practice as disseminated by a central authority. So intent were the Chinese upon presenting a unified and consistent cultural image, in fact, that imperial historians regularly revised history to bring past actions into accord with current policies. As Wolfram Eberhard has observed, for the official dynastic historians, "history" was not so much an impartial record of events as a portrayal of ethics based on example (Eberhard 1950: 2). In recent years scholars have challenged this monolithic and static view of Chinese culture and history (see, e.g., Fairbank 1992: 163).

Nor did the Chinese necessarily seek to diffuse Chinese culture to non-Chinese people. One of Von Glahn's most interesting observations is that "for the most part, Song statesmen expected little in the way of cultural assimilation" on the part of the indigenous people (Von Glahn 1987: 16).[15] The frontier, it seems, was expected either to remain an area of high cultural diversity or to be rid completely of the non-Chinese peoples (both consequences were common in the past). Nonetheless, the emphasis on Han Chinese homogeneity has sharply affected the ability of Chinese and foreign researchers alike to identify such concepts of cultural variation as "frontier" for Chinese society. More often than not, the image of the Chinese cultural landscape is one of sharp contrasts and boundaries between Chinese and non-Chinese, with little regard for potential zones of transition and intercultural influences and adaptations.[16]

Cultural diffusion from or through the frontier regions took place during the pre-1949 era both within frontier settlements and across the vast expanses of the frontier regions. Micro-scale diffusion can be seen, for example, in the Chinese adoption of local building practices for vernacular architecture in frontier cities. Macro-scale diffusion can be seen in the spread of Islam, Buddhism, and Manichaeism into China, as well as the adoption of aspects of material culture, technology, and agricultural and military techniques. Denis Sinor cites an early example—that one result of fourth-century B.C. contacts between the Chao (Han) and the nomadic Xiongnu was the adoption by the Chao of the wearing of trousers and the use of mounted artillery (Sinor 1969: 86). A considerable amount of diffusion also took place on the frontiers between the non-Chinese peoples. Tibetan Buddhism spread to the Mongols via China's frontiers, for example. And again, much of the frontier architecture, monumental as well as vernacular, displays evidence of such cross-cultural influences.

The Development and Maintenance of the Chinese Frontiers

Many of the succession of states dating from at least the third millennium B.C. that have been collectively known as "China" have had expansionist policies aimed at controlling new territories. The most successful of these states fashioned elaborate policies aimed at the systematic expansion and exploitation of their frontier regions. Such policies embraced both diplomatic and military measures, including the construction of chains of forts and outpost cities, planned migrations, the establishment and taxation of controlled markets, and settlement schemes like the *tuntian* policy of the Han dynasty, in which garrison troops were expected to open up the "wastelands" and support themselves by farming in the frontier regions in which they were posted.[17]

Yet while China has long laid claim to vast areas of the continent, much of this territory remained frontier regions. Only in the former frontier region south of the Yangzi did much land become part of China proper over the past millennium. Thus there has long been a relatively clear and long-established distinction along much of the perimeter of China between the core area and the frontier zones. Moreover, since the Chinese concept of the heartland was ethnic as well as spatial, regions of largely non-Chinese population remained consistently outside the perceived core area, regardless of their proximity to the heartland. Thus, for example, though much of Inner Mongolia is closer to the Chinese culture hearth at the great bend of the Yellow River than the Yangzi River region is, it has always been and remains "frontier," whereas the Yangzi region became a part of the core area once the Chinese successfully supplanted the indigenous populations and established a solid cultural foundation there.

In effect there were two frontiers. An inner frontier zone stretched between the limits of Chinese agricultural settlement and the lands inhabited by the non-Chinese peoples. Here, around the edges of the core of the eastern China heartland, was a zone of continued and intensive intercultural contact such as has been maintained for centuries, for example, in Gansu, Qinghai, Sichuan, Inner Mongolia, and Yunnan. The outer, larger frontier zone extended as far as the Chinese conceived of the borders of their empire and established their forts to hold it—deep into Central Asia during the great Han empire and in the Tang (and again under Manchu rule during the Qing). The current national boundaries of the PRC roughly correspond to the far limits of the outer frontier under the Qing dynasty. G. William Skinner uses a similar framework in his discussion of urban hierarchies in China, putting the "inner frontiers" at the borders of regions and provinces and identifying as "outer frontiers" the south and southwestern border areas, the inner Asian territories, and the coastal or maritime frontier (Skinner 1977: 318–19).

Rather than attempt to convert the non-Chinese to their way of life, the Chinese often turned the differences between them to their advantage. Many of the Chinese dynasties worked to create local elites indebted to them for their support. Typical was the first Ming emperor, who manipulated the religious hierarchy of Tibet to carry out his policy toward border peoples in Tibetan regions. This policy, "yong qisu er rou qiren" (use their customs to tame them), encouraged Lamaism in order to influence the Tibetan political and economic system. Promoting Lamaism had direct economic benefits for the Ming, since the Tibetan religious hierarchy collected wealth from the lands they held surrounding the monasteries, and in turn were required to pay tribute to the Ming court (Chen Meihe 1986: 7). The Qing adopted a similar policy—"yi suxi wei zhi" (take [their] system of customs in order to rule)—that allowed for limited contact between the Chinese and the non-Chinese, to the benefit of the gentry on both sides (Chen Meihe 1986: 10). Mediating groups developed to facilitate this relationship. For example, Chinese traders served as agents for transactions both between Chinese and Mongolians and among Mongolians. This intermediary system was facilitated, in part, by Mongolian tribal organization, which barred Mongolians from becoming traders. The system survived with only slight modifications into the late nineteenth century, when the Qing dynasty established a school in Beijing to train Mongolian and Tibetan elites to become imperial officials in the frontier regions (Dreyer 1972: 419).

Another important mechanism for the maintenance of Chinese control in the frontier zone was the establishment of markets for trade with the local peoples. Some scholars argue that these markets were one of the fundamental mechanisms, along with tribute and marriage alliances, by which "Chinese courts sought to institutionalize interaction and thereby stabilize frontier relations" (Jagchid & Symons 1989: 79; see also Barfield 1989). Though these markets are often referred to as "tea-and-horse" markets, many other goods were traded in them. In fact, although tea was long traded with the Tibetans, it did not gain popularity among the Mongolians until about the sixteenth century. Until then the trade had centered on the exchange of cloth and grains for horses. Horses were one of the most coveted frontier trade items for the Chinese, who valued them for use in the military (Jagchid & Symons 1989: 80, 165).

Though the frontier peoples managed to maintain their own societies despite considerable contact, they could not help being impacted by the Chinese presence. In some places, Chinese supplanted local people in important occupational niches. In Qing times Chinese craftsmen came to usurp the position of Mongolian craftsmen in the Inner Mongolia region. A striking example is the blacksmith trade, an occupation vital to the Mongolian way of life that was completely taken over by Chinese smiths during the Qing dynasty (Lattimore 1940: 92–93). Moreover, some non-Chinese elites went to great lengths to adopt Chinese practices. Lattimore explains that, in the system of frontier feudalism, "it was impossible to prevent [non-Chinese leaders granted Chinese feudal titles and privileges] from drawing into their 'tribal' pasturages Chinese traders, artisans, and even cultivators, from building for themselves rather outlandish imitations of Chinese palaces and 'cities,' and from diversifying their revenue as far as they could" (ibid., p. 548). As both Lattimore (1940) and Barfield (1989) have observed, those non-Chinese elites who began to play the Chinese game may ultimately have benefited from it.

The immense region that I define as the western frontier—today's Xinjiang, Tibet, Qinghai, and parts of Gansu and Sichuan—has been the homeland of many different peoples over the more than two millennia that the Chinese have from time to time (and for centuries at a time) claimed and administered it. These peoples have undoubtedly had their own perspectives on the "Chinese" frontier. For some, such as the Tibetans, stretches of the "inner Chinese agrarian settlement frontier" has also for centuries been their own settlement frontier. In periods when the Chinese empire asserted its claim over the "outer" frontier regions, many of these peoples must have perceived the Chinese as intruders and conquerors, and their forts and cities as enclaves of outsiders in their homelands. From this perspective periods of Chinese retrenchment would have been perceived as opportunities to reclaim political sovereignty over areas that they may never have ceased to regard as theirs.

On the other hand, times of Chinese imperial weakening and the retraction of frontier administration may also have undermined political and economic linkages between non-Chinese and Chinese in ways that caused considerable concern to some societies and individual leaders. The weakening of the relationships of what Lattimore called frontier feudalism may have been regretted particularly by some non-Chinese groups, such as some of the nomadic groups (and especially by their elites) that had long been accustomed to Chinese economic subsidies and political support. Barfield (1989), for example, argues that these resources were intrinsic to the political organization and lifestyles of a number of nomadic peoples on different parts of the northern, northwestern, and northeastern frontiers across a span of time dating from the Han dynasty until Qing dynasty days.[18] He suggests, to give just one striking example, that intensified Mongol raids against northern China in the Ming dynasty were a nomad response to the initial Ming refusal to establish regular trade (including horse markets) and to grant the Mongols economic subsidies and titles (Barfield 1989: 15–16, 245–46). Similarly, the famous Tibetan raid on Chang'an during the Tang dynasty, which followed a period of Tibet's expansion east at Chinese expense and a century of Chinese policies of royal-level marriage alliances with members of the elite, as well as other signs of recognition and economic support, was a response to China's refusal to forward the annual "tribute" payment of 50,000 rolls of silk that the Tibetans had come to count on as a continuing "peace offering" (Richardson 1984: 28–30).

This was but one instance when the rhythm of recurrent Chinese expansion into the far frontier regions was disrupted by non-Chinese peoples expanding their own territories outward—sometimes for centuries at a time—at Chinese expense, either restricting Chinese administration to southeastern China or supplanting it altogether. The Qidan (Khitan) Liao empire (916–1125), the Ruzhen (Jurchen) Jin dynasty (1115–1234), the Mongols, and the Manchu all invaded the core region of eastern China and established administration over parts or all of it at various times between 916 and 1911. For the Qidan, the Mongols, and the Manchu, Beijing was once a frontier city.[19]

Contemporary Frontiers in China and Abroad

Frontiers are often based as much in cultural contact as in political boundaries. Often—as in the case of China—frontiers are now zones of interaction between states and nations, between governments (states) that represent the culture and society of one or several peoples of a country's core area and other peoples (nations) whose homelands are located in the periphery. Most of the world's armed conflicts today reflect nations' struggles for autonomy in a world defined by states. Contemporary (post-1965) frontier situations often derive from the increasing number of conflicts over frontiers and definitions of states in the postwar period. Many, if not most, of these conflicts are between nations demanding independence and the states that surround or divide them. The historical literature of both China and the West tends to identify inhabited frontiers as the frontiers between sedentary and nomadic peoples. But many nomadic peoples have been sedentarized and confined to the point that this distinction is no longer clear.

For the purposes of this study, I will limit my analysis of the contemporary frontier dynamics to the manifestation and expressions of national identity in urban morphology and architecture. The most significant factor in issues of national identity in China is the extent to which its outward expressions are carefully managed by the state. This management of expression, long a hallmark of Chinese-style governance, has undergone a series of major policy shifts during the era of the People's Republic. Early pride in a heterogeneous nation, with coalitions between national groups, was eventually supplanted by a growing emphasis on homogeneity that reached its height in the Cultural Revolution of the late 1960s and early 1970s, only to be reversed in the 1980s with state-imposed efforts toward controlled expressions of national identity and local character.

That China's west remains a frontier region to this day, not only in political, economic, and cultural terms but also in demographic terms, is illustrated in Map 2. The "Aihui-Tengchong" line on this map is a useful device for delineating in the most simple terms the concentration of the Chinese population in the east. In 1982 roughly 94 percent of the population occupied the 30 percent of the land area east of that line, leaving just 6 percent to occupy the 70 percent of the land area that makes up China's western frontiers.

The political organization of the PRC, moreover, lends itself to a continued differentiation between core and frontier. Most of China's western frontier regions (see Map 1) are governed by "autonomous" units of administration (regions, prefectures, and counties), which receive different treatment on the basis of their relatively high percentages of non-Chinese populations. This system, modeled after the former Soviet Union's "Autonomous Republics,"[20] ensures that frontier peoples remain under an entirely different system of representation and administration. The first autonomous region, Inner Mongolia, was established in 1947, before the Chinese Communist Party gained full control of China. The other four autonomous regions were established after the PRC was founded: Xinjiang Uygur, in 1955; Guangxi Zhuang and Ningxia Hui, in 1958; and Tibet, in 1965. Autonomous regions have the status of provinces and send their own representatives to regional and national governing organizations. In addition, they are allowed some exemptions from the economic and social laws that apply to the provinces.

Some of the more marginal frontier regions receive economic dispensations or subsidies from the national government (see Epstein 1983). But

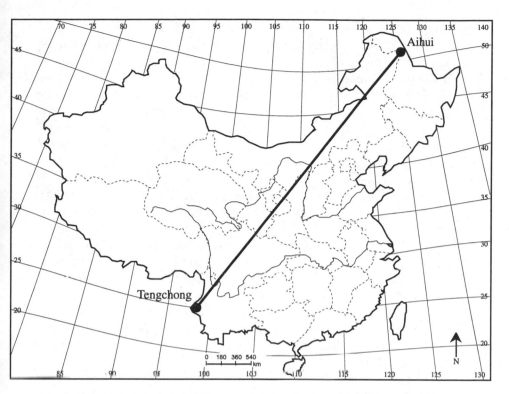

Map 2. The Aihui-Tengchong division of China. In 1982 the region west of the line, 70 percent of China's land area, contained just over 6 percent of the population. Source: based on data in Kirkby 1985: 260.

even as these regions receive aid in social and development programs, there has been a concerted effort to extract resources from them for the benefit of the core area. In his famous 1956 statement "On the Ten Great Relationships," Mao Zedong explained, "We say China is a country vast in territory, rich in resources and large in population, [but] as a matter of fact it is the Han nationality whose population is large and the minority nationalities whose territory is vast and whose resources are rich, or at least in all probability their resources are rich" (cited in Berger 1979: 174). During the decades of development planning after 1949, considerable efforts went into development in the frontier regions, which served the joint purposes of providing resources for the core area and augmenting the defensive buffer zone around it. According to Kang Zhixin, "Large-scale capital construction changed the geographical distribution of China's industry. In the past 30 years, about 40% of China's capital investment went into the construction of projects in the hinterland and in areas inhabited by minority people. Investment in the hinterland accounted for 54% of total investment in 1979, compared with 39% in 1952. The number of factories and mines operating in northwest and southwest China increased from 300 in 1952 to 80,000 in 1979" (Kang Zhixin 1980: 549). Though these economic development efforts in the frontier provinces and autonomous regions have been aimed at raising their standards of living, as well as exploiting their natural resources, these areas are far from achieving economic and development parity with the rest of the country.

The perpetuation of the frontier is no less a cultural and intellectual activity than the product of political and economic policies. Xinjiang, Qinghai, Tibet, and Inner Mongolia all remain the frontier in the minds of the eastern Chinese. And even today the long-standing images of the historical frontier are perpetuated in Chinese books, movies, and television programs. The Tang dynasty epic *The Journey to the West* (currently available in China as a novel, as a long-running television serial, and as a series of children's books) remains perhaps the most popular of China's classic tales. The frontier as depicted in this work about the travels of the monk Xuanzang to India via the Silk Route, aided by the notorious Monkey King, is a land of strange landscapes, unusual peoples, and many dangers and challenges.

The Han Chinese have had much more personal experience with the western frontier in the post-1949 era than they had in the past as a result of a series of population movements, including both the permanent resettlement of Han Chinese in the frontier regions and the temporary sojourns of Chinese "sent down" there during the Cultural Revolution and earlier periods. Perhaps as a result of this experience, the frontier of today is also a popular subject in contemporary literature and film. Recent movies, such as "Season of Love," set in Inner Mongolia, and "Sacrificed Youth," set in Yunnan, both of which tell stories of Beijing teenagers sent down during the Cultural Revolution, address the themes of the "foreign" nature of life on the frontier and the interaction between Chinese and non-Chinese people.

Peoples of China's Western Frontiers

Frontiers are regions of interaction between different groups of people. The identification of these groups, with their interests and characteristics, is important to policy makers and frontier analysts alike. As noted, under the PRC frontier peoples must apply for official recognition by the central government. Fifty-five peoples are currently formally recognized as *shaoshu minzu* (minority nationalities). Formal recognition is a complex process, involving an analysis of language, customs, history, settlement patterns, and other factors to determine whether or not a group is eligible for minority (non-Chinese) status, and, if so, whether it falls into some already identified category, such as the Tibetans, or is culturally unique. Official status as a minority nationality is extremely important, since political and economic policies often differentiate between Chinese and non-Chinese people. For example, non-Chinese people in some circumstances are allowed to legally marry at a younger age than the Chinese and may have fewer legal restrictions on the number of children they can bear.

By 1955 over 400 groups had applied for status as minority nationalities. More than 260 of these groups came from the culturally complex mountain areas of Yunnan Province. As of 1957, only 11 groups had been officially identified (Fei Xiaotong 1981: 60–61). Even in the mid-1980s, after almost half a century of study and classification, the PRC had yet to classify nearly 800,000 people by nationality.[21] The 28 largest currently designated *shaoshu minzu*, with their populations, are listed in Table 1. In this book I will rely primarily on these modern categories, with the understanding that they do not necessarily match precisely the definition or self-identification of culture groups in the pre-1949 era.

For the purposes of this study, however, I prefer to divide the peoples of China into four broad cultural groups, based on their distinct urban

TABLE 1

Officially Recognized Minority Nationalities, 1990

(populations greater than 100,000)

Nationality	Population	Nationality	Population
Zhuang	15,489,630	Hani	1,235,952
Man (Manchu)	9,821,180	Kazak	1,111,718
Hui	8,602,978	Li	1,110,900
Miao	7,398,035	Dai (Tai)	1,025,128
Uygur	7,214,431	She	630,378
Yi	6,572,173	Lisu	574,856
Tujia	5,704,223	Lahu	411,476
Mongol (Mongolian)	4,806,849	Dongxiang	373,872
Tibetan (Zang)	4,593,330	Va	351,974
Buyi	2,545,059	Sui	345,993
Dong	2,514,014	Naxi	278,009
Yao	2,134,013	Qiang (Chang)	198,252
Korean	1,920,597	Tu	191,624
Bai	1,594,827	Kirgiz	141,549

SOURCE: Zhao Songqiao 1994: 120.

traditions and settlement practices: the Han Chinese, the Islamic peoples, the Lamaist peoples, and the peoples of the southwest.[22] In the following pages I will provide a brief introduction to each of these groups.

The Han Chinese

The Han Chinese are united by many common traditions and beliefs, as well as a common written language and shared history. Leo Moser (1985), in one of the few books to make a thorough presentation of cultural variations among the Han Chinese, notes a number of key cultural traits shared by all of them. These include the use of the same written language, the belief in an ancestral cult, and a strong sense of association and loyalty to their native place. Though the belief in the ancestral cult is discouraged today and has been abandoned in much of mainland China, the unity imparted by a shared written language and a strong sense of association and loyalty to native place endures. Yet there is considerable regional variation in spoken dialects, subsistence practices, settlement patterns, and a number of cultural practices such as dress and food preferences. One striking example is the difference between the Mandarin and Cantonese dialects. Another is the striking difference in rural lifestyles between the Han Chinese in the wheat- and sorghum-based agricultural regions of the north and the rice-based agricultural regions of the south.

According to the PRC, about 93 percent of China's population is ethnically Han. Some scholars contend that the use of the term "Han" in such a broad sense is a modern political construct. The anthropologist Dru Gladney presents this argument clearly in his 1991 work, *Muslim Chinese*. For the purposes of this book, I will focus on the evolution of the "Chinese" as following two often, but not always, linked paths: the evolution of the culture of "Han ren," those people who trace their origins to the early civilizations centered on the great bend in the Yellow River, and the evolution of the Chinese empire, a political entity that can be traced through centuries of dynastic history in spite of boundary and capital changes and even changes in the ethnicity of those who ruled it.

Chinese culture is usually traced to the peoples who inhabited the region of the great bend in the Yellow River about 3,000–4,000 years ago.[23] Over a period of centuries, these peoples fanned out eastward from the heartland of the North China plain, to occupy the land and politically and culturally integrate its peoples into the empire. The core area for Chinese settlement was more or less established by the time of the Han dynasty, though the Chinese empire was subsequently fragmented by political divisions and would remain so for several centuries. This traditional area established during the Han reaches from the Great Wall boundary north of Beijing to the south coast, and from the east coast to the eastern edge of Tibet in the west. Many of the beliefs and practices that form the basis for Chinese culture were established by the end of the Han era. By then the Chinese already had a strong sense of cultural identity and identified themselves as "civilized" people distinct from their neighbors.

An unusual aspect of Chinese culture is a tendency to maintain plural belief systems rather than to adhere to one or another of the world's major faiths. Throughout their history, the Chinese have taken a synthetic approach to religion, often embracing more than one major faith at any time. The major religions developed by the Chinese are Confucianism and Daoism. Buddhism, imported from India, has also been important in Chinese culture. While religious professionals have usually kept strictly to their doctrines, it has been common practice in Chinese popular religion to combine practices derived from all three faiths.

The empire itself vacillated between periods of strong rule by the Chinese, periods of domination by foreign dynasties, and periods of fragmentation. The three great epochs of Chinese rule, after the Han, were the Tang (618–907), Song (960–1280), and Ming (1368–1644) periods. During each of these periods, the Chinese controlled vast areas and managed extensive frontier zones through their frontier settlements. But one of the remarkable aspects of Chinese culture over the long span of history is its survival during times of foreign domination, particularly the Mongol Yuan dynasty (1279–1368) and the Manchu Qing dynasty (1644–1911). Chinese culture continued to flourish and remained strong not only in the everyday lives of ordinary citizens, but in the very rule of the foreign dynasties as well. Thus the Mongols built their capital at Beijing according to ideals of Chinese urban planning, and the Manchu walled their garrisons, just as the Chinese did.

Today the Chinese culture region extends far beyond the political boundaries of the People's Republic, to Taiwan, Hong Kong, and Singapore, and to scattered communities throughout the rest of the world. Within the People's Republic, some aspects of Chinese culture have been altered through both the natural changes that occur with development and modernization and the intense efforts of the PRC to change what it disliked about traditional China. Despite these changes, however, the Han Chinese have retained a culture that can still be traced to the practices of the Han era and earlier.

Islamic Peoples

Islam reached China in the mid-seventh century via sea traders from Arabia and Persia. These merchants carried on a lively trade in the ports open to foreigners, of which Guangzhou, Quanzhou, and Hangzhou were the most significant. The form of Islam they brought with them, traditional Sunni, Hanafi Islam, became known as Gedimu (the Old Sect) in China (Gladney 1987b: 15; 1991: 37). During the Tang and Song dynasties, Islam also reached what is now western China via the overland Silk Routes north and south of the Tianshan range. Here the movement began with the introduction of Sufi practices in Kashgar in 955 and spread eastward, to arrive in the Tarim basin by the mid-eleventh century, where it eventually supplanted both Buddhism and Manichaeism (Sinor 1969: 235–36). Traders from Persia and Afghanistan brought Islam to much of the vast northwestern frontiers of China and even as far east as Qinghai, Gansu, and the region around Chang'an (Xi'an; Wu Jide 1986: 46–47).

During the thirteenth century, after the Mongols conquered China and established the Yuan dynasty, many Islamic peoples migrated to China from Central Asia, Persia, and Arabia (Wu Jide 1986: 47). Islam spread under the patronage of Khubilai Khan's grandson Ananda, and with the travels of Islamic "merchants, envoys, military officers, and others" (Jagchid & Hyer 1979: 195). The net result of these Islamic migrations was the establishment of settled Islamic communities across most of China. Those in the west often included several different Islamic peoples living in close proximity. Those in the east are in general much smaller and almost entirely composed of Hui; many of them developed in place as a result of earlier conversions before the Mongol era.

The development of Islam among the Hui is particularly interesting because it has often involved the fusion of traditional Chinese beliefs with Islam. Sufism became widespread among Hui believers in China during the seventeenth century, with the rise of various orders that were based on saintly lineages and made use of saints' tombs and shrines as centers of devotional activity. At least one of the Sufi orders that developed at this time among the Hui combined Sufism with elements of Confucian moral tenets, Daoist mystical concepts, and Buddhist folk rituals (Gladney 1987b: 19–22). For the next 200 years or so, Islam in China developed in relative isolation from the rest of the Islamic world, and in some cases became infused with distinctive Chinese practices. In the early twentieth century a renewal of ties with Islam brought a wave of reform to Hui Islam.[24] As a result, the Hui returned to a veneration of the scriptures rather than saints (ibid., pp. 28–31).

Under the PRC, Islam has undergone much the same experience as other religious beliefs and organizations. It was more or less tolerated during the early years of the People's Republic, vilified during the Cultural

Revolution, and permitted more open expression and revival during the 1980s. There are ten officially recognized Islamic "minority nationalities" in China today, namely (in order of population): the Hui, Uygur, Kazakh, Dongxiang, Kirghiz, Sala, Tajik, Uzbek, Bonan, and Tatar peoples. However, some of these ethnic categories may be more politically than culturally constructed (see, e.g., Gladney 1991: 34 on the Dongxiang, Baoan, and Sala).

The Hui. The Hui, China's third largest "minority nationality," have often been referred to as "Chinese Muslims" or, in the pre-1949 era, Dungans. The term "Chinese Muslims" is a misnomer, implying as it does that they are simply Han Chinese people who believe in Islam. Though the Hui speak Chinese dialects and may have Chinese ancestors, they have a distinct (though widely varying) culture and history. The frequent incorrect equation of the Hui and the Chinese derives in part from recent observations of the small groups in eastern China who have lost much of the religious practice of Islam and are more or less integrated into Chinese society, retaining only a few remnant cultural practices. For example, the Hui near Quanzhou in Fujian Province are now distinguished primarily by their ancestral lineages and do not observe Islamic practices. Dru Gladney found that this depiction is substantiated by the Fujian Hui's self-description and identification (Gladney 1991: 262). The Hui are more culturally distinct in other parts of China, and particularly on the frontiers, where their settlements are relatively large. The largest populations are in Gansu, Ningxia, and Henan provinces. There is also a large population of Hui in Xinjiang, perhaps reflecting a mass immigration of Hui from Gansu and Shaanxi that took place in the late eighteenth century, with the encouragement of the emperor (Schinz 1989: 441). But Hui people can be found in every province of China, particularly in the urban areas.

The Hui are thus a diverse group. According to Gladney, "The people now known as the Hui are descended from Persian, Arab, Mongolian and Turkish Muslim merchants, soldiers and officials who settled in China from the seventh to fourteenth centuries and intermarried with local non-Muslim women. Largely living in isolated communities, the only thing that some but not all had in common was a belief in Islam" (Gladney 1991: 96–97). The Hui engage in all manner of occupations, but traditionally they were particularly concentrated in occupations such as "restauranteer, innkeeper, shepherd, cavalryman, caravaneer, butcher, tanner, tea trader, jeweler, interpreter and clergyman" (ibid., p. 30). Before 1949 some Hui were renowned as traders, using donkey caravans to serve as middlemen between Chinese and nomadic peoples on the northwestern frontier. And some Hui in the northwest, particularly in Datong, north-west of Xining, also made a living as gold miners (Chow 1949: 110). In the southwest the Hui of Yunnan have been both urban and rural dwell-ers. During the Qing dynasty, some Hui also labored as mineworkers for the Chinese in Yunnan. The famous fifteenth-century naval commander Zhenghe, a Hui from Yunnan Province, and Ma Bufang, the warlord of Qinghai in the early twentieth century, are but two examples of the many Hui who actively participated in China's government and history.

During the post–Cultural Revolution period, and particularly after 1980, the Hui have been very active in the reconstruction of mosques throughout China. Many of these reconstructions are being carried out without any outside funding and attest to the continued dedication of the Hui to their religious communities.

The Uygur. The establishment of the Xinjiang Uygur Autonomous Region on October 1, 1955, reified in spatial terms the designation of the Uygur as one of China's largest minority nationality groups. As with the Hui, however, the designation of the Uygur as a single people masks re-gional variations in a diverse and widespread group. The name Uygur it-self seems to have been revived during the twentieth century, after several centuries of nonuse. The extent to which the present-day people are de-scended from the original Uygur tribes as they were known in the eighth century remains an open issue.

The Uygur emerged as a unified Central Asian people by about A.D. 700 in what is now Outer Mongolia (Schwarz 1984: 3). In 762–63 the Uygur ruler Mou-yu was converted to Manichaeism during a stay at the Chinese capital of Luoyang. He returned to Mongolia with four Mani-chaean priests and made Manichaeism the state religion. Sinor notes that this represented the first adoption of an international religion by a Central Asian nomadic group (Sinor 1969: 114–15). In the latter half of the eighth century, the Uygur built a capital city on the Selenga River with "a magnificent royal castle" and "twelve iron gates of huge size" (Mackerras 1972: 13).

The Uygur were defeated by the Kirghiz in 840, and many fled to China for refuge. Thirteen tribes got as far as North China and were ap-parently absorbed into the population there. Fifteen others fled to the west and southwest, and established a city-state in the Dunhuang region and the Turfan basin. The Uygur established a sedentarized lifestyle and built a grand capital at Gaochang, near the present-day city of Turfan. Accord-ing to Sinor, paintings from the walls of Gaochang indicate that the Uygur were probably living at that time in Chinese-style courtyard housing.

Most of the people in this multicultural kingdom seem to have been either Buddhists or Nestorians, but Gaochang was apparently tolerant of a variety of peoples and religious practices (Sinor 1969: 115–21). The remains of Gaochang's extensive city wall and some monumental structures have been excavated and remain a lasting monument to the Uygur urban civilization.

Between the tenth and sixteenth centuries, the Uygur were gradually converted to Islam. At the same time the fall of the Mongol empire led to a breakdown of the great trading networks that had supported the oasis kingdom of Gaochang. As the Gaochang kingdom faded, so, too, apparently, did the concept of the Uygur as a people. The people who had been the Uygur became identified with or were absorbed into the population of the widely dispersed oases they inhabited.[25] The term "Uygur" fell into disuse. It was not until the Yaqub Beg rebellion (1864–77), in which Islamic peoples rose up against the Chinese empire, that a more unified Islamic nationalism developed in Xinjiang. The term "Uygur" itself was revived and used to describe these peoples in both the Soviet Union and China in the early twentieth century (Gladney 1990: 8–14). It may be, as Edward Allworth indicates, that the term was first revived by Soviet organizers for the local people they met in Tashkent in 1921 (Allworth 1990: 206).

The Uygur were one of the first peoples to be identified by the PRC as a *shaoshu minzu*. Today there are more than seven million Uygur in China, most of whom live in small villages and towns in Xinjiang. The remainder of the world's Uygur live primarily in Kazakhstan and Kyrgyzstan.

The Sala and the Dongxiang. The Sala and the Dongxiang are identified as distinct peoples by the Chinese government. Both live in relatively small communities near Xining and Lanzhou.[26] The origins of the Sala are "murky at best" (Li & Stuart 1990: 40). Some believe they are descendants of migrants from Samarkand who came to Qinghai after Chinggis Khan's western expedition and there mixed with Tibetans, Chinese, and Hui to form a distinct group (Xin Jiguang 1987: 32). Others trace their presence in China to as early as the Tang dynasty or emphasize the role of the Tibetans in their ancestry. Most accounts agree, however, that the Sala had Central Asian origins (Li & Stuart 1990: 40–43). The late-nineteenth-century traveler William Woodville Rockhill remarked that "the Sala have retained their original language and still speak it with such purity that it is perfectly intelligible to the traders from Ho-tien and Kashgar who come to Hsi-ning [Xining] and Ho-chou" (Rockhill 1894: 40).

There are approximately 70,000 Sala in the PRC, 70 percent of whom live in the Xunhua Sala Autonomous County near Xining. The Sala live in flat-roofed adobe houses with courtyards filled with fruit trees, and earn their living primarily by growing melons, grapes, apricots, dates, apples, and walnuts. There were at one time at least 74 mosques in that county alone (Schwarz 1984: 39–46).

The Dongxiang, the fourth-largest of the Islamic peoples in China, number more than 373,000 people, two-thirds of whom live in the Dongxiang Autonomous County in Gansu. Most of the others live in the cities of Lanzhou and Xining. The name "Dongxiang" is derived from the local name for the Gansu region. Prior to 1949 these people were known as Dongxiang Hui or Mongolian Hui. Although their origins are uncertain, they are probably descended from Mongol troops garrisoned in the region who intermarried with Chinese women. Their language is related to Mongolian, and they continue to practice some Mongolian customs (Schwarz 1984: 97–106).

Lamaist Peoples

The most populous Lamaist groups living on the Chinese frontiers are the Tibetans and the Mongolians. Though quite distinct, with different territories and histories and many divergent cultural traits, these two groups are linked by their adherence to Lamaism (Lamajiao), or Tibetan Buddhism. Both peoples have a long history of interaction with the Chinese before the advent of Lamaism.

Lamaism is a form of Buddhism that developed in Tibet through a synthesis of traditional Tibetan religion (Bon) and Buddhist traditions imported from India, Nepal, and China. Buddhism was introduced to Tibet in the mid-seventh century, and the first Buddhist temples there were built during the reign of King Songsten Gampo (Songzanganbu; r. 608–50). During the mid-ninth century, however, Buddhism was suppressed in central Tibet, and it was not reestablished there until the middle of the tenth century. From that time on Lamaism developed in a number of different sects and traditions.

The most influential strain of Lamaism is the Yellow or Yellow Hat sect, a branch of Mahayana Buddhism founded by the Tibetan religious reformer Tsong Khapa (Zongkapa; 1357–1419).[27] The tradition of the Dalai Lamas of the Yellow Sect was established in 1577, when Tsong Khapa's third successor, Sonam Gyatso, was given the title Dalai Lama by Altan Khan, a Mongolian prince (Richardson 1984: 40–41).[28] Thus Tibetans and Mongolians are closely tied by common religion and religious organization, as well as through some commonalities of nomadic lifestyles shared by the Mongolians and a segment of the Tibetan population.

The Tibetans. Nomadic peoples known to the Chinese as the Qiang and the Tufan inhabited the Tibetan plateau as early as the second century B.C., ranging over not only the plateau itself, but also far into Central Asia and what is now northwest China.[29] The many clans of Qiang were unified by a leader in the Yarlung valley of central Tibet, Namri Songsten, in about A.D. 600. His son, Songsten Gampo, established Tibet as an empire and powerful military state during his rule from 627 to 650. He also moved the capital of Tibet to Lhasa, where it has remained ever since. During those early years Buddhism and writing were introduced from India, and secular law from China (R. A. Stein 1972: 45–61). Other aspects of Chinese culture were introduced by Chinese princesses who married Tibetan rulers and by other Chinese travelers.

The Tibetan empire continued to grow during the eighth century. This Tang-era empire bore little resemblance to the Tibetan theocracy of modern times. It was a militaristic and expansionist state that controlled a vast territory, at times including cities in southern Xinjiang, as well as Qinghai. In 763 Tibetan forces even succeeded in sacking the Tang dynasty capital of Chang'an (today's Xi'an). At the beginning of the ninth century, however, the Tibetans entered a prolonged period of political and cultural upheaval following the death of the last king of Songsten Gampo's line, who had persecuted Buddhists and was assassinated by a Buddhist monk. For the following four centuries, Tibet existed as a fragmented state with contending factions maintaining power bases at separate monasteries and cities. Tibet remained divided until the thirteenth century, when the Mongols used military force to assist in its reorganization as a political state centered on the Lhasa-Xigaze region. The Gelukpa (Yellow Hat) sect emerged with the rise of Tsong Khapa in the fourteenth century, and had spread throughout Tibet and Mongolia by the seventeenth century. Tibetan society coalesced into a theocracy based on the leadership of the Dalai Lamas in the seventeenth century, after Mongol military leaders assisted the Fifth Dalai Lama to power over a unified Tibet. From the eighteenth century onward, the issue of Tibetan sovereignty became increasingly complex. The Qing dynasty declared Tibet a protectorate in 1720,[30] stationed a garrison in Lhasa, exacted annual tribute, and actively participated in Tibetan affairs of state until 1912, when Tibetan independence was restored and the thirteenth Dalai Lama, who had been living in exile, returned. To make matters more complex, the Tibetans were also paying tribute to Nepal during this period, after having suffered a military defeat at the hands of the Nepalese (R. A. Stein 1972: 61–91).

The Tibetans enjoyed only 39 years of independence. The PRC annexed Tibet in 1951, and in 1959, after a long period of resistance, agreements, and disillusionments, followed by an abortive uprising in Lhasa, the Dalai Lama fled to India, and Tibet was placed under Chinese military and advisory control. In 1965 the PRC established the Tibetan Autonomous Region.

There are many regional variations in Tibetan culture, including differences in languages and lifestyles. There are nomadic Tibetans, and Tibetans who practice settled village agriculture, and Tibetans who live in cities. A distinctive group of Tibetans who occupy the margins of the Huangshui valley, the Xiningfan, are of particular concern in this study. They cultivate barley, oats, and peas and other vegetables. Some live in mixed Chinese/Tibetan/Hui villages. Villages of Xiningfan at higher elevations are solely Tibetan. There are four groups of Xiningfan—the Changjia, the Niuzu, the Shardin, and the Runjia—of which the last two live nearest to Xining (Chow 1949: 120–21).

The Mongolians. The Mongolians are one of the eight peoples who dominated the steppes of Inner Asia during traditional times, the others being the Xiongnu, the Xianbi, the Ruan-ruan, the Tujue, the Uygur, the Qidan, and the Manchu. The name Mongol and the clans associated with the name date only from the thirteenth century, when Chinggis Khan, convinced that the Sky God Mongke Tenggeri had given him responsibility for unifying the Mongolians and ruling the world, brought several clans together to form the Mongol empire (Jagchid & Hyer 1979: 1–19; Rossabi 1988: 4). Unification was accompanied by a growing ethnic consciousness (Rossabi 1988: 4). The empire under Chinggis Khan and his successors was widespread and powerful. In the thirteenth century the Mongols conquered China, which they ruled as the Yuan dynasty until they were overthrown in 1368. During the period of their domination of Asia, Mongolian people dispersed widely across the continent, and they and their collaborators had great impact on the formation of Asian continental cultures. At its height the Mongol empire controlled a broad expanse of land reaching from the Pacific Ocean to the shores of the Mediterranean.

The period of Mongol control in China (1264–1368) saw a great increase throughout the empire in multicultural interaction and the integration of a variety of cultural forms. For example, when Khubilai Khan organized the construction of Khanbaligh (Beijing), he hired a Chinese to design the city, a Muslim to serve as architect, and a Mongol to supervise the project. Large yurts were still used as palaces in the city as late as 1353 (Wright 1977: 66–67). And in the frontier city of Kunming, the Mongols' appointed governor of Yunnan, a Muslim military leader of Central

Asian origin, sponsored projects that promoted Confucianism, Daoism, and other Chinese religious practices, as well as Islam (Yu Xueren 1987: 22–28).

After the fall of the Yuan dynasty, the Mongols retreated to what is today Inner and Outer Mongolia. In 1578 the Mongolian prince Altan Khan was converted to Tibetan Buddhism during a visit to Mongolia by Sonam Gyatso. Other Tibetan lamas carried the message to Mongolia, and in less than 100 years, most of the Mongolian people were converted to Tibetan Buddhism. The Mongols in turn played a prominent role in the evolution of Tibetan Buddhism and the Tibetan theocracy when Gusri Khan, a Mongol prince, defeated the Tibetan king in 1642 and supported the Fifth Dalai Lama as Tibet's supreme religious leader, while taking the secular leadership of Tibet into his own hands (Richardson 1984: 41–42).[31] From the seventeenth century to the twentieth, the Qing government of China exercised considerable influence in Mongolia, and sought to further "divide and rule" the Mongols by creating numerous ranks and titles that eroded their traditional ability to organize and defend themselves against a strong nation. The Qing offered independent Mongolian leaders security in return for allegiance (Jagchid & Hyer 1972: 245–300).

From about the eighteenth century on, the Mongolians were increasingly caught between the expansion of the Qing dynasty northward and the expansion of Tsarist Russia southward. China and Russia ultimately agreed to divide Mongolian territory between them. The Mongolian People's Republic was established in 1924 as a client state of the USSR and, after a long period of socialism and relative isolation, is now beginning to open to the world. The Inner Mongolian Autonomous Region of China was established with the founding of the People's Republic of China in 1949.

Peoples of the Southwest

The mountainous regions of China's southwest have the greatest cultural diversity in China. Yunnan Province alone is inhabited by 24 officially recognized national minorities, as follows (in order of representation): Yi, Bai, Hani, Zhuang, Dai, Miao, Lisu, Hui, Lahu, Va, Naxi, Yao, Tibetans, Jingpo, Bulang, Pumi, Nu, Achang, Benglong, Juno, Shui, Mongolians, Bouyei, and Drung. These diverse peoples represent a wide spectrum of cultural and historic traditions, from the nomadic traditions of some groups of Tibetans and other mountain peoples to the sedentary society of the Bai. The non-Chinese peoples of the southwest can be classed into three broad groups on the basis of religious belief: the Islamic peoples, primarily Hui; peoples who practice forms of Buddhism, such as the Tibetans and the Dai; and peoples who practice a variety of indigenous, usually animistic beliefs, and who are most closely related to the peoples referred to as "hill tribes" in highland Southeast Asia. Linguistic classifications of the peoples of the southwest classify most as speakers of one or another of the Tibeto-Burmese languages within the Sino-Tibetan language family.[32] I myself prefer a finer distinction that singles out six major cultural "types" in the southwest, namely: (1) those peoples who have maintained a distinct culture but also borrowed elements from Chinese culture as a result of a long history of contact and interaction with the Chinese, such as the Bai; (2) remnant populations introduced to the southwest during the course of the Mongol invasion, particularly the Hui; (3) peoples who trace their origins to the Tibetan plateau and who retain some aspects of Tibetan cultural practices, such as the Pumi; (4) peoples who trace their origins to and retain some cultural affinity with the peoples of northern Thailand and Burma, such as the Dai; (5) peoples who may have migrated from Cambodia and Vietnam, and maintain cultural and linguistic practices from upland Mon-Khmer culture, such as the Va; and (6) peoples who have developed relatively distinct cultural and linguistic traits, such as the Miao and Yao. The peoples most directly involved with urbanism in Yunnan Province, the focus of this study in southwest China, are the Bai, the Dai, the Sani (Yi), and the Hui.

The Bai. The Bai are the descendants of a people who have long urban and agrarian traditions and who developed a major and long-lasting kingdom on the borders of China.[33] The Bai Nan Zhao kingdom was established in the Dali and Kunming region of Yunnan more than 2,000 years ago and endured as an independent state until the Mongol conquest of the thirteenth century. Although the Bai had not previously been incorporated into the Chinese empire, they had had numerous dealings with the Chinese over the centuries and had adopted many Chinese practices. Unlike most of the other non-Chinese peoples in the southwest, the Bai established a tradition of sedentarized agriculture very similar to that of the Chinese by the time of the Sui and Tang dynasties. Their principal traditional crops were irrigated rice, including locally developed varieties that produced well at relatively high altitudes, and millet. Maize also became important in late imperial times. In addition the Dali region is famous in China for its marble resources, so famous that the Chinese word for marble is Dalishi (Dali-stone). The Bai controlled the quarrying, carving, and trade of this prized stone, which was exported on a large scale to adorn the imperial palaces of Chang'an and Beijing. The Bai adopted many aspects of Chinese religion over their long history of contact with the Chinese and constructed Buddhist pagodas and temples as early as the Tang dynasty. The Bai utilized Chinese ideals in the layout of the city of Dali. Nonetheless, the Bai have retained their own identity, with a distinctive language, style of dress, and domestic architecture.

The Dai and the Sani Yi. Although the Bai were the major ethnic group and cultural elite of the Nan Zhao kingdom, the Dai were an important part of that kingdom as well. Today the Buddhist Dai are perhaps the most well known of the Yunnan minority nationalities in China; thanks to their colorful festivals and ways, they are much portrayed in Chinese film and literature and are something of a domestic tourist attraction. The Dai are members of a larger group with a common language and set of customs known as the Baiyue, which includes peoples in Yunnan, Guangxi, Sichuan, and Guizhou (the Zhuang, Dong, Shui, Bouyei, and Li), as well as peoples in northern Laos, Thailand, Burma, and India. The Dai are Hinayana Buddhists and share strong similarities in some facets of culture with the Thai of mainland Southeast Asia.

The Sani Yi, one of the subgroups of China's Yi people, were also members of the Nan Zhao kingdom. The Yi practice Buddhism and Daoism. Approximately 50,000 Sani inhabit the Lunan Yi Autonomous County. Their homeland is the "stone forest" area, a region of eroded limestone karst pinnacles about three hours from Kunming by road. Many Sani also live within Kunming itself, and they have become one of the most visibly identifiable minority groups in Kunming in recent years because of their wearing of colorful ethnic dress and marketing of handicrafts. Margaret Swain has traced the recent visibility of the Sani in Kunming to their entry into the tourist industry in Kunming around 1984. From that time, the Sani have been in increasing evidence in their traditional clothing in Kunming, selling handbags and other handicrafts to tourists, and, in more recent years, participating in money-changing operations as well (Swain 1990).

These diverse peoples are the contemporary survivors of a long history of frontier interaction with the Chinese empire. As the Chinese empire waxed and waned, these distinctive peoples also developed. Other frontier peoples who will appear in the next chapter, such as the Xixia, the Xiongnu, and the Tangut, also played substantial roles in the making of China's persistent frontier regions, though they themselves were subsumed in the tides of history.

The Chinese frontiers, then, are inhabited frontiers subject to cycles of domination by the Chinese empire, all the while maintaining a sometimes delicate balance between conflicting allegiances and identities. They mark the limits of both the expansion of Han Chinese culture and the expansion of non-Chinese cultures, such as those of the Tibetans, the Mongolians, and the Uygur. In the following pages, this book will explore the roles Chinese cities played along this great zone of multiculturalism: as both bastions of core cultures and places of multicultural exchange where new ways of life developed.

The Historical Development of the Five Cities

Iranian fire worshippers and musicians were to be found in all of [the cities of the northwestern frontier during the Tang dynasty], and all were of doubtful allegiance: one year the Chinese Mandarins were in residence, quoting the sages and counseling virtue; the next year the Turks rode in, waving their bows; often Tibetan princes were their lords.

—Edward Schafer, *Golden Peaches of Samarkand,* 1963

Each of the cities in this study has long served as an outpost of Chinese settlement in non-Chinese territory. Kunming, whose mild temperatures have earned it the nickname "City of Springtime," is a Chinese outpost in the fertile mountains of the Yunnan-Guizhou plateau. Yunnan Province borders on Burma and Laos, and has the most culturally complex population of any of China's provinces: 24 non-Chinese groups account for about a third of the total population of the province today (and for substantially more than that in the past). Lanzhou, whose early fame was earned as a key trading center on the Silk Routes, is the first city along the upper reaches of the Yellow River as it winds its way east toward the heart of China. This city of the loess region has a substantial Islamic population and lies just north of the northeastern reaches of the Tibetan culture region. In recent years Lanzhou has exchanged its role as a trading center for that of the northwest's most industrialized city. Xining, a city that continues to serve as a primary gateway to Tibet, lies on the northeastern reaches of the Tibetan plateau, near the westernmost reaches of the Chinese loess plateau, where Chinese, Mongolian, and Tibetan civilizations meet. In addition to these groups, there is a substantial Islamic population in Xining. Qinghai itself is sparsely inhabited, and the city of Xining accounts for nearly one-quarter of the total population of the province. Hohhot, whose Mongolian name is "The Blue City," was developed by Mongolian, Chinese, Manchu, and Hui peoples over the course of several hundred years as both a trading post linking the world of the steppe to the Chinese realm and a religious center for Mongolian-Tibetan Buddhism. It is located in Inner Mongolia, a once sparsely inhabited region that has undergone localized heavy industrial development and substantial Han Chinese settlement since 1949. Urumqi lies just north of the ancient Silk Routes' string of oases, nestled on the plains at the foot of the Tianshan mountains in Xinjiang. Once a small military garrison town, whose founders erected a red walled temple to Guandi,[1] Urumqi is now a bustling, cosmopolitan center for trade and industry. Xinjiang long had an overwhelmingly non-Chinese population, with only scattered settlements of Chinese in the cities. Today the numbers of Han Chinese and Uygur in Xinjiang are about even.

Each of these five cities is a regional administrative center. Xining, Lanzhou, and Kunming are provincial capitals, and Hohhot and Urumqi are the capitals of autonomous regions (which have a national political status similar to that of provinces). All have witnessed major population and industrial growth since 1949, as have the regions they administer. Table 2 shows the population growth in their home provinces between 1885 and 1985. Much of this growth is the product of in-migration rather than natural increase, and represents a substantial change in the cultural character of these regions. The bulk of migration to the western provinces since 1949 has been a migration of Chinese people from the east, and a significant portion of these newcomers have settled in urban areas, especially in the capital cities. This substantial increase in frontier urban popu-

TABLE 2
Population by Province/Autonomous Region, 1885–1985

Province	1885	1922	1953	1985
Yunnan	11,700,000	9,839,180	17,472,737	33,620,000
Gansu	5,400,000	5,927,997	12,928,102	20,160,000
Inner Mongolia	—	—	6,100,104	19,850,000
Xinjiang	2,491,000	—	4,873,608	13,440,000
Qinghai	—	—	1,676,534	4,020,000

SOURCES: 1885, Qing census of 1885, as reported in *The China Yearbook, 1924* (the Xinjiang figure is from the Mingchengpu census, 1910); 1922, Post Office estimate, as reported in the 1924 yearbook; 1953, Tregear 1970: 103–4; 1985, PRC, State Statistical Bureau 1985.

NOTE: The figures are only approximations, since the boundaries of these political units have been redefined several times over the last 100 years.

lations has resulted in near-complete transformation of these capital cities from frontier garrison towns to large industrial centers.

This chapter provides sketches of the history of each of the cities, with an emphasis on processes of formation and growth. The material is compiled principally from Chinese sources, including both historical gazetteers and local histories and contemporary academic works. With the exception of the works of Paul Hyer (1982) and William Jankowiak (1993) on Hohhot, and a few pages on each city by Alfred Schinz (1989), there has been little description or discussion of China's frontier cities in the English literature on Chinese urbanism. Works in English that address frontier cities are primarily limited to either pre-1949 travel accounts or recently published travel guides. I have included in the text a few quotes from these popular accounts to illustrate some common nonacademic observations and characterizations of frontier cities.

Historical sources reveal some basic patterns of development among these cities, such as their founding as seats of administrative power, their development as trade centers, and their settlement through long-distance migration prompted by military, political, or economic circumstances. These common patterns will be discussed in further detail in later chapters.

Lanzhou, the City of Golden Walls and Metal Ramparts

The British consular officer Eric Teichman was much taken with Lanzhou as it appeared in the early part of the twentieth century:

Lanchou Fu . . . is by far the most attractive of the provincial capitals of China I have visited. . . . The greyish yellow city walls and towers blending with the yellow waters of the river and the desolate yellow grey hills all around, the whole relieved by the bright green of the irrigated fields in the valley, combine to form an attractive picture which will long remain with those on whom the deserts and mountains of the North West exercise their mysterious charm. (Teichman 1921: 115)

Some 700 miles west-southwest of Beijing, Lanzhou today is a bustling industrial city that sprawls along the Yellow River where, still relatively narrow, it cuts through the Gansu loess. The city has a long history as an important stop for caravans on the Silk Routes, an administrative center for the northwestern frontier territories, and a center for trade between the Chinese and the peoples of the frontier. The main developed area lies on the south bank of the river at an altitude of 1,520 m (5,016 ft.). Loess bluffs rise abruptly on the north side of the river, allowing only a narrow strip of settlement along the bank. The south bank is about 3 km wide at its widest point. The line of the southern hills curves on either side of the city, cutting off the plain east and west.

The compact old city on the south bank remains the heart of Lanzhou. Here shops, some retaining traditional Chinese facades, line narrow streets, with courtyard housing filling in the blocks behind. The Gansu Provincial Government complex stands at the junction of the main cross streets behind an imposing traditional gateway, the site of the former imperial government representative's headquarters. The area of the old city, with its dense settlement and single-story residential courtyards, contrasts with the sprawling multistory residential compounds and factories built in Lanzhou in the post-1949 years. South and east of the old city, there is a large new development with wide streets and modern buildings. There is also a narrow strip of new development between the hills and the river to the west of the old city. Beyond this lies a new industrial area called Xigu District (Xigucheng). Traditional houses and some new development stand on the north bank, which is dominated by Baitashan Park, a former Buddhist temple complex stretching from the banks of the river to the top of the hills. Another temple complex (also now a public park) rests on the hills south of the city.

Lanzhou has a long settlement history, with archaeological evidence for the first human habitation of the area between 4,000 and 5,000 years ago. During the Qin period the earliest Great Wall extended out into this area. Between 115 B.C. and 111 B.C., the Han emperor sent armies to explore the area and to conscript local people as laborers. A few decades later, the Han court established two fort-cities here: a single-walled fort-city, located south of the present old city area, and a smaller one, to the west, at the site of today's Xigu District. The main city was named Jincheng, or Metal Ramparts,[2] after a proverb—"Well-tempered metal, take it to be a strongpoint"—that harkened back to China's ancient Moist philosophers, for whom a strongpoint was a city with ramparts of metal and a moat of boiling water. Jincheng was located at the foot of the mountains, just south of what was then the shore of the Yellow River, at a place that had been the northwesternmost point of the Qin Great Wall. The other settlement served as a ferry terminal for trade across the river, the first leg of the long Silk Routes that led west through the Gansu corridor to the Tarim basin and beyond. Thus Lanzhou was a caravansary and exchange point along the old Han Silk Route, as well as a river-crossing point and a base for Han defensive forces. Jincheng also administered a large area in the northwest. During the Han dynasty the lord of Jincheng had control over Qinghai's Minhe county northwest of Lanzhou, as well as territory in present-day Gansu (Xian Xiaowei & Chen Lijun 1982).

The period from the Eastern Han to the Tang was a time of social unrest and change in Lanzhou. Its prosperity declined along with the decline of the Silk Route in the late Han dynasty, and the city fell into relative obscurity as the Xiongnu (a nomadic people of Central Asian origin) invasion forced the Chinese to retreat out of the northwest.[3] The Lanzhou region subsequently came to be controlled (from A.D. 304 to 439) by the Xiqin kingdom of the Xianbi empire.[4] The Xiqin king established his capital at Lanzhou in 385. It lost that status in 412, when the capital was moved to Linxia after the death of the king (*Lanzhou fenglai* 1987: 3–4). During this period the course of the Yellow River gradually shifted to the north, enlarging the Dongpingyuan (eastern plain), the city's best agricultural land. In response to this shift, the city was expanded at the beginning of the Sui dynasty (581) to include land farther north, toward the new riverbanks (Xian Xiaowei & Chen Lijun 1982). This was the first of several expansions and relocations of the city site, each of which followed a northward shift in the course of the Yellow River (see Map 3).

During the Tang dynasty trade on the Silk Routes revived, and from the Tang to the Ming dynasty, Lanzhou again flourished as a transport and trade center. It also became a major center for the important regional horse-and-tea trade that was carried out between the Chinese and local nomadic peoples such as the Qiang (Chiay) and the Tufan (Tibetans). Tea grown in Hunan, Hubei, Sichuan, and Jiangxi not only was exchanged with nomads for horses but was also sold or bartered there for transport on to Qinghai, Xinjiang, Tibet, and Mongolia (Xian Xiaowei & Chen Lijun 1982).

Lanzhou continued to grow under the Song dynasty. During this era the city site was again moved north following a northward change in the course of the Yellow River. In 1081 the Song reconstructed the Tang city. Then, in 1083, they constructed a significantly larger city just to the north. This square city occupied a site that later became the southwest corner of the Ming walled city.

During the Ming dynasty Lanzhou once again served as the center of northwestern government and military affairs. Its importance as a regional administrative and commercial center enabled it to remain a significant trade and transportation hub even after the second decline of the Silk Routes. In 1377 the city was expanded and surrounded by a rectangular

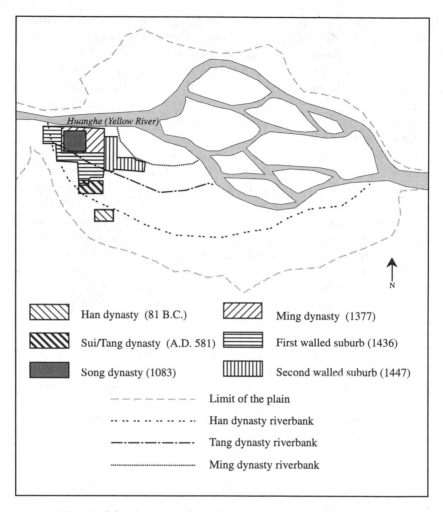

Huanghe (Yellow River)

N

Han dynasty (81 B.C.)   Ming dynasty (1377)

Sui/Tang dynasty (A.D. 581)   First walled suburb (1436)

Song dynasty (1083)   Second walled suburb (1447)

⸺⸺⸺⸺⸺   Limit of the plain

·· ·· ·· ·· ·· ·· ·· ··   Han dynasty riverbank

—·—·—·—·—·   Tang dynasty riverbank

················   Ming dynasty riverbank

Map 3. Historical development of Lanzhou, 81 B.C.–1949. Changes in the course of the Yellow River are shown in gray. Source: adapted from Xian Xiaowei & Chen Lijun 1982.

brick-faced rammed-earth wall. Significantly stronger than the previous earth walls, this new city wall had four gates, one facing each of the cardinal directions.

Within the space of a half century, settlement expanded beyond the Chinese city as a substantial population of Hui merchants, craftsmen, and shopkeepers settled just outside the walled area. Between 1426 and 1436

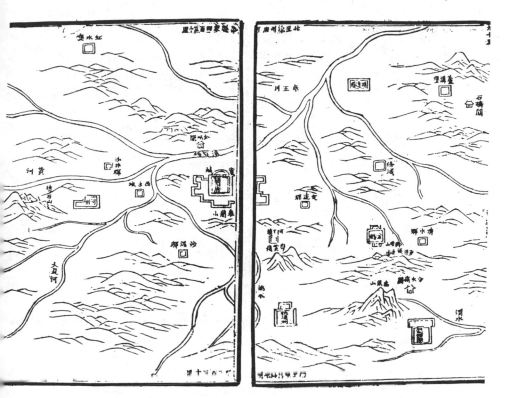

Fig. 1. Qing dynasty map of Lanzhou and surrounding area. The city is split across the center of the two panels. Note that the double wall is evident here but minimized in Fig. 2 from the same source, *Lanzhoufu zhi* 1834.

the city government built new walls to enclose areas to the west, south, and southeast as a suburb for the Hui. This suburb was expanded in 1447, with the addition of a walled area enclosing the neighborhood outside the east gate of the city. By this time the outer wall around the suburbs had nine gates and enclosed at least as much area as the original Ming city wall. In 1497 the eastern suburb was expanded still farther to provide space for troops traveling through the region (Figs. 1, 2).

Lanzhou continued to play a key role in the administration of vast areas of the northwest under the Qing dynasty. During the seventeenth and eighteenth centuries, it was the seat for the Qing administration of Mongolia, Tibet, Qinghai, and Xinjiang. The Manchu built a separate walled fort just to the southwest of the old walled city. This fort was about one-fifth the size of the walled city. By the end of the nineteenth century,

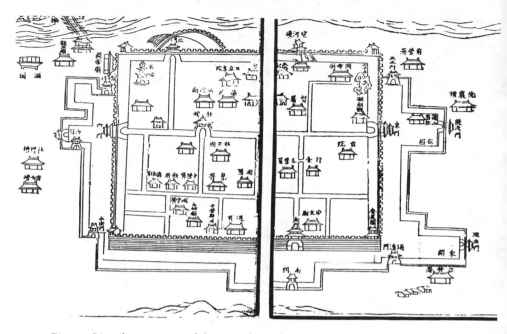

Fig. 2. Qing dynasty map of the city of Lanzhou. Note the minimizing of the walled suburb area. Source: *Lanzhoufu zhi* 1834.

however, Rockhill described this Manchu garrison as "sparsely populated" (Rockhill 1891: 35).

The importance of Lanzhou during the Qing dynasty was reflected in the improvements made to its city walls. The crenellated inner wall had a circumference of about 3 km. In 1738 the east, west, and south walls were reconstructed and covered in brick, and the northern wall was given a stone facing to guard against flooding from the Yellow River. Ten defensive towers were constructed in 1890 (Xian Xiaowei & Chen Lijun 1982). Map 4 shows the city's configuration at the turn of the century.

A number of Westerners who passed through Lanzhou in the first half of the twentieth century remarked on its size and prosperity. For example, L. Richard describes Lanzhou in his 1908 geography of the Chinese Empire as "a very commercial city. Its environs are well cultivated: gardens, orchards, tobacco-plantations, poppy-fields. . . . The land near Lanchow Fu [is] too valuable to cultivate [corn] thereon" (Richard 1908: 37).

Lanzhou also became a center of modern industry for northwestern China during the first half of the twentieth century. Long known for traditional industries, such as gold and silver smithing and wine production,

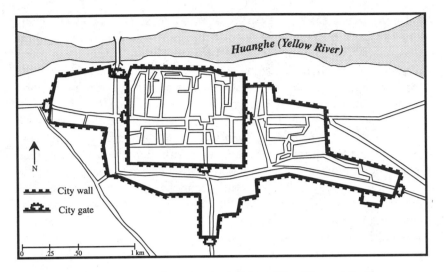

Map 4. Lanzhou, ca. 1900. Source: adapted from Xian Xiaowei & Chen Lijun 1982.

Lanzhou became a center for new industries such as papermaking, cement production, and machine-tool manufacturing as the Nationalist government and private entrepreneurs developed industries in response to the Japanese disruption of trade and transport that effectively cut off the supply of goods to the area during the Sino-Japanese war. The Nationalist government granted funds to Lanzhou to start up a paper industry, for example, when the flow of imports was blockaded by the Japanese. Between 1937 and 1942 the number of factories in Lanzhou increased from 10 to 42.

Lanzhou grew considerably during this time. There was enough motor traffic by 1939 that new gates were opened on the east, south, and west sides of the city walls to accommodate it. Two years later, another gate for motor traffic was opened on the east side of the city, and three of the old gates were widened to allow two-way traffic. At that time the population was 148,000. Just seven years later, the figure had increased by nearly a third, to reach a total of about 195,000 (Xian Xiaowei & Chen Lijun 1982). During these years of rapid population growth, the city sprawled far beyond the original walled area. The bluffs to the west became covered with settlements of inexpensive single-story loess-walled courtyard housing, in contrast to the more costly brick-and-wood multistory houses of the traditional city center.

Development has been even more rapid since 1949, and especially since 1953, when Lanzhou was one of the seven inland cities targeted for industrial development under the PRC's First Five Year Plan (along with Xi'an, Luoyang, Taiyuan, Datong, Chengdu, and Baotou). Thereafter the city grew rapidly, not only in the area it administered, but in population and built-up area as well. In 1949 the built area of the city center was just over 2 km². In 1953 the area administered by the city grew to 450 km², and this area was expanded again in 1957 to 660 km². By 1970 the total area administered was over 2,000 km². Although these jurisdictional changes do not in and of themselves indicate substantial changes in population or built area, real growth did occur. In 1980 the built area was estimated at more than 1,100 km², of which approximately 365 km² was devoted to housing (Xian Xiaowei & Chen Lijun 1982: 27). As early as 1956 the Dean of Canterbury was struck by the changes since his first visit, in 1932, noting that none of the development outside the east suburb gates had existed at the time (Alley 1957: 23).

The character of Lanzhou's population has changed substantially as well. Once the PRC targeted the city for development, large numbers of migrants began to arrive from eastern China, many of them skilled workers. One Lanzhou resident remarked to me that, for a time, it seemed that all the skilled jobs were held by outsiders, with Lanzhou natives left to perform the more routine tasks. The importance of migrants from the east was brought home to Rewi Alley during his visit in the mid-1950s, when he noted that the Shanghai dialect could be heard throughout the city and remarked, "I was surprised at the amount of custom in the bigger Lanchow shops, and noted that many of them and their staffs had come from Shanghai, including one very spick and span large barber's establishment (Alley 1957: 21, 24).

The industrial growth begun at Lanzhou during the 1950s was resumed after the Cultural Revolution. Lanzhou is now a city of heavy industry, with a population well over one million and a landscape marked by smokestacks and large industrial compounds. Its chief industrial products are refined petroleum, chemicals, machine tools, nonferrous metals, and wool textiles. It also supplies electric power.

Xining, Gateway to Tibet

Xining has been underappreciated by Western travelers. And it will no doubt remain so for those who accept a judgment like this, from the popular and influential travel writer Paul Theroux: "only its altitude made Xining breathtaking. In other respects it looked like what it was, a frontier town: square brown buildings on straight streets, surrounded by big brown hills" (Theroux 1988: 427). Situated on the northeastern edge of the Qinghai-Tibet plateau, Xining has been a true Chinese frontier outpost for the centuries it has served as the last major Chinese stronghold on the route to Tibet. Twentieth-century western travelers making their way inland dismissed it as yet another Chinese city—perhaps the last to be seen before crossing the border. Travelers moving from west to east often viewed it as the first evidence of the constraint of Chinese civilization: the end of the freedoms of the steppes and grasslands of Tibet and Central Asia. Yet Xining had far more to offer than these travelers recognized, as even Theroux ultimately acknowledged: "Xining was the sort of simple ramshackle place I had come to like in China" (1988: 430). The city's history eludes the casual observer. But it is a history as rich as that of any American frontier town.

With an elevation of 2,261 m (7,461 ft.), Xining is second only to Lhasa in altitude among the major cities of the PRC. It lies on the south bank of the Huangshui River, flanked on both the north and the south by hills. The bluff to the north is honeycombed with caves connected by a superstructure of covered catwalks to form Xining's "North Temple." At the southern edge of the city, the South Temple stands on top of the first of a series of gently rolling hills. A small tributary creek that once defined the city's western border now serves as a mid-city divide between the older neighborhoods and the post-1949 sprawl.

For all its recent spreading growth, Xining retains the feel of the small city it has long been, with city life focused on the intersection of the two main streets of the old city. These streets have been widened and lined with modern concrete structures; traditional courtyard housing lies along narrow streets behind. Sharp contrasts in architectural styles make the boundaries of the old city still clear, even though most of the city wall has been dismantled. East and west of the old city there is modern development, primarily on a long strip flanking the main east-west through road.

Archaeological evidence indicates that the Xining area was inhabited by peoples of the Yangshao civilization about 4,000 years ago (Chow 1949: 64). The area was later the home of the ancestors of the Qiang (Tibetan) people in the Shang and Zhou periods (1766 B.C.–770 B.C.; Liu Man & Zhao Yun 1986: 434). Urban settlement began in 121 B.C., when the Chinese established Xipingting, a walled garrison outpost of the Han army, for defense against the Xiongnu and Qiang (*Qinghai lishi jiyao* 1987: 11–12). This type of outpost, established under the tuntian policy, included not only the walled fort, but also elements of infrastructure, such as roads, a postal stop, and bridges. In this sense it served as an urban or proto-urban frontier settlement despite its relatively small size.

The subsequent political and settlement history of the region does justice to its reputation as a turbulent area. In the year A.D. 221, a resident of Xiping assassinated the local governor and attempted to seize control of the region. Shortly after the assassin was himself assassinated by a Qiang. Order was quickly restored by the imperial government, which responded by building walled fortifications around the old fort. During the fourth century A.D., when the Jin dynasty was waning, several groups of non-Chinese peoples gained control of the northwest, including the Xining region, and established a base at present-day Wuwei in Gansu Province. The alliances formed by these groups were known as the Former Liang and the Later Liang. In the late fourth century, however, a number of rebellions were staged against these alliances. A Xiping resident led an uprising against the Former Liang, and though he himself was killed, the Former Liang lost its hold on Xiping. Control was regained eventually by the Later Liang, only to be lost again at the end of the fourth century to the Xianbi.

The Xianbi established the Southern Liang state with their capital at Xiping. The Hutai (Tiger Mounds) in Xining, where there is one large mound of earth and four smaller mounds, is said to have been constructed by the Xianbi army during the fifth century. While in control of Xiping, the Xianbi adopted Chinese-style schools and agricultural practices (*Qinghai lishi jiyao* 1987: 29–34). After their defeat in the mid-fifth century, the Xianbi lived in mixed settlements in eastern Qinghai with the Qiang and were gradually assimilated into the Qiang culture (ibid., pp. 38–39).

From the Northern and Southern Dynasties period (A.D. 386–589) until the Tang dynasty, the control of Xining passed back and forth between the Northern Wei dynasty, the Sui dynasty, and the Tuyuhun, a branch of the Xianbi who came from what is now Liaoning Province in northeastern China. The Northern Wei dynasty (386–534) captured the region, and toward the end of its reign, in 526, established a regional administration at what it called Shanzhou (modern Xining). During this Northern Wei period, however, the region was primarily under the control of the Tuyuhun. In the latter half of the Northern and Southern Dynasties period, Xining served as a major trade center for the trade routes linking the Central Asian interior to the international sea trade at the southeastern coast of China. Persian silver coins unearthed along Xining's Jiefang (Liberation) Road in 1956 are believed to date from the years 459–83 (*Qinghai lishi jiyao* 1987: 42, 49; Liu Man & Zhao Yun 1986: 436).

In 584 the Tuyuhun presented themselves at the Sui court at Chang'an, and the Sui subsequently gained control of Xining. In 607 the Sui shifted their regional capital to Ledu, 50 km east of Xining. After the fall of the Sui dynasty in 618, the Tuyuhun took over again, only to lose control some 10 years later to the Tang dynasty, which established a local administration at Shanzhou (*Qinghai lishi jiyao* 1987: 58–63).

During the early Tang dynasty, Xining was an important stop on the trade and communication route between Chang'an, Lhasa, and the capital of the Tufan, who gradually supplanted the Tuyuhun in the Xining region. The last 30 years of the seventh century witnessed considerable discord between the Chinese and Tibetans in the Xining region, and communications and trade broke down between Lhasa and Chang'an. Relations between the two peoples improved after 710, when the Tang court sent the Tang princess Jincheng to wed the Tibetan ruler in Lhasa. Relative calm prevailed for about a century and a half, until the Tufan staged a major military action and dislodged the Tang from much of the Qinghai region, including Xining, which they made their capital. This capital, which the Chinese called Qingtang Cheng, was the center of a thriving Tibetan administration under Gusiluo (997–1065), who established the Xifan kingdom and reigned from 1015 to 1065.[5] The Xifan kingdom endured into the twelfth century. During its existence it carried on an active trade with both the Gaochang kingdom in the west and China, and its people adopted some Chinese cultural practices, particularly in the areas of architecture, medicine, and making use of the Chinese zodiac (*Qinghai lishi jiyao* 1987: 70–71, 74–75, 85–86, 91–93).

Qingtang Cheng was a walled city about 10 km in circumference,[6] with a population of at least a thousand Tibetan families. A north-south wall ran through the center of the walled area and divided it into two sections called the East and West cities. The West City was the home of the elite. Its most imposing structure was Gusiluo's palace, which stood just inside the city's west gate. The entrance to the palace was flanked by two towers, with the central gate and the ceremonial gate behind. Inside the ceremonial gate, on the east and west sides, were the earth-roofed residences of Gusiluo's concubines. These were located approximately on the site of the Nanshen Temple in present-day Xining. The main hall, with a tile roof, was located just north of the ceremonial gate. The pillars of this great hall were elaborately painted, and the exterior was decorated with glazed tiles. Inside the great hall there was a large golden Buddha image, clothed in pearls. The West City also contained three altars, which lay just east of the palace. In contrast to this exclusive western district, the East City was the home of about 100 families of traders of many different nationalities. The suburbs surrounding the city contained several Buddhist monasteries (*Qinghai lishi jiyao* 1987: 96–98). This basic layout, with the ruling ethnic group in the west, a multiethnic trading community in the east, and monasteries in the outlying area, was to remain the form of Xining until 1949.

At the beginning of the twelfth century, the Song government attempted to topple the Xifan kingdom by persuading its citizens to revolt against heavy taxes. This revolt was followed by Xixia attacks on the Xifan,[7] as well as Jin (Ruzhen) military activity in the region, and then the Song dynasty's attempt to oust both and impose its own rule (*Qinghai lishi jiyao* 1987: 104–5). The Xixia emerged as the victors in these many conflicts in September 1220 (*Qinghai fangzhi ciliao leipian* 1987: 1653).

But the Xixia did not keep their hold on Xining for long. In 1227 Chinggis Khan's Mongol army reached Xining and overcame them. From that time until the end of the Yuan dynasty (1368), the Mongols administered the area from Lanzhou (*Qinghai lishi jiyao* 1987: 106–8). Mongol rule contributed to a change in the city's ethnic composition as Central Asian Muslims migrated to and settled there in the Yuan years. During this period, Islamic migrants were settling in other frontier communities in China as well.[8] Xining's Islamic population continued to grow throughout the thirteenth and fourteenth centuries. At the beginning of the Ming dynasty, many Muslims from Shanghai and its environs were resettled in the Xining area, further swelling the Islamic population (ibid., pp. 116–22). Thus a highly varied Islamic population developed in Xining and the surrounding area.

The first Ming armies reached the northwest in the 1370s and established a military stronghold at Xining. The Ming maintained a strong military presence in Xining; by 1488 the stronghold was manned by more than 9,000 horse and foot soldiers. To enhance its strong defensive position at Xining, the Ming government built new city walls in 1386 to replace walls that had fallen into disrepair. About 4.5 km in circumference, the new city walls surrounded half the area that the old walls had: a significant portion of the southern half of the old city that had been primarily agricultural land was left outside the walls. Like many of the walls built by the Ming, the new walls were impressive. They were constructed of rammed earth, about 16 m high and nearly as thick. Each of the four gates was surmounted by a watchtower, and lesser watchtowers were posi-

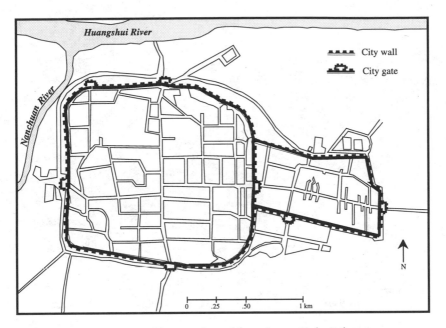

Map 5. Xining, ca. 1900. Source: adapted from Japan, Koka Rikugun 1939.

tioned at points in between. A walled suburb was built on the eastern side of the city for the Islamic population. These first Ming walls at Xining stood as they had been originally built for nearly 200 years. After that, between 1575 and 1576, they were repaired and faced with a protective layer of brick (*Qinghai lishi jiyao* 1987: 129–30). Map 5 shows the city walls and gates in about 1900 (see also Figs. 3, 4).

Xining became a trading center after 1397, when it was made the site of one of the four tea-and-horse markets the Ming established in the region. Some investment was also made in Ming times in local industry. Traditionally, Xining had imported all of its iron from Shaanxi. In 1595 soldiers from the Xining regiment, with the help of experts from Shaanxi and Shanxi, set up their own smelting plant to process iron ore imported from Gansu. The North Mountain smelting plant was located a few miles north of Xining (*Qinghai lishi jiyao* 1987: 124–25, 132–34, 147–48).

Despite the Ming's efforts to pacify the western frontier with a strong military presence, peasant uprisings erupted in Shanxi, Shaanxi, Hebei, and Henan in the seventeenth century and then became a full-fledged revolt, spreading to Gansu and Qinghai as well. Tibetans joined the movement, and fighting broke out inside the city of Xining in December 1642.

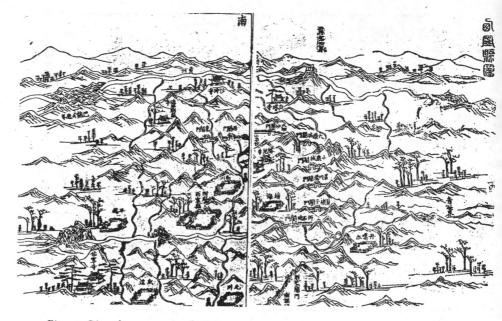

Fig. 3. Qing dynasty map of Xining and surrounding area. Xining is the double-walled city at the right edge of the left panel. Source: *Xiningfu xinzhi* 1930s.

The Ming representative there was murdered as the rebellion spread into his own army. The region remained under the control of the revolutionary army until 1645, when imperial power was restored by the new Manchu Qing dynasty (*Qinghai lishi jiyao* 1987: 150–51).

Xining became the base from which the Qing negotiated with the Mongols who, by and large, controlled the surrounding region during the mid-seventeenth century (*Qinghai lishi jiyao* 1987: 159).[9] Determined, like the Ming, to maintain a strong presence on this frontier, the Qing made some investment in Xining, and in 1745 built three main complexes of new government buildings in the center of the city (*Xiningfu xinzhi* 1930s: 355). Once again, however, Xining proved a difficult position to hold. When Islamic revolts erupted throughout west and southwest China in the mid-nineteenth century, the Qing government lost its hold on Xining; it did not regain control of the city until 1872.

By the accounts of Western travelers who passed through the city, in the late Qing years, Xining was a thriving outpost of Chinese civilization. F. Grenard's first impression was of "a very imposing, bustling, noisy, populous city" (Grenard 1891: 202); Rockhill considered it "commercially and strategically the most important town in Western Gansu"

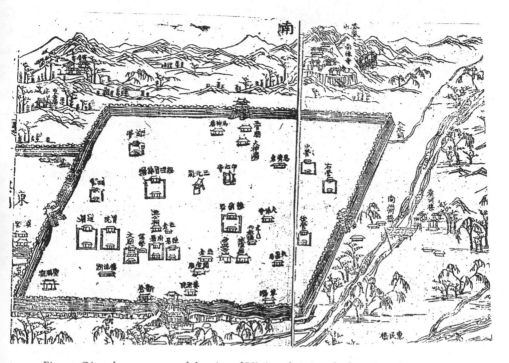

Fig. 4. Qing dynasty map of the city of Xining showing the location of its monumental structures. Note that the walled suburb is not pictured. Source: *Xiningfu xinzhi* 1930s.

(Rockhill 1891: 48); and L. Richard described it in his geography as a city, "at an elevation of more than 7,000 feet, and with a population of 60,000 inhabitants, [which had] important commercial relations with Tibet [and had been] recaptured from the [Muslim] rebels only in 1872" (Richard 1908: 37). But the city stagnated in the Republican era, when it fell under the control of a powerful warlord, Ma Bufang. Little development took place during this time, and Xining remained a relatively small, though locally important, trading city well into the twentieth century.

Qinghai became a separate province in 1928, with Xining as its capital. But Xining remained a Chinese outpost in a non-Chinese region through the end of the Nationalist regime and beyond. Even the immediately surrounding area continued to be populated primarily by non-Han peoples. In the early 1940s there were 73,000 Hui in the Xining and Datong areas of the Huangshui valley. The Hui in Datong were primarily engaged in gold mining, those in the Xining area primarily in farming. At that time there were also about 11,000 Xiningfan (Tibetan agricultural villagers) living in the upper margins of the Huangshui valley (Chow 1949: 110, 120). The Chinese population of Xining remained a minority in the regional context well into the twentieth century.[10]

That picture has changed considerably with the massive post-1949 influx of Han Chinese into both Xining and the surrounding region. During the Great Leap Forward in 1956, for example, thousands of Chinese were sent to the frontiers to "reclaim" arable land. This resettlement policy was successfully carried out despite local resistance in Xining to the first in-migration of 5,000 Chinese (Schwarz 1963: 67–68). Further settlement by Chinese migrants has taken place since that time. Today the Han Chinese outnumber the Tibetans in the province.

Despite substantial gains under the PRC's development policies, Xining remains relatively underdeveloped compared with other provincial capitals. Though it now produces such items as metallurgical instruments, mechanical parts, chemicals, and building materials, the city's major exports consist of wool blankets and other traditional products. Priorities for future development are focused on light industries, including the processing of hides, woolen textiles, and building materials (PRC State Statistical Bureau 1987: 172).

Hohhot, the Blue City

"As to cities," a visitor wrote a half century ago, "there are two: the new city and the old city, facing each other at a distance of four or five *li*. The new city is filled with the offices of the bureaucracy; the old city is filled with commerce and industry" (Chen Kangya 1936: 40). In 1936, when Chen Kangya penned these words, he was quick to identify the most striking feature of Hohhot at the time: the pair of cities facing off across the plain, one still retaining the monumental air of Qing dynasty bureaucracy, the other still the center of the community's economic and spiritual life. These two "cities" remain visible in Hohhot today.

The city of Hohhot today consists of three different urban developments that have been integrated to form a continuous settlement. In the northwest lies the former Manchu city, with rectangular blocks, some modern development on the main east-west street, and traditional shops on the north-south street. On the northwest corner of the intersection of these two streets, there is a large traditional Chinese *yamen* complex that once housed the military government of the city and region. Both the complex and a 100-foot-long spirit wall associated with it, which stands in the middle of the east-west street, have been restored. Southeast lies the old

Mongol/Chinese city, with a few new buildings and many traditional shops on the main north-south thoroughfare, and a maze of courtyard housing, temples, and former temples on either side of the main axis. Just north of this area, there is a large Hui settlement. Hohhot's modern development lies between the old Manchu city and the old Mongol city. Here department stores and government buildings flank wide avenues. From this primarily commercial and administrative area the character of the modern development gradually shifts, giving way finally to industrial districts south and east of the old towns.

Some 400 km west of Beijing, Hohhot is the capital of the Inner Mongolian Autonomous Region. Despite the city's proximity to Beijing, it is as much a part of the steppe environment of Mongolia as it is a part of China. Hohhot stands on the north bank of the Dahei River, a tributary of the Yellow River, on a plain 2,000 m (6,600 ft.) above sea level that is bordered on the south by the hills marking the edge of the North China loess plateau and on the north by the Yin mountains. The Inner Mongolian plateau stretches beyond these mountains northward toward Mongolia.

Although Hohhot has a relatively recent history as a Chinese city, it has a long settlement history. According to Rong Yang of the Inner Mongolian History Institute,[11] the earliest written Chinese reference to the area is found in the *Shiji* (Records of the historian; 104 B.C.–91 B.C.), which says that during the Warring States period (403 B.C.–221 B.C.), this was the home of a people called the Linhu (Forest People), so named because they were thought to have migrated to the steppes from some more heavily forested area.[12] The population at that time numbered only a few thousand. During the preceding Zhou (1122 B.C.–771 B.C.) and Spring and Autumn (722 B.C.–481 B.C.) periods, the population is estimated to have been just slightly over a thousand people (Rong Yang 1979: 2–4). On reaching the Hohhot area in 306 B.C., representatives of the Warring States built a defensive wall at the base of the Yin mountains (just north of present-day Hohhot) and named the area Yunzhong (Among the Clouds) Prefecture (*Huhehaoteshi dimingzhi* 1985: 9). The Qin and Han dynasties retained this name for the prefectures they established in the area, which included all the land from modern-day Hohhot south to the Great Wall. During that period the Xiongnu inhabited the area (Rong Yang 1979: 2–4), the Qin and Han prefectures being primarily defensive garrisons.

Though Xiongnu settlers flooded into the area beginning in the spring of A.D. 50 and thoroughly outnumbered the Chinese population, the area remained a Han prefecture under Chinese supervision. According to records of the Later Han era, the Chinese population of the whole of Yun-zhong prefecture then comprised something over 13,000 households, or nearly 70,000 people, compared with about 34,000 Xiongnu households, or 237,000 people. The Chinese thus made up only about 21 percent of the total population (Rong Yang 1979: 22–23).

In the second century A.D., the Xianbi joined with the northern Xiongnu to form a powerful new state based in the Hohhot area (Rong Yang 1979: 23; Hyer 1982: 59). The site of the Xianbi capital was 80 li (approximately 42 km) south of Hohhot, at the present site of Tucheng village in Helin county. There may well have been a Chinese fort on that site, since, according to Rong Yang (1979: 24), the Xianbi built all their cities on former sites of Qin and Han fort-cities. In A.D. 259 the Toba, one of the most powerful families of the Xianbi, established their own capital, Shengle, about 12 km north of Hohhot at the site of an old Han garrison. They constructed walls around the settlement in 313, creating a multiple-walled city, with the former Han garrison town forming one wall, and a second adjacent enclosure for the Toba. The Toba established the North-ern Wei dynasty in the year 386.[13]

As the Toba turned toward the affairs and culture of China, they lost control of the frontier steppe lands. A northern nomadic group, the Ruan-ruan, moved in, and the city of Shengle (Hohhot) became a frontier mili-tary outpost. The Toba state by that time was centered in the Henan Prov-ince area (Hyer 1982: 59).[14] From the time of the Wei to the beginning of the Tang dynasty, the urban centers in the Hohhot area remained popu-lated, though no substantive changes were made to the city walls, which indeed were not even repaired over the centuries. Thus, according to Rong Yang, the urban landscape remained relatively fixed (though decaying) throughout the period (Rong Yang 1979: 24).

The Tang empire asserted control over the area after military offensives against the Tujue in the years 629 and 630 (Dai Xueji 1981: 21). The Tang established a county seat near Hohhot, which included a military base (Rong Yang 1979: 26). They eventually established three separate prefec-tural seats in the area, including one on the site of Yunzhong city (Tuoke-tuo county). The Tujue continued to resist Tang advances. In response, in 708 the Tang built three military forts around Hohhot—East, Central, and West Shojiang cities (Dai Xueji 1981: 21; Rong Yang 1979: 27–28).

After the Tang, control of the Hohhot area passed from the Chinese to the Liao dynasty.[15] The Liao established a city, Fengzhou (Plentiful Re-gion), in the area currently known as Baita (White Pagoda) village in the eastern suburbs of Hohhot.[16] According to Dai Xueji, the Liao people transformed much of their economy and culture and established permanent agricultural settlements after contact with the Chinese people in the area (whether that contact induced them to settle is another question). Archaeologists have determined that Fengzhou was a walled city 4.5 km in circumference, with palaces, temples, pagodas, and other works of monumental architecture. Most of the Liao wall is buried under earth today, but a remnant of the southeastern corner is still visible. Where the northwest corner of the wall once stood, there is today a large eight-sided, seven-story brick pagoda, commonly known as the White Pagoda (Rong Yang 1979: 30; Dai Xueji 1981: 24–25). The ruins of temples and pagodas within the bounds of present-day Hohhot not only confirm the existence of the Liao settlement, but also indicate that considerable use was made of brick for monumental architectural construction.

During Liao times the Hohhot region was a major center of valuable export production and trade. The Liao controlled an active salt industry there. Moreover, many gold and silver mines were opened in the area between the Yellow River near Hohhot and the Yin mountains. These also contributed to the wealth of the Liao state. Fengzhou became an important trading place, where the nomadic peoples from the north procured *sijuan* (a thin, tough silk) and other goods from Chinese itinerant traders in exchange for wool. The Liao created a taxed market at Fengzhou in order to profit from this trading activity as well (Dai Xueji 1981: 25–26).

Hohhot continued to grow under the Song (960–1127) and Jin (1115–1234) dynasties, although it remained an island of urbanism in a largely nomadic region. According to the *Jinshi, dilizhi* (History of the Jin Dynasty, Geographical Annals), Fengzhou had about 22,000 households in Jin times (cited in Rong Yang 1979: 31). In 1115 the Jin established a walled military settlement, also called Fengzhou (Cheng), southwest of the Tiandongjiao White Pagoda (*Huhehaote shi* 1985: 9). Paul Hyer observes that throughout the twelfth century, "the society and culture of the region around [Hohhot] was dominated by traditional nomadic institutions with an impress mainly of the Khitan" (Hyer 1982: 60).

There continued to be a city at Hohhot through Yuan dynasty times, as reported, for example, by Marco Polo, who passed through the area on his way to Beijing (then called Khanbaligh) to see Khubilai Khan (Hyer 1982: 61).[17] Hyer asserts that

in fact it should be made clear that during the fifteen hundred year period of history discussed to this point [the point at which the Mongolian empire began to decline], while [Hohhot] was an important point of contact between various peoples and a strategic military point in the confrontation between various forces, particularly the Chinese and the nomads, at no time could one really talk of the place as one of magnificent, permanent buildings and palaces with a large population. More probably the usual scene, as the fate of the place rose and fell with contending powers, was a collection of nomadic dwellings, a conglomeration of semi-permanent buildings at best in peak periods. (Hyer 1982: 61)

This assessment of the significance of Hohhot is probably fairly accurate in terms of the functions of the city. But Hyer's assertion that the settlement contained "semi-permanent buildings at best" may underestimate the place, which at times had a substantial population and which, as the extant ruins from the Liao dynasty suggest, was characterized by some substantial monumental architecture as well.

The form of modern-day Hohhot was established in the late Ming and early Qing periods by the Mongols. In 1557 the Mongol prince Altan Khan had the first true walled city built on the site, making use of the labor and skills of Chinese refugees fleeing the persecution of the White Lotus Buddhist sect (Bailianjiao), as well as captured Chinese artisans and corvee labor provided by local Chinese villagers (Jankowiak 1993: 11; Hyer 1982: 61).[18] Hyer suggests that Hohhot was "the first city built by the Mongols after the decline of the Mongolian empire and the collapse of the Yuan dynasty" (Hyer 1982: 61). Altan Khan named Hohhot his capital and used it as a symbol of the new permanence of Mongol power. This was actually a fairly small walled fort, less than 1 km in circumference. The old wall of the fort, located in the northern part of the old city district, remained intact until the beginning of the Republican era, when all of the wall except the north gate was torn down. What is today known as the "old city" gradually developed between this walled administrative compound and a number of lamasery compounds.

The establishment of Hohhot in the sixteenth century transformed the region from a military garrison to a center of diverse social and economic activity and a religious center for Buddhism. At the same time as Altan Khan ordered the city built, he ordered the construction of two lamaseries, Dazhao Temple and Xiaozhao Temple, on auspicious sites as determined by Tibetan Buddhist monks in the immediate vicinity. Hohhot became a place of some significance for the officials in Beijing as a northern base for the expansion of Chinese commercial and political power. The Chinese attempted to gain control of the city by granting titles to Altan Khan and renaming it Guihua Cheng (The City Returned to Chinese Culture).

During the seventeenth-century Ming-Qing transition, Hohhot became a pivot point for the rising Manchu. The Manchu defeated the Mongols there in 1634 in their drive to consolidate their power on China's northern frontiers (Hyer 1982). Subsequently, Hohhot served as a base for the Manchu invasion of northern China at the beginning of the Qing dynasty, just as the city of Kunming had served as a base for the Mongol invasion of southern China at the beginning of the Yuan dynasty. Later in the seventeenth century, Hohhot also served as a base for Manchu military forays into Mongolia.

The Manchu built their own city at Hohhot in 1736, during the reign of the Qianlong Emperor. They named this city (now known as New City) Suiyuan (City for the Pacification of Remote Areas). Located just over 2 km northeast of Guihua (the Old City), it housed a growing Manchu political bureaucracy and military (see Map 6). Suiyuan remained the venue of administrators and military personnel until the end of the Qing

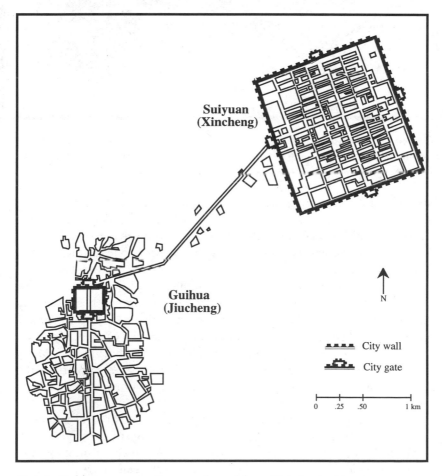

Map 6. Hohhot, ca. 1900. Source: adapted from *Huhehaote shi* 1985.

Fig. 5. Qing dynasty map of Hohhot and surrounding area. Guihua, the Mongolian/Han city, is on the left; Suiyuan, the Manchu city, on the right. Source: *Guisui quanzhi* 1910.

dynasty (1911). Few businesses were established within its walls. The commercial center of the area continued to be located in Guihua. The two cities together became known as Guisui. This twin urban form, with two separate walled areas, one for the Manchu garrison, one for the Chinese town, became common during the Manchu era on the frontier (Figs. 5, 6).

After the construction of Suiyuan, Guihua flourished as a center for trade. Hui migrants from Shanxi Province became some of the most active merchants in Guihua. The regional population also increased in the late Qing years, when the government officially encouraged Chinese migration to Hohhot in an effort to ease population pressure in China proper. Many of these migrants took up farming near Hohhot. In 1904, in particular, a large amount of the surrounding land was brought into cultivation (Hyer 1982: 68).

Though politically integrated as a single city since 1914, the two cities maintain their distinct characters even now. Nonetheless, both have changed substantially in the twentieth century. As noted, most of the wall around the old city garrison was torn down in the early days of the Chinese Republic. This was only the first of a series of attempts to modern-

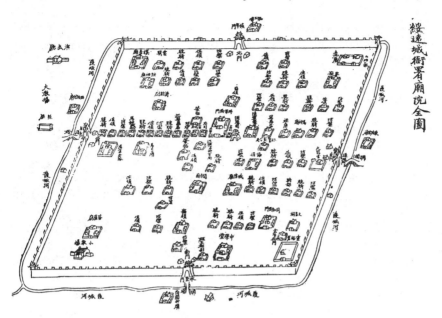

Fig. 6. Qing dynasty map of the Manchu city at Hohhot showing the location of its monumental structures. Source: *Guisui quanzhi* 1910.

ize both "cities" The railroad from Beijing reached Hohhot in 1919, bringing both increased economic development and increased Chinese in-migration. The balance between Han Chinese and Mongolian populations shifted as a result, to the point where the Chinese finally became a majority in the Hohhot area; they have increased their proportion of the population year by year ever since (Hyer 1982: 63, 70). Nonetheless, the old city district as Verne Dyson saw it in the 1920s was hardly modern, with its "dilapidated walls [and] narrow winding streets, each devoted to some particular trade, and swarming with people, children and dogs" (1927: 35).

Since 1949, Hohhot has grown and developed substantially. Much of this growth has been associated with the necessity of creating a modern city to be the capital of Inner Mongolia. The focus of new construction has been in the area between the two former cities. But some development has also taken place within them as well. Large areas of both cities, but particularly the new city, have been redeveloped with massive concrete factory compounds and institutions. The old walls around the new city were torn down between 1954 and 1957, and the north gate tower of the old city was finally dismantled between 1958 and 1960 in order to facilitate traffic (Guan Xiaoxian et al. 1987: 227, 228). Today, Hohhot's skyline is punctuated not by the curved roofs of the gate towers, but rather by tall brick smokestacks reaching toward the vast blue Mongolian sky.

Urumqi, City of the "Old Red Temple"

Che Muqi, a Chinese author who visited Urumqi in the late 1980s, wrote: "Entering the city proper, I felt that Urumqi differed from cities on the Central Plains. . . . Gurgling streams lined the streets, watering the towering Lombardy poplars. . . . Anyone who found people's attire in Beijing and Shanghai too monotonous would feel satisfied here" (Che Muqi 1989: 141).

Urumqi, the capital of the Xinjiang Uygur Autonomous Region, lies at the northern foot of the Tianshan range in a broad fertile valley that ranges from 680 m to 920 m in altitude. It is the largest city between Lanzhou, the westernmost city on the Yellow River, and the cities of Kyrgyzstan, Uzbekistan, and Kazakstan. Urumqi is sometimes described as the world's most inland city, and, at more than 43° north latitude, it is the northernmost of the cities under study.

Urumqi today is composed of three types of districts: recently developed areas, an old Chinese city, and an old Muslim city. The north and northwestern areas of the city, as well as the southernmost limits, have all been developed since 1949, with modern five- and six-story concrete buildings set in large compounds. The central section is the old Chinese city: much renovated, but with far narrower streets than more recently developed areas, and with courtyard-style housing and old shops scattered throughout. South of the old Chinese city lies the Muslim city, where modern development touches only the buildings lining the main street. Behind these one-story shops are mazes of courtyard housing interspersed with alleys. The domed roofs of mosques and minarets reach above the flat roofs of the houses. Several street bazaars punctuate the neighborhood, and many small restaurants and stalls offer noodles, kebabs, and the fresh-baked flat bread characteristic of Central Asia.

Urumqi is the most recently established of the cities discussed in this book. Its site, located just off the main Silk Routes, was of little concern to the Chinese until the eighteenth century and was only seasonally inhabited and used for pastureland by several different nomadic peoples until then (Yu Weicheng 1986: 1). Although some Chinese traders passed through the region as early as the second century A.D., and a branch of the northern Silk Route from Hami passed through Urumqi and over the Yili

River, no permanent settlements were established in the area (Zan Yulin 1983: 4). The Gaochang kingdom extended its control to the area and held periodic circuit courts there. During the Yuan dynasty the Mongols called the region Bishbalik, or Five Cities, referring to five settlements that ringed the site of modern-day Urumqi (Yu Weicheng 1986: 1).

According to Ming dynasty records, there was an indigenous settlement or city at Jiujiawan, 5 km west of present-day Urumqi, during the Ming. It was apparently burned down when the Manchu of the Qing period first arrived to settle in the region (Zan Yulin 1983: 7). During Ming times Mongolians also used the region as a herding ground. What brought the Manchu to the region was the Chinese government's recognition of its strategic importance for securing the western frontier regions. In 1755 (or in 1758, according to Zan Yulin 1983: 8), the Qing army fought and defeated the Dzungarian Mongols who controlled the area, and built an earth-walled enclosure that they called Urumqi (Wulumuqi).[19] This, the first walled settlement in the area, was located east of the present-day city, at the base of the eastern mountains of the Urumqi plain. The Manchu soldiers who settled the region also built a vermillion-walled Guandi temple on top of Pingding mountain overlooking present-day Urumqi. This temple gave Urumqi its nickname of Red Temple, and some residents still refer to the city as Old Red Temple today. In 1760 the Qing established a *tongzhiguan* (an information post) at the fort. At that time Urumqi and the region it administered had a population of 50,000 (Zan Yulin 1983: 8, 23; Yu Weicheng 1986: 1).

Five years later the Manchu started work on a walled city, Dihua. Auspiciously located at the southern foot of Hongshan, a rock outcrop in the center of the plain, it encompassed what is today downtown Urumqi. The city, completed in 1767, had four great gates facing the cardinal directions. Only four years later, in 1771, the Manchu built yet another city, Gongning Cheng, about 2.5 km northwest of Dihua (see Map 7). Gongning Cheng became both an exclusively Manchu city and the seat of the government, giving Urumqi a twin-city form similar to Hohhot's. Gongning Cheng was about 3.5 km in circumference; had four gates, each of which bore inscriptions in Manchu, Mongolian, Uygur, and Chinese scripts; and contained more than 6,500 rooms of barracks for the troops, and 9,500 rooms for the families of troops and for shops. Several temples were also constructed in the city. Gongning Cheng remained the administrative center into the nineteenth century, while the older city, Dihua, developed as a trading center. After 1765 Urumqi expanded its military and commercial functions. Some 3,500 Qing troops from Gansu, Ningxia,

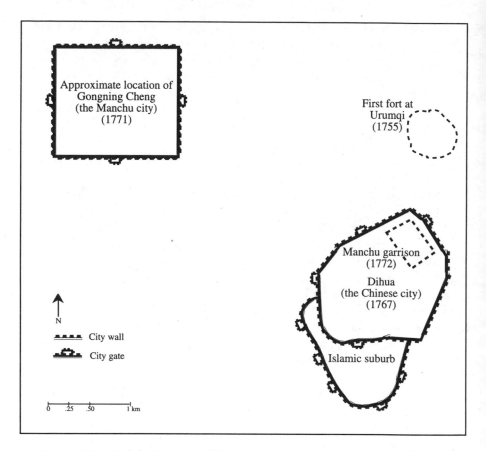

Map 7. Historical development of Urumqi, 1755–1800s. Source: adapted from Japan, Koka Rikugun 1939.

and Shaanxi were posted there in 1772. These non-Manchu troops were garrisoned, not in the Manchu city, but rather in the northeastern corner of Dihua (Yu Weicheng 1986: 1; Zan Yulin 1983: 8, 23–24).

In 1864 the northwestern Muslim rebel army led by Yaqub Beg captured Gongning Cheng, killed the Qing administrator, and burned the city to the ground. Gongning Cheng was abandoned, and the Manchu fled to the garrison in the northeastern corner of Dihua. Gongning Cheng was never reoccupied. In the 1930s a normal school was built on its ruins. This school was later used as a headquarters for the Guomindang (Nationalist) forces, and after 1949 an agricultural college was built on the site (Zan Yulin 1983: 26; Yu Weicheng 1986: 2). A portion of the Gongning Cheng city wall is still visible on the western edge of the college campus.

Yaqub Beg's forces remained in control of much of the Urumqi area after they destroyed the Manchu city. This was something the government would not long tolerate because the region was considered a critical buffer zone between the Chinese and Russian empires, and Urumqi was seen as a key link in regional security. In 1875, Cou Congtang (Tso Tsung-t'ang), the Manchu army general who eventually won back Xinjiang for the empire, wrote to the emperor, "Since our forces recovered Su-chou by a total victory, which was followed by the liberation of Anhsi, Hami, Barkol, and Chi-mu-sa, only the area of Urumqi is still in the hands of the rebels. . . . To stop all the troops outside and inside the Great Wall at present does not make sense. Your Majesty said: '. . . If China does nothing to recover Urumchi, both the northern and western frontiers will be in constant danger'" (quoted in Chu Wen Djang 1966: 175).

The government regained control of southern Xinjiang in 1878. In 1884 it elevated Xinjiang to the status of a province, with Dihua as the capital. The city wall was expanded in 1886 to encompass about 6.5 km, and three new gates, a lesser east, lesser south, and lesser west gate, were opened. Several temples and public buildings were restored at the same time (see Map 8). The city population rose to nearly 39,000 people (Zan Yulin 1983: 9).

For many of the Chinese who were stationed in or who passed through this region so far from the centers of Chinese culture, Urumqi was an outpost of civilization. The Qing author Shi Shanchang, for example, wrote of Urumqi, "Wine and tea gardens, no different from China proper" (Yu Weicheng 1986: 2). Another Qing writer went so far as to call Urumqi the "Jiangnan outside the border" (Zan Yulin 1983: 9).[20] By this era walled suburbs had developed north and south of the old Chinese city. Qing authors described lively night markets in these suburbs (Yu Weicheng 1986: 2). Even allowing for some degree of poetic license in these depictions, it seems that the Chinese had attempted to recreate some of the urban life and landscapes familiar to them from eastern China.

Urumqi was a multicultural settlement from the outset, with Chinese living in Dihua, Manchu in Gongning Cheng, and Uygur, Hui, and other Muslim peoples and even foreigners from outside China in the suburban districts. The Chinese population was itself diverse, embracing migrants from many regions. There were scholars from southern China, traders from Tianjin, and peddlers from Shanxi and Gansu. The most well-represented Chinese groups in Urumqi were from Gansu, Shaanxi, Shanxi, and Hunan (*Xinjiang dilizhi* 1914: 166). Strict divisions were maintained between the Chinese, non-Chinese, and Manchu residence

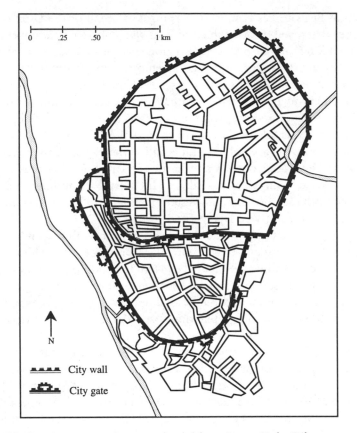

Map 8. Urumqi, ca. 1900. Source: adapted from Japan, Koka Rikugun 1939.

areas. The Chinese referred to the gate between the Chinese city and the southern Muslim suburb as the gate that divided heaven (within the Chinese walls) from earth (the suburb) (Zan Yulin 1983: 37).

The presence of foreign traders added to Urumqi's multicultural atmosphere. Russians were particularly prominent. Russians were trading in the Urumqi region as early as 1696. In 1762 the Chinese began taxing that trade in all Xinjiang, a practice they continued until an 1881 treaty granted Russians free trading privileges in the region. An office to oversee the Russian trade was established at Urumqi in 1896. By the early twentieth century, Britons, Germans, and Americans had joined the Russians in conducting business in Urumqi, and some had settled just south of the southern walled suburb, creating an international enclave. Indian, Afghani, and Turkish traders also conducted business in Urumqi. The Russians, the Americans, and the Europeans established schools, presses, a telegraph and radio office, churches, and pharmacies in the city. The Russians lost their free trade privileges after the 1917 revolution, but even with the renewal of Chinese taxes, they continued to be prominent participants in Urumqi's businesses.

Urumqi was a bustling trade center during the early twentieth century. L. Richard found it a lively city of 50,000 people, marked by "a large trade especially in skins and furs" and an ethnic mix of Uygur, Chinese, Manchu, and a few Mongol inhabitants. He estimated that the Uygur composed one-fourth of the population (Richard 1908: 532).

In 1927 the recently established Nationalist government in Urumqi took over the Great Mosque, located near the north wall, and transformed it into a Confucian temple, and Islamic people were no longer allowed to enter the city on the way to their prayers. The new government also established another temple, the God of Wealth Temple (Caishenmiao), 200 m south of the south gate, in the traditionally non-Chinese suburb (Zan Yulin 1983: 37).

During the 1930s there were major revolts in central Xinjiang, led by a Hui from Gansu, Ma Zhongying. On April 12, 1933, the rebels reached Urumqi and stormed the provincial government headquarters within the city walls, forcing the provincial chairman to flee for his life; the revolts continued until a final surrender at Kashgar in 1935 (Norins 1944: 42–43, 84). In the midst of these turbulent years, Communist Party workers came to Urumqi, tore down the south gate, and burned down the God of Wealth Temple (Zan Yulin 1983: 38). But they also built roads and schools, and made other infrastructure improvements. There is a museum in Urumqi today honoring Mao Zedong's brother, Mao Zemin, who resided in the city during this period.

Since 1949 Urumqi has become an important industrial center, with massive metallurgical, chemical, and machine works. There are also coal mines and oil refineries just outside the city. This industrial growth has given much of Urumqi a new look that overwhelms for many visitors the charm of its traditional neighborhoods and park areas. The verdict of a popular guidebook on China, for example, is that "Urumqi is an interesting place to visit, but it's got to be one of the ugliest cities on the face of the earth" (Samagalski et al. 1988: 769). This seems unfair, for much of the city simply reproduces the uniform post-1949 landscapes of most Chinese cities, and many of its neighborhoods retain their older charm and special character.

The industrialization of Urumqi has been accompanied by a substantial in-migration of Han Chinese from the east. In 1965 T. R. Tregear reported that "Urumchi is essentially a Uygur town, Uygur being the official language. . . . The population is almost entirely Moslem" (Tregear 1965: 294). But he may well have been mistaken, if Richard's earlier estimate of Uygur population at only 25 percent in 1908 was correct. Since then considerable numbers of Han Chinese from eastern China have migrated to Urumqi. Today its Islamic population is less than 20 percent.

Kunming, China's "City of Springtime"

Kunming is a city where the modern visitor can still experience the flavor of traditional southern Chinese market streets. Entire neighborhoods behind the main north-south thoroughfare are lined with two- and three-story wooden shops with residences upstairs. Street markets alive with the cries of street vendors advertising their wares mark the city's older neighborhoods. Long blocks of red and green wooden houses contrast sharply with both the visual discord of multicolored modern development and the monotony of the gray and brown factories that line the newer streets. The charm of these traditional housing neighborhoods has been widely recognized by foreign tourists, and some popular guidebooks describe them. They have also been appreciated recently by the city government, which has adopted measures for the preservation of these traditional areas. Nonetheless, Kunming today is very much a city undergoing substantial change, and the traditional buildings in the west of the city are rapidly giving way to modern high-rise buildings. The eastern portion of the city is already modern, with wide tree-lined avenues and multistory concrete structures.

Kunming lies on the northern shores of Lake Dian (Dianchi), surrounded by the mountains of the Yunnan-Guizhou plateau, and immediately east of the dramatic escarpment known as the Western Hills. The city is located some 390 miles southwest of Chongqing and 340 miles northwest of Hanoi, at an elevation of about 1,895 m (6,253 ft.) above sea level. In 1985 Kunming, a city of about 1.5 million inhabitants, administered an area of just over 2,000 km^2 (with a population of 3.2 million). With a relatively high altitude at a location just north of 25° latitude, the climate is mild, earning Kunming the name Quncheng (City of Springtime) among the Chinese.

Long before the Han dynasty was established in northern China, the first settlements in the Kunming area were scattered along the eastern banks of Lake Dian. At that time the lake stretched all the way to the foothills on its north side, but by the Han dynasty the broad plains we see today had been uplifted and were being cultivated by people who called the place Guchang (Fertile Valley). By then agriculturalists had also formed settlements at the southern end of the lake.

Some of these early settlers were Chinese. During the third century B.C., a Chinese general representing a prince from the Yangzi River valley settled at Lake Dian with his followers when they were cut off from returning home by their enemies. He declared himself the king of Dian and established a small capital near present-day Kunming. His descendants intermarried with the local people and ruled for two centuries. During the Han dynasty Chinese troops again reached Lake Dian and were received by the king of Dian.

It is likely that this early capital was more a large village or town than a city. Little is known of its size or character. The first urban settlement at Kunming on which there is some substantive evidence was established 500 years after the collapse of the kingdom of Dian by the Nan Zhao kingdom. The establishment of this settlement marks the first of four periods of urban development at the site: the Nan Zhao–Dali kingdom period, the Mongol Yuan period, the Ming-Qing period, and the twentieth century.

The Kunming area became part of the Nan Zhao kingdom in the eighth century, when power was consolidated by a prince who had declared himself the Prince of all the South (Nan Zhao) after assassinating five other ruling princes in the area. The Nan Zhao kingdom and its successor, the Dali kingdom, survived as an independent state from 732 until 1253, when it was conquered by Khubilai Khan's armies. The Nan Zhao armies took over the site of Kunming proper in 748 (Ding Shuiren 1987: 17–19).

In 765 the Nan Zhao army built a walled city, known as Tuodong Cheng, at Kunming. Though initially conceived as a defensive outpost against the Tang dynasty, by 809 the city had become a secondary capital of the Nan Zhao–Dali kingdom (Schinz 1989: 291). Tuodong Cheng had three walled areas; the main city was constructed in two sections, on the east and west banks of the Panlong River, with a smaller square compound to the southeast, on the eastern bank of the Jinlong River. The north walls of the main city reached but did not enclose the two hills, Wuhua Hill and Dade Hill, that mark the center of modern Kunming. The Dali state, which established its capital at Dali, northwest of Kunming, also used the walled city at Kunming as a secondary capital and renamed it Shanchan Cheng. The city was expanded toward the west during the tenth century (Yu Xixian & Yu Xiqian 1982: 162).

The Mongols conquered the Dali kingdom in 1254 and used Yunnan as a southern base from which to attack the Song empire and secure their trade routes to Burma and Annam (Rossabi 1988: 22, 28). When the Mongol troops arrived at Shanchan Cheng, they sacked the old city and built a new walled city, Zhongjing Cheng, west of the Panlong River. Soon after they established this stronghold, they overthrew the Song dynasty and made Zhongjing Cheng their administrative center for the Yunnan area, with about 1,000 families in residence (*Kunming xianzhi* 1887: 13).

The Mongols' walled city extended farther north than the old walled city, now enclosing Wuhua and Dade hills. At that time the waters of Lake Dian were higher than they are today, and the western wall followed the shore of the lake. The new city had five gates: two on the east, and one each on the north, south, and west. On the other side of the Panlong River, the Yuan built a temple (Yuan Baita) outside the eastern wall of the former Shanchan Cheng. Two bridges gave access to it, the Zhizheng bridge, which stood opposite the northern of the two eastern gates, and the Dade bridge, which stood opposite the southern of the two eastern gates. The Yuan also bridged the creek that ran through the center of the city (the Tongji bridge).

The Mongol invasion and subsequent establishment of an administrative city at Kunming had a substantial impact on the city's cultural character. The first Yuan dynasty governor of Yunnan was a Central Asian Muslim named Saiyid Ajall Shams al-Din. He established Zhongjing Cheng, a multicultural city built at the site of Kunming, overseeing the construction of a Confucian temple and a Buddhist temple, as well as two mosques. The overall form of the city he built, however, was Chinese, not Mongol or Central Asian in style (Rossabi 1988: 201–3).

The city was made all the more cosmopolitan by an influx of Chinese from many parts of the empire. According to a late Qing gazetteer, the surrounding hills were dotted with graveyards dating back to the Yuan that had been established separately by people originating from Jiangxi, Shandong, Shanxi, Zhejiang, Shaanxi, Fujian, Guangxi, Sichuan, Anhui, and Hubei (*Kunming xianzhi* 1902: 155–56).[21] The existence of these place-of-origin-associated graveyards not only indicates that the city came to have a diverse population of Chinese in the Yuan period but shows that these people were intent on maintaining their connections to their place of origin though they lived and died on the frontier.

Yunnan and the Kunming region figured ever more importantly in the empire's economy during the Yuan era. The new rulers discovered rich metal ore and mineral deposits in the region and actively exploited them.

By the end of the dynasty, Yunnan had become a leading producer of minerals in China, with eleven gold mines, five silver mines, two copper mines, and six iron mines. Yunnan has remained a mining center ever since, and the mines have played a prominent role in its history. Kunming was thus the capital of an increasingly wealthy region. By the time Marco Polo visited it, Kunming was, by his description, a very great and noble city.

The Ming built a new city called Yunnanfu Cheng at the Kunming site in 1381. There was a major growth in the city's population during this dynasty, much of which resulted from the settlement of migrants from the north. Three or four million people migrated from the core area of China to Yunnan during this time. In 1389 alone an estimated 2.5 million people made the journey. These migrants were primarily political exiles from eastern China. At the beginning of the dynasty, many residents of Nanjing who had opposed the Ming accession were sent to the southwest frontier, along with people from Jiangxi, Jiangsu, and Anhui. The first Ming emperor, trying to clear his new capital at Nanjing of potential enemies, ordered as many as 300,000 local men and their families to relocate to Yunnan. Loyalists were also sent to the southwest to administer the newly founded Yunnan Province (Mote 1977: 144; Yu Xixian & Yu Xiqian 1982: 164). The result was a decided shift in the ethnic composition of Kunming. Until this time the majority of the population had been non-Chinese descendants of the Dian kingdom, Mongols, and Islamic peoples of mixed descent. The Chinese who had moved to the area in earlier times had intermarried with local residents. After the influx of migrants from the Nanjing region, however, the balance of population in the city was Chinese, and there was far less intermarriage between Chinese and non-Chinese (Yu Xixian & Yu Xiqian 1982: 164). Ming-era graveyards around Kunming show an even greater diversity in the Chinese population than in Yuan times. Zhejiang, Anhui, Jiangxi, Hubei, Hunan, Guangdong, Guangxi, Fujian, and Shaanxi are all represented (*Kunming xianzhi* 1887: 156). They also suggest that more of the Ming population was of southern Chinese origin.

The Ming walled city was built to the northwest of the previous cities, encompassing Wuhua and Dade hills at its center, as well as the Green Lake, or Cuihu (which was then just a swamp), and reaching just north of Yuantong Hill in the northeast. The city, now called Yunnanfu Cheng, had a squarish but somewhat irregular shape with rounded corners. In addition to six gates (one each on the north and south sides, and two on the east and west sides), the Ming city was surrounded by a moat, which was bridged at each of the gates.[22] The northern gate and bridge led directly to

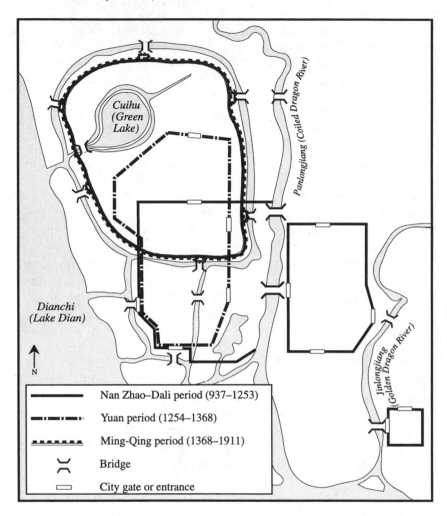

Map 9. Historical development of Kunming, 937–1911. Source: adapted from Yu Xixian 1981: 162.

Shang Mountain. The southern east gate was aligned with what had been the northern one in Yuan times, and a new bridge across the Panlong River (the Yongjing bridge) was built opposite the new northern east gate. Map 9 illustrates the development of Kunming from the Nan Zhao and Dali periods to the Ming and Qing periods.

The Qing city retained the six gates of the Ming with a wall nine li (about 5 miles) in circumference (see Fig. 7; *Kunming xianzhi* 1887: 39). The drum tower and bell tower were located just inside and to the east

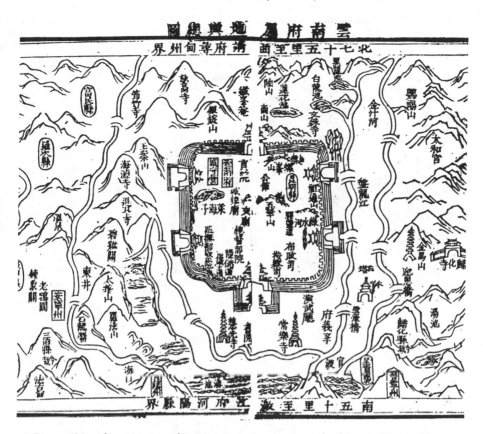

Fig. 7. Qing dynasty map of Kunming. Source: *Yunnanfu zhi* 1967 (Qing ed.).

and west of the south gate. The flourishing local economy attracted traders and craftsmen from many parts of China, and population growth led to expansion outside the walls (see Map 10). Some of the earliest to arrive during this period were groups of calligraphers and porcelain craftsmen from Jiangxi and Hunan and silk and glass merchants from Sichuan. The most important trading streets in Qing times were Embankment Alley (Tangzi Xiang), First in the Palace Exams Hall (Zhuangyuan Lou), and Southern Trade Market (Nanjiao Chang; Yu Xixian & Yu Xiqian 1982: 165).

During the eighteenth century the Chinese used Yunnan as a base for military maneuvers against Burma. Tribute was thereafter transported from Burma to Kunming via a route similar to the Burma Road of the Second World War. This important trade route, sometimes referred to as

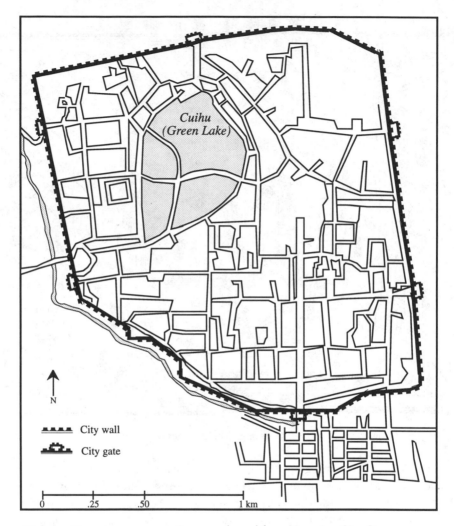

Map 10. Kunming, ca. 1900. Source: adapted from Kunming City Government map, 1924.

the Southern Silk Route, served as the primary means of communication between the Chinese empire and Burma.

From the mid-1850s to the mid-1870s, Yunnan was shaken by rebellion. What started as mostly labor disputes between Muslim mine workers and their Chinese supervisors grew into a full-fledged revolt by non-Chinese peoples against the empire. In the course of this movement, Muslims destroyed most of the Buddhist temples and monuments in Kunming, along with a number of government buildings and the houses of the elite. The rebellion was put down in 1873 by Chinese troops. Many rebels were killed, including most of the Muslim residents of the city of Dali. L. Richard observed the devastation wrought by these rebellions in Kunming as late as 1908; he attributed the city's low population (which he estimated at 45,000) to the impact of the Muslim rebellions and their suppression.

At the turn of the twentieth century, the British and the French vied for entry into Yunnan, hoping to gain trade access to the interior of China, to create inland linkages for their Southeast Asian colonies, and to draw on the province's rich deposits of tin and copper. The French won the concession to build a railway from Hanoi to Kunming; the line was completed in 1910. They also established a residential quarter in Kunming south of the south gate, and French traders and bankers set up businesses in this area. The influence of French architectural styles is still apparent in this section of the city.[23]

The next period of change for Kunming came during the late 1930s and early 1940s. The city became a refuge for a wave of university professors, other intellectuals, and professionals who fled the Japanese occupation in 1937. Many of these refugees brought substantial collections of books that they contributed to an ever-growing library at Yunnan University (or the Southwest Associated University of Kunming, as it was then called). Other refugees brought dismantled factories and other infrastructure to reassemble in Kunming. Between 1937 and 1939 the Chinese worked to construct the Burma Road connecting Lashio, in eastern Burma, with Kunming as a supply line for the resistance against the Japanese. The Japanese captured Lashio in 1942, shutting down communications with Kunming until American forces arrived and, under the guidance of General Joseph Stillwell, constructed a new link connecting the Burma Road to Ledo, India.[24] Kunming also served as a command base for General Claire Chennault's American Volunteer Group, better known as the Flying Tigers, from 1942 to 1945.

Today about 3.7 million people live in the area under Kunming's administration. Fully 625,000 of these people live in the densely crowded (about 46,000 residents per km²) central city, made up of the old Ming walled area and its surrounding suburbs—the local government's attempts to prevent the city center population from growing beyond 600,000 notwithstanding.

Kunming has a multiethnic population, though most of the non-Han Chinese, except the Hui, live outside the central city. There are approximately 360,000 non-Han residents, divided roughly as follows: 220,000

Yi, 50,000 Hui, 30,000 Bai, 20,000 Miao, 5,000 Dai, 3,000 Hani, and 32,000 peoples from a variety of backgrounds (Ding Shuiren 1987: 35–40). The non-Han share of the population has remained relatively constant over the past 30 years, accounting for just over 11 percent of the entire city's population in 1964 and just over 11.5 percent in 1982 (*Kunming shiqing* 1987: 84). In the two city center districts, however, non-Han residents make up only 5 percent of the population; nearly 18,000 of these people (58 percent of the 30,000 non-Han total) are Hui (*Yunnan dizhou shixian gaikuang* 1987: 53, 64).

Kunming has become an economically diverse industrial city. Among its industries today are metallurgy, machine tools, electric power, electrical instruments, cosmetics, building materials, textiles, food products, and paper manufacturing. Nonetheless, it is a city whose landscapes retain strong ties to its past. Development during the post-1949 period has until recently been largely focused on the eastern part of old Kunming and the expanding periphery of the city. A relatively high percentage of traditional structures and entire neighborhoods remain intact in the western half of the city. A number of old monuments (particularly Buddhist temples) remain as well. These are open today as tourist attractions, frequented primarily by domestic tourists. And Kunming's neighborhoods still have their own distinct characters based on their differing histories of migration and settlement.

3

The Functions of Cities on the Frontiers

With the exception of a few pioneering works such as those of Richard Wade (1959) and John Reps (1979, 1981), cities have not been a focus of frontier studies.[1] Yet particularly in China, cities are crucial to an understanding of the frontier relations between Chinese and non-Chinese people, not only at the macro-level of political policy and exchange, but in day-to-day cultural and economic life and interactions as well. Cities on the frontier, like cities elsewhere in China, serve as centers for a variety of activities involving the residents and neighboring rural populations, such as trade, administration, crafts production, and cultural events, and fulfill several functional roles at the regional and national level as well. But cities on the frontier often take on a disproportionate share of some of these functions, which might more typically be shared by numerous cities of varying size. Frontier cities are similar in function to primate cities: they are anomalous points of high population density in the midst of large regions typified by a dispersed rural population.[2] In the following pages I will survey both the overall functional significance of Chinese frontier cities and specific aspects of urban functions, including their role in conquest and administration, transportation, trade, finance, and industry.

Cities, Settlement, and Urban Functions on the Frontiers

Frontier cities in China do not fit neatly into any of the conventional methods of categorizing cities within national city-systems. These cities tend to have exaggerated regional and national significance in relation to their size. Like primate cities, they may usurp all urban functions for a substantial distance in all directions. Unlike primate cities, however, they have not experienced rampant economic and population growth except where it has been fostered by state-mandated development and migrations. Their hinterlands tend to be too sparsely populated to generate large numbers of rural-to-urban migrants, and they are by and large too remote to attract large numbers of migrants from the country's major population centers. Now that state controls on migration are becoming less strict, this situation may change. But, even so, the current trend is for rural migrants to seek out the cities of eastern China. In the post-Mao years, many Chinese who were sent to the western frontier cities to work returned to the east as well.[3]

In the study of any urban frontier, and for that matter, any frontier settlement pattern, one of the most important concepts is that of first effective settlement, that is, the analysis of the first settlements established in a new region that survive long enough to be considered effective settlement, and especially those that form the basis for settlement that endures (Zelinsky 1973: 13). This concept is highly biased toward the unidirectional analysis of the frontier and fails to credit successful indigenous settlements that predate so-called frontier settlements.

The concept of first effective settlement so often applied to studies of historical settlement patterns in the West takes on new dimensions in the Chinese context. In the Western case the first effective settlement is the beginning of continuous settlement on a site. In discussions of Chinese urban history, a somewhat different approach is taken. Chinese cities have been built, abandoned, and rebuilt time and time again on the same site. Sometimes several hundred years may pass between successive cities on a site. Nevertheless, the Chinese perceive a city as dating back to the first settlement at the location, regardless of whether or not that settlement was subsequently abandoned and only later succeeded by other settlements. In this view of first effective settlement, settlement does not need to have been continuous. This perspective is particularly relevant in the case of the frontier, where cities are traced to the first establishment of a fort or garrison on a site, even if there were intervening years during which the fort was unmanned and in ruins.

This frontier perspective on settlement is quite different from the perspective on the core area. Arthur F. Wright asserts that the Chinese "did not regard the city as the prime unit—practical or symbolic—of their penetration of new territory," and that what counted most was the establishment of Chinese agriculture, with the building of stockades following only after the region was tamed (Wright 1977: 33).[4] Richard von Glahn has suggested that this was also true in remote Sichuan (Von Glahn 1987).

Nonetheless, stockades, forts, small fortified towns, and cities were often critical to the securing of the frontier when Chinese settlement was opposed by the local inhabitants. And in frontier areas reliant on trade rather than agricultural settlement, such as vast areas of the far northwest and much of Inner Mongolia, the establishment of cities generally preceded Chinese rural settlement (if it took place at all). These proto-urban settlements were the key to Chinese settlement of the frontier. In the far frontiers, forts were the first settlements, and soldiers attempting to support themselves were often the first Chinese agriculturalists.

Still, in such cases, the distinction between frontier garrisons, towns, and cities is often very fine and open to interpretation. In the sparse settlement context of the frontier, I suggest that urban places (cities and towns) must be identified in terms of function rather than size.[5] If a walled settlement with a relatively high population density historically carried out a number of urban functions on the frontier, such as serving as centers of administration, trade, and nonagricultural production, I treat it as an urban place regardless of its size. For former garrisons, this also requires a transition in functions from strictly military to multifaceted activities. The larger question, perhaps, is whether or not the settlements were truly viable as urban places. Thousands of garrisons and settlements that were established on the Chinese frontiers over the long stretch of Chinese history failed. Most frontier settlements had to be regularly supplied from the core area and were incapable of surviving long periods of time on their own. One of the distinguishing features of the cities I have identified in this study is their ability to survive as urban settlements despite significant changes in policy, government, and regional control. It may be that this ability to survive, to remain viable as urban places, is the single most important factor justifying their identification as cities from their earliest days.

The frontier functioned as a zone of contact and interaction between the Chinese empire and its neighbors, and frontier cities in turn functioned as the focal points of that political and economic interaction. Chinese administrators planned the establishment of cities on the frontier to provide a venue for communication and control.

Frontier Cities as the Vanguard of Territorial Conquest and Control

"A certain congruence may be noted," G. William Skinner suggests, "between the defense function of many frontier cities and the special character of other administrative functions in the more remote portions of regional peripheries":

It was along China's regional frontiers that local society assumed its most heterodox and variegated guise. . . . In dealing with such elements, normative strategies of administration were largely ineffective, and frontier administrators necessarily relied on repression, containment, and divide-and-rule strategies. (Skinner 1977: 322)

As Skinner observes, China's frontier cities were charged with administering regions far more diverse than any in the core area. On the western frontier, the most important functions of the cities have typically been military and political. Those cities were often designated as "secret" strategic posts and thus assigned primarily military functions with, according to Skinner, a narrow band of control (Skinner 1977: 319–21).[6] The Chinese usually carried out the conquest of frontier lands through a combination of military action, cooptation of local leadership, and settlement. These strategies were often pursued in tandem. Regions were usually considered to be secured once a series of forts was established and maintained along strategic routes. During the Ming period, for example, forts were established at even intervals ten days' march apart. Professional armies were maintained in such regions: armies that built citylike structures and may have spent three of the four seasons farming and only one season in military training. Sometimes soldiers were divided into two groups: one with true military duties and one whose primary duty was to carry out agriculture and other tasks necessary to the survival of the military establishment (Elvin 1973: 56, 96). Once a region was secured, it was placed under the jurisdiction of a regional governor and bureaucratic administration. It was in this process of transition to civil authority that cities were formed on the Chinese frontiers. The transition was in some senses ceremonial. Many walled forts functioned as cities before the transition and changed little after it. Other forts never became much more than local garrisons with slightly expanded functions even after they came under civil authority.

Defense was clearly an ongoing and critical function. As noted earlier, cities in the northwest in particular were subject to frequent raids. Some were lost from Chinese control and not regained even for hundreds of years. Late-nineteenth-century revolts throughout the frontier lands are evidence that even at that late date, the frontier had yet to be truly integrated into the empire.

The transition from military to civil administration usually involved the naming and official recognition of the region as a part of the Chinese empire and the import of various civil officials from the core area. As in all Chinese administrative cities, the civil bureaucracy was headquartered in the center of the city (or fort) in a complex called the *yamen*. The central placement of the yamen was symbolic of its central function in the administrative life of the city.

Difficult as it was to maintain frontier cities, imperial authorities went to considerable lengths to do so. These outposts enabled the Chinese to buffer the core area against potential invasions, to control valuable long-distance trade routes, and to gain access through local and regional trade to the natural resources of the frontier. The wealth and power of the empire was based on tax revenues generated by a settled population that included both farmers and city-dwellers. The most important form of public revenue was land-based and production-based tax assessment. Thus it was in the Chinese interest to create a mechanism on the frontier for the approximation, in legal and economic terms, of the sedentarized system of the east, to supplant the nomadic systems of the west.

The Chinese did not subjugate and control all the frontier peoples directly. Rather, as discussed in Chapter One, they instituted regional forms of what Owen Lattimore has called "frontier feudalism" to govern and extract revenue from the local populations. The Chinese empire also controlled trade as much as possible by establishing taxed markets and declaring untaxed trade illegal. The frontier cities provided a mechanism for the management and enforcement of these policies.

Cities on the frontier formed a super-system above the hierarchical power structure established under frontier feudalism. As permanent settlements commanding specific territories, they were the antithesis of the local clan-based system of social organization and administration. As the representatives of the long arm of Chinese rule in the frontier regions, they were both symbolically and concretely the ultimate expression of that rule: local leaders who had been granted titles and authority to rule territories outside of the cities still needed permission to enter the central walled administrative complexes.

Large frontier cities were the administrative centers for vast territories—territories considerably larger and more diverse than those administered by any level of administrative city in eastern China save only the imperial capital itself. The degree to which their administrative authority was ceremonial or actual varied considerably with the changing fortunes of the empire as a whole. For example, Lanzhou at times officially administered lands far into Tibet and the northwest, by the authority of the empire, though Lanzhou had no real power, control, or recognition in those areas.

Transportation

Transportation and communication were great challenges on the frontier. The miraculous nature of successful travel on the frontier is illustrated by the mid-nineteenth-century traveler Evariste-Regis Huc, who observed: "Enfin, grace à la bonté de Dieu, nous arrivâmes sans accident à Si-Ning [Xining]" (1845). The development of reliable, fast, and efficient transportation routes is a key element in integrating a frontier into a core system and at the same time expanding the core system into the frontier. Rail, road, and air access to the frontier have facilitated greater changes in the relationships between core and periphery within the past hundred years than were possible in the thousand years preceding. Travel in China today is considered difficult by many Western travelers; it was extraordinarily so in the frontiers of China before 1949. George Cressey, one of those hardy travelers of the pre-1949 era, reports that "Chinese distances are not to be measured in miles but in time, and in discomfort and danger" (Cressey 1955: 334). This was particularly true on the frontier, where modern means of transportation were slow to come. Certainly the inconvenience of transport has long been a primary factor in the persistence of the frontier over the centuries. Nonetheless, it is important to note that none of the cities in this study has been truly isolated, despite the difficulties of terrain and climate. All are located on one or more major and long-established trade routes. The general trend of transportation development in the frontier regions since 1949 has been to dramatically increase connectivity with the core area. This goal is not unique to the frontier region; there has also been an emphasis on connecting other remote or inaccessible areas more effectively with the core area. What makes the frontier regions distinctive in this respect is both the far greater distances involved and the far greater change that the new connectivity could bring.

Intraurban Transportation

The streets of most Chinese cities were generally unpaved and uneven even as recently as the nineteenth century. Rain and snow frequently rendered them impassable. Nor was there much development of public transport before the twentieth century, though there were various forms of transportation for hire such as rickshaws and carts. Indeed the vast majority of people continued to travel by foot on unpaved roads in China's cities for some time after the founding of the People's Republic. Only the more prosperous or powerful cities could boast of paved streets. China as a whole did not undergo the experience of a Western industrial revolution, with its concomitant infrastructural improvements. Those improvements that were instituted here and there before the 1949 revolution were ad hoc undertakings at best, reflecting the whim of local leaders rather than any unified effort to fundamentally change urban life. Hankow, for example, got paved streets in the nineteenth century, thanks to the sponsorship of the city's guilds (Rowe 1984: 304–5). In general, however, few streets in frontier cities were paved even in 1949.

Another aspect of intraurban street patterns in traditional China was that there were few through streets, and that these were established when the city was founded. Other than the primary axial streets, urban streets typically led into dead-end mazes of courtyards or market areas. These streets were subject to varying levels of control by the residents, and might very well be closed off at night for the purpose of neighborhood security. As a result of this street layout, it was (and remains) rare for Chinese to pass through residential neighborhoods unless they had a specific reason to be there. This characteristic of Chinese urban form may have contributed to the maintenance and formation of ethnic enclaves in frontier cities. Cities were subdivided and compartmentalized not only by their walls but by their street patterns as well.

The adoption—even at a very small scale—of the automobile altered China's traditional structure. In Urumqi, for example, there was speculative and promotional transport development during the Republican era. In 1921, 36 cars set out for the city from Tianjin as a bank promotion. Only one car reached Urumqi, where it was heralded as the first ever to enter the city. Urumqi saw its first regular use of European motorcars in the 1930s, when they were acquired for local government officials. In the 1940s several local companies began to offer Russian-manufactured vehicles for hire to the general public. The most popular was a kind of modified truck capable of carrying five or six passengers. These vehicles were also used as attractions at temple fairs and for tourists. Trucks and motorized carts were used at this time by local families involved in the timber industry for hauling lumber. And a few platform-bed trucks were used for intraregional transport in the first half of the twentieth century. Passenger tickets were available from local companies for these trucks (Yang Bin 1986).

In 1939 two public bus routes were inaugurated in Urumqi. One ran from the north gate to the Xinjiang Academy (today's south campus of Xinjiang University) in the southern suburbs. The bus made four stops in between. The other line ran from the old east gate (today's Tianshan Building) to the great west gate (today's front gate of the Xinjiang Central Theater). After the revolution the street system was improved to provide four major north-south arteries and six major east-west ones. Streets were paved, and islands and traffic circles were added, and planted, for safety and landscape improvement. Today there are seven public bus routes within the city center, as well as seven suburban routes (Yang Bin 1986).

Automobiles and private bus lines were also introduced in Lanzhou and Kunming in the Republican era. The warlord Ma Bufang introduced them in Xining. Although motor vehicles remained beyond the affordable reach of most citizens, the increasing use of cars, trucks, and buses, as well as increases in traditional forms of transport, did begin to have an impact on urban form even before 1949. The most significant early result has already been touched on: the widening of city gates and the creation of new gates to accommodate traffic. In Lanzhou, as we saw, there was enough motor and cart traffic in 1939 that new gates were opened on the east, south, and west sides of the city walls; and in 1941 another new gate was opened on the east side of the city, while three older gates were widened to allow two-way traffic (Xian Xiaowei & Chen Lijun 1982). During the same period a space was opened in the Kunming city wall to accommodate the road leading away from the train station (Smith 1940: 173). Similar widenings of city gates were taking place in Xi'an and Beijing at this time.

Since 1949 the government has been relatively even-handed in its efforts to improve transportation in all cities, with no noticeable pattern distinguishing the frontier regions from the core area. All provincial and autonomous region capitals, and most large and mid-size cities, now have paved streets and bus systems, and as Table 3 shows, the frontier has been brought up to parity with the rest of the country in both departments.

Interurban Transport

Traditional interurban transport in China was by foot, animal, or water. In southern China the water buffalo was the most common beast of burden; in the north donkeys and mules served a similar purpose. Bactrian camels were used in the northwestern desert regions, and the yak was then, as it is today, the most important pack animal on the Tibetan plateau. Horses were long the prestige animal for transport in most of these regions, but were used only by the elites in China proper. They were more

TABLE 3
*Area of Paved Road and Number of Public Buses
per 10,000 Persons in Core and Frontier Cities, 1986*

Core area city	Paved road (m²)	Public buses	Frontier city	Paved road (m²)	Public buses
Beijing	3.82	8.30	Xining	2.97	3.89
Shanghai	1.87	7.40	Kunming	1.49	3.81
Guangzhou	1.37	4.87	Urumqi	2.38	4.38
Xi'an	2.51	3.26	Lanzhou	3.00	3.49
Wuxi	2.71	3.47	Hohhot	2.37	1.44
Anyang	2.83	1.39	Lhasa	6.49	5.83[b]
Guilin	5.06	2.59			
Shenzhen	17.52[a]	7.23			

SOURCE: PRC, State Statistical Bureau 1986: 369–72.
[a]This unusually high figure has to do with the PRC's development of Shenzhen as a special economic zone tied to nearby Hong Kong.
[b]In fact only one bus operated inside the Lhasa city limits in 1986, going back and forth and making stops about once every two hours. The figure in the source must include regional routes, suggesting that the other data could be similarly inflated.

widely used by Mongolians, Tibetans, and other nomadic groups on the frontiers. Long-distance travel by all of these means was, of course, relatively slow and unreliable. For protection against the gangs of bandits who roamed much of the countryside, traders commonly traveled in large groups or caravans.

Highways have played a key role in linking the frontier cities with each other and the core. From the time of the Qin emperor on, there was an extensive imperial highway system in China, although long stretches of road were often in a state of disrepair. Highways were built and maintained with varying success. Much of southern China was traversed by flagstone highways; the "highways" in the loesslands of the north were mere earthen paths. There were about 2,000 miles of imperial highways by the thirteenth century (Cressey 1955: 153, 269).

The imperial highway system, in its best years, included way-stations at regular intervals; some were only the most basic of inns, but others could be elaborate establishments complete with postal services, jails, and permanent staffs of government representatives. On the frontiers the cities provided the anchors for this system. Not only did they serve as particularly well-appointed way-stations, where travelers could stop and resupply; they were also the places where the government controlled traffic in and out of China. Permits for trade and passage were issued through the imperial representatives in frontier cities.

In modern China highways serve primarily as a means of transporting goods. There are few private automobiles, and buses and trucks still account for most of the traffic. Travelers tend to prefer trains over buses for long distances, despite higher fares.

The PRC's national strategy for highway construction is to create intraprovincial networks of highways focused on and radiating from the provincial capitals, and then to link these through an interprovincial network. But the choice of provincial capital sites is based primarily in historical precedent, which may or may not have relevance to modern transportation needs. Thus, for example, while Hohhot is the designated transportation hub of the Inner Mongolia Autonomous Region, the region's most heavily industrialized city, Baotou, is three hours by train to the northwest. As a result substantial railyards and road systems have had to be constructed at Baotou, as well as Hohhot, so the Autonomous Region actually has two transportation centers. In general, however, the designation of the provincial capital as the transportation hub works relatively well in the frontier regions, since the provincial capital in each has, for some time, been the largest city in the region, and more often than not is located on good natural transportation routes.

All of China's provinces have made significant improvements in roads since 1949, and the frontier regions, in this context, have fared relatively well. Although the improved road networks in the frontier regions do not cover the land area in as thorough a net as they cover some of the eastern provinces, all of the frontier provinces now have a number of modern and well-maintained roads. Many of these were built by the People's Liberation Army, and their routes have been guided by strategic considerations. The military importance of these highways is fortuitous for the frontier regions, for the army's concern ensures that they are built to a high standard and kept in good condition.

Of course, the large expanses of the frontier, combined with low population density, make highway statistics deceptive because they inevitably result in relatively high length of road per capita. The Chinese provinces and autonomous regions with the highest length of road per capita are Tibet and Qinghai, where the construction of basic road links with the east has been a priority, and vast ribbons of highway now stretch as far as Nepal, Xinjiang, and Sichuan. Yet they are also regions in which many residents live several days' walk from the nearest road. Nonetheless, these roads have become major interprovincial commercial and passenger routes linking the frontier with the core area far more effectively than was possible in the past.

Xining is a good example of the improvement in Chinese long-distance road networks under the PRC. Before the mid-twentieth century, road travel to Xining, and journeys onward to Lhasa, were quite time-consuming. In 1924, when the geographer George Cressey traveled from Beijing to the Xining area and back by train, pack animal, foot, and boat, the round trip took 109 days (Cressey 1955: 269). Today the same route by public bus might take three or four days, and by train as little as two. Negotiating the cart and wagon road from Xining to Lhasa was a 50- to 54-day affair at the turn of the century (Richard 1908: 553). Today the journey takes about three days via train to Golmud and bus to Lhasa.

The first road suitable for motorized transport in Qinghai Province was built in 1935; it connected Xining to Xiangtang, 90 km east. In the late 1930s the Nationalist government granted a number of requests for assistance in further road building after having been successfully lobbied by Ma Bufang, the warlord of Qinghai. Roads to Sikang (present-day Sichuan) and to Tibet were partially constructed between 1942 and 1944. And a road between Qinghai and Xinjiang was started in Xining in 1946 and reached Mangnai in the northwest corner of Qinghai in 1947. The project was halted in 1948 (but has since been completed). For all these gains, long stretches of these roads were not suitable for motor vehicles, and in 1949 there were just 472 km of motorable roads. But then there was little traffic to bear, for in the absence of any repair shop in all Qinghai, only four of the province's 216 motor vehicles (most of which were owned by Ma Bufang) were operable (*Qinghai lishi jiyao* 1987: 465–67, 491–93; *Qinghai shengqing* 1986: 294; *Qinghai sanshiwunian* 1985: 161).

The 1950s saw the commencement of construction on an intraprovincial network of roads centered on Xining and on the highways that were to connect Xining to Lanzhou, Urumqi, Chengdu, Lhasa, and other destinations. The most famous of these highways, the Qinghai-Tibet Highway, which crosses from Xining west to the center of Qinghai at Golmud, then turns south to Lhasa, is nearly 2,000 km long and is one of the world's highest in terms of average elevation. By 1983 Qinghai had more than 15,000 km of roads and highways (*Qinghai sanshiwunian* 1985: 161–62).

Neighboring Xinjiang entered 1949 with a much more extensive road network than Qinghai and Tibet. It had about 3,000 km all told. But the road conditions were such that a journey between Urumqi and Kashgar, in the far west, might take two or three months. After 1949 the highway system was greatly improved and was focused on Urumqi. The most important highway is that constructed from Urumqi east through Hami to Gansu Province (linking with a highway to Lanzhou). Highways were also built or improved from Urumqi to Tacheng on the Soviet border and to Kashgar. By 1983 Xinjiang had a total of 22,000 km of highways; 35 percent of these were asphalt paved under a program that was started in 1958 (*Xinjiang weiwuer zizhiqu gaikuang* 1985: 160–63).

In imperial times Kunming stood at the junction of three flagstone-paved imperial highways. One led east toward Guangzhou (Canton), another led north to Chengdu in Sichuan, and the third led northeast to Guiyang in Guizhou, to branch north for a direct connection to Beijing and west to Burma. The road to Sichuan was a relatively poor one, and so was the road to Burma, a difficult track through the mountains (Cressey 1955: 228).

As noted in Chapter Two, in the Second World War Kunming became the goal of the greatest allied road-building project in Asia, the Burma Road. Though it served its purpose of moving matériel all the way from India to the wartime capital at Chongqing, the road was only for the hardy. It was built in seven months, and the frequent rains in the area tended to work loose the large flat stones with which it was surfaced, making travel conditions less than ideal.

Since 1949 Kunming has become a regional transportation hub for both highways and rail transport. In 1954 an 873-km road was completed between Kunming and Xishuangbanna, the Dai nationality region in the south of Yunnan Province near the Burma border; it was paved in asphalt in 1976 (*Yunnan—keai de difang* 1984: 316). Construction began on a highway linking Yunnan to Tibet in 1950, with a terminus at the Yunnan city of Dali, which in turn is linked with Kunming. This Yunnan-Tibet highway, which also connects with a Sichuan-Tibet highway, passes through incredibly difficult terrain and was not completed until 1973 (ibid., pp. 317–18). Parts of the Burma Road have been maintained from 1958 on, particularly the section from Kunming to Dali, which has been improved considerably.

Inner Mongolia had about 2,300 km of unpaved roads in 1949. In 1958 a program was initiated to pave roads with *taoli* (ceramsite, made from crushed kiln-fired brick) in order to make use of local materials. Since then, a variety of other paving methods have also been employed. By 1985 the Autonomous Region had a total of 38,000 km of roads, including 24,000 km of "high quality" highway (*Tuanjie jianshezhong de neimenggu* 1987: 218–19).

The building and improvement of interurban highways connecting frontier cities with both their own hinterlands and China's core regions has been a force for development and national integration. But because of the limited availability of motor transport in the PRC, their full economic, social, and cultural impact has yet to make itself felt. The expanded use of motorized transport may well fundamentally alter key relationships between the frontier cities and both their hinterlands and the core area.

Railroads. On the frontiers of China, as in the nineteenth-century frontier regions of the United States and Australia, the building of the railroads was one of the most important modern transportation developments, playing a principal role in "opening up" the frontier for development and establishing stronger linkages with the core region.[7] Railway development in China as a whole began in the mid-nineteenth century at the impetus of foreign investors and Chinese businessmen, despite initial resistance by the Qing government. The central government encouraged railway development at the end of the nineteenth century. By the end of 1906, there were about 5,600 km of railway lines open (Richard 1908: 431). By 1911 the extent of Chinese railways (including Taiwan, then controlled by Japan) had jumped to about 9,600 km. Although railway development was of particular concern to Sun Yatsen as a way to create national unity out of a highly fragmented China, his efforts were largely unsuccessful: the pace of development during the Nationalist era was not what he had hoped it would be (Leung 1980: 47, 88–89; Richard 1908: 431).

In fact railways did not reach the western frontier until rather recently. There was little or no service to China's frontier regions in 1949. In the 1930s trains operated west only as far as Xi'an. In the succeeding years railway development remained so concentrated in the east that in 1949 less than 20 percent of the track was located west of the Beijing-Guangzhou (Canton) line (Xue Muqiao 1982: 582). The pace of railway development in China during the Nationalist period had been hampered by a number of difficulties, including the weak authority of the central government and the relative power of local warlords, a lack of adequate capital, and local opposition based on concerns about the ill effects of rail line construction on the auspicious geomantic balance of the landscape.

Railway building has not only been a significant element of PRC development policies since 1949; it has been a key point in the effort to develop and integrate the frontier regions. In general, it can be said that between 1949 and 1963, national railway development was primarily directed toward that end. By C. K. Leung's estimates, the frontier area's share of operating railways rose from only 12 percent in 1949 to about 33 percent in 1963. Since then the stress on major railroad construction in the frontier regions has slackened, although two significant lines have been completed—between Kunming and Chengdu (1970) and between Xining and Golmud (1984) (Leung 1980: 156–58).[8]

Hohhot was the first frontier city to be linked by rail to China proper. Railway development took place there relatively early, perhaps as a result of the city's proximity to Beijing. Construction of a line between Beijing and Hohhot began in 1905, but with the disruptions of the Nationalist revolution and later a workers' uprising (see Gan Xulan 1987), it was not completed until 1921. An extension to the industrializing city of Baotou, southwest of Hohhot, was completed in 1923 (Guan Xiaoxian et al. 1987: 88). Between 1955 and 1958 the line was further extended to Lanzhou, linking Beijing and Inner Mongolia with the northwest (*Tuanjie jianshe-zhong de neimenggu* 1987: 216). In Inner Mongolia as a whole, the length of rail line increased from about 1,500 km in 1947 to over 4,500 km in 1985, at which point all but two of the Autonomous Republic's 16 cities were connected to Hohhot (ibid., p. 217).

Gansu had only 50 km of railway in 1949 (Xue Muqiao 1982: 798). In 1952 the Shanghai-Qinghai (Longhai) rail line reached Lanzhou (Zhao Shiying 1987: 137), the initial step in the city's development as China's northwestern rail hub. As noted, a Baotou-Lanzhou link was added in 1958, providing a connection to Beijing via Yinchuan, Baotou, and Hohhot.[9] The line was immediately pushed on westward to Xining in 1959. And the long stretch of rail following the old Silk Route through the Gansu corridor and across the desert to Urumqi, linking eastern China to the petroleum and other natural resources of Xinjiang, was completed in 1963. Lanzhou's importance in China's rail system is further emphasized by the fact that it is the site of the Lanzhou Railway Institute (one of 11 institutions in the country that train railway professionals).

Urumqi was formerly a very long journey from the eastern core of China. As late as 1932 the lack of transport facilities and disruptive conditions on the frontier forced the Chinese official Aitchen Wu to travel from Beijing to Urumqi by an incredibly circuitous route. He proceeded from Tianjin by ship to Kobe, then crossed Japan by rail to Tsuruga, where he caught a steamer to Vladivostok. From there he rode the Trans-Siberian railway all the way to Novosibirsk, where he caught a local train to Semipalatinsk (Kazakhstan) and then another local train to Ayaguz (Kazakhstan). From Ayaguz he traveled by truck and sleigh to Qoqek (Tacheng, Xinjiang) and then completed his 36-day journey by automobile to Urumqi. This route was considered faster and considerably safer than trying to cross directly from Beijing to Urumqi overland through northwestern China and Xinjiang (A. K. Wu 1940). George Cressey reports that, before the 1940s, the overland route from Beijing to Urumqi, making use of the train to the end of the line at Xi'an, required at least 113 days (Cressey 1955: 333).

The Lanzhou-Urumqi railway (the Lanxin line) was begun in 1952 and completed in 1963. It roughly follows the northern Silk Route of the Han and Tang eras much of the way, passing through the narrow Hexi corridor in Gansu, then crossing into Xinjiang and continuing through the desert to Urumqi. A southern branch was later constructed from Turfan to Korla (Kuerla). Tracks and facilities were apparently severely damaged during the Cultural Revolution, and regular services did not resume until 1978 (*Xinjiang weiwuer zizhiqu gaikuang* 1985: 156–60).

Railroad development in Yunnan was not oriented toward a connection with Beijing at all until the PRC came to power. The first railroad in the province was a short local line started in 1904 by the French and extended by 1910 from Kunming (where the station was built in French architectural style; Smith 1940: 172), to Hekou on the Vietnam border (where the Red River crosses from China into Vietnam), and from there to Hanoi, so providing an alternative route of entry via the South China coast for French and British trade (see Chandran 1971). Known in the West as the Tonkin-Yunnan railway, the line was constructed by 200,000 to 300,000 Chinese laborers, including many who came from as far away as Guangdong, Guangxi, Sichuan, Fujian, Zhejiang, Shandong, and Hebei provinces to work on it. They were joined by more than 20,000 Vietnamese workers (Yu Jiahua et al. 1986: 533–35).[10] This 645-km rail line climbs from near sea level to an altitude of 8,000 ft. and passes through 152 tunnels and 3,422 bridges (Cressey 1955: 228). A 178-km stretch was destroyed during the Japanese occupation of China, along with the great bridge over the Red River at Hekou on the Vietnam border. The Yunnan portion of the line was not repaired until 1956–58 (Yu Jiahua et al. 1986: 537).

The early Yunnan lines, such as the Kunming-Hekou, Kunming-Zhanyi, and Gejiu-Shiping lines, were narrow gauge. They have all been upgraded under the PRC; the Kunming-Hekou line was rebuilt at meter gauge in 1980, and the others were rebuilt at standard (British) gauge (4'8"), which has been used for all the lines in Yunnan added since 1949 (Xue Muqiao 1982: 923). Yunnan was not linked into the national rail system until 1966, when a 643-km line was completed between Kunming and Guiyang, the capital of Guizhou Province. In 1970 the People's Liberation Army completed construction of a stretch between Kunming and Chengdu, the capital of Sichuan Province. Forcing a rail line through the mountains was a major engineering challenge, requiring an average of one bridge every 7 km, and 427 tunnels all told (Yu Jiahua et al. 1986: 536; *Yunnan — keai de difang* 1984: 313).

The railroad reached Qinghai in 1959, when Xining was connected to eastern China via a 188-km line from Lanzhou. In 1960 construction began on the first leg of a line planned to connect Xining to Lhasa via Golmud; the Xining-Golmud segment was completed in 1984 (*Qinghai shengqing* 1986: 300). The line from Golmud to Lhasa is still in the planning stages. In the meantime a highway linking the two cities is the main overland route. There are also a number of short rail lines in Qinghai. These include a line from Xining to Datong, 36 km to the north, which was opened in 1968, and a branch line from the Xining-Golmud line to Qinghai Lake, 7 km distant, completed in 1965. Several lines have also been built to service the major salt-rich areas in Qinghai's interior drainage lakes, including a 51-km stretch completed in 1974 that provides access to the salt production areas of the Qaidam Basin (*Qinghai shengqing* 1986: 300). At Chaka Lake, for example, I observed a narrow gauge line that runs out over the salt crust on the lake to the salt-mining areas. Salt and workers are transported back to the processing plant on this line, which in turn is linked with the standard gauge line to Xining.

Air and water transportation. Commercial air transportation was not developed in China until after the Sino-Japanese War, and even then, there was only limited service to Lanzhou and Urumqi and occasionally to the other frontier cities. When the Nationalists fled the mainland, most of the commercial airplanes were flown to Taiwan or other locations, and it was several years before the PRC was able to reestablish air service and begin manufacturing airplanes on its own (Tregear 1965: 198). With the assistance of planes provided by the USSR, the PRC put an integrated air transportation system into operation in 1960. It was based on three main hubs, at Beijing, Wuhan, and Xi'an, and three secondary hubs, at Urumqi, Lanzhou, and Chongqing. The frontier cities of Urumqi and Lanzhou were thus important early on in the development of Chinese air transport (Buchanan 1970: 260).

All the frontier capitals now have regular air service. Kunming is well served, with direct flights to a number of cities in China, notably Beijing, Xi'an, Shanghai, Guangzhou, Chengdu, Chongqing, Guilin, and Hangzhou; international flights to Hong Kong, Thailand, and Burma; and intraprovincial flights to Simao, Baoshan, and Zhaotong. In 1984 the Kunming airport handled 160,000 passengers and just over 3,000 metric tons of cargo (*Yunnan dizhou shixian gaikuang* 1987: 26).

Urumqi's airport handles international flights west, as well as internal flights throughout Xinjiang Province and to points outside of Xinjiang, such as Lanzhou and Beijing. Lanzhou has flights to Beijing, Shanghai, Guangzhou, Shenyang, and Urumqi, as well as intraprovincial flights to Qinyang, Jiuquan, and Dunhuang. The airport is located two hours by bus outside the city proper. Hohhot has international flights to Mongolia, as well as domestic flights to other cities in the province and to nine of China's major cities. The first airport at Xining was built in 1933, but this small strip was little used before the founding of the People's Republic (*Qinghai lishi jiyao* 1987: 356). Xining today is connected by air to Golmud, Lanzhou, Xi'an, and Beijing. It has only a few scheduled flights a week, and these are cancelled frequently. In 1985 Xining processed only 5,000 passengers and 66 tons of freight, compared with 72,000 passengers and 1,700 tons for Lanzhou. But there were plans in the mid-1980s to construct a second airport at Xining to handle large passenger planes and provide more regular service (PRC, State Statistical Bureau 1986: 85, 171).

Air transportation remains a luxury in China; it is still used primarily by government officials, business people, and foreign tourists. Few Chinese have the means to purchase air tickets for personal use, although this is starting to change under the post-Mao economic reforms. Nor is air freight common, although a few lines, such as the Chengdu to Lhasa line, serve as alternate freight routes to the frontier. In short, air transportation has not had much of an impact in most of China's transport markets. Nonetheless, the distances and time involved in travel to the frontier cities (particularly Urumqi) lend a greater significance to the speed of air travel in enabling more effective communication and trade between the frontier and the core region.

Long-distance water transportation has not been much of a factor in any of the cities in this study. Though Lanzhou lies directly on the Yellow River and Hohhot is located near it, the upper reaches of the river cannot be navigated by large ships. Consequently, lightweight rafts, used for short-distance transport, were and are the only water transport serving these cities. Rafts made of inflated goatskins were used for river crossings on the overland route between Lanzhou and Xining at places where there were no bridges (there has long been a bridge at Lanzhou itself). Rivers were not important in transport in the Kunming region either, although Lake Dian was and continues to be used as a major transport route connecting the settlements that surround it.

Trade

Except for the Kunming area, the regions under study were not primarily settler frontiers in historical times. The Chinese empire did not seek to control them in order to gain new territories for agricultural production and settlement. Rather, these frontier areas were secured primarily for two purposes: dominion and trade. By "dominion" I mean that the state's aim is to control vast territories for the wealth and the prestige this brings and to establish political and military buffer zones and lines of defense around the core area. But the desire to expedite trade can be an important incentive for territorial expansion and the maintenance of frontier zones. Sechin Jagchid and Van Jay Symons's central argument in their book *Peace, War and Trade Along the Great Wall* supports the thesis that trade was the primary factor influencing relationships between the Chinese empire and the nomadic inhabitants of the northern frontier (Jagchid & Symons 1989). The five cities in this study played important roles in realizing the objectives of Chinese frontier trade policy.

The Silk Routes and Traditional Trade

In the northwestern regions of China, all long-distance trade of any significance before the twentieth century was plied along the famed Silk Routes that connected the empire with Central Asia, the Middle East, and Europe. Other trade routes that are also sometimes referred to as Silk Routes extended through China's southwest. There are reports of trade and transport on this southwestern route between China and South Asia as early as the Han dynasty (Bian Kui et al. 1986: 3). The Silk Routes that passed through the northwest were established as early as 115 B.C. and were heavily used into the third century A.D. After the Han dynasty the Chinese section was cut by a series of conflicts between the nomadic Xiongnu people and the Chinese and ceased to be safe for travel. The route was revived during the Tang dynasty and lasted through the disintegration of the Mongol empire in the fourteenth century.

The Silk Routes operated as a chain of exchange. They stretched about 5,000 miles from the shores of the Aegean and Mediterranean seas to Chang'an (Xi'an) and Luoyang in central China. Goods traveled the entire length of the routes, but few of the merchants involved ever completed a round trip or even went all the way in one direction. Long-distance east-west travel did not become routine on the routes until the late thirteenth century and ceased to be routine by the mid-fourteenth century. This period, commencing with the travels of Marco Polo, was made possible by what has been called a brief *pax Mongolica* (Franck & Brownstone 1986: 3), when most of the route fell directly or indirectly under Mongol rule and influence.

The Silk Routes within what is now China are often considered to begin at Chang'an, though in fact there were feeder networks that brought silk and other goods from eastern China to Chang'an to be forwarded on. From Chang'an there was a single route westward as far as Lanzhou. The bulk of the trade continued in a northwest direction through the Gansu corridor, to Wuwei and Dunhuang. A secondary route led from Lanzhou due west to Xining and on to Dunhuang from there.

From Dunhuang the route split into three branches. The northern branch crossed north to Hami, then turned west and followed a series of oases north of the Tarim basin through Korla, Kucha, and Aksu to Kashgar. A central branch crossed due west to Loulan, then cut north to Turfan to join the main northern route. The southern branch followed the oases south of the Tarim basin, passing through Shanshan and Khotan along the northern flanks of the Kunlun mountains, then splitting at Yarkand, with one route joining the more northerly routes at Kashgar, and the southern and western routes continuing either west to Babylon (later Baghdad) or south through modern-day Pakistan to the Indus River.

From Kashgar one route led west to Babylon, then north to Antioch and Sardis or through Ankara to Sardis. Another went across the steppes north of the Aral and Caspian seas, arriving at the northeastern shores of the Black Sea and the Sea of Azov. There was also a northern steppe route that left the main route at Jiuquan (in Gansu), and passed through the Mongolian steppe north of the Altai Mountains, then followed the Volga and Don rivers to the Black Sea and beyond.

The Han and Tang Silk Routes varied somewhat, with a greater diversity of routes during the later period, but the overall structure of the system was similar in the two eras. Lanzhou and Xining both played important roles on the northwestern Silk Routes, and Kunming was connected with the southwestern routes.

The Silk Routes were not the only early long-distance trading routes in China. There were trade routes connecting all the major cities in eastern China, and trade routes connecting the frontier cities to the interior as well. At times when China had control of the frontier region, these routes were maintained and protected by Chinese garrisons posted along them.

The most important trade between the empire and the northern and northwestern peoples was the famed horse-and-tea trade (for details, see Jagchid and Symons 1989; and Rossabi 1970). To foster this trade, the

Chinese established markets from the Tang dynasty onward in a number of strategic locations along the frontier. Despite the name, many other kinds of goods were traded in these markets, which served as an exchange point between the Chinese imperial representative and the local peoples as a mechanism to control frontier relations, and as local markets as well. Markets were usually taxed or regulated through permit systems, but their ability to control trade varied considerably. The official prices sometimes collapsed when the economy outgrew the state's ability to control it (Fairbank 1992: 85). And though the markets were often closed for years at a time in periods of disorder, they were continually reestablished once peace was restored (Jagchid & Symons 1989: 79–113). Despite the elaborate system of regulation imposed by the Chinese, there were apparently many instances of illicit transactions (such as trading the best horses to someone other than the imperial representative or disguising opium as tea) in these markets (Jagchid & Symons 1989: 80). Horses and other livestock were traded in the southwest as well, in periodic markets and fairs. The frontier markets did, however, serve as the primary economic link between the Chinese empire and the frontier peoples. The frontier cities became centers for regional and local trade as well. For much of the frontier region, then, there were three primary trade activities taking place in or near the cities: the long-distance trade typified by the Silk Routes, the specialized national/regional trade carried out in the horse-and-tea markets, and regional and local trade.

Lanzhou, crossing point on the Silk Routes. During the Tang dynasty Lanzhou served as a collection and forwarding point for tribute and goods of all sorts entering China from the northwest, ranging from exotic items of Tibetan and/or Mongolian origin like marmots, musk, and flakes of gold to staples like salt, wool, and horses (Schafer 1963: 91). Outward-bound traffic encompassed all the goods for which the Silk Routes are famous: tea, spices, and silk itself.

As an important trade center on the Silk Routes, Lanzhou had relatively highly developed markets and craft industries. Here raw materials for both export and import were processed, and the needs of long-distance trade were provided for. An extensive system of market streets developed within the city walls that persisted until the 1949 revolution. Metallurgy and trade in metal implements and jewelry, for example, was carried out along the two main intersecting streets in the city (the Great West Street and the Great South Street (today's Zhangye Road and Jiuquan Road). The elaborate shops along these streets had wood and glass cases on their counters displaying jewelry and other small items. Larger products were displayed behind the counter, and the workshop was located at the rear of the building. The finest goods were sold inside the shops. Well-made jewelry and other products manufactured within the city were also sold in markets just outside the city gates, as well as by peddlers who traveled the countryside. Lesser quality and utilitarian goods for the night markets and traveling peddlers were produced and sold outside the central walled city. These goods were not permitted to be sold within the city markets (Zhang Shangying 1987: 21–22). The differences between these markets reflected the class distinctions within the Chinese community, and between the Chinese and other peoples. The government and the guilds were less concerned with regulating the quality of goods traded to the lower-status Chinese and non-Chinese who lived and traded outside the walls.

There were three horse-and-tea markets in the Lanzhou region—at Lanzhou, Xining, and Zhuanglang. From the Tang dynasty until the end of the Song (1280), the horse-and-tea market in Lanzhou was administered by the government through the Zhuanglang Horse and Tea Company (headquartered about 240 km west of Lanzhou in today's Xueluo Cheng). The trade at Lanzhou continued through the Qing dynasty, when the administration of horse and tea trade in the region was moved to Lanzhou, thus expanding its market. The tea traded in Lanzhou came primarily from the province of Hunan, south of the Changjiang (Yangzi) River, via horse cart and camel caravan (Ji Nong 1987: 38).

Lanzhou persisted as an important regional trade center. A Russian firm attempted to establish shops in five cities in the Gansu region. However, by the end of the 1880s, all but the Lanzhou shop had failed. This suggests there was a greater market for trade in Lanzhou than in the region's smaller settlements. The Russian shop dealt in cloth, brassware, rugs, hardware, matches, and other items, which Rockhill believed were primarily for Tibetan and Mongolian customers (Rockhill 1891: 36–37).

The horse-and-tea trade at Xining. Xining served as a point for the exchange of goods between the (mostly) nomadic west and the sedentary east. For Grenard, writing in the late nineteenth century, the contrast of cultures in the city's shops and markets was striking: "The great number of saddlers, felt-makers and sellers of hides, skins and furs indicate the neighborhood of a nation of horsemen, herdsmen and hunters; but, close at hand, in carpenters' shops, those great displays of substantial coffins, giving out a good smell of dry wood and presenting their inviting and comfortable interiors to the public, recall old China, sedentary and slumbering in the coffin of her traditions" (Grenard 1891: 205).

Xining was a major stop along one of the southern branches of the Silk Routes and the route to Lhasa over the Tibetan plateau. During the peak Silk Routes eras, Persian goods and representatives are reported to have traded in and passed through Xining (Li Shengcai 1985: 405). There has been a trade route between Xining and Lhasa (and continuing on to India) since at least the beginning of the Tang dynasty. The Tang princess Wencheng traveled it on the way to her marriage at the Tibetan court; and from that time, if not earlier, it was the principal means by which knowledge was transmitted back and forth between Tibet and China, carried by the sons of Tibetan officials who went to the Tang capital at Chang'an (Xi'an) to study and by the many Chinese monks and scholars who visited Lhasa and other parts of Tibet. Goods like paper, ink, wine, and wood were traded along this route as well (Chen Qiaoyi 1986: 435).

The regional tea-and-horse trade is thought to date back to an initial exchange of these items between the Tang and the Tufan (Tibetans) in 733 near present-day Xining. During much of the Song dynasty, when the Xining region was under Tibetan control, the Song court sent emissaries to carry out the trade in a number of locations in eastern Qinghai, but not at Xining itself. In 1081 a market was established exclusively for this purpose at Xining. During the Tang and Song periods, Xining became an important trade center linking the Gaochang kingdom (centered in today's Turfan region of Xinjiang) and the east. Large numbers of traders from the west resided, either temporarily or permanently, in the city's eastern suburb, outside the Little East Gate (Dongxiaomen). Goods traded at Xining during the eleventh and twelfth centuries included pearls, elephant tusks, jade, frankincense, and other exotics, which were exchanged for Chinese agricultural products, gold, silver, medicines, and, particularly, tea (*Qinghai lishi jiyao* 1987: 94–97, 131–32).

Like its predecessors, the Ming dynasty sponsored the tea-and-horse trade throughout the northwestern frontier regions. As early as 1371 the Ming established a regional tea-and-horse market at Xining. Most of the tea traded there came from Sichuan, especially from the Ya'an and Huzhou regions. Tea from Hunan was also popular. The market was hard hit later in the century when a glut of tea and a shortage of horses brought a dramatic drop in prices. In order to bring the trade closer to the Tibetans and their horses, the Ming established three more markets: in Hezhou, Taozhou, and Gannan. They also forbade the private transportation of tea to Qinghai from the two main sources, Hunan and Sichuan, and transferred tea transport to military control. Trade was normalized soon after. In the sixteenth century, in the hope of further encouraging the tea-and-horse trade, the Ming dynasty established a national bonus system for traders who could sell the most tea: a high-quality horse for 120 *jin* (approximately 60 kg) of tea sold, an average horse for 70 *jin* (approximately

35 kg), or a low-quality horse for 50 *jin* (approximately 25 kg) of tea. At its peak in 1591, the Ming tea-and-horse market at Xining traded 902 horses. In the following year the total fell to 625 (*Qinghai lishi jiyao* 1987: 131–34).

Trade at the city of Xining itself was supplemented by the active trade carried out at nearby Kumbum Jampa Ling Monastery. Early Western travelers mention making trade and resupply stops there, and as late as 1949, Lusar (Lushaer), the adjacent town, was still "one of the most important trading centers for Tibetan goods, especially during periods of festivities" (Chow 1949: 108).

During the Qing dynasty Xining continued to serve as an important trade center. In the nineteenth century all trade between Chinese, Mongolians, and Tibetans was controlled by the Amban (governor) of Xining; no one was allowed to buy or sell goods without purchasing a permit from the Amban's office. According to Rockhill, these permits often expired before transactions were completed, so traders were vulnerable to heavy fines. He thought that this probably discouraged more active trade from taking place (Rockhill 1891: 53). Even so, at the time of his visit, Xining not only had a monopoly on the tea trade with both Mongolia and Turkestan (Grenard 1891: 293),[11] but handled a vast array of products, including locally produced or obtained oil, wool, musk, rhubarb, lambskins, furs, gold, salt, and cloth, as well as such imported goods as silks, guns, Hami raisins, and chinaware. Rockhill noted that imported cloth did not sell well in Xining because the local people found it inferior to Chinese products; the reverse was true of other items like Russian red leather and foreign paper, pens, and pen holders. A Russian trade firm had set up shop in Xining in the late nineteenth century, probably dealing in similar goods to those offered by its counterpart in Lanzhou, but the venture was unsuccessful and had closed by the late 1880s (Rockhill 1891: 36, 50).

Xining was eclipsed as a major trade center by Lanzhou for centuries, though some observers believed it should have been more successful. W. Karamisheff, in his 1925 assessment of trade in Mongolia and western China, thought Xining was in a particularly advantageous position for trade, and that in light of both its access to "Xining Wool" ("the best wool in China") and its favorable geographical location in relation to Tibet, it ought to have "in general a great interest for European firms" (Karamisheff 1925: 32). Despite Karamisheff's optimism, Xining remained a relative backwater in China's national trade networks.

The markets of Hohhot. Trade has long been an integral part of life in Hohhot. Altan Khan, the Mongolian founder of the monastic settlement at Hohhot in the sixteenth century, encouraged the development of "intense economic demand for regular channels of exchange for the surplus products of a growing cattle industry in return for Chinese handicrafts and agricultural goods" (Zlatkin 1964: 100, as translated in Sinor 1969: 206). Active trade developed at Hohhot after its founding, though this trade was often interrupted by skirmishes between the Ming and the Mongolians along the frontier. The Mongolians traded horses, donkeys, cattle, and sheep, as well as pastoral products such as horsehair and wool, for grain, cloth, tea, iron pots and pans, and other manufactured items for daily use.

According to Dai Xueji, after Amidan Khan was given a local title (Shunyiwang) by the Chinese in 1572, conflicts between Mongolians and Chinese in Hohhot decreased, and trade picked up considerably. There were then five kinds of exchange and markets in Hohhot: the tribute exchange of the imperial court (*chaogong*), government markets (*guanshi*), people's markets (*minshi*), night markets (*yueshi*), and small local markets (*xiaoshi*). The tribute system functioned like trade in the sense that local leaders brought their tribute to the representatives of the empire and were given gifts in return. The government-controlled markets were primarily involved in regulating the horse trade and tended to be limited to transactions between Mongolian chiefs and the representatives of the Ming court. The people's markets and the night markets were the sites of common trade between Mongolians and the Chinese, with the Mongolians bringing horses, camels, cattle, sheep, hides, horsehair, horse tails, felt, salt, fodder, wood products, gold, and silver to exchange for grain, tea, cotton, and other agricultural products, cotton cloth, spun thread and yarn, silk and satin, and kitchen and farming implements. Mongolians from outlying regions often came once or twice a year to Hohhot to trade at special markets (Dai Xueji 1981: 37–39). The atmosphere at one of Hohhot's camel markets has been vividly described by Verne Dyson:

A large main-place, to which the principal streets of the town lead, is filled with the camels which are for sale. They are lined up side by side. The noise and confusion of these markets is almost indescribable. To the shouts of the buyers and sellers, who quarrel and vociferate as though a popular rising were in progress, is added the long moaning cry of the camels being pulled by the nose to persuade them to kneel and rise, their skill in which action is a measure of their value. (Dyson 1927: 36)

Urumqi's bazaars and trading companies. Urumqi was a major trading center for both regional and international trade. The bulk of the international trade was with Central Asia and more distant Russian regions. There was also some trade with merchants from what are now Pakistan and Afghanistan.

The volume of Russian trade in Xinjiang grew considerably during the nineteenth century, particularly after the Russian empire gained control of parts of Central Asia. By then Russian merchants were well established there, having set up trade in Kashgar (Kashi) and Khotan (Hetian) as early as 1755. The primary trade between the Chinese and Russians in Xinjiang was for tea, silk, rhubarb (*dahuang*),[12] and local wool and hides in exchange for spun thread and woven cloth, manufactured food products, kitchen implements and tools, and kerosene. In 1762 the Qing government began to levy taxes on all Russian trade in Xinjiang. This policy sparked uprisings among local traders, moving the Russian government to lodge official protests, and after much negotiation, the Qing established preferential trade centers ("enclosures") in a number of Xinjiang's cities, including Urumqi in 1881. After Urumqi was declared the capital of Xinjiang in 1884, most of the Russian trade came there. By 1911 Urumqi had 30 Russian trading firms, with 800 local shopkeepers and traders. These "Russian" firms were usually operated, and sometimes owned, by Uzbeks and Tatars (see Table 4). They were joined, in the Republican era, by American, German, and White Russian firms (Zan Yulin 1986). In addition to the 13 foreign firms listed in the table, there were British, Indian, and Afghani traders in Urumqi.

TABLE 4

Establishment and Management of Selected Foreign Trade Firms in Urumqi, by Nationality, 1850–1930

Firm	Founding date	Established by	Managed by
Russian *Zhisheng* Co.	1850	Tatar	—
Russian *Renzhongxin* Co.	1852	Uzbek	Uzbek
Russian *Tianxing* Co.	1860	Tatar	Tatar
Russian *Jiyangpu* Co.	1861	Tatar	Tatar
Russian *Maosheng* Co.	1862	Uzbek	Uzbek
Russian *Jili* Co.	1880	Uzbek	—
Russian *Dehe* Co.	1881	Uzbek	Uzbek
Russian *Desheng* Co.	1883	Uzbek	Uzbek
Russian *Dali* Co.	1911	Russian	—
German *Shunfa* Co.	1917	German	German
American *Anli* Co. (Bank)	1918	American	American
American *Bili* Co.	1918	White Russian	American
American *Huamei* Co.	1930	White Russian	—

SOURCE: Zan Yulin 1986: 173–74.

The Russian firms in particular were highly sophisticated, well-integrated capitalist ventures. The Jili company, for example, owned a tea-processing factory in Hankou, and thus controlled the source of the tea it exported to Russia. The Dali company imported cotton from the Turfan region to its own spinning factory in Moscow, then exported finished cotton back to the markets of Urumqi. The Dade company (not shown in Table 4) and the Zhisheng company owned grasslands and herds in the Urumqi and Tacheng regions, from which they exported pastoral products to Russia. The Jiyang and Desheng companies jointly established a large wool-washing facility in the area between today's Xinjiang Central Broadcasting Station and the Yan'an Street Public Park (Zan Yulin 1986: 173–74).

The foreign trade district in Urumqi, which was also a residential area for foreigners, extended outside the walls of Urumqi from today's Erdaoqiao Road south to Tuanjie Road, and from the Russian Public Cemetery Hill west to the southern stretch of Hetan Road. The district operated in much the same way as the foreign trade concessions of Tianjin and Shanghai. The foreign community was exempt from Chinese taxation and had its own schools and other infrastructural establishments, including an Evangelical chapel opened by an English missionary and a Catholic church opened by a German missionary, which had a primarily White Russian congregation.

After the 1917 Russian revolution, foreign businesses were once again taxed in Urumqi. White Russians living in the area were concerned about Soviet reprisals and possible Soviet incursions into the border areas and, with the exception of three families, the Russians in Urumqi fled into China proper (Zan Yulin 1986).

The non-Chinese peoples of the Urumqi region also had their own market outside the walls. Located south of the south gate of the Chinese city, this market, which dated from about 1767, catered to the local trade between the Chinese and non-Chinese peoples. The principal trade goods were cotton, tobacco, and brick tea. The Hunan Anhua Tea company, which sold "black-brick tea," had a monopoly on the tea trade, but rumor had it that this was merely a cover for opium trading. Opium is said to have been one of the primary currencies in this local market during the Nationalist era (Er Chang 1986).

Retailing became particularly important in Urumqi under the influence of the "Eight Great Families" who controlled the city in the late nineteenth century. These families were immigrants from eastern China, a few of the more than 200 peasants from the Tianjin region who came to

Urumqi in 1876 with the Xinjiang-Qinghai army. Many carried goods from the east with them to trade and peddled these as they traveled across the country to Xinjiang. Some eventually set up general stores in Urumqi in the Anjia area. The most successful of these retailers, the Eight Great Families, owned and operated what were called "Jingjin Zahuo" (Beijing & Tianjin mixed goods) stores. Though the retail trade in Urumqi was initially monopolized by these and other families from the Beijing-Tianjin region, competitors eventually moved in from Shanxi, Shaanxi, and Gansu. Some non-Chinese traders from the region, who had been selling specialty goods for some time, began dealing in general goods as well. By the 1930s, with more than 200 families running general retail stores in Urumqi, shopkeepers had become the largest of the city's trading classes (Liu Zhuxi 1986).

The goods they handled were brought in from Beijing and Tianjin by land and water as far as Lanzhou, and the rest of the way by camel. The trip took four months or more. The retailers developed a return trade-barter system, in which they exchanged wool, camel hair, cotton, medicinal goods, hides, and other local items, which were then carried back to their suppliers in the Beijing-Tianjin region, in return for eastern goods. As this trade developed, Chinese retailers began to import goods specifically targeted for the non-Chinese consumers of the region. These goods included multicolored silk, patterned woolen cloth, paper, cooking implements fashioned to local tastes, and *hada* scarves for the religious use of Buddhist Mongolians (Liu Zhuxi 1986: 2–3).

Trade was undermined throughout Xinjiang during the upheavals of the 1930s. Transportation between Urumqi and the east all but broke down. Some retailers went out of business; others began dealing in Soviet products. Several merged to form larger companies, such as the Weixin Gongci company, which specialized in the hide and fur trade with Soviet traders. But unrest continued, and a number of Urumqi's retailers were murdered. In late 1939 retail trade nearly stopped in Urumqi. Some trade with eastern China resumed after the Japanese retreated from China (Liu Zhuxi 1986: 4–5).

Kunming, a city of markets. Yunnan has long been integrated into several long-distance trade networks. Trade with Burma and other parts of Southeast Asia has been particularly important in Kunming's history, along with trade to Tibet. During the Song dynasty, the Chinese empire received tribute from the Dali kingdom, which had its capital at the site of Kunming, in the form of swords, rhinoceros hides, armor, carpets, saddles, bridles, and a deep blue-green stone called *bi gan* (Schafer 1963:

230). The variety of these goods—particularly the *bi gan* (possibly malachite) and the rhinoceros hides—indicates that the Dali kingdom was trading with peoples to the south, probably in Burma. Kunming served as one of three major trade centers in Yunnan, along with Dali and Lijiang to the west. Besides their market streets and market areas, both Dali and Lijiang continue to hold periodic regional markets. In addition to weekly markets, once a year Dali holds a Third Month Fair in the spring where the Bai people trade with the local Chinese, Naxi, and Tibetans for a variety of goods. Traditionally, the most important trade item at this fair was Tibetan horses.

Kunming's mixed Chinese population contributed to a lively and varied trade history, reflecting many different trade linkages with eastern China. There were both specialty street markets within the walled city and markets just outside the walls. Before the Qing dynasty the most active Chinese traders were pen-and-ink and porcelein traders from Jiangxi and Hunan and silk, glass, and leaf tobacco traders from Sichuan. Qing times brought new traders from Guangdong, Guangxi, and Beijing and the development of a trade district in the area of Tangzi Alley, Zhuangyuan Tower, and Nanjiao Market. Today's Jinbi Road was once the home of traders from Guangxi and Guangdong. The market areas outside the city walls were substantially damaged during the rebellions of the Xianfeng (1851–62) and Tongzhi (1862–75) eras. Of all outside groups engaging in commerce in Kunming, those from Shanxi and Zhejiang had the largest-scale business, including control of the banks. The banks invested in the export of local goods such as tea, salt, minerals, medicines, and livestock products to other parts of the country. The list of trade goods also included cotton cloth, paper, and gold and silver jewelry, all of which were offered in markets at the gates of the city. By the end of the Qing period, there were three *fang* (large) markets and 24 *pu* (relatively small) markets in Kunming (Yu Xixian 1981: 84–85).

Contemporary Trade

Today the distribution and availability of consumer goods have been monetarized and, to a degree, standardized throughout China. Goods shipped to frontier regions from the core area, such as tea, are subsidized, and prices are controlled, so that consumer prices are fairly uniform across the country in state-controlled stores. However, collectively and privately run stores are now competing with the state-run stores, so that the pricing system is changing rapidly. Small retail shops can be found in nearly every district of every city and town in China selling similar arrays of canned foods, cigarettes, candy, cookies, instant noodles, soft drinks, paper, pencils and other useful small household items. As a result of the Great Leap Forward of 1958–63, when cities were encouraged to become self-sufficient in production, many of these goods are now locally produced, particularly easily manufactured items such as cookies and matches. The distribution and supply of non–locally produced goods tend to be sporadic and highly uneven, leading to a high demand for certain chronically understocked items. There has rarely been brand choice in these stores, although this is starting to change with China's recent economic reforms. Shops typically carry one, or maybe two, brands of each item, with the exception of cigarettes, liquor, and soft drinks.

In general and perhaps contrary to expectations, frontier cities have relatively more retail units per capita than core areas. For example, whereas Beijing had only about 44 and Shanghai only 60 retail units per 10,000 people in 1986, Lanzhou, Urumqi, and Xining had 75, 90, and 101 units, respectively (PRC State Statistical Bureau 1986: 396–97). These figures may be deceptive, however, since they do not indicate the size of the enterprises. Cities with large Islamic populations seem to have relatively high numbers of small retail establishments. The Hui people, in particular, continue to operate actively, at a small scale, in the retail sector. Whereas residents of Beijing might be more likely to visit a department store on their shopping trip, residents of frontier cities are perhaps more likely to frequent five or six separate shops or stalls.

The effect of a relatively poor national consumer goods distribution system, combined with the local productive infrastructure legacy of the Great Leap Forward, perpetuates the differentiation of retail activity and product availability in the state-sponsored retail sector. This situation is further complicated by the success of private entrepreneurs in establishing free markets in recent years. Perhaps the greatest implication of the free markets for the frontier regions is the potential for the reintroduction of trade in local products and the reestablishment of local economies. And, ironically, the realization of that potential in turn implies the possibility of direct and indirect participation in international economies.

For example, there is an active trade now in goods for use by non-Chinese peoples for non-Chinese activities in the frontier cities. All of the cities in this study have at least several sellers of books in Arabic and/or Chinese specifically relating to Islam (as well as copies of the Koran). Some of these books are printed locally; others are printed and distributed from specialized presses in Shanghai, Beijing, and Ningxia. In the Lamaist regions of Inner Mongolia, Qinghai, and Tibet, stalls and street peddlers offer an array of religious paraphernalia, including incense, prayer scarves, prayer wheels, printed prayers, and ceremonial cups.[13] Locally manufactured items of traditional clothing for non-Chinese peoples are also sold in frontier cities: Uygur men's hats and cloth for women's clothing in Urumqi; Hui men's hats and cloth in Xining and Lanzhou; Tibetan clothing items in Xining, Lhasa, and other cities of the Tibetan Culture Region; and Bai embroidered goods in Kunming. Private dealers in these goods seem to have largely supplanted the state distributors. Tibetan carpets produced in Xining and Lhasa, and Central Asian carpets produced in Urumqi, are examples of important traditional items still produced by state-run factories. Stores selling state-manufactured non-Chinese goods are still operating, such as the Kunming Minzu Trade Store (Kunmingshi Minzu Maoyi Shangdian) in downtown Kunming and a similar store in the northwestern part of Xining. But these state-run ventures carry only a few minority items and operate primarily as regular general stores.

A new market has developed for the sale of minority goods with the arrival of Western, Japanese, Taiwanese, and Hong Kong tourism in the frontier regions. The colorful Bai embroidered goods sold in Kunming are primarily purchased by foreign tourists. And the production of carpets now serves both the local market and international export demand. Uygur caps are popular souvenirs among those tourists who find the Uygur neighborhood in Urumqi, but these are few and far between. Similar items are available for purchase in hotel lobbies and "friendship stores," albeit for somewhat higher prices. Nevertheless, most sales of minority handicrafts in frontier cities are still primarily directed at local people. For example, there is a row of shops about a quarter mile long lining both sides of the street leading to Ta'ersi, the lamasery outside of Xining. These shops, run primarily by local Hui, buy and sell Tibetan goods ranging from hair ornaments and ceremonial bowls to saddles and large metal temple ornaments. There are clearly more shops and goods here than could be supported by the small international tourist trade (nor could tourists readily transport or ship many of the large items). Though foreign souvenir hunters do patronize these shops, the majority of the shoppers are Tibetans from outlying regions who have come to the monastery on pilgrimage. In addition, I have twice observed Tibetans purchasing an entire truckload of temple-roof ornaments, enough to refurnish an entire temple.

The majority of non-Chinese handicraft items bought by foreigners are purchased in state-run and joint-venture hotel lobby shops. A selection of these goods is available in the friendship stores and hotel lobbies in Beijing and Shanghai. They are probably produced by the state-run collectives, which also supply goods for the minorities' department stores in frontier cities. Certain general department stores in Hohhot, Xining, and Urumqi also carry some minority-targeted items.

The increasing opportunities for entrepreneurial activities in China will likely bring a resurgence in the private local trade that helped to sustain the economic life of frontier cities before 1949. For example, the reopening of night markets in Lanzhou has already led to an increase in specialized retailing in the city's neighborhoods. A continuation of the trend toward growing affluence (and differentiation in wealth) in post-Mao China will further encourage the growth of retail and international trade on the frontiers. Trade with the new Central Asian republics, in particular, may become a factor in Urumqi's future growth.

Banking and Finance

Moneylending is an ancient practice in China, the work of guilds, clans, or professional moneylenders. But modern institutionalized banking of the sort found in present-day capitalist countries was a late and short-lived development, an institution that came and went during the turbulent half-century between the declining years of the last dynasty and the founding of the PRC. The first modern Chinese commercial bank was the China Trade Bank (Zhongguo Tongshang Yinhang), established by the Qing government in Shanghai in 1897 (Cui Jianwen 1987: 16). Its successors were all either closed or nationalized in 1949. During this brief window of Western-style banking and finance development, the new practices spread through China even as far as the frontier cities. Banks came relatively early to the frontier, the product of attempts to capitalize on and invigorate the economic life of these areas and Nationalist efforts to unite the country by pulling the frontier regions more fully into the national economy. The establishment of banks serves as evidence of both local economic activity and the degree of integration with the core economic system.

Six banks were opened in Urumqi during the late nineteenth and early twentieth centuries (see Table 5). The first was the Monetary Office of the Urumqi Government (Wulumuqiguan Qianju), which was established in 1884, with the founding of Xinjiang Province, as the official lending agency.[14] It was also responsible for issuing paper currency on the basis of gold and silver deposits. By 1889 the bank had opened branches in six other cities in Xinjiang. The institution continued to operate after the fall

TABLE 5
Banking History of Urumqi, Xining, Lanzhou, and Hohhot, 1884–1947

City and banking firm	Founding date
Urumqi	
Monetary Office of Urumqi (Wulumuqiguan Qianju)	1884
Russian Imperial Bank (Di'e Daosheng Yinhang)	1906
Xinjiang Provincial Bank (Xinjiangsheng Yinhang), then	
Xinjiang Commerce Bank (Xinjiang Shangye Yinhang)	1930[a]
Central Bank (Zhongyang Yinhang)	1947
Peasant's Bank (Nongmin Yinhang)	1947
Xining	
China Peasant's Bank (Zhongguo Nongmin Yinhang)	1938
Bank of China (Zhongguo Yinhang)	1939
Central Bank (Zhongyang Yinhang)	1940
Qinghai Province Bank (Qinghaisheng Yinhang)	1945
Qinghai Merchants Bank (Qinghai Maiye Yinhang)	1946
Lanzhou	
Lanzhou Government Banking Office (Lanzhouguan Yinqianju)	1906[b]
Northwestern Bank (Xibei Yinhang)	—
Gansu Workers and Peasants Bank (Gansu Nonggong Yinhang)	1928
China Peasant's Bank (Zhongguo Nongmin Yinhang)	1934
Gansu Province Bank (Gansusheng Yinhang)	1939
Hohhot	
Bank of China (Zhongguo Yinhang)	1914
Suiyuan Peaceful City Government Office (Suiyuan Pingshiguan	
Qianju)	—[c]
Trade Bureau Bountiful Industry Bank (Shangban Fengye	
Yinhang)	—[c]
Shanxi Province Bank (Shanxisheng Yinhang)	—

SOURCES: Chai Jisen 1984; *Qinghai lishi jiyao* 1987: 490; Cui Jianwen 1987; Dai Xueji 1981: 177–78.
[a]Taken over by the CCP in 1939 and renamed.
[b]Became the Gansu Government Bank (Gansuguan Yinhao) in 1913 and the Peaceful City Government Money Office (Pingshiguan Qianju) in 1922.
[c]Taken over by the Japanese in the 1930s and combined to form the Mongolian Frontier Bank (Mengjiang Yinhang).

of the Qing dynasty in 1911, and until 1928 it dealt in all the currencies in use, including its own notes. These notes were pegged to the rate of inflation and fluctuated daily (Chai Jisen 1984: 99–109).

In 1906 the first foreign bank branch was opened in Urumqi. The Russian Imperial Bank (Di'e Daosheng Yinhang), founded in 1895, already had branches in major eastern Chinese cities, including Beijing, Shanghai, Harbin, and Jilin, and was involved in those regions in the printing of paper currency. The bank began its expansion into Xinjiang in 1900, with branches planned for Yili, Kashgar, and Tacheng, as well as Urumqi. The Urumqi branch, located on today's Shengli Road, specialized in transactions with Russian and other foreign traders in the region. After 1917, the

Paris branch took over control of the China branches. The Xinjiang branches had relied heavily on Russian currency, which was useless after the revolution, and were closed in 1920 by order of the Paris branch.

The Xinjiang Provincial Bank (Xinjiangshen Yinhang) was founded in 1930 on Confucian Temple Street (Wenmiaojie). It accepted deposits, made loans, issued notes, and was able to grow in spite of the political turbulence of the Nationalist era. Within years of its founding, however, it was beset with the same economic crises as all other banks of the time. In 1934 it traded about five provincial notes per silver dollar; by 1938 the rate had inflated to 4,000 (Chai Jisen 1984: 104–5). In 1939 it was taken over by the Chinese Communist Party and renamed the Xinjiang Commerce Bank (Xinjiang Shangye Yinhang). By 1946, when it moved into a new building at the intersection of Urumqi's Great South Street and Mingde Road, the bank had branches in 13 towns in Xinjiang. Two national banks of the Nationalist government moved into the province the next year. The Central Bank established branches in both Hami and Urumqi, and the Peasant's Bank opened an Urumqi branch (ibid., pp. 99–109).

Urumqi's banking history is basically one of early action by local government and private sources, as well as of strong Russian influence (before the Russian revolution). The Commerce Bank was the first to be controlled by a nationally organized group; and the first banks truly integrated with the core did not arrive at this frontier outpost until close to the end of the banking era.

In Xining there were five banks or bank branches opened between 1938 and 1946 (see Table 5). The Central Bank (Zhongyang Yinhang), the Bank of China (Zhongguo Yinhang), and the Peasant's Bank (Zhongguo Nongmin Yinhang) were all national banks that issued printed money in exchange for gold and silver. The Central Bank of the Nationalist government had the primary responsibility for issuing notes in the area. But in late 1948, as the Nationalist government was crumbling, the warlord Ma Bufang began issuing his own notes in small denominations through his Qinghai Merchants Bank (Qinghai Maiye Yinhang), established two years before (*Qinghai lishi jiyao* 1987: 488–99).

The first bank in Lanzhou was established in 1906 by the city government. Called the Lanzhou Government Banking Office (Lanzhouguan Yinqianju), it was responsible for issuing paper notes. The name of this bank was changed to Gansu Government Bank (Gansuguan Yinhao) in 1913, and then to Peaceful City Government Money Office (Pingshiguan Qianju) in 1922. Another bank, which had been operating under the name Northwestern Bank (Xibei Yinhang), established a second institution, the Gansu Workers and Peasants Bank (Nonggong Yinhang), in 1928. The China Peasant's Bank and the Gansu Province Bank came to the city in 1934 and 1939 (Cui Jianwen 1987).

At least as early as the eighteenth century, Hohhot had an active class of money changers who converted silver and gold to various foreign currencies in local use. But the city did not have a modern bank until 1914, when the Bank of China established a Hohhot branch. Two local government banks were also established in the early twentieth century, the Suiyuan Peaceful City Government Money Office (Suiyuan Pingshiguan Qianju) and the Trade Bureau Bountiful Industry Bank (Shangban Fengye Yinhang). During the 1930s these two banks were taken over by the Japanese and combined to operate as the Mongolian Frontier Bank (Mengjiang Yinhang). In the years between the end of the war and the revolution of 1949, banking was never really reestablished in the city (Dai Xueji 1981: 177–78).

By the time the Communists came to power, then, the frontier cities had a scattering of modern banks. Nonetheless, banking on the frontier was necessarily an uncertain venture in those uncertain times. Several regional banks issued their own currencies, and banks changed hands or folded with regularity. Finance on the frontier was tenuous at best.[15]

Industry

In general cities on the frontier were involved far more in trade than in production in traditional times. Much of the traditional industrial activity was devoted to such enterprises as wool processing and leather work, making use of goods obtained from local non-Chinese peoples. There was also a role for industries in support of the cities' military functions. Many came to have metal works for the production of weapons, for example. And all frontier cities had brick kilns, carpentry shops, and other facilities for preparing construction materials. The Nationalist era brought some modern industrialization to the cities, but for the most part, the process came later than it did in eastern China, where industrialization in the late nineteenth and early twentieth century had been heavily influenced by the presence of foreign companies searching for cheap labor. Local development of modern industries on the frontier began, in most cases, in the late 1930s and 1940s.

Since 1949 the PRC has promoted industrial development in all cities in China, including those on the frontier. As a target for industrial development under the First Five-Year Plan, Lanzhou was the first of the frontier cities in this study to become a truly industrial city. Urumqi, Xining, and Kunming were targeted for development under the Second Five-Year Plan. In all of these cities, planned, high-speed industrialization resulted in massive labor migrations from eastern China to the frontier, and fundamentally altered the physical, economic, and social landscapes.

As in most frontier cities, Lanzhou's traditional nonagricultural production was primarily focused on handicrafts. Drawing on raw materials from both long-distance trade and local mining, for example, the city's jewelers attained a relatively high level of production of fine items such as gold and silver jewelry. In the middle of the nineteenth century, the governor attempted unsuccessfully, at great expense, to establish a woolen factory at Lanzhou utilizing the latest European machinery. In the late nineteenth century tobacco processing was the principal industry. It was largely controlled by migrants from Shaanxi Province. Factories in Lanzhou dried and processed locally grown tobacco into cakes of three levels of quality for both local trade and export (Rockhill 1891: 34–36).

Other modern industries were not developed in Lanzhou until the war years of the 1930s and 1940s. In response to the Japanese disruption of supplies, Lanzhou's first modern-style factory—a paper-making operation—was established. Other enterprises followed in the 1940s, notably an electric power plant, a machine tools factory, a woolens factory, several flour mills, and an automobile parts factory (*Dangdai zhongguo de chengshi jianshe* 1990: 485). But as late as 1949, the whole of Gansu Province had no more than 1,000 small "factories, mines and handicrafts workshops," employing about 7,000 people (Xue Muqiao 1982: 797). After the revolution the making of fine jewelry and other handicrafts was discouraged, and attention was focused on the development of heavy industry. Lanzhou's targeting as a "city of pivotal construction" in the First Five-Year Plan led to the establishment of oil refining, synthetic rubber, nitrogenous fertilizer, petroleum processing equipment, chemicals, machine tools, cement, and pharmaceuticals factories as well as spinning mills (*Dangdai zhongguo de chengshi jianshe* 1990: 485; Buchanan 1970: 233, 274). This industrial development was accompanied by a large labor migration. The city rapidly grew past the million mark.

Lanzhou is now a city of heavy industry. Its primary industry today is oil refining, followed closely by chemical processing, machine building (for the petroleum industry), and nonferrous metals. Textiles, instruments and meters, pharmaceuticals, and processed foods also account for a significant share of the industrial output value.[16]

Lanzhou also has a uranium-enrichment plant that plays a vital role in China's nuclear weapon industry (see, e.g., Shinz 1989: 154). By 1985 the city had more than 1,000 industrial enterprises employing more than 400,000 people (PRC State Statistical Bureau 1987: 83). These include plants of every kind and size, producing items ranging from automobiles and aluminum to television sets and thermos bottles. This type of diversified industrial base has become common in the other frontier cities as well, and indeed in most of China's cities, under the PRC.

Production at Hohhot was limited in traditional times to the handicrafts directly associated with the interaction between nomadic and settled peoples on the frontier, such as blacksmiths' shops and saddleries. Before 1949 the city had only a handful of factories: a few small electric generating plants, a flour mill, a small coal factory, a brick factory and a small woolens mill (PRC State Statistical Bureau 1987: 67; *Tuanjie jianshezhong de Neimenggu* 1987: 184). In addition, there were small commercial enterprises for the production of wine, soy sauce, iron, and woven straw products (Guan Xiaoxian et al. 1987: 28). After 1949 woolen textiles became the largest industry, but other industries were also developed, including iron and steel smelting, electronics, and chemicals. Under the First Five-Year Plan, new factories were established for the production of agricultural tools and machinery, electricity, and pharmaceuticals, and the few existing enterprises were expanded or improved (ibid., pp. 28–29). By 1985 the city had more than 700 industrial enterprises employing about 133,000 workers (PRC State Statistical Bureau 1986: 67).

Kunming has long been a center for both traditional crafts production and the processing of the copper and iron output of the nearby mines. Kunming's modern industrial development came relatively early for a frontier city, thanks to the technological expertise of the refugees from eastern China who settled there in the late 1930s. Kunming received considerable support in its industrial development after 1949. Although the machine tool industry alone now accounts for 25 percent of its industrial output, Kunming has the greatest range of industries of all the frontier cities. Among its other major products are synthetic detergents and phosphate fertilizers. In 1985 Kunming had about 21,000 industrial enterprises (PRC State Statistical Bureau 1986: 78).

Urumqi acquired a diverse set of handicraft industries in the late eighteenth century. The first craftsmen, of course, came with the military. In 1758, while Dihua was still a fort, the local soldiers required 7,000 agricultural implements, and 3,800 carts. At the same time local enterprises were developed for the production of building materials, such as brick, tiles and stone (Liu Yintong 1986: 11). The first iron foundry in the region was established in 1765 in Urumqi's northeastern suburbs, the second, in 1784, at Dongtiechanggou (East Foundry Gulch).

In 1949 Urumqi had 10 small factories and about 50 handicraft workshops. Large-scale industrial development began there in 1952, with the establishment of industrial enterprises ranging from a spinning mill and an iron and steel factory to an automobile repair yard, a flour mill, and a cement plant (*Dangdai zhongguo de chengshi jianshe* 1990: 554). Today Urumqi's main industries are machine building, petroleum, and textiles. Chemical processing, metallurgy, building materials, electricity, and food processing are secondary industries. In 1985 the city had 236 industrial enterprises with a work force of nearly 200,000 (PRC, State Statistical Bureau 1987: 148).

Xining has a long tradition of iron and building materials production, dating back to 1386, when the Ming government established facilities to supply its troops (*Dangdai zhongguo de chengshi jianshe* 1990: 272). As late as 1891, however, Xining primarily exported agricultural products. The most important of these was bean oil, which was sent to Lanzhou and the city of Ningxia (Yinchuan) during the summer via raft. Other exports at that time were wool, musk, rhubarb, lambskins, furs, gold, and salt (Rockhill 1891: 50–51). Although Xining continued to be primarily a center for trade and small craft production before 1949, the warlord Ma Bufang established several industries during the 1940s, notably a spinning mill, a chemical plant, a carpet factory, a machine shop, a tannery, a brick kiln, a glue factory, a porcelein factory, a tile factory, and a charcoal factory (*Qinghai lishi jiyao* 1987: 495).

After more than 40 years of industrial development under the PRC, Xining now has a wide variety of enterprises similar to those of other frontier cities. Like the industries of Hohhot, these include industries for processing the products of grasslands herding activities, as well as a variety of other enterprises for both local urban life and farming.

Though cities on the frontiers function in a similar manner to cities in the core area, China's frontier cities took on a disproportionate share of these functions in their regional contexts. The frontier cities acted as the primary representatives of the empire on the frontier. Frontier cities were not just cities of local trade and commerce; they were control points that exercised influence over both politics and economy in far-flung hinterland areas. The frontier cities fulfilled an important set of functions for the non-Chinese peoples as well as the Chinese. Not only did they serve as the primary conduit to the Chinese empire for trade, military support, and other services, but they also served as common ground on which a variety of different peoples could meet. Tibetans, Mongolians, Uygur, and other non-Chinese peoples traded among themselves as well as with the Chinese in the setting of the frontier city.

4

Chinese Urbanism and the Frontiers

The following three chapters discuss the form of cities on the frontier in the context of cities elsewhere in China. Here form should be understood as it is manifested in three modes: the physical form of each individual city as it exists or has existed in time and space, the generalized characteristics of city form as they have been identified, discussed, and created by the scholarly community, and the values and ideals about form as passed down by the people who build and maintain cities. Each of these three modes is important for analyzing urban form on the Chinese frontiers. This chapter will explore these modes as they are expressed in traditions of Han Chinese city building. Chapter Five will address similar themes for Islamic and Lamaist traditions of city building, and Chapter Six will bring the Chinese and non-Chinese traditions together to discuss form on the frontiers.

Urban-Rural Distinctions in Traditional China

Urbanism has long been an important issue in discussions of Chinese culture and society. Classical analyses based largely on the idealistic and utopian renderings of Chinese annalists have identified Chinese society as essentially rural, a society that by and large shunned the city and regarded life in rural or wilderness areas as the ideal civilized existence.

Traditional Chinese philosophy embraced a three-tiered hierarchy for the ideal locale of human existence. At the pinnacle of this hierarchy is the ideal of living in nature: the life of the poet contemplating life from his cave or cottage in the wilderness. Second to this was the life of the rural gentry residing in the countryside surrounded not only by the pastoral scenes of the rural landscape but also by the controlled nature of the classical Chinese garden. The urban life was the least desirable: too removed from nature to enable a truly harmonious life and detached from the family ties of rural China as well. As Arthur F. Wright notes, the glorification of rural life as virtuous and the vilification of urban life as rife with vice and corruption are basic Confucian tenets (Wright 1977: 34). Chinese historians, who were for the most part Confucian scholars, were thus naturally led to reify these beliefs in their descriptions of traditional Chinese life. The very fact that officials maintained country addresses even though they spent nearly their entire lives in the cities illustrates the rural ideal. And the fact that the Chinese shunned or criticized city life indicates that there was some fundamental difference perceived between urban life and rural life.

Some scholars have been led by the Chinese idealization of nonurban lifestyles to suggest that there was little basic difference between rural and urban life in China. For Max Weber, the extreme concern with native place on the part of the Chinese suggested a lack of identification with urban places (Weber 1951: 90). And Frederick Mote has argued that there was little urban-rural distinction in China.[1] Moreover, he suggests that there was no architectural distinction between town and country in traditional China: town houses and country estates were identical in design and size. Nowhere did one find the increased building heights, smaller lots, or other urban adaptations that took place in traditional Europe (Mote 1970, 1977: 116).

The early idealization of China as a rural society and the fact that the population has always been predominantly rural may have slowed the investigation of Chinese urbanism. Until recently studies of Chinese urbanism have been further hampered by a focus on monumental structures to the exclusion of other aspects of urban form. Even today Chinese scholarship on urban morphology places little emphasis on vernacular form and architecture beyond simple descriptions of typical traditional housing styles. In much of the literature on Chinese urbanism, the Chinese city is portrayed only in the framework of monuments.

But in fact, despite the strong basic similarities of architectural form between urban and rural places in some areas, urban and rural architectures are distinct in China, particularly since the Tang dynasty development of permanent shops outside of designated markets in Chinese cities allowed for an increased variety of architectural styles, such as shophouses, specifically adapted to the urban situation. The varied and specialized occupations of urban dwellers, with their organization along occupational and place-of-origin grounds, have long made for distinct urban organization, and even architecture. Nowhere in the countryside would there be similarly concentrated dwellings and shops of like occupation—nowhere would there be a street of jewelers, for example, occupying buildings constructed with storefronts and workshops on the street frontage and dwellings to the rear. City dwellings devoted less space to animal and fodder storage, and more space to commercial functions, than rural houses. Though individual homes in the cities may have had a strong resemblance to homes in the countryside of origin of their owners, the varied origins of city dwellers naturally led to a distinctive melange of styles, creating unique residential landscapes uncommon in rural areas. Urban architecture has also tended more toward multi-story construction than rural architecture. Yet multi-storied houses have rarely been discussed in Chinese historical literature. As Jacques Gernet notes in regard to Hangzhou, "Western travelers so frequently mention multi-storeyed buildings in Hangchow that we cannot doubt their existence, despite the lack of information in Chinese sources, which only contain vague references" (Gernet 1962: 32). He might have added that multi-storied shop houses also figure prominently in scroll paintings of cities like Suzhou and Kaifeng in the late imperial era.

Moreover, cities did in fact serve distinct functions. As Wright observes, elites used the cities as centers for both wealth and power alike (Wright 1977: 34). Chinese cities not only served administrative and trading functions not found in the rural areas, but also carried out a diverse set of economic activities with large proportions of their populations engaged in nonagricultural activities.

The concept of cities as a spatial and cultural contrast with non-urban surroundings has been raised before. A somewhat dated but nonetheless interesting work, *The Formation of the Chinese People* (1928), by Li Chi, makes the argument that city walls are the clearest evidence of the presence of Chinese identity in a given area. To Li, the building of city walls is a clear expression of settled Chinese culture and can thus be used to trace the spread of Chinese culture and identity. He develops a statistical analysis of rates of city construction and abandonment in an attempt to map the diffusion and consistency of Chinese culture over long periods of time. Though this venture as a whole may present too many difficulties to be useful in and of itself, it does illustrate that walled cities can be considered an integral and distinctive aspect of Chinese culture (even if it fails to recognize that non-Chinese peoples within China have also historically built their own walled cities).

Scholars have recently begun to reassess the significance of cities in Chinese culture as a result of further analysis of the actual, rather than the ideal, life in historic China (see, for example, Buck 1984; Kirkby 1985; Rowe 1984). And cities have become increasingly important in Chinese national life since the treaty port experience of the nineteenth century. Today the cities, and particularly those of the eastern seaboard, are the focus of major economic and social changes. These changes are only gradually filtering down to the countryside and the poorer cities of the interior.

Chinese Urban Traditions and Ideals

Chinese city forms grew out of the heartland of Chinese culture. As Wright asserts, "All the normative ideas and techniques of city building were developed in the North China Plain, the nuclear area of Chinese civilization. The availability of flat sites made orientation to the cardinal points easy, and construction with pounded earth or mud brick was universal" (Wright 1977: 51–52).

Four basic features of Chinese urbanism have been quite thoroughly identified and accepted as fundamental to the analysis of Chinese cities for most historical periods before the post-1949 era. That it has been possible to identify a set of key characteristics across so many centuries attests to the remarkably consistent nature of Chinese urban planning and construction. These features are the ceremonial center, the city wall, the organization of city space on the basis of status, and the use of cosmology/geomancy for city siting and orientation.

The basic principles for the spatial organization of settlements developed between the twelfth and eighth centuries B.C. on the North China Plain. Among them, for example, were the construction of a city wall to enclose industry and artisans, residences, and markets, the construction of an inner walled area for the city's ceremonial and administrative center, geomantic principles such as siting the city on level land whenever possible, and the north-south orientation of streets, buildings, and the walls themselves. These form the basis for a great tradition of city building that in the most general sense was practiced throughout China consistently into the nineteenth century. Passages in the *Kaogongji* (Record of craftsmen) section of the *Zhou li* (Rituals of the Zhou) describe a city built in a square, with three gates on a side and nine regularly spaced north-south and east-west streets. This city had a number of ceremonial structures, including an ancestral temple, altars of soil and grain, and, at the center of the city, an audience hall with markets behind (to the north)

(Wheatley 1971: 411–26). Later other guidelines were set, specifying the placement of key temples, administrative centers, and bell and drum towers at the center of the city and the use of spatial divisions for class and ethnic demarcations.

Walls and walled fortifications, at every scale form the family courtyard to the city wall, are one of the most distinctive elements identified with the Chinese city.[2] There have been changes through time in the function and use of city walls throughout China. The extent to which urban activities were contained within various types of walls and thus subject to restricted access and participation is an indicator of the Chinese urban social milieu at any given time or place.

Several basic principles governed the placement and character of walls at all scales. For example, walls were to be built following as square a path as possible, as a representation of the Chinese conception of the earth (heaven, in contrast, was round), and this square form was to be oriented on the cardinal directions. Walls were to be pierced by gates at regular intervals. Within the walls main thoroughfares were laid out connecting the gates to the central administrative area of the city. These were always as straight as possible, oriented on the cardinal directions, and built in widths mandated by the city's position within the imperial administrative hierarchy. The location of the most important structures, such as the administrative center and the temple to the town god, was determined at the time of the city's founding and was usually near its center. The major boulevards that converged at the center of the city did not pass through these central administrative and religious areas but rather led to their gates.

From early times, as early as the Qin dynasty, centralized planning emerged in the form of imperial edicts setting out the specifications for various types of cities, particularly those at different levels in the administrative hierarchy. These "decreed" requirements are especially important in an analysis of the cities of the frontier, where it is often difficult to relate their size, placement, and form simply to their economic or military roles.

Apart from the city walls, major thoroughfares, and monumental architecture, the Chinese city was relatively free in structure, though always within the bounds of convention concerning construction and the control of economic activities such as markets (S.-d. Chang 1961, 1963, 1970). City wards, for example, were controlled by families or, in late imperial times, by guilds, rather than by the municipal government, and the planning and administration of those wards were to some degree at the discretion of the residents.

The Chinese system of cities as a whole was based on a complex interweaving of imperial passions and functional practicality. Whereas most of the cities built before the late imperial period were established directly by imperial decrees, those of newer vintage were far more likely to have grown organically out of market towns. One might expect such economically derived cities to be more irregularly shaped than cities established by edict (Mote 1967: 155), but the distinction is not easily drawn. Some cities established by imperial decree were in fact "established" on the sites of existing, economically viable cities.

Chinese Urban Ideals

Scale and the Ethical Form of the City

The primary controlling feature of the establishment, planning, and administration of cities throughout the long history of Chinese culture has been the effort to achieve both uniformity and an idealized form dictated by beliefs in a cosmo-magical universe and a well-defined sociospatial order. The ideal Chinese city is a rigid representation of the Chinese cosmological order. The square central city is a representation of the world; streets divide it into regions. The square administrative complex is a microcosm of the cosmos, composed of a succession of courtyards, each square a more perfect representation of that cosmos, until the ultimate order is achieved in the innermost courts. The entire plan of the city, down to the level of the design of individual quarters and the placement of furniture, was laid out with great attention to geomancy, numerology, and the harmonizing of human settlement with the natural and spiritual worlds. Even achieving the ideal in image, if not in reality, was important. Published plans of imperial capitals were thus sometimes altered in order to make the city appear as more "ideal" than it actually was. Nancy Steinhardt cites several examples of this phenomenon, including a nineteenth-century depiction of thirteenth-century Lin-an (Hangzhou) that considerably idealized the rather irregular shape of the original settlement (Steinhardt 1990: 147; see also pp. 83, 146, 160, 161, 171).

The ideals of traditional Chinese architecture and urban planning are inextricably linked within the requirements of cosmological representation. These specify shape more than size, making Chinese architectural practices non-scale-specific in their ideal forms. This also means that considerations of ideal shape, proportion, and placement are appropriate at every level within a settlement. The planning of furniture layout is a miniature of the planning of the construction of the house and house site, and the planning of the city is an enlarged projection of the planning of an individual house or temple complex. These idealized conceptualizations of house and temple form were extended to city form as well.

Traditional ideals for Chinese architecture and urban planning encompassed the building process as well as architectural form. This mix of precepts is clear in what Liang Ssu-ch'eng (Liang Sicheng), a noted Chinese architectural historian, identifies as the four primary characteristics of traditional Chinese architecture and urban construction:

> All architectural activity is conditioned by ethical concepts.
> Layout and ground plan are of great significance.
> [Construction] neither seeks permanence nor values the use of materials assuring permanence.
> The architectural arts were transmitted from craftsmen to apprentices; books and written records were unimportant in this process. (Liang Ssu-ch'eng, as quoted in Mote 1977: 112)

These points are worth examining in turn. That all architectural activity was traditionally conditioned by ethical concepts is reflected in Chinese city planning in the way that the cities were carefully laid out according to cosmo-magical principles, within the limitations of site, materials, and functional considerations. Moreover, the application of the process of geomantic planning was an act of ethics: it would have been both unconscionable and a danger to the well-being of the community to establish a city without taking geomantic principles into consideration.

The ordering of urban space also embodied Chinese conceptions of social order: basic tenets of Confucian ethical philosophy that assigned separate identities and characteristics to heaven, man, and earth, and sought to reproduce this natural order in human creations of spatial design. There was a strong correlation in the ideal conception of the Chinese city between social structure and the physical structure of the city itself. Just as in the cosmos in which China stood at the center of the world, so, too, the central enclaves of the city were the realm of enlightened administrators at the top of the traditional social pyramid. This relationship was an enlargement, particularly in the Qing dynasty, of the structure of the city's administrative center, the yamen.[3] As John Watt has noted, the physical layout of the yamen emphasized the differentiation and hierarchical order of public and private places. There were four sequential divisions within the yamen: two outer courtyards and two inner courtyards. Intercommunication between these divisions was restricted to the large gateways between them. The structure of the yamen reflected public and private realms and social hierarchies. The public was confined to the out-ermost courtyard, and business concerning the public took place in the second. The first of the inner courts was for the private staff of the govern-ing official, who had no direct dealings with the public. The last was the private residence of the official himself (Watt 1977: 378–79).

The cosmic representation of the city described above also supports Liang's second tenet, that the layout and ground plan were of primary significance. The siting of thoroughfares, temples, administrative com-plexes, and the like was carried out with extreme care for the unity and auspicious grouping of the entire assemblage.[4] Thus for all that the Yuan dynasty was Mongol, its capital, Dadu (the future Beijing), is held to be a close approximation to the Chinese ideal of city building because it in-cluded the appropriate placements of walls, an ancestral shrine, altars of the state, the court (yamen), and markets, all laid out upon a flat plain (Mote 1977: 112).

Yet the highly defined and rigid spatial conception of the ideal Chinese city was, in fact, limited to only a few elements: the walls, and, in a general sense, the area contained by them; the orientation of the city as a whole and of its major thoroughfares; and the placement and internal structure of the monumental architecture. Beyond this grand level, any adherence to tenets seemingly harmonious with the overall ideals was based purely on individual decisions and the dictates of geomancy and other folk prac-tices, and not through any effort to legislate or plan the city as a whole in the sense that modern planning is conceived of in the West. City planning stopped with the siting and construction of monumental structures, and thus as long as new structures did not conflict with the original conception of the city, they were permitted. This established a fundamental disjunc-tion between the carefully structured monumental realm and the ad hoc vernacular realm. On the frontier this compartmentalization of planning concerns became a key factor in the ability of the Chinese to adapt their urban forms to multicultural situations.

Ideals may also have entered into urban development in other dimen-sions suggested by Liang Ssu-ch'eng. The lack of value placed on per-manence meant that cities were both continually rebuilt and continually changed. The vernacular aspects of the city, such as housing blocks and shops, were particularly vulnerable to deterioration, and therefore change. Within the otherwise rigid ideals for the city plan, consequently, there was considerable flexibility in the "impermanent" precincts of the city. But the principle of lack of permanence did not hold true in the case of the city walls, which by their very nature, and particularly after the Ming dynasty's widespread application of brick facings, were quite long lasting. Likewise, the paths of major thoroughfares were fixed from the start and were intended to remain in the carefully planned, cosmo-magically sanctioned patterns of their founding. Unless a city was perceived to have particularly bad luck, to change the position of its key elements was to invite disaster.

Liang Ssu-ch'eng's final tenet concerning an apprenticed rather than written tradition is probably accurate. Mote notes that in all his in-depth survey of documents relating to the founding of Nanjing, he was unable to locate any written record of the "sources of the ideological, practical and technical knowledge employed by the planners and builders, or about who they were and how they worked." This lack of material on the individuals involved in the planning process makes discussion of "authored landscapes" in Chinese history difficult, but it also suggests that design and construction techniques were handed down through apprenticeships. Nonetheless, there is no lack of physical and inferential evidence that Nanjing, like most Chinese cities, was planned with a "fully worked out conceptualization of what a capital city should be, how its parts should relate to each other, and what symbolic or functional significance those parts should have" (Mote 1977: 112–13).

Principles of urban planning were passed from generation to generation of geomancers and administrators involved in high levels of government. This in turn would suggest that, without texts to refer to, the "urban planner" of traditional China would have been limited to his own knowledge of society's ideals. And in the frontier areas, where in the early years scholars were few and architectural projects were typically carried out by the military without access to the most elite and subtle practitioners of geomancy, it is reasonable to assume that many cities were laid out on the basis of a relatively simple understanding of those principles. Though some extraordinary military expeditions had geomancers among their members, as did, for example, the imperial navy during the fifteenth-century explorations of Zhenghe, few ordinary border missions would have been as fully staffed. Moreover, the fact that military cities along the Great Wall were built on a standard military plan, with relatively little attention to the site, and were quite consistently square in shape, with relatively simple structure (L. Wu 1986: 113–21), suggests that frontier outposts tended to be laid out without the benefit of specialists to fine-tune them to their specific sites.

The ideal Chinese city, then, was a rigid conceptualized plan of a highly structured organization of urban space infused with cultural beliefs about the relationship of spatial organization to the well-being of the inhabitants. At the same time it was a place in which such attention was given to only some elements of the city, with the result that the ideals were not realized in all areas of the city.

Chinese Geomancy

The ideals and applications of Chinese geomancy are thus worth a closer look because they contribute to an understanding of the motivations and priorities of the Chinese on the frontiers. Of the many factors influencing the traditional urban landscape in China, including urban ideals, economic or political functions, and even environmental conditions, most are linked in one way or another with an underlying system of beliefs concerning the relation of the material and environmental aspects of urban life with the immaterial. These systems, including the ancient Chinese art of *fengshui* or *kanyu*, as well as a broad spectrum of religious practices, are all forms of geomancy.

Geomancy, the determination of auspicious locations for human occupation of the land, is a practice common to many cultures, both ancient and modern. Hong-key Yoon describes it as "a unique and comprehensive system of conceptualizing the physical environment which regulates human ecology by influencing man to select auspicious environments and to build harmonious structures on them" (Yoon 1980: 341). Although Yoon refers primarily to geomancy as a distinctive Chinese form, his definition could be applied to forms of augury and geomancy employed, for example, by the Etruscans, and later the Romans, to determine auspicious locations for cities.

The Chinese system of geomancy (*fengshui*) is much celebrated as an ancient practice that has been pervasive in Chinese societies for centuries and that has survived to the present day (in Chinese societies other than the PRC, where it has been officially discouraged). Historically one of the primary sets of beliefs influencing the formulation of architecture and urban space in China, fengshui is a system of rules for the siting of man-made objects in the landscape. At its heart is the belief that the landscape is infused with lines of force, which may be strengthened or blocked whenever some new man-made object is introduced. The object of fengshui practice is to position such objects in a way that will take the best advantage of, and cause the least harm to, the natural forces (*qi*) surrounding and passing through the site. Man-made objects in this sense might be as small as a chair or as large as an entire city.

Fengshui is only one part of a broader tradition of divination used to locate both auspicious places and times. Though astrological divination, for example, is generally associated with time, it is also related to place to the extent that it can be used to calculate the most auspicious times for building or changing a structure. Fengshui, in contrast, is associated with the earth and most commonly relates to place rather than time. But time is also a factor in fengshui, since the forces of nature are modified hourly with the shifting positions of sun and moon, the flow of the tides, and changes in the weather.

Three basic aspects of nature are critical to the fengshui system. The first is the actual and representative forms of natural elements. Certain shapes of landscape elements are considered auspicious or inauspicious by their association with various mythical beasts or objects. For example, the most auspicious mountain forms are those with a sharp ridge, as on a dragon's back, and those with undulations in a form that is associated with tigers. There are, furthermore, five shapes of hill associated with the five phases (*wu xing*): wood, fire, earth, metal, and water. These must be combined in complementary ways for good fengshui.

Landscape elements also have male and female (yang and yin) characteristics that must be balanced. The combination of yang and yin is one of the key elements in the second aspect of fengshui, that of the circulation of nature's "breath" through the landscape. Yang sites for buildings or cities (such as the north banks of rivers) tend to be open to many auspicious influences; yin sites (such as the south banks of rivers) tend to be inauspicious positions requiring modification.

Finally, geomancy incorporates numerological beliefs derived from the mystical proportions of nature. In this complex system several different auspicious numbers based on nature (such as the twelve signs of the zodiac, the five elements, the five central planets, and the ten heavenly stems of the Chinese calendar) are combined into a round "compass" that can be read for the determination of auspicious time and place.[5] This compass is believed to be the origin of the magnetic compass in China (Ronan 1978: 200).

Fengshui is usually practiced by a professional retained for the purpose of either locating the appropriate site for a project or determining the best course for readjusting an ill-omened site. The fengshui practitioner analyzes a proposed site for a grave, house, or city with the aid of an astrological compass and the use of a wealth of knowledge concerning the hidden lines of force in the landscape. A well-known illustration from a late Qing work, the *Shujingtu shuo*, depicts a geomancer in the act of selecting a city site. Standing in an area bordered by a mountain in the background and water in the foreground, the geomancer consults his compass as his assistants study the detail of the landscape. Noblemen, perhaps those who commissioned this process, look on (Ronan 1978: 201).

The best fengshui landscape is one that permits the invisible forces embodied in nature to flow freely, without obstruction, or that is so situated as to collect good and strong aspects of fengshui for the benefit of the residents. Thus, for example, tall, pointed structures are a danger since they pierce the sky, thereby blocking the free flow of forces there. Flowing water is often considered auspicious (depending on its location), since it aids in the movement of these forces. It is inauspicious only if it carries too many of the forces of the landscape away from the site.

For the siting of a city, the most important elements are hills or mountains and water. Mountains block lines of force; rivers carry lines of force (as do the wind and the earth itself). Particular care must be taken with mountains linked to dragons or tigers, for they can attack by causing ill fortune when offended and will protect when appeased. A city should never be placed on the ridge of a hill, precariously perched on a dragon's back.

The relationship of the city to elements in the surrounding landscape is partially determined by beliefs concerning the cardinal directions. In Chinese cosmology north is evil and south is good. North is associated with winter and the military, and is depicted by a black tortoise; south is associated with summer and administration, and is depicted by a red bird. East and west may be good or bad, depending on the situation. East is associated with springtime and is depicted by an azure dragon; west is associated with autumn and is depicted by a white tiger. Traditionally, however, the western side of the city tended to be the abode of wealthier residents, while the east of the city was the home of poorer residents (Wu Liangyong 1986: 123). The northeast is a particularly bad direction, associated with an inauspicious and threatening wind, both natural and spiritual. Though careful north-south orientation is usually critical for good fengshui, exceptions are made when the site has such a favorable combination of mountains and water that it is possible to have auspicious siting without strict adherence to the cardinal directions.[6]

Chinese town planning has been influenced by beliefs in geomancy since ancient times. Many of the tenets of geomancy as it relates to urban organization were established as early as the Shang and Zhou periods. These tenets continued to be at the core of urban planning in China until the establishment of the PRC. They include such principles and practices as precise alignment with the cardinal directions, with south as the ritually favored orientation; rectangular forms; the use of divination; the articulation of cities into functional zones; the use of double enclosures (separation of the administrative center from the rest of the city); the need to balance the dual forces of good and evil (yang and yin), the male and female principles; and the need to take into account the five elements (*wu xing*) that make up the universe (Wright 1977: 37–38).

It was believed that the internal organization of cities could be made auspicious as well by ensuring that certain buildings were properly placed. And, as with the overall siting of the city, it was possible to improve the geomantic layout of the internal structure by strategically manipulating and reshaping the natural environment. All of these beliefs regarding fengshui applied equally to any later modifications. The placement of spirit walls and other structures to take better advantage of or ward off natural and spiritual forces often took place after the initial building was completed, when it was determined that the geomantic position needed strengthening. The most common practices for correcting the fengshui of an existing structure or site included building spirit walls or placing mirrors to fend off ill forces, relocating or blocking entrances to buildings, adding pools and streams of water to landscaping to encourage favorable forces, raising artificial hills, and tree planting. "Coal hill" in Beijing is a good example of such an attempt to improve a site's fengshui. This artificial hill, created out of dirt dug to build a moat, was placed directly north of the large palace complex to better defend the imperial residence against the ill fortunes of the north. But the most basic practice, particularly in the simplified context of the frontier, was to place as many temples and government buildings as possible near the center of the city. Since this space obviously could not accommodate all the city's important structures, urban planning necessarily involved evaluations of relative importance and a hierarchy of placement.[7] The most important secular structure was usually the yamen. In cities containing more than one yamen, such as those that served as provincial-level administrative centers but also had separate quarters for the city government, preference was usually granted to the highest level of administration (though there were exceptions). Other structures important to locate near the center of the city were the temple of the town god, the Confucian temple, and the bell and drum towers.

The Application of Chinese Geomancy on the Frontiers

Beliefs carefully and professionally applied to city building in China proper were perhaps rigidly adhered to but more amateurly executed on the frontier. Frontier outposts, as noted, were often designed and built by military men without the aid of skilled practitioners of geomancy and with an eye mostly to practical or defensive considerations (Wu Liangyong 1986: 113–16). In some cases, like Lanzhou and Xining, the city site itself was relatively poor in terms of geomancy. But even in those cases, the city's interior plan conformed to the fengshui ideal. It is interesting to note that these ideals seem to have been upheld also in cities such as Hohhot and Beijing that were sponsored by the Mongols. Although the Mongols had little experience with city building, they were adept at using Chinese planning experts and skilled labor to create cities that came close to the Chinese ideal. The cities of Yunnan built by non-Chinese (but perhaps with Chinese advisers) and the garrison cities of the Manchu during the Qing era also maintained these fundamentally Chinese ideals.

The Selection of City Sites

Fengshui seems to have been an important consideration in the siting and construction of Dihua (Urumqi). It was established south of Hongshan (Red Mountain), a rocky outcrop near the center of the plain that reaches a height of 910 m at its highest point, about 100–200 m above the altitude of the city proper. This site, just south of a hill on a plain, was the best to be found for a considerable distance. A recent description of Urumqi, which today surrounds Hongshan, depicts the hill as a dragon sleeping in the city center (Liu Weidiao 1988: 20). It is no coincidence that Hongshan became the local Buddhist center and pilgrimage site. At the time of Urumqi's founding, the hill was likely perceived as a dragon protecting the northern bounds of the city. The dragon spirit believed to live there was said to have flown down and settled at the hill from Bogda Peak, the nearby high and much revered snow mountain.

But the otherwise perfect geomantic site for Urumqi was blemished by the Urumqi River, which skirts the west side of the hill and then flows south in such a manner that the city was of necessity built slightly southeast of the hill, rather than due south. The river's inauspiciousness was demonstrated in 1785–86, when it flooded and destroyed many homes. Local tradition held that this occurred because the spirit of Hongshan wanted to unite with the spirit of Yamashan, a local mountain, by transforming the site of Urumqi into a great sea. In 1788 pagodas were built on both mountains to appease the spirits. Since that time, there have been no more problems with floods (Zan Yulin 1983: 11–13).[8] Though the Manchu city at Urumqi, Gongning Cheng, built due west of Hongshan, had a relatively less auspicious site than Dihua, it was protected by Pingdingshan, a less dramatic but perhaps nearly as auspicious hill.

Kunming has one of the best fengshui locations in all of China: a lake to the south, streams to the east and west, and hills to the north. There are two ranges of hills to protect the city and provide good fengshui siting. Wuhua Hill stood immediately north of the city until it was encircled by new city walls during the Ming dynasty, while Luofeng and Dade hills, farther to the north, remained well positioned to protect the city from ill winds rising out of the north.[9] The highest point in Kunming proper (1,926 m), Wuhua Hill was first built upon in 1277, when the governor of Yunnan had a Buddhist temple constructed there.[10] Many different temples were subsequently built on its slopes. The government offices of both Kunming and Yunnan Province have been located there since Ming times.

Traditional names for topographic features in Kunming make reference to their function in the fengshui scheme. The lower section of East Huashan Road was traditionally referred to as the "four auspicious masses." And the neighborhood of Yunnan University near North Green Lake Road was known as Jade Dragon mass (Yulongdui; Wang Xueshi et al. 1987: 183).

The entire Ming city at Kunming, nestled between the hills and the water, with ample southward-flowing watercourses, is a textbook example of the ideal geomantically balanced city, with the external structure of the site complementing the internal structure of building placement and orientation. Both Xining and Lanzhou, in contrast, have relatively poor geomantic sites, even though all the elements for good fengshui—hills, a plain, and a river—are present in both cases. Here everything is backwards because the rivers are on the north between the cities and the mountains. Ideally, they would be south of the city, so that its north edge backs up against and is protected by the mountains, and the south edge opens onto the water.[11] In neither case is there much room for urban development on the north side of the west-to-east-flowing river, however, and the wide plain that contains the city is located south of the river. Military and practical considerations seem to have overridden geomantic concerns; both cities are strategically well positioned to control the river valleys they are located in.

The indifferent nature of the site of Xining has been improved through the placement of temples north and south of the city. South Temple stands on the hilltop to the south of the city, with a commanding view of both the city and the Nanchuan River, a placement aimed at better connecting the city with the favorable winds of the south. By contrast, North Temple, a combined Buddhist and Daoist complex, is secreted in a series of caves in the northern cliffs, high above the plain. These buildings face the south and thus avoid direct contact with the ill winds of the north.

The builders of Xining also contravened geomantic practice by putting the main gates on the east and west sides of the city. This allowed the authorities to control the region's principal east-west road, the primary northern route between China and Tibet, which passed directly through the city.[12] Nonetheless, the internal structure of the walled city remained geomantically sound, with the most important yamen auspiciously located in the northwest quadrant of the city, adjacent to the central intersection and facing south, and the main axes of the walled inner area oriented with the cardinal directions.

Pre-twentieth-century Lanzhou was bordered on the west by streams and on the north by the Yellow River. Like Xining, Lanzhou has temples on both the northern and the southern hills, perhaps correcting the inauspicious nature of the site (though the northern complex stands at the crest of the hill, with views both north and south). Lanzhou adheres to a classic geomantic pattern internally. The main axial streets within the boundaries of the inner city wall form a "T," as in many Chinese cities, about two-thirds of the way north from the south wall.

Hohhot has a relatively better geomantic site than either Xining or Lanzhou, despite the fact that the site was chosen long before the Chinese were an important influence. It lies at the center of a flat plain, surrounded by mountains, with a watercourse running along the western edge of the old city. The new Manchu city, Suiyuan, has a large pool of water, Manchu Capital Sea, southwest of the walled area. This pool may well have been constructed in an attempt to improve on the geomantic conditions of Suiyuan, which is oriented along southeast-northwest and southwest-northeast axes. Internally, Suiyuan was structured much like Xining and Lanzhou, although it diverged somewhat from true orientation with the cardinal directions. The Chinese/Mongolian city at Hohhot was only partially articulated into this form, with a north-south axial street but no significant east-west axis. As with Xining, function dictated part of Hohhot's road and gate pattern. Suiyuan's west gate connects to the primary thoroughfare linking that city with the north gate of the Chinese city to the southwest.

What is most significant in this connection is that in all of these frontier cities geomantic considerations have been applied only to the Han Chinese and Manchu sections. In Xining, Lanzhou, and Urumqi, geomancy seemingly played little role in the construction of the walled Muslim suburbs, except perhaps in the extension of major axial streets from the inner city to preserve its carefully established geomantic order. In Lanzhou especially, as the outer walled suburb came to surround the inner city, the streets broke the cardinal-direction-oriented grid, and the district as a whole gave the city a highly irregular outer-wall shape. So, too, the walled Muslim suburbs at both Xining and Lanzhou break the careful geomantic ordering of the cities.

The Siting of Administrative Centers and Temples

All of the five cities discussed in this book served as centers of multiple levels of administration and thus had to see to the proper siting of several different administrative structures. Because the administrative nature of the cities changed over time, it was not possible to plan in advance for all of the administrative yamen that would later be required. But these complexes were often reused (or rebuilt on the same site) by successive administrations, and the rebuilding of cities with the advent of dynastic change usually included the construction of administrative facilities early in the rebuilding process. In Qing dynasty Lanzhou, for example, the regional (provincial) government yamen, which was the highest level of government organization in the city, was located centrally, on the north side of the "central intersection" in the northern third of the city. The county and city administrative headquarters were relegated to a lower status and were located in the western half of the city, about half way along the south to north axis, some distance from the regional government center (*Lanzhoufu zhi* 1834: 6–7, 192–94.

In contrast, Kunming, well positioned as it was between the hills and water, was able to give all three of its major administrative centers good sites (see Map 11). Here the topographical complexity of the site meant that siting in the center of the city was less important than siting in relation to beneficial topographical features. The provincial yamen was located in the northwest corner of the walled city, with the lake to its south and southeast; the county yamen was located in the northeast corner, nestled in the folds of the Yuantong hill; and the city yamen was in the south (*Kunming xianzhi* 1902: 49).

In Hohhot the provincial yamen was placed in the most auspicious site in the new Manchu city, on the northwest corner of the central intersection at the former headquarters of the military governor. The county yamen (built in the 1720s), however, occupied a relatively poor site outside the northwest corner of the old Chinese/Mongolian city. The position of this county yamen reflects its construction prior to the construction of the new city.

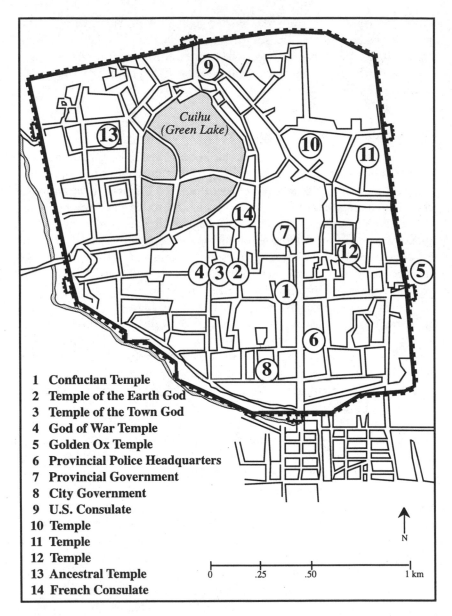

Cuihu
(Green Lake)

1 **Confucian Temple**
2 **Temple of the Earth God**
3 **Temple of the Town God**
4 **God of War Temple**
5 **Golden Ox Temple**
6 **Provincial Police Headquarters**
7 **Provincial Government**
8 **City Government**
9 **U.S. Consulate**
10 **Temple**
11 **Temple**
12 **Temple**
13 **Ancestral Temple**
14 **French Consulate**

0   .25   .50   1 km

N

Map 11. Sites of selected structures in Kunming, pre-1949. Sources: adapted from two French maps in the China Map Collection of the Library of Congress, "Yunnan-sen" (1948) and "Yunnan-fou" (1908); and from Wang Xuepei et al. 1987.

Other key structures that were often placed early in the planning of the city in accordance with good geomantic siting principles included the temple of the town god, the Confucian temple, and the city's bell and drum towers. The most important of the temple structures for the city as a whole was the temple of the town or city god, also known as the temple of the god of the city wall and moat (*chenghuangmiao*). Town god temples had become prevalent in Chinese administrative cities by the Song era (Taylor 1977: 34).[13] As the focus of the practice of some aspects of Chinese popular religion, Romeyn Taylor argues that town god temples became places where common people gathered and could be controlled or coerced by the local government (Taylor 1977: 39). In fact they have been explicitly described as "a point of interaction between state and society" (Feuchtwang 1977: 588). Though these institutions were governed by official rites and regulations, they had a social character as well, becoming the sites of markets and other popular activities (Feuchtwang 1977: 607). The merchant-employer class, which became prominent after the eighth century, is believed to have contributed significantly to the development of the town god temples (Johnson 1985). There was no specific prescription for positioning them, but as with the administrative yamen and the Confucian temple, the most auspicious site was as near to the center of the city as possible.

Unlike the temple of the town gods, the Confucian temple, or *wenmiao*, was the realm of the administrative elite and the focus of formal ritual activities. A city might have several Confucian temples, though one usually served as the official temple for state rites. Stephan Feuchtwang refers to such an official temple as the *xuegong*, or school temple, because it functioned as a center for preparing scholars for the imperial examinations (Feuchtwang 1977: 607).

Kunming's Temple of the Town God and Confucian Temple were both well sited. The town god's temple was near the center of the city, two blocks west of the main administrative complex, one block south of Green Lake. The Confucian temple (today's Kunming City Arts Center for the Masses) was adjacent to and directly south of the main administrative complex. During the Qing dynasty the Temple of the Town God housed not only the spirit of the city (on the left side of the altar), but the spirits of the county and the province (on the right and in the center, respectively; *Kunming xianzhi* 1902: 64).

Lanzhou's town god and Confucian temples were also near the city center. The Temple of the Town God (today's Workers' Club) was adjacent to the main administrative complex, near the center of the city's east-west axis, in the northern half of the north-south axis. The Confucian Temple (today's No. 2 Middle School) was several blocks to the south.

Each of the two cities at Hohhot had a town god temple. The one in Suiyuan, the Manchu city, was located near the center of the city on the east side of the main north-south street; it was built around 1768. Its counterpart (ca. 1730) in the Chinese-Mongolian city of Guihua, how-ever, was located in a very unusual position. It was built outside the city walls, beyond the north gate (*Guisui xianzhi* 1946: 225). (Both the Great Mosque of Hohhot and one of the city's two Catholic churches are also in this area.) Various explanations are possible for this unusual placement. The site was perhaps considered particularly auspicious or was the only available space for building at the time. Historical sources are silent on the rationale for this particular choice of site.

Similarly, and even more curiously, the Confucian Temple in Gongning Cheng, the Manchu city at Urumqi, was built outside the east gate, whereas the town god's temple was cosmologically well sited, positioned in the fore (southern) portion of the north-south axial street, near the cen-ter of the city (Zan Yulin 1984: 24).

Architectural Elements and Decoration

The application of geomancy is also important in micro-scale elements of architectural design and decoration, such as structures to block ill forces from entering buildings and clusters of buildings, ceremonial gate-ways designed to encourage the entrance of good forces, and mirrors to ward off evil. Many of these elements have become abstracted and gener-alized over the years. The *yingbi* and the *zhaobi* (spirit screen or wall), for example, underwent such a change in architectural meaning and purpose. These design elements were originally developed out of the belief that de-mons and ill winds could only travel in straight lines. Thus a screening structure placed just inside or outside a doorway would make it impossible for a malign spirit to enter the building (Rossbach 1983: 75).[14] These struc-tures vary widely in size and application, from the smallest homes to impe-rial palaces. Although many of the larger ones have been dismantled or al-lowed to fall into disrepair, a few striking examples are still standing. One of the most dramatic is the long wall south of the entrance to the old mili-tary governor's yamen in Hohhot's former Manchu city. This imposing gray brick wall, half a block long and about two feet thick, runs down the middle of the main east-west street all the way to its intersection with the main north-south street. A similar wall in Hohhot, covered with the remnants of old posters, south of the former palace of the Chinese princess Haibang, occupies a vacant lot behind some dilapidated housing.

Spirit screens are so much a part of Chinese architectural design that they are often used even in churches and mosques. Their presence in such unexpected places may signal that the belief in fengshui is so basic to Chinese culture that it transcends the teachings of foreign religions. But it might alternatively signal adherence to a tradition in which such elements are reflections of architectural fashion rather than belief. That is almost certainly true of the screen in the Zion Christian Church on Jinbi Street in Kunming, for example, which is just inside the main entrance (an entrance that defies the precepts of geomancy by facing north).[15] A number of frontier mosques, including the recently constructed Shuichengmen (Water Gate) mosque in Xining, have elaborate spirit screen and moon gate entrances. Like most mosques in China, the Xining mosque as a whole is oriented with its entrance on the east so that the direction of prayer is to the west. But the outer-wall entrance to the compound faces north and is protected by a spirit screen just inside the moon gate. The use of these elements in a complex that is otherwise Central Asian in style may indicate that the spirit screen was in this case placed for geomantic purposes.

Just as the spirit screen was designed to keep out ill winds and evil demons, so the ornamented multiple-arched wooden gateway known as the *bailou* was designed to invite good fortune into a city or building complex. In traditional Chinese architecture, these gateways had three or more arches, so that the gods and the emperor could enter by a separate path from the paths used by ordinary people (Jochim 1986: 99). The only traditional buildings to have such gates were yamen and temples. In Hohhot, for example, an elaborate bailou is the sole visible evidence from the street of the old Xiaozhao Lamaist temple behind. But this type of structure too has now become commonplace, separating vehicular from pedestrian traffic, rather than the routes of gods from mortals. Like the spirit screen, the bailou has been abstracted beyond its traditional significance. Notable examples in Chinese frontier cities include the gate to the Minorities Academy in Xining and the gate to the provincial government compound (formerly the yamen) in central Lanzhou.

Fengshui mirrors are a smaller-scale aspect of efforts to influence the geomancy of individual urban structures. Sometimes referred to as *bagua*,[16] these mirrors (which in earlier days could be quite large) are primarily a phenomenon of South China and were not a significant part of the urban landscape in the north or northwest even in traditional times. Bagua are typically placed on the outside of houses to keep malign spirits from entering and are regarded as the cure for many geomantic shortcomings, such as badly placed roads, evil spirits, or unpleasant neighbors. Traditional bagua usually have the eight trigrams incorporated into their design; fancier versions may have a warrior god as well. But any reflecting object will do—including common household items such as woks (which are apparently especially popular in Hong Kong and Taiwan), or broken pieces of mirror. Since the mirrors are believed to deflect evil in a path perpendicular to their surface, a family that lives across the street from a family that has put up a bagua might have to erect its own mirror to avoid ricochet effects (Rossbach 1983: 68–69).

Many houses in Kunming today are adorned with fengshui mirrors. By far the most common form is a small round mirror (about 2 inches in diameter) that looks like the cheap makeup or shaving mirrors sold in stores throughout China. But there are larger round mirrors as well, and some rectangular or square ones. (The last are rotated and suspended by one corner so that they appear diamond-shaped.) Most of the mirrors are hung over both doors and windows, usually at the first-floor level.[17]

Fengshui mirrors can be seen on older houses in a number of neighborhoods throughout Kunming, but they are most prevalent on Golden Ox (Jinniu) Road. By my count, 18 of the 150 houses in one block alone had mirrors mounted on them. Several houses along Following the Wall (Shuncheng) Street were also so adorned. The most elaborate display I saw was on a house at the northeast end of the bridge at People's (Renmin) Road, just across from Golden Ox Road. There, mounted outside a second-floor window, the owner had placed a cast of a tiger's head and four fengshui mirrors.

Both Golden Ox Road and Following the Wall Street are in the city's Muslim neighborhoods. These are also areas of almost exclusively traditional housing. It is unclear why the use of mirrors is so much more pronounced here than in the other neighborhoods. Possibly the residents are unusually conservative in their practice of tradition or unusually bold in so visibly displaying faith in what is often written off as superstition. Or it may be that there are especially large numbers of demons to be warded off along those streets. Kunming's Muslims are not the only non-Chinese people in the province favoring fengshui mirrors. They are very common among the Dai people of southern Yunnan. They are also common in the Bai city of Dali.[18]

*

The Chinese have rich and highly formalized urban traditions in which cultural values, including cosmological conceptions, play key roles. These traditions are an important example of the ways in which Chinese culture and society place great value on the structuring of space and spatial relationships. This value is one of the basic elements of Chinese culture that is challenged on the Chinese frontiers.

5

Non-Chinese Urban Traditions
on the Frontiers

There has been little discussion of non-Chinese urban development and morphology in China in U.S. or Chinese academic literature. The analysis of non-Chinese urban traditions presents difficulties in the historical and contemporary analysis of both indigenous non-Chinese urban forms and non-Chinese neighborhoods within Chinese cities. This book focuses on Chinese cities in frontier regions, rather than indigenous cities such as the Central Asian cities of Xinjiang or the Bai and Naxi cities of Yunnan. Of the five cities I address in this study, Hohhot and Kunming had non-Chinese origins but have been Chinese cities for centuries.

The urban traditions of non-Chinese peoples pose several challenges for the identification of urban forms. The cities of Mongolia and Tibet, for a start, historically included such movable structures as tents and yurts as part of the monumental landscape, in violation of basic Western and Chinese images of urbanism. Moreover, some of the non-Chinese urban forms of the frontier exist today only as archaeological sites, or have been so sinified that they cannot be clearly distinguished from Chinese forms. The cities of Gaochang and Xiahe near Turfan, for example, stand as grand ruins of the urban civilization of the Gaochang kingdom, but we can only speculate about many aspects of their form. And the towns of the Dian kingdom in Yunnan have been rebuilt over the centuries in increasingly Chinese forms.

As for the role non-Chinese peoples played in the creation of multicultural cities, here too the record is unclear and the extent of their participation cannot be fully measured. Power relationships between the Chinese and the non-Chinese were often highly unequal. It is unlikely that non-Chinese had much of a hand in the overall layout of the cities (with the

obvious exceptions of the ones they established), but they often significantly affected the shape of their own districts within the cities.

There have been a number of significant non-Chinese urban traditions
over the course of history on the Chinese frontiers. The Gaochang kingdom established thriving and sophisticated cities, and other Central Asian
cities along the Silk Routes also attained substantial size and distinctive
forms. Early kingdoms of the steppes such as the Liao also built cities and
monumental architecture, and the Mongols fused Chinese city-building
ideas with their own grand yurts and Lamaist temple forms to build cities
like Urga (now Ulan Bator). In Tibet cities were formed around the large
monastic communities that dominated the spiritual and, ultimately, the
political and economic life of the people. And in the south, the Dian and
Nan Zhao kingdoms built cities, as did the Mongols, with a fusion of local
and Chinese practice.

There were a number of other urban cultures on the frontiers in the
traditional era, including, in the southwest, the Bai and the Naxi, and in
the north and northwest, remnant Christians (such as Nestorians), and, at
some periods, other foreign trade communities (Nepalis, Russians, and
West Europeans, among others). But if the influence over Chinese urban
structure of the Islamic and Lamaist communities was limited, the influence of these other groups was virtually nonexistent. The most cohesive of
them, the Bai and the Naxi, both adopted many aspects of Chinese urban
structure into their own urban traditions quite early on, so that it is difficult to separate their designs from those of the Chinese. Most of the other
groups mentioned were too small and uninfluential to leave a permanent
mark on even local architecture. In the following pages I will review some
of the urban traditions that did influence the landscape-shaping activities
of non-Chinese peoples in Chinese frontier cities.

Islamic City Forms

Whether or not there is an "Islamic city" has been a matter of much
scholarly debate. The consensus view now seems to be that the urban
forms throughout the Islamic world are too varied to constitute a truly
uniform city type. Nonetheless, there are some common elements in urban
areas with high proportions of Islamic residents. The Friday mosque and
the market are typical focal points in the "full-fledged Muslim town" (von
Grunebaum 1961: 145). A. H. Hourani and S. H. Stern, while noting that
there is great variation between Islamic cities, offer the following as possible general characteristics of Islamic cities: a citadel; a royal "city" or

"quarter"; a central urban complex composed of the Friday mosque and secondary mosques, schools, a central market, with special places assigned to specific kinds of craftsmen or traders, and the houses of wealthy merchants; a core of residential quarters, with each quarter separate and ethnically or religiously distinct from the rest; and suburbs and outer quarters containing "recent and unstable immigrants," such as traders and practitioners of undesirable occupations (e.g., tanners; Hourani & Stern 1970: 21–23).

This and most other characterizations of Islamic cities are based primarily on the example of North African and West and South Asian cities. Few scholars of Islamic architecture include the easternmost part of Central Asia (Xinjiang) or any of the Islamic regions of China in their studies; and maps illustrating the distribution of Islamic settlement in the literature seldom indicate any such population inside China.

There are three possible explanations for this omission. First, many in the field consider the sparsely inhabited region of Chinese Central Asia a region of nomadic settlement, without highly developed architectural and urban traditions. As Denis Sinor observes, "The Central Eurasian way of life has never been conducive to the development of architecture. Few cities were built, and in them the skills and tastes of non-native craftsmen— Greek, Iranian, Chinese—remained predominant" (Sinor 1969: 123– 24). Second, scholars of Islamic architecture and urbanization may omit Chinese Central Asia and Islam in China simply because there is a dearth of published material, even in Chinese, on this eastern frontier of Islam. And finally, because China as a whole contains a number of quite distinctive Islamic groups, each with its own architectural and urban traditions, the phenomena of Islamic settlement have perhaps been too widely diffused and diverse to receive attention from scholars of Islam.[1]

There are some predominantly Islamic cities in Xinjiang—cities founded by and still populated primarily by Islamic peoples (usually Uygur). These demonstrate many of the characteristics of cities in the rest of the Islamic world, particularly the Central Asian region. Kashgar, for example, in far western China, preserved Islamic form, with widely distributed mosques, at the close of the Qing dynasty. Its mosques, 126 in all, serving 40,000 people, were said to be on every street (Liu Zhiping 1985: 8). Islamic settlements within Chinese cities, however, cannot demonstrate all of the features that would characterize cities and towns planned and controlled by Muslims. Yet, as later chapters will demonstrate, a number of features of Islamic town structure, to the extent that they can be generalized, are compatible with Chinese urban structure. What is interesting for the present study is the degree to which they have been incorporated into the multicultural Chinese cities on the frontiers.

Islamic Urban Ideals

One argument for the discussion of Islamic city forms is that the practice of Islam ideally requires a specific physical and social structure. This ideal physical and social structure is, in a sense, an ideal for urban form. At the most elemental level the mosque and the marketplace are the primary monumental features of the Islamic city. Mosques should be distributed to facilitate easy access by Islamic residents. Marketplaces would be similarly distributed. There has also been a concern in Islamic tradition with land assignment for religious/secular structures other than mosques, notably those devoted to education and to medicine. And finally, the concept of the Friday mosque is central to the Islamic city. This structure ideally serves as the physical, spiritual, social, and economic center for the entire Islamic community.

According to von Grunebaum, in the classic Southwest Asian Islamic city, the main Friday mosque is located at the crossing of the two main thoroughfares,[2] a position that allows it, and the square at its entrance, to function as the political as well as the religious center of the city. Usually an administrative structure lies directly behind the mosque (von Grunebaum 1961: 145–46). In planned Islamic settlements, though not always in Islamic cities of non-Islamic origin, the mosque is usually centrally located (Alsayyad & Boostani 1989: 461).

Space in the ideal Islamic city of Southwest Asia is divided into separate quarters for national or religious groups and is characterized by strong quarter or group loyalty. This practice derives in part from the congregating tendency of Islamic society. Separate walled wards were often constructed for different nationalities. Arabs and Turks, for example, would live in their own walled quarters, and each would have its own mosques, baths, and markets (von Grunebaum 1961: 146, 149).

The markets in these cities are often organized by trade, with market lanes devoted to particular products. The lanes are laid out in relation to the mosque, with religious and intellectual goods such as books and writing materials closest in. The next section is usually devoted to leather goods, textiles, and precious materials and may be roofed and gated so that it can be locked at night. Still farther out come carpenters, locksmiths, coppersmiths, and other craftsmen. Other markets and trade activities take place in areas well beyond the Friday mosque. For example, caravanserais for itinerant merchants and related service groups, such as saddlemakers, are typically located near the city gates, and the area outside the gates is home to a fair for trade with extraterritorial traders and to undesirable enterprises like tanning (von Grunebaum 1961: 146–47).[3]

Obviously, all facets of the ideal Islamic city cannot be realized in Chinese cities where the Muslims are a minority population. At best, in these cities, Muslims have some control over their own walled districts. The concept of an Islamic quarter within a Chinese city is in fact antithetical to the Islamic ideal that requires living in a place governed by Islamic law. Nonetheless, as the following pages will illustrate, the Chinese city has not entirely precluded the development of some Islamic patterns for urban space. Islamic groups in Chinese cities have tended to create quarters not unlike, perhaps, the ones Arabs and Turks established in Islamic cities in North Africa. The tendency of Islamic urban spatial organization toward developing district cultural quarters means that it is possible for Islamic groups to fit into the Chinese system of segregated quarters.

Islamic Architecture

The mosque is one of the key markers for Islamic neighborhoods throughout the world. The siting and orientation of mosques has been highly formalized since A.D. 624, when Muhammed decreed that the *qibla* (direction of prayer) wall, with its *mihrab* niche containing the Koran, face toward the Kaaba. In theory, then, all mosques are oriented with the back, or qibla, wall facing Mecca, so that worshippers may be assured that they are sending their prayers in the right direction. This ideal is realized throughout the Muslim world, regardless of the placement of the surrounding buildings and roads. In North Africa and West Asia, the requirement has produced elaborate systems for determining the precise angle of orientation for Mecca (Bonine 1987).

Contrary to the dictates of the faith, however, not all mosques are accurately aligned. For example, Michael Bonine has found several incorrectly sited mosques in North Africa. These fairly exceptional misalignments appear to have been the result of minor miscalculations measured by a few degrees (Bonine 1987). But in China misorientation seems to be the rule rather than the exception: the Chinese builders' fixation with the cardinal directions has tended to triumph over Islamic tradition: the majority of mosques are oriented along an east-west axis, so that the orientation of the qibla is due west throughout China. In China Muslims thus typically pray not toward Mecca, but in alignments fixed by concepts of building orientation rooted in Chinese tradition. Fully 21 of the 27 mosques whose orientation I have determined from plans in Liu Zhiping's

TABLE 6
Orientation of Mosques in Selected Cities

City	Orientation	Deviation from due west
Quanzhou	Northwest	26° north
Dali	Southwest	25° south
Zhengzhou	Northwest	20° north
Tianjin	Southwest	17° south
Hebei, Xuanhua County	Northwest	16° north
Kashgar	Southwest	30° south

comprehensive study of mosques in China (1985) are oriented on an east-west axis; only six are oriented along non-cardinal axes.[4] Of the six that are not cardinally oriented, only the Tianjin and Kashgar mosques approach the correct orientation. It is significant that most of the six either were established by non-Hui Muslims or date from a much earlier period (as in Dali) than the bulk of the mosques whose structures still stood in the early 1960s (see Table 6).

Islamic Architecture and District Structure on the Frontiers

Virtually all of the mosques I studied in frontier cities were oriented along east-west axes, with the entrance on the east side and the qibla facing due west. This was true of both very old mosques and more recently built mosques, and of mosques of both Central Asian/Southwest Asian and Chinese style. It is possible that the misalignment of mosques in China may derive not only from the cardinal orientation imposed by Chinese building practices, but also from a misunderstanding of the location of Mecca, or a fortuitous interpretation of its location as being due west. Liu Zhiping, for example, writes that mosques in China are oriented toward Mecca, "which is west of China" (Liu Zhiping 1985: 233). It is possible that in some cases, though the building itself is not oriented toward Mecca, the mihrab niche in the qibla wall, whose purpose is to indicate the direction of Mecca, is angled correctly. I suspect that this is not the case. During the course of the research for this study, however, I was unable to conduct close measurements of the orientation of the mihrab niche. My visual inspection, however, suggests that the mihrab was in line with the qibla wall in all cases. In any event, the worshippers I observed at prayer always kneeled due west.

Mosque design in China often reflects the adoption of Chinese architectural styles. Through most of the history of Islam in China and in much of the country, including the frontier regions, mosques were built in the style of Chinese temples and were virtually indistinguishable in architectural ornamentation from them. For the Hui, a Chinese-style mosque is an architectural reflection of their distinctive mixture of Chinese and Islamic traditions in daily life and practice, similar to their use of chopsticks, the Chinese language, and the *kang* (heated platform) bed.

Islamic residential districts in the frontier cities do share similarities with each other. Most are separate from Chinese districts, both as a result of Muslims' desire to congregate as a community and as a result of Chinese practices that segregated them from the Chinese. Each district has at least one mosque,[5] a market associated with the mosque, and a nearby concentration of Muslim dwellings. Most frontier Islamic communities have a hierarchy of mosques, so that here, as in Southwest and Central Asia, some are designated as Friday mosques, and the rest are reserved for local functions. Finally, different Islamic ethnic groups within a city typically form their own communities, with Hui, for example, living near and worshipping at Hui mosques and Uygur living near and worshipping at Uygur mosques.[6]

In the Islamic traditions of Southwest Asia, unlike the Chinese geomantic tradition, there is no emphasis on orienting houses toward the south. In China, many Hui houses *are* sited along north-south axes, just as Chinese houses are, but the Uygur of the northwest do not orient their courtyard houses to the south or, indeed, in any of the cardinal directions. They conform instead to what Von Grunebaum suggests is the most important orientation for the Islamic house, which is away from the street (Von Grunebaum 1961: 148).

At times the Chinese and Islamic ideals for appropriate architecture have come into conflict. As we have seen, in the Chinese tradition, buildings canted off the cardinal directions may disrupt the geomantic harmony of entire cities, and this is particularly true of relatively large structures such as mosques. Minarets were often considered a problem because they pierced an otherwise balanced landscape, and there have been cases in which a Chinese administration ordered them dismantled to preserve the city's geomantic character (Rossbach 1983: 94).[7] For this reason, no doubt, Chinese-style mosques tend to have no minarets at all or to have modified ones in the form of a squat pavilion or, in recent structures, a tall spire topped with a gently curved tile roof similar to the roofs of a pagoda.

Similarly, Chinese control of the urban plan precluded the Islamic preference for centrally sited monumental elements. For the Chinese, allowing the Friday mosque to stand at the intersection of the two main roads of the city was unthinkable; this was precisely the most auspicious location for their own temples and administrative centers. Indeed, Islamic peoples were often not even permitted to reside in the heart of the walled central city and were welcome only for the conduct of business and other activities during the daylight hours. But Muslims were allowed to place their mosques where they wished within their quarters. Mosques in Lanzhou and Xining were centrally located within the walled Islamic settlements.

Lamaist Cities

Tibetans and Mongolians are not generally thought of in connection with cities and urban traditions. Mongolians are typically linked to the nomadic way of life, and Tibetans to nomadism and high-altitude village-based agriculture. Nonetheless, both peoples do have traditions of building large compact settlements in which the majority of the residents made their livelihood through nonagricultural means. These settlements can be traced to two interrelated traditions: that of the fortified castle of the lord, and that of the monastic settlement. There were also earlier practices of establishing large formally organized royal camps that had proto-urban characteristics in both societies. The Tibetan word for "palace" also means "military camp." The royal Tibetan summer camp that was pitched on the plains north of the Tsangpo River in 822, for example, was effectively a city of thousands. The whole was bounded by a stockade formed of 100 spears inserted in the ground every 10 paces. There were three concentric enclosures, each with a monumental gateway. The tent of the king stood on a platform at the center of the complex (Stein 1972: 109–17). A thousand years later, when important Tibetan leaders such as the Dalai Lama traveled outside their capitals, as was common in the spring and summer months, they usually moved with an extremely large entourage and set up camp in vast, carefully ordered tent cities.

Similarly, the Mongols organized their royal camps of vast numbers of yurts in citylike forms. Even after they built their fortified city at Beijing, it is believed that at least in the summer the nobility resided in tent cities-within-the-city. Large yurts were still used as palaces in Beijing as late as 1353 (Wright 1977: 66–67). Urga (now Ulan Bator, the capital of Mongolia) was long a yurt city as well.

Tibetan urban civilization dates back at least 1,300 years. Lhasa, the earliest known urban settlement, remains Tibet's preeminent city to this day. Xigaze and Gyantse are also centuries old. Lhasa, founded by the Tibetan king Songsten Gampo in the seventh century, has long been the political and religious center for Tibet, but all three of these cities functioned as both monastery towns and trading centers. All three had outdoor markets and permanent shops. The market areas were owned by the monasteries. Both Lhasa and Gyantse were long surrounded by defensive walls (Stevens 1992: 6–7).

The most striking structures in Lhasa today are the Potala Palace and the Jokhang Temple.[8] The original Potala, built as a fort-palace by Songsten Gampo, was destroyed by lightning fires in the ninth century and was not rebuilt until 1645, during the reign of the Fifth Dalai Lama. The city that developed at Lhasa was centered around the Jokhang Temple, about a mile away, rather than around the Potala itself. The primary temple of Lhasa (and of all Tibet), the Jokhang is surrounded by a more or less circular road called the Barkhor, which serves as both a pilgrim's path and a lively market that has long drawn traders from India, Nepal, and China, as well as Tibet. This permanent economic settlement is interdependent with the religious settlement: pilgrims to Lhasa support urban merchants, as well as the religious life of the city. The large monasteries in the area immediately surrounding Lhasa, particularly Sera and Drepung, are often considered part of the city, though they are even farther from the secular settlement than the Potala is. Though the structure of Lhasa is similar in its component parts—monastery, fort, and secular market settlement—to other cities, such as Xigaze and Gyantse in central Tibet and Leh in Ladakh, India, it by no means served as a model for all Lamaist cities. Many lack one or more of the three components. The largest and densest urbanlike settlements in Tibet, aside from the few cities mentioned above, were probably the monasteries themselves.

Before the turbulent events surrounding the incorporation of Tibet into the PRC, most of the larger monasteries of Tibet and Mongolia were for all practical purposes small cities—diversified complexes incorporating not only religious structures, but housing, storehouses, kitchens, administrative centers, and associated markets for thousands of people. The great monasteries of Tibet—Drepung, Sera, and Ganden near Lhasa, Tashilunpo near Xigaze, Kumbum Jampa Ling outside of Xining, and Labrang in southern Gansu—all functioned as cities. Several had monastic populations numbering in the thousands.[9] Since most monasteries controlled domains in the surrounding countryside along with the peasants commended to them, and traders and agriculturalists lived just outside the monasteries in compact villages as well, the total size of these settlements was considerably larger than the monastic population alone.

Perhaps influenced by their knowledge of cities in China and Central Asia, the Mongols built permanent urban settlements from the thirteenth century onward. Their first imperial city was probably Karakorum (Khara-Khorum), established by Ogodei Khan in 1235 near the Orkhon River. Karakorum was a multicultural settlement, which probably consisted of two quarters, one for the Mongols and other northern nomadic peoples, with both government structures and markets, and another for the Chinese, who served primarily as artisans. The city was walled and had four gateways. During the same century Khubilai Khan built the city of Shangdu near Dolonor in present-day Inner Mongolia. Shangdu was built with the aid of a Chinese adviser and had many features consistent with Chinese imperial urban planning (Steinhardt 1990: 120). Both cities were later destroyed and little is known of their form.

Better records survive for other Mongol cities. Yingchang Fu, the administrative seat of the Mongol prince of Lu, was constructed in 1271 and bore a strong resemblance to the Chinese ideals of the Tang period. This square-walled city incorporated Chinese-like symmetry, wide axial streets leading from the gates, and an administrative compound in the center north area. Abandoned in 1370 after a century of settlement, it may have been the only Mongol city to emulate the Tang rather than later Chinese-Mongol urban schemes (Steinhardt 1990: 120, 148–54). The most famous of the Mongol cities of the thirteenth century was Khubilai Khan's capital at Beijing. Dadu (Khanbaligh), on which construction began in 1267, was built to Chinese specifications with the aid of Chinese architects and planners. Hohhot, built by Altan Khan toward the end of the sixteenth century, was probably the third great Mongol city, after Karakorum and Khanbaligh. Urga, or Ulan Bator, was also a major Mongolian urban settlement. Urga was long a fairly permanent tent camp, with the prince's yurt and later the tent temple of the living Buddha placed at the center of a ring of yurts (Jagchid & Hyer 1979: 67–69). By 1908 it had three districts: the monastery, the Lamaist district (with lesser monasteries), and the commercial district, "where important dealings (in cattle, camels, horse, sheep, piece-goods, milk, etc.) [were] carried on between Russians, Mongols and Chinese." The population at that time included 13,000 monks and 25,000 Chinese and Mongolian inhabitants (Richard 1908: 517).

In Mongolia, as in Tibet, citylike settlements sometimes grew up around the local temples. Like the monasteries, some of these temples leased the land they owned in the surrounding areas for marketplaces, thereby attracting trade. In Hohhot, for example, the Dazhao Temple owned land just beyond its grounds that it let to merchants and artisans, creating a small commercial district/marketplace.

According to Frederick Mote, because "the cities of China were not keystones in an important religious institutional structure," they were "deprived . . . of one of the elements that contributed most conspicuously to the importance of cities elsewhere" (Mote 1977: 115). Though Mote clearly overstates the case, since many of the world's cities do not serve significant religious functions, religion did play a central role in both urban morphology and urban functions in Mongolia and Tibet; and consequently, their religiously founded cities diverge fundamentally from the secular cities of China.

Characteristics common to many Lamaist cities include, besides forts and monasteries located near or within the settled area, tight nucleated settlement with narrow streets and multi-story structures, small temples and shrines, pilgrim paths, and market areas. The spatial relationships between these elements vary considerably from place to place. In general the settled area itself is densely packed with buildings, and markets and other enterprises that require open space are located adjacent to, rather than within, this tightly settled area. The location of monasteries, temples, and shrines within or near the settlement shaped the later development of the cities.

Lamaist Geomancy and Cosmology

As in China, architecture and complexes of architecture in Tibet are often conceived as representations of the cosmos. Whereas the Chinese cosmos is a square earth with a round heaven above, the Tibetan cosmos is round in plan, or spherical in three dimensions. Thus, for example, the hemispherical dome in the midsection of many Lamaist stupas (Tibetan *chorten* or shrine) is a replica of the dome of the cosmos (Speiser 1965: 169).[10] One of the most important elements in the design of Tibetan temples and cities is the incorporation of a series of concentric circumambulation routes at different scales, ranging from routes within temples to routes around monastic complexes or an entire city. If there is a monastery, temple, or shrine within the city, then the streets and buildings around it will accommodate a path surrounding the entire structure for circumambulation.[11] The Jokhang Temple at Lhasa, for example, is at the center of three concentric routes: the inner route within the temple, the Barkhor surrounding the temple, and the Lingkor surrounding the city (Qiao Xi & Yang Yusheng 1985a: 113).[12]

The city of Lhasa, with its concentric plan around the Jokhang Temple, is a fairly good approximation of the Tibetan cosmological circular form. The extent to which these ideal representations are incorporated into complete city plans varies considerably; although all cities with temples have circumambulation routes, many do not attain the near-perfection of Lhasa's form.

Geomancy has a long tradition in Tibet, where it has been associated primarily with temple design and placement. Elements of Tibetan geomancy and augury predate the Tibetans' adaptation of Chinese concepts, but Tibetan geomantic practice has been influenced by traditions from China since at least the seventh century, when the Tang princess Wencheng came to Tibet to marry King Songsten Gampo. When Princess Wencheng set out from China in 640, she and her substantial entourage brought divination charts in the form of a "striped scroll of trigrams" that allowed her to calculate favorable conditions and evil impediments. She later consulted these charts to find the best sites for temples in the Lhasa area, including the Jokhang, the most holy temple in Tibet. But another Chinese princess, who arrived there in 730, probably made a more important contribution. The books about fengshui she brought with her would have been of more use than the few scrolls of Princess Wencheng (Aris 1980: 12, 14, 22).

This is not to say that Tibetan geomancy is simply a borrowing and adaptation of the Chinese system. In fact it is a synthesis of Chinese ideas and older Tibetan traditions of shamanism and Bon religion. According to Keith Dowman, all the emperors before Trisong Detsen (r. 754–97) were "deeply involved in pre-Buddhist shamanism and the 'black arts' of astrology, geomancy and divination," although they also practiced Buddhism (Dowman 1988: 286). This "shamanistic science," called *tsuklak*, included elements of both Iranian Manichaeism and the oldest animistic traditions of Tibetan religion. Dowman explains that though the ancient Bonpos of Tibet probably did not have the kind of formalized geomantic system the Chinese had, they did seek auspicious sites on the basis of combinations of natural elements like caves and rocks. Traditional identification of these places as auspicious was so strong that temples continued to be built on sites auspicious to the Bonpos even when, in later years, their construction contravened Chinese-style geomantic principles (ibid., pp. 286–88).

Chinese geomancy was interpreted in a distinctive manner in Tibet. Whereas the Chinese developed an image of the world as a landscape of dragons and power, the Tibetan cosmos was manifested as a demoness. The Chinese princess Wencheng contributed to the development of a Tibetan system of geomancy by divining that the whole of Tibet was "like a Demoness fallen on her back" (Dowman 1988: 284). Thus, the first 12

Tibetan temples, for example, are said to have been carefully sited so as to control the demoness embodied in the Tibetan landscape by pinning down her arms, legs, and other body parts (Aris 1980: 15). The demoness lies with her head in the east and her feet in the west, with limbs spreadeagled toward the northeast, southeast, northwest, and southwest. The Jokhang Temple in Lhasa is literally at the heart of this system: it is said to hold down the demoness's own heart (Dowman 1988: 284–86).[13] So auspicious was the Jokhang's site that the temple was built on it even though a pond was located there. In fact the divination indicated that a pond was the appropriate site for the temple. The pond was drained and filled in, as shown in wall paintings inside the Jokhang, but Tibetans believe it still lies beneath the temple.

In addition the Tibetans reinterpreted or changed certain aspects of Chinese cosmology. Though they adopted the idea of associating the cardinal directions with colors and animals and indeed with the tortoise, dragon, bird, and tiger, for example, they matched these animals with different directions (see Table 7). It is not clear whether these shifts originated in reinterpretation or simple error. A number of Tibetan beliefs regarding the orientation of buildings to directions and topography differed from Chinese beliefs as well. The Tibetans held that a building was best sited with the land "open" to the east, "heaped" to the south, "straight" to the west, and "curtain like" to the north (Aris 1980: 21). The ideal Tibetan site would thus appear strikingly different from the Chinese choice, facing mountains on the south rather than the open space and water source preferred by the Chinese.

Tibetan beliefs about temple siting are relevant to studies of Tibetan urbanism since many urban settlements followed or were concurrent with the development of temples. According to the reincarnate Tibetan lama Thubten Legshay Gyatsho, the requirements are a tall mountain behind (on the north; see below) and many hills in front, with two rivers converging in front from the right and the left, all in a central valley filled with

TABLE 7
Chinese and Tibetan Associations with the Cardinal Directions

Cardinal direction	Chinese association	Tibetan association (animal / natural feature)
North	Black tortoise	Black tortoise / bearded rock
East	Azure dragon	Striped tiger / whitish path or rock
South	Red bird	Azure dragon / river and/or verdure
West	White tiger	Red bird / red earth or rock

SOURCES: Aris 1980: 21; Thubten Legshay Gyatsho 1979: 29.

rocks and meadows resembling heaps of grain. The features surrounding the site are sometimes referred to as the four earth pillars: (1) a wide expanse in the east, (2) a hill in the south, (3) a rounded, low hill in the west, and (4) a mountain like a draped curtain in the north. This confirms Michael Aris's observations and suggests that the "tall mountain behind" is probably on the north side ("a mountain like a draped curtain"). The southern side is thus perhaps the "front," and the north the "back." At the same time there are several features that must be avoided, notably ravines in a lower valley on the east, water plummeting into a cavern on the south, pitfalls in the path on the west, and seething, roiling water on the north. Moreover, a road leading southwest means friends and good fortune, but a road leading to the northwest is a portent of demons and enemies (Thubten Legshay Gyatsho 1979: 29).

Thubten Legshay Gyatsho also outlines some strategies for verifying a good site. One is to dig a hole in the ground about 18–20 inches deep, then refill it. If there is more than enough dirt to fill the hole, it is a good site. Insufficient dirt indicates a bad site. This seems to indicate a preference for clay soils and a dislike of sandy ones. So does a second test, in which a hole of similar depth must be able to retain water long enough for a person to walk 100 paces away and return (Thubten Legshay Gyatsho 1979: 30).

Naturally, no site is perfect, and there are, as in the Chinese system, methods for fixing inauspicious elements, and for purifying the site as a whole. Bad characteristics can be overcome by a careful placement of stupas, religious paintings, and other objects, the recitation of prayers, and the performance of rituals. And an entire site can be purified by drawing a serpent-bellied earth deity there according to a prescribed set of geometric proportions so as to locate the deity's right armpit. Treasure must then be buried at that spot before building commences (Thubten Legshay Gyatsho 1979: 30–32). Here, again, in contrast to the Chinese system, the site is equated with a living being whose form and demeanor influence the placement of objects and performance of rituals. These are carried out at points that represent different parts of a humanlike figure.

The siting of Tibetan Buddhist temples was not based on geomancy alone. In the early years monasteries were built on valley bottoms in secluded and protected sites, and the forts of the elite on prominent sites. The Fifth Dalai Lama, however, bent on giving Buddhism a higher profile, advocated constructing monasteries at more visible sites that commanded a view of the surrounding area, with the result that from the mid-seventeenth century on, new monasteries were built on hilltops and overlooking the countryside (Snellgrove & Richardson 1986: 199). Such sites also gave them both the spiritual advantage of spatial separation from the adjacent valley settlements and a defensible position, an important factor in Tibet's often turbulent political history. Hills, particularly those in the vicinity of monastic settlements, were sometimes considered holy or auspicious. The hill on which the Potala Palace stands is a holy one, as is Chokpori Hill, adjacent to it.

Lamaist Geomancy in the Frontier Cities

Tibetans do not constitute a sizable population in any of the cities in this study (though many live just outside of Xining), and Mongolians are numerically significant only in Hohhot. In this section I will concentrate on the geomantic aspects of the structures that are the most visible contribution of the Lamaist people to the urban landscape of these places—the monasteries and temples.

The Kumbum Jampa Ling Monastery outside Xining combines Tibetan and Chinese architectural styles. Though the geomantic aspects of the site are acceptable in Tibetan terms, many of the Chinese-style buildings in the complex are not well sited by Chinese standards. The entire Kumbum Jampa Ling complex lies on the sloping sides of a stream valley along a southwest–northeast axis. Important structures are ranged along both sides of the stream, with the main gates in the temple courtyard on the north side and the doors into individual buildings varying between north-facing and west-facing entrances. It is clear, then, that there has been little adherence here to the rules of Chinese geomantic siting, even though the influence of Chinese architectural practice is very strong, with a number of buildings appearing completely or partially Chinese in style.

For example, the Tsong Khapa Memorial Hall, one of the most sacred buildings in the complex, is aligned on the cardinal directions, with the entrance on the east. This orientation fits relatively well with Aris's scheme for Lamaist geomancy, which calls for an entrance on the "east" or "open" side. The positioning in this case was guided by the most sacred object at the monastery, the tree associated with Tsong Khapa. The Tsong Khapa Memorial Hall was built with its entrance adjacent to this tree. In Chinese geomancy a tree at the entrance to any building is quite ill-omened (Lip 1979: 44). The Dafosi, a Tibetan temple in Xining, also had a tree in the courtyard immediately adjacent to the main temple entrance.

The Third Reincarnate Lama Hall at Kumbum Jampa Ling is oriented on the cardinal directions, with the entrance on the north. The Great Illumination Temple (Dazhao), however, is constructed along a southeast-northwest axis, with the entrance on the southeast side of the building—this despite the fact that the building is quite Chinese in style. The hall for the Protection of the Buddha-Truth maintains a southwest-northeast axis, with the main entrance on the southwest. The Great Hall of the Scriptures is oriented only slightly off the cardinal directions, built on an east-west axis, with the entrance on the east side.[14] None of the complexes where living Buddhas and monks reside are aligned with the cardinal directions. Thus, though the Tibetans who occupied these temples made extensive use of Chinese-style architecture, they borrowed its surface forms without following the conventional Chinese siting principles.[15]

The Lamaist temples in Hohhot, in contrast to those in Tibet, Gansu, and Qinghai, adhere closely to Chinese-style geomantic principles. The Dazhao and the Xilituzhao Lamaist temples are aligned along north-south axes like Chinese temples, and front entrances to buildings are on the south side, also in accordance with the Chinese system. Unlike the Tibetans, who combined their own architectural system with the Chinese system, the Mongolians did not have an indigenous architectural tradition appropriate to Lamaist temples. The Mongols may have made even more use of Chinese craftsmen than the Tibetans did at Kumbum Jampa Ling. We know that at the time the temples were being constructed, the Mongols were employing Chinese refugees from the White Lotus Sect purge as architects and builders of other structures in the city (Hyer 1982). In Mongolian temple architecture both Tibetan and Chinese elements were borrowed, but Chinese geomantic principles were adhered to in Hohhot in preference to Tibetan principles.

Nonetheless, the temples of Hohhot have a distinctly Mongolian look and feel. The Xilituzhao temple, for example, while constructed in a mixed Chinese/Tibetan-style architecture, is faced in brilliant blue tile—a color favored by Mongolians but rarely if ever employed by the Chinese or the Tibetans. Decorative elements such as paintings, roof ornaments, and carved balustrades at all of Hohhot's Mongolian temples likewise tend toward Mongolian themes. And, in earlier times, it would have been common to see yurts pitched in and about the temple courtyards, because though the Mongolians so often used Chinese- and Tibetan-style structures for their monumental edifices, they continued to prefer yurts for residences.

Though the non-Chinese peoples of the northwestern Chinese frontiers did not possess urban traditions as uniform and highly structured as those of the Chinese, they did have a number of beliefs and customs regarding the shaping of urban space. These beliefs in the ideal conception or construction of settlements had an impact on the participation of the non-Chinese peoples in Chinese frontier cities. While they were constrained by the physical expression of Chinese urban form, they were also acting within their own cultural bounds.

6

City Forms on the Frontiers

This chapter will explore how multicultural interactions have influenced urban form on the frontiers.[1] Of course, over China's long history there have been variations in the ways in which Chinese and non-Chinese co-existed in frontier cities and the ways in which these social relationships affected urban morphology and landscapes. In both the Tang dynasty and the Yuan dynasty, multicultural expression was tolerated within city walls to a far greater extent than in other historical eras. During the Yuan period administrators even permitted the construction of non-Chinese (and non-Mongolian) temples and mosques inside the city walls. A resurgence of Chinese nationalism with the advent of the Ming dynasty led to greater segregation between peoples. This spatial segregation continued and was in some ways increased by the Manchu during the Qing dynasty.

All of the cities in this study, as was discussed in Chapter Three, have long been dominated by the Chinese and by Chinese urban practices. Each, as was argued in Chapter Four, embodies the classic principles of Chinese urban planning in its morphology. Indeed, frontier cities seem to meet some of the fundamental dictates of Chinese cosmological ordering of city form more closely than the cities of eastern China. Frontier cities were built along basic conceptual patterns that had been stripped down to their essentials and show little evidence of the subtle modifications of basic patterns that were often introduced in eastern cities in response to site-specific conditions. For example, as I will demonstrate later in the chapter, frontier cities tend to have been built in square or rectangular forms more frequently than eastern cities.

At the same time, however, multicultural values and urban structures did produce certain features that became characteristic on the frontier.

Multiple-walled forms and ethnically differentiated suburbs outside the walled core, for example, served to accommodate the multicultural situation within the basic cultural and social framework of Chinese cities. The Islamic districts—particularly those in walled areas just outside the gates of the central cities—were characterized by distinctive patterns of spatial and social organization that contrast with those in the Chinese sections of the cities. They are still the most readily identifiable of the non-Chinese neighborhoods in the frontier cities. As William Jankowiak has observed in Hohhot, for example, the Hui formed true ethnic enclaves that survived even the massive influxes of Chinese and Mongolians after 1949 (Jankowiak 1993: 31).

It is more difficult to generalize about the impact of Lamaist peoples on frontier city morphology. As noted, relatively few Tibetans live within the cities under study. Some have settled in Xining and Lanzhou, but the districts they live in do not display any distinctive Tibetan morphology.[2] Most reside in nucleated settlements at a slight remove from the two cities. And while there are greater concentrations of Mongolians in certain parts of Hohhot than in others, there are no readily apparent morphological differences. Nor does the architecture give any clue to the existence of ethnic neighborhoods.[3] This undoubtedly is a reflection of the high degree of cultural assimilation of Hohhot Mongols noted by Jankowiak (1993: 5).

Walled Cities

One of the most fundamental features of Chinese urban morphology is the shape of the walled city. The first effort to identify and analyze Chinese city form on the basis of the pattern of city walls was carried out by Ishiwari Heizo, who conducted field investigations and collected city maps while on military assignment during the Japanese occupation of China.[4] Sen-dou Chang developed the first English-language analysis of the distribution of different types of Chinese walled city forms and highlighted the variety of city shapes found in China and their differing regional importance (S.-d. Chang 1961, 1970). Chang found that rectangular wall shapes were particularly characteristic of imperial capitals and important cities in North China, that round shapes were more common in the south, and that irregular shapes were likely to occur in regions of rugged topography. He also noted that "cities with multiple walls were of high political or strategic importance, usually imperial capitals, provincial capitals or, in a few cases, frontier towns with military significance" (S.-d. Chang 1970: 67).

The literature has lately been enriched by the contributions of Nancy Schatzman Steinhardt and Wu Liangyong. Several of the forms Steinhardt identifies in her book on imperial city planning (1990) bear a striking resemblance to frontier forms, suggesting that frontier cities are in some ways straightforward replications of ideal types for administrative cities. Wu Liangyong, a professor of architecture at Beijing's Qinghua University, has provided a useful classification of Chinese traditional urban forms (published in English), which is particularly valuable for his finding that irregular walled city shapes are correlated with the market and handicraft towns that developed during the Ming and Qing dynasties (Wu Liangyong 1986: 110, 124).

Wall Forms in Imperial China

I have classified 233 Chinese cities by their pre-1949 wall forms on the basis of plans, drawings, and photographs culled from a number of sources.[5] This classification is based on an analysis of inner wall forms, rather than on the shape of the entire settlement (which might also include outer walled or unwalled suburbs). The shape of the innermost city walls most directly reflects the planning, policies, and attitudes of those who established and maintained the cities. These walls usually represent concerted efforts by administrators to raise or rebuild entire walls as a whole, rather than the process of piecemeal accretion through which outer walls and settlement patterns were often shaped over a period of centuries by many different administrators and planners.

Most but not all of the 233 cities were county (*xian*) capitals before 1949. They varied considerably in their population and size. There was no way to determine the exact sizes, in either area or population, for many of the cities on the basis of the maps, and accordingly I did not classify them by size or use a minimum size as a basis for disqualification. The data for the survey were not strictly representative. The materials available are richer for some parts of the country than others. In particular the province of Shandong may be overrepresented. Northwestern China may also be overrepresented to the extent that I have included a larger proportion of small cities from that region than from other regions (particularly the cities taken from Mannerheim 1940). The large number of Shandong cities, however, may be appropriate to the extent that it is reasonable to suppose that Shandong, then as now, had by far the highest percentage of China's total urban population and the densest concentration of xian capitals. And the smaller walled cities and towns in Xinjiang and Gansu are worth including, given the generally smaller size of urban places in the far

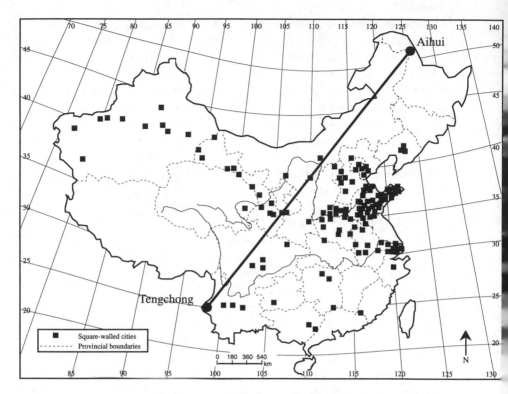

Map 12. Square-walled cities, ca. 1900. Note that the cities in Gansu and Xinjiang follow the main Silk Route.

west and their significance as urban centers in these regions of low population density.[6]

I have analyzed regional variation in city shape using three different definitions of 'west" to compare western China with eastern China: the Aihui-Tengchong division discussed earlier in this book (which I have indicated on Maps 12–15),[7] the 105° east longitude line, and the 110° east longitude line. The Aihui-Tengchong division enables comparison with other published discussions of the Chinese frontier. The 105° line divides China's area approximately equally east and west, while the 110° line includes more of the western provinces of Ningxia, Gansu, Sichuan, and Guizhou in the western region.

I initially classified the cities into five categories: square, almost square, round, almost round, and irregular (see Table A.1). I then collapsed these categories into three—square, round and irregular—on the assumption

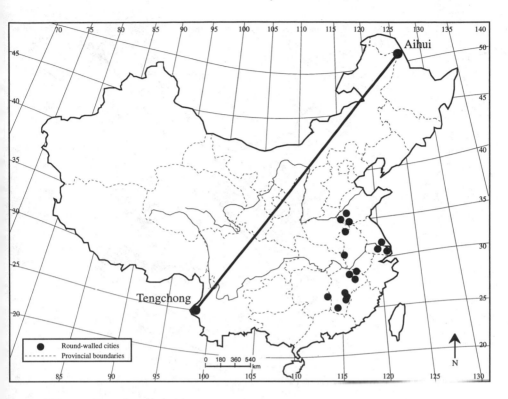

Map 13. Round-walled cities, ca. 1900.

that cities that were almost square, with only slight irregularities, represented attempts by their builders to create square forms, and that those that were almost round were intended to be round.

In undertaking this survey, my primary goal was to examine the degree of correlation between the walled city and Chinese ideals for its orientation and shape. But determining the outline of the former walls can be a considerable challenge. Many traditional Chinese gazetteers and maps indicate cities with a stylized rectangle or oval rather than an accurate representation of the walls. And historical maps of individual cities sometimes portray them as far closer to the ideal in shape than seems to have been the case (see, e.g., Steinhardt 1990: 83, 146, 147, 160, 161, 171). To avoid this error of idealization, I attempted, whenever possible, to employ multiple sources and to cross check information with contemporary street patterns and other indicators.

The classification is reasonably accurate for the forms of the cities as

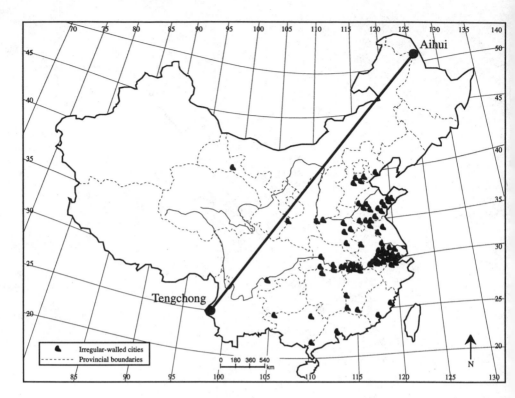

Map 14. Irregularly shaped cities, ca. 1900.

they were in approximately 1900, before significant destruction of city walls began. At that point the cities were still by and large of the shape they were given during the massive reconstruction of city walls during the Ming dynasty. There are some notable exceptions, however. Some cities on China's eastern seaboard were significantly modified during the period of European influence and occupation in the nineteenth century. But even so, this influence on the morphology of the municipality as a whole rarely affected the basic form of the walled Chinese city, which typically became a district of an enlarged and Westernized city. More pertinent to urban morphology on the western frontier was the fairly widespread tendency of the Manchu to construct walled garrison cities adjacent to existing cities. The construction of such garrisons was perhaps the most dramatic contribution of the Qing era to urban form in China, and accounts for many of the "twin cities" identified in this survey.

The set of cities I examined generally conformed to the Chinese urban

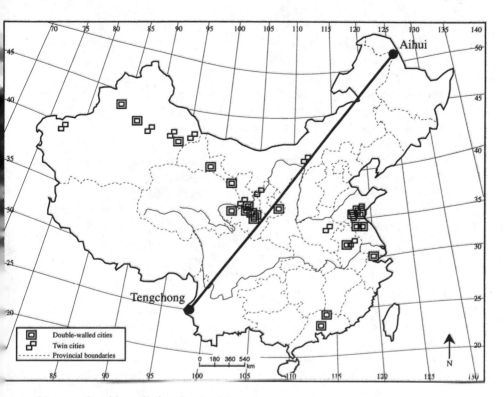

Map 15. Double-walled and twin cities, ca. 1900.

ideal in terms of their orientation (see Table A.2). Alignment on the cardinal directions with a southward orientation was by far the most consistent pattern. Some 84 percent of all the cities met this goal. Cities west of the Aihui-Tengchong line had a higher tendency to be oriented on the cardinal directions, with 97 percent of those cities oriented on a north-south axis. Results were similar when the other two definitions of west were used: 90 percent of the cities west of 105° east longitude and 88 percent of cities west of 110° east longitude were oriented with the cardinal directions.

Achieving a square or even a rectangular city shape proved to be less important than proper orientation. Only 61 percent of all the cities were square or rectangular in shape. A full 32 percent were quite irregular in shape. Only about 7 percent were round. As can be seen in Maps 12–14, all of the round cities and nearly all the irregular cities were in the east, with the round ones concentrated primarily in the riverine and mountainous regions of central China, and the irregularly shaped cities concentrated especially along the course of the Yangzi River. About equal numbers of cities in eastern China were either irregular or square/rectangular. Frontier cities, however, demonstrate a strikingly greater adherence to the ideal square city form. All save one of 29 frontier cities west of the Aihui-Tengchong line were square (97 percent). Using alternative definitions of the west, 97 percent of cities west of 105° and 88 percent of cities west of 110° were square.

Frontier cities were also much more likely to have double or twin walls than were the cities of the east (see Map 15). By my definition for this survey, double-walled cities had two or more walled areas that share at least one common wall. Twin or multiple cities had two or more spatially separate walled areas which were administered jointly (see Fig. 8).

Only 15 percent of the 233 cities in the survey fell into the twin/multiple and double-walled categories, with slightly more double-walled cities than twin cities. There is, however, a significant correlation between both of these forms and the frontier regions. Well over half (62 percent) of the cities west of the Aihui-Tengchong line were twin or double walled. Nearly half (47 percent) of cities west of 105° east longitude, and 44 percent of cities west of 110°, had multiple or double walls. In contrast, only about 8 percent of cities east of the Aihui-Tengchong line, or east of 110° east longitude, were twin or double walled. About 10 percent of cities east of 105° east longitude were twin or double walled.

In sum, there was a striking spatial differentiation in traditional Chinese urban forms, and though ideals for urban form were often realized, deviations from the ideal were very common. Frontier cities in this sense seem to better fulfill the ideals that originated in the core area than do those of the core itself. As noted earlier, this probably reflects the character

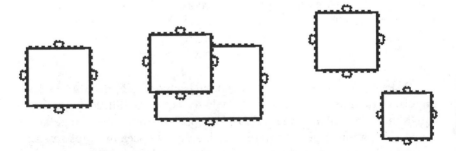

Fig. 8. Generalized Chinese city forms on the frontiers. From left to right: single-walled, double-walled, and twin-walled forms.

of frontier forms as simplified replications of the ideal. Cities in the east may demonstrate a more sophisticated understanding on the part of their builders and designers of both the nuances of the ideal form and the high-level geomantic processes through which, for example, the sharp corners of a square city might need to be rounded to better integrate with auspicious features of the landscape such as water and hills.

Wall Forms on the Frontiers

While the central-walled areas of frontier cites are usually square in shape and carefully oriented to the cardinal directions, the settlement areas outside the central walls tend to be far more complex and to reflect Chinese adaptation to the multicultural characteristics of frontier life. About 45 percent of the frontier cities surveyed were either twin cities or double-walled cities. All but one of the five primary cities in this study are in one or the other category. Both of these complex forms derive from ethnic differentiation and from cultural and social relationships between ethnic groups. All are "new" forms introduced by the Chinese during the course of their occupation of frontier territories. Unlike many of the world's invading forces, the Chinese usually did not take over indigenous cities to use for their own purposes. Rather, they nearly always built their own cities, either on the ruins of indigenous cities or adjacent to still-functioning ones. In the construction of city walls, the Chinese left a relatively long-lasting physical representation of the socio-spatial relationships between peoples on the frontiers.

The earliest walled frontier cities established by the Chinese were invariably single walled. This form, which usually began as a simple fort or citadel, was often maintained in subsequent expansions or rebuildings. During the relatively cosmopolitan eras of the Tang and the Yuan, Chinese and non-Chinese peoples sometimes lived together within single-walled cities. The construction of double or multiple walls tended to be a response to substantial growth in the size of the Chinese population (a rare phenomenon on the frontier in traditional times) or the development of non-Chinese communities in the immediate vicinity of the cities. These became more common during and after the Ming era. This rising incidence may reflect the dynasty's promotion of more rigid distinctions between peoples. The twin or multiple-walled city became widespread under the Qing, an outgrowth of the preference of the Manchu to construct separate walled quarters for themselves whenever possible.

The single-walled form: Kunming. Most cities in the core area had only a single wall. But in times of relative peace, auxiliary settlements might develop outside the wall, clustered around the gates and lining the approaching streets. These settlements were populated by both non-Chinese peoples and relatively low-status Chinese. Some Chinese lived outside the gates by choice to avoid the taxes levied on city residents. In late imperial times these settlements outside the gates sometimes grew to become much larger and more populous than the walled city area itself.

The Ming city at Kunming, the most recent of the walled cities on the site, resembles the Chinese late imperial single-walled form. As is common for southern cities, its square form is rounded at the corners, in this case a reflection of topographic and possibly geomantic considerations. The city's single wall was surrounded by a moat. From at least the early nineteenth century on, large trade communities lay outside the south and east gates. These clustered settlements contained a relatively high proportion of non-Chinese residents, and much of the city's economic life took place there. For example, the largest and most active markets were located in the Hui neighborhood outside the south gate. The area to the south was also where the French and other Westerners settled during the late nineteenth and early twentieth centuries.

Double-walled forms: Xining, Lanzhou, and Urumqi. The most notable and well-described double-walled city in all China is Beijing. It is typical in the sense that this form was often adopted for imperial capitals, as a means of clearly separating the city of government from the city of commerce, or, particularly from Tang times onward, of accommodating and controlling the foreign populations that gathered at the seat of empire. Steinhardt traces this pattern back to as early as the Warring States period.[8] The capital of one of the Three Kingdoms, Shu (modern-day Chengdu), was clearly a double city, though Steinhardt notes that there is some question whether the two cities were actually attached. Here the adjoining cities were referred to as the greater city and the lesser city, with the greater city serving as the site of the palace city, and the lesser as the abode of nobles and merchants. Steinhardt traces the use of the double city for imperial capitals onward through the Northern and Southern Dynasties, Liao, and Jin periods (Steinhardt 1990: 89–90).[9]

Double walls were employed on the frontier also as a means of dealing with multicultural situations in the urban environment. The multiple-wall system served as a means of differentiating and defining status among various non-Chinese groups. The outer walled suburbs, usually called *guanxiang* or *guo*,[10] were the abode of high-status non-Chinese peoples, as well as lower-status Chinese, such as traders. Most often the non-Chinese residents were Muslims, who gained their status in Chinese society through the key role they played as merchants and bankers. And many of these high-status Muslims were Hui, a group sharing relatively more cultural traits with the Chinese than others. The construction of secondary walls tends to correlate with the development of a large Islamic population; most were erected after the Hui's emergence as a distinct group during the Ming dynasty, which was also a time of active wall construction throughout China.

Little or no attention was given to preserving the square form of a city in the addition of secondary walls around suburbs. The double-walled forms reflect the Chinese view of the cosmos, with the square, ordered Chinese world surrounded by the less-ordered (by Chinese standards) world of the non-Chinese. Although the outer walls of the walled suburbs were attached to the primary city wall, and thus changed the city's overall shape, they seem to have had little effect on the cosmic significance of the central square inner wall.

Xining, Lanzhou, and Urumqi are among the many cities of the northwest with walled Muslim suburbs (see Maps 4, 5, and 8). Xining was a single-walled fort-settlement until the early Ming, when the enclosed area was reduced by about half (for a new circumference of about 4.5 km), and a walled suburb was constructed outside the east gate to house the Muslim population (*Qinghai lishi jiyao* 1987: 129–30). Soon after the suburb was completed, in 1380, the Great Mosque of the Eastern Suburb (Dong guan Qingzhen Dasi) was built. Initially a small structure, it was later expanded several times to become one of the four great mosques of the northwest (Zhu Xianlu 1985: 173–75). The suburb continued to grow during the Qing dynasty. By the end of the nineteenth century, this "considerable suburb, peopled almost exclusively by Moslems," had an estimated population of nearly 10,000, as against some 15,000 Chinese within the city proper (Grenard 1891: 204).

The complex nature of social relations as they are articulated in ethnic segregation is further evident in Xining's Tibetan community. Although Xining was a double-walled city, from the Yuan through the Ming and Qing dynasties, some Tibetans, unlike Muslims, lived within the inner walls. At least one Tibetan Buddhist temple was established in Xining proper. This was the Great Buddha Temple (Dafosi), on Great Western Street near the center of the walled city. Thus there was likely a small Tibetan-Mongolian monastic community within the city walls as well (see *Qinghai lishi jiyao* 1987 for a photograph of the temple).

Lanzhou also remained a single-walled city until the Ming dynasty. In the early Ming years the walled city center was about 3 km in diameter.

During the Xuande era (1426–36), a 7-km-long wall was built to form a suburb that wrapped around the city from the northwest to the southeast (see Map 4). Then, in 1447, another suburb was attached to the first, enclosing the eastern side of the core area. This configuration survived into the twentieth century (Liu Man & Zhao Yun 1986: 423). During the Qing dynasty a separate walled Manchu fort was built southwest of the walled city as well.

Urumqi had the most complex structure of the cities in this study. Not only was it a twin city, but the city of Dihua was double walled as well. The Chinese said of the gate between Dihua's northern area and the southern Muslim suburb that those inside the gate lived on wines and meats, while those outside lived on bones.[11] The suburb was inhabited by a mix of communities differentiated not only by ethnicity but also by place of origin. There were, for example, a Uygur community, several Hui communities (such as those from Qinghai and Shaanxi), and a community of Tatars. The foreign community (primarily Russian but also German and American traders) that established itself in the early twentieth century lived within or just south of the suburb (Zan Yulin 1983: 37).

Twin cities: Hohhot, Urumqi, Lhasa, and Xiahe. Twin cities were typically the result of occupying forces establishing a new city or fortified settlement adjacent to an existing indigenous settlement without destroying it. The two settlements were administered as one, and many urban functions were shared between the two places.[12] Although there were twin cities before the Qing era, this settlement pattern was particularly favored by the Manchu, who often established a walled city-fort just outside an indigenous (or Chinese) city for administrative purposes. The Manchu may have created as many as 34 twin cities in the north and northwest alone by the late eighteenth century (S.-d. Chang 1977: 92).[13] This practice seems to have been adopted from the exclusionary policies of the Chinese. Only Manchu lived in the Manchu city, though other peoples were allowed inside the walls during the day. Both Hohhot and Urumqi are examples of this form. The formation of twin cities allowed for the survival of the indigenous city, but, at the same time, had significant impact on the city and its residents.

Hohhot's status as a twin city may date back as early as the fourth century, when the city of Shengle (12 km north of the present city) had two walled areas, one for the old Chinese garrison and the other for the Toba (northern Wei) administrators.[14] In any case it assumed the twin form in the eighteenth century, when the Manchu established the garrison city of Suiyuan approximately 2 km north of the Chinese/Mongolian city of Guihua. Suiyuan, built between 1735 and 1739 as headquarters for the eighth army, was much larger than Guihua, enclosing not only barracks and housing for a sizable support staff but also agricultural fields (see Map 6). Some attempt had been made to link the two cities both practically and symbolically by placing a bell tower (normally found near the center of the city) at the crossroads of the roads that passed between them (Dai Xueji 1981: 49–50). In the economic boom that followed, a large Muslim community developed, sprawling north and east from Guihua toward Suiyuan. Guihua retained its earlier character, however, unwalled except for a small Chinese administrative settlement cloistered in a square compound in the northern section of the town and with narrow, twisting alleys leading away from a single straight north-south street. The city's life continued to be shaped by its numerous temples.

Urumqi, as mentioned earlier, was both a twin city and a double-walled city. Dihua, the first city, was built on Manchu orders in 1767 by Chinese craftsmen and workers, who were allowed to live within its irregularly shaped walls as the work proceeded. But soon after the city was completed, the Manchu established another city 2.5 km to the northwest. Gongning Cheng, built in a perfect square, was reserved exclusively for the Manchu. A river flowed between the two cities (Zan Yulin 1983: 23).

The twin-city pattern is a contemporary as well as historical Chinese city form. In recent times twin cities have emerged on the frontier as a result of the establishment of new Chinese settlements adjacent to existing indigenous ones to house the influx of Han Chinese into the frontier areas. Lhasa and Xiahe (Gansu) are good examples of this phenomenon, as is Lijiang, the Naxi and Chinese city in northwestern Yunnan.

Lhasa is a study in contrasts. The old city, in the eastern section, is a compact settlement of two- and three-story Tibetan "row houses," with shops lining the first floor frontage along the wider streets. This dense settlement, as discussed earlier, is centered around the Jokhang Temple; the main street, the Barkhor, encircles the temple as both a circumambulation route and a bustling market street lined with shops and stalls. Side streets are narrow and crooked, mere alleys in most cases to provide access to the courtyard residences.

In contrast the recent (post-1959) Chinese settlement area that sprawls to the west, east, and north of the old Tibetan town has wide tree-lined avenues and large work-unit compounds spaced widely apart that combine residences, offices, and factories. This new town, with its tin-roofed buildings of cement or cement block, has the air of a rapidly constructed Nevada boom town. The Chinese Lhasa carries on little trade; it is primarily engaged in production, administration, and military activities.

Xiahe, in southwestern Gansu Province, is the site of both a Tibetan settlement associated with Labrang Monastery and a Chinese settlement associated with Xiahe's position as the prefectural capital of the Gannan Tibetan Autonomous Prefecture. The population of the town, which administers an 8,600-km^2 area, was about 12,000 in the early 1980s. From all appearances the Chinese settlement adjacent to Labrang is a post-1949 phenomenon, and data on the development of industries and social services indicate that it grew relatively slowly in the first PRC years. Before the Cultural Revolution, development here was essentially confined to equipping the town with the kind of basic services, "cultural" institutions, and education facilities that are common to most Chinese towns today. These efforts brought a post office (1953), a cadre school and a food products factory (1955), a bookstore, a cultural palace and a movie theater (1956), a middle school (1958), a radio station (1960), a teachers' school (1962), a fuel company and an auto repair shop (1971), and an elementary school for minorities (1974). After the stagnation of the Cultural Revolution, the emphasis switched to a more locally oriented program. The years 1979–80 saw the founding of a hospital and research institute for Tibetan medicine, and 1983 brought a factory for the production of Tibetan carpets. A more sweeping measure came in 1984, with the prefectural government's passage of a resolution calling for an increased exploitation of the area's natural resources such as forestry and pastoralism (*Gannan zangzu zizhiqu gaikuang* 1987: 15, 252–69). Many of the buildings I saw seemed only a few years old. Among them were several shops catering to the tourist trade, a department store, and two hotels. Improvements were also being made to the basic infrastructure, particularly the main roads running through the town.

Districts

During the period from the Han to the Tang dynasty, the basic unit of organization within the Chinese city was the ward: a walled area with one to four gates that were normally closed at night and could be defended against unwanted intrusions. Each ward contained a number of courtyard dwellings whose residents usually had clan or native-place ties. There was little commerce on the streets of Chinese cities during this period, and trade took place primarily in designated markets or in the wards themselves with itinerant peddlers (Y.-c. Kao 1981: 27–48).

Little is known about the precise location and arrangement of these internal elements of Chinese cities, since most historical city maps show only the walls and prominent landmarks.[15] Steinhardt observes, for example, that the wards and markets of Han Chang'an were not shown on any plan (1990: 67). Nonetheless, written accounts and archaeological work suggest that the wards were, more often than not, placed in fairly uniform grid patterns, and that designated markets might appear in almost any square of the grid, within or outside the walls, save only the ceremonial center itself.

Significant changes in the socioeconomic system, such as the growth of commercialism, led to change within the organization of the Chinese city during the latter half of the Tang dynasty. Shops began to appear outside the designated markets areas, first within residential compounds, and later on the streets themselves, in order to take advantage of business after the wards were closed for the evening. Land within residential wards became available for purchase, and land rents became differentiated according to commercial access. Shops were built on the streets along the ward walls, creating commercial districts with residences arranged in courtyard blocks behind (Y.-c. Kao 1981: 48–54). Specialized trade districts developed, to give rise eventually to trade guilds (ibid., p. 55). Other districts began to specialize in services such as warehouses. Tea shops, wine bars, and general stores were established throughout the city (He Yejiu 1980). What resulted was a city akin in many respects to the mercantile cities that developed in Europe during the Middle Ages.

The transition throughout China from cities organized on the ward system to a more outward and commercially based neighborhood structure coincided with the development of truly multicultural cities, based on a Chinese model. The increasingly open mercantile nature of the cities created more opportunities for non-Chinese to participate in the urban economy. The development of occupational districts also made the establishment of separate non-Chinese quarters an easy and relatively logical extension of the city. Since non-Chinese districts usually specialized in different trades from those practiced by the Chinese, they were easily separated from them. Non-Chinese enclaves became both ethnic enclaves and distinct economic districts within the urban system.

Bazaars and Market Districts

Open stall markets have long been a part of the Chinese urban landscape, and outdoor night markets were especially popular in traditional China. Despite repeated closures (followed by reopenings) during the Maoist period, they have been in service in most cities since the late 1970s. Street markets are particularly interesting in the frontier context, not only as a means through which nonresidents of the walled city—usually non-

Chinese peoples or rural farmers selling produce—could trade inside the walls, but also, in the case of the Muslim traders of the frontier, as a key aspect of the articulation of Islamic urban forms.

Islamic markets were similar enough in form to Chinese markets that they were easily incorporated into the fabric of the Chinese city as a whole. Bazaars combining street markets, mosques, and courtyard housing were incorporated into the large unplanned blocks between main thoroughfares in the outer suburbs of the traditional Chinese city. The spatial and social patterns established by this form have survived beyond the dismantling of city walls and massive development of the post-1949 period.

Islamic markets continue to flourish in frontier cities today. In Xining, for example, the traditionally Islamic area around the Great Mosque remains the liveliest market district in the city. Modern development, however, has overtaken the main thoroughfare, which has been widened and lined with modern shops. Market stalls selling both goods and food now line the side streets and back alleys of the neighborhood. Map 16 shows the location of the city's open-air markets in relation to the former city walls.

Here, as in other frontier cities, the mainly Hui-operated outdoor markets and bazaars serve as outlets both for city products and for products

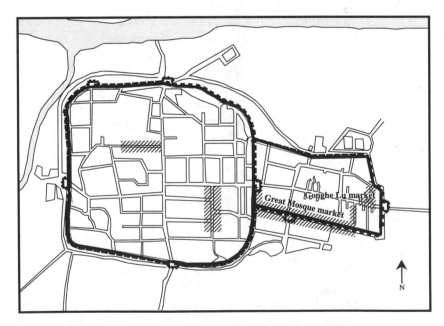

Map 16. Street markets in Xining in relation to former city walls.

of the city's hinterland. The Hui have long acted as middlemen, for example, for Tibetan goods. Tibetan traders sell wildcat pelts, horns, traditional medicines, and woven goods to the Hui merchants of Xining, who then retail these items in their stalls. Hui merchants also run shops and market stalls outside of Kumbum Jampa Ling Monastery and Labrang Monastery that stock goods for a Tibetan clientele.

In Urumqi this enterprise is concentrated in the southern (formerly walled) suburb area, where markets line many of the back streets honeycombed between the mosques (see Map 17). There has been some attempt at state control of this activity: the market streets here are roofed, and merchants are assigned stall numbers and identification cards. This market has many of the features of a Central Asian bazaar, with a large number of stalls specializing in carpets, brassware, Islamic religious parapher-

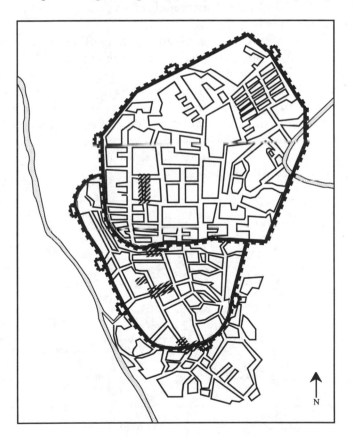

Map 17. Street markets in Urumqi in relation to former city walls.

nalia, shish kebab, and flat breads. Urumqi also has an active street market district at the southern base of Hongshan. This market may have developed out of the temple fairs associated with the cluster of temples at the base of Hongshan during the pre-1949 (and particularly the pre-1911) era.

Lanzhou has several street market areas (see Map 18). One is in the Qilihe district, between the west train station and the Yellow River. This large Islamic market, sprawling into several side streets off the main east-west road (street marketing is not permitted on the main street itself), offers a wide array of goods, including clothing, spices, prepared and bulk foods, vegetables, shoes, and household products. The market is as lively at night as it is in the day, with flocks of customers coming in to eat or drink tea at one of the many Muslim-run noodle shops in the evenings. There is another large Islamic market closer to the old walled city to the east, at the Xiaoxihu bus stop.

Lanzhou also has a Chinese street market in the alleys near the former Temple of the Town God (which is now a community center). It dates to the time when this quadrant of the central walled city contained several temples and adjoined the seat of local government. It has stalls for services such as tailoring and shoe repair, as well as for clothing and produce. A relative latecomer is the street market that developed in conjunction with the development of the Railway Workers' Village with the coming of the railroad to Lanzhou in the 1950s. This is a large, covered bazaar with booths for all sorts of merchandise.

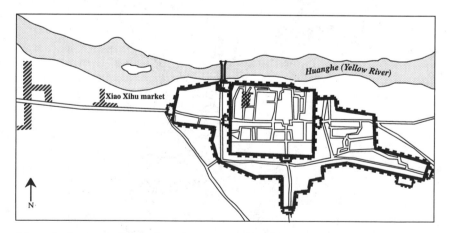

Map 18. Street markets in Lanzhou in relation to former city walls.

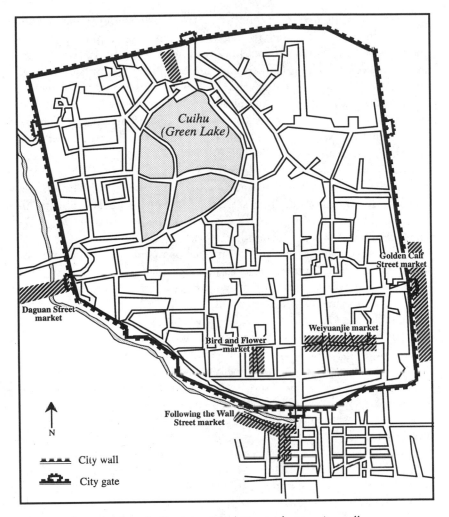

Map 19. Street markets in Kunming in relation to former city walls.

Kunming, more than any of the other cities in this study, is a city of street markets (Map 19). This is partially attributable to a year-round mild climate that is ideal for outdoor markets and to its character as a southern Chinese city. Those cities tend to have more street markets than the northern cities have. The largest market is located on Following the Wall Street (Shuncheng Jie), which once paralleled the city wall outside the south gate. A predominantly Muslim market in a district with three mosques and a high proportion of the city's Muslim population, it contains whole streets devoted to vegetables and meats, plus numerous noodle shops and bread shops selling traditional Hui foods. Another Islamic market runs along Golden Calf Street (Jinniu Lu) outside the old east gates. This area was once part of a narrow strip of development between the wall and the Panlong River. The market was traditionally known for the sale of beef, horse, and sheep meat and products and as the tanners' district (Wang Xuepei et al. 1987: 184–86). A third street market, also outside the old walls, lies in the south, along the road to the Daguan Temple—one of several temples (most important, White Horse Temple, or Baima Miao) that once stood along this road. The market probably developed originally to serve the temple traffic. It is a mixed Chinese and Hui market, but primarily Chinese, with a wide variety of goods. The Hui in the main operate noodle shops.

There were also at one time a number of markets and shopping or service districts within the central walled area that contained permanent shops as well as open stalls. Downtown streets in pre-1949 Kunming were known for specializing in certain goods (see Wang Xuepei et al. 1987 for a list), including Guanghua Road, known for its tailor shops and hat and boot shops; Fuzhao Road (also known as Xiyuan Street), known for tailor shops and copper and jadeware shops; Minzhu and Minquan streets, also known for tailor shops and copper shops; Changchun Road, known for food and drink shops, hide and fur goods shops, and curio shops; and Weiyuan Street (also known today as the number-two vegetable market), which was a vegetable marketing area. South Huashan Road (or Suyuan Street) was known for embroidery shops, painting and calligraphy shops, and framing shops; it was a meeting place for the cultured and educated citizens of Kunming. West Huashan Road (or Maixian Street) was a street for sellers of thread. Jingxing Street (or Liangdao Street), starting from the Liangdao Yamen (Provisions and Food Administrative Center), was lined with small hotels and inns; and Gongyuan Street (or Qingyun Street) was a street of tea shops. There was a famous flower market as well (ibid., pp. 184–86).

Today the primary street markets still active in central Kunming are the bird-and-flower market, which runs south of Victory Auditorium (Shenglitang), a vegetable market that runs east-west on Weiyuan Street downtown, and a vegetable market north of Green Lake. The bird-and-flower market, where pets and houseplants are sold, is so famous that anticipation of bird shopping was a popular subject of conversation among businessmen I met on the long train journey from the northeast.

Hohhot: spirit wall outside the former governor's yamen near the center of Suiyuan, the Manchu city at Hohhot. The wall runs east-west and stands about 15 m south of the south gate of the yamen. See Chapter Four.

Kunming: district of migrants from Guangdong (see Map 20). Note the light stucco exterior, with shop fronts on the first floor. See Chapter Six.

Kunming: district of migrants from Jiangsu. Note the light stucco exterior on the first floor, with wooden facade above. These structures are strictly residential.

Kunming: district of wealthier migrants from Guangdong.

Kunming: district of "older Yunnan families" (Ming dynasty migrants).

Lanzhou: Temple of the Town God. Typical Chinese temple style, with courtyard and drum tower to the left of the entrance hall. See Chapter Seven.

Xiahe, Gansu Province: Labrang Monastery. See Chapter Seven.

Roof detail from Labrang Monastery.

Xining: Tibetan ceremony carried out in the Chinese-style courtyard of Kumbum Jampa Ling Monastery. Note the Tibetan-style roof ornaments. See Chapter Seven.

Detail of doorway at Kumbum Jampa Ling Monastery. Note the Chinese-style form, with Hui-style carved flowers and a Tibetan-style roof ornament.

Hohhot: Xilitu Temple. Mixed Tibetan and Chinese-style architecture decorated with blue brick. Blue is the preferred color in Mongolian design. See Chapter Seven.

Courtyard of Xilitu Temple. Chinese-style architecture, with a baita-style pagoda.

Lanzhou: Central/Southwest Asian–style mosque, constructed in the mid-1980s, overlooking the Yellow River. See Chapter Seven.

Xining: Railway Workers' Village Mosque. The dome is purely ornamental; the main hall of the mosque does not have a domed ceiling. See Chapter Seven.

Xining: the Great Mosque. Chinese-style structure with Tibetan-style roof ornaments.

Detail of Tibetan roof ornaments on the Great Mosque.

Urumqi: the Great Shaanxi Mosque. A Hui mosque built in Chinese style. See
Chapter Seven.

Urumqi: the Qinghai Mosque. A Hui mosque under reconstruction (1988) in the
Central/Southwest Asian style.

Hohhot: the Great Mosque. A Hui mosque built in Chinese style, with minaret. See Chapter Seven.

Detail from the Great Mosque in Hohhot. Note the Chinese-style eaves decorated with Islamic crescent moons and a depiction of the Koran.

Detail from the Great Mosque in Hohhot. Lamaist temple-style roof ornament.

Most of the customers in this market are Chinese, although some Bai shop there as well.

The vast array of produce available in the Weiyuan Street market demonstrates three levels of trade linkages. Products such as eggs, fish, and tomatoes represent the market gardening and trade activities between people in Kunming city center and the surrounding villages. Alongside such produce as pineapples and bananas brought in from the southern provinces (including Yunnan) are carefully wrapped pears and apples, shipped all the way from Tianjin and Shandong, to be sold (at a relatively dear price) as rare and highly valued commodities in Kunming.

Another market, which operates near the entrance to Kunming Normal University, demonstrates a different sort of diversity. Both patrons and merchants are more ethnically mixed than in any of the city's other markets, with peoples from southern Yunnan, such as the Dai, coming to trade vegetables and other food products with the Bai and other nationalities of the Kunming region.

Hohhot's street markets are closely linked with the old city forms. The main north-south streets of both the old Manchu city and the old Mongolian-Chinese city are centers for street market activities. Other street markets, in the streets south and southwest of the train station and in the street running past the university, are of relatively recent origin.

What is striking about the markets in Chinese frontier cities today is the extent to which they have persisted in their traditional locations. Even though the walls have long since disappeared, Chinese people still tend to conduct much of the trade inside the former walled areas, and Hui and other Islamic groups still operate markets outside them. This perpetuation of the social and spatial divisions established by city walls holds true for residential patterns as well.

Residential Districts

Before 1949 urban residence tended to be differentiated more by place of origin or ethnicity than by wealth, though wealth could be a factor within or between place-associated districts. Unlike economic differentiation, social differentiation does not necessarily engender architectural or morphological differences. Nonetheless it was a significant variant in the landscape for the residents of traditional Chinese cities.

Since 1949 many people have been relocated on the basis of work assignments, so that the formerly consistent nature of place-associated neighborhoods has been altered by both in-migration and out-migration. Even so, there is still a fair amount of differentiation by place or ethnicity in frontier cities. In part this is because most of the post-1949 in-migrants have been housed in new built-up areas. But there has also been a tendency to organize occupational groups into work units within traditional neighborhoods. For example, Hui butchers have been organized into butchers' cooperatives without any necessity for changing their place of residence or work.

Much of the population of Kunming reflects historical migrations. Descendants of the people exiled from Nanjing by the First (Ming) Emperor, now considered "Yunnan" people, occupy the core of the old walled city (Map 20).[16] Adjoining them is a district peopled by families of Cantonese origin, one of two differentiated on the basis of the wealth of the ancestral families. The houses in the less historically wealthy Cantonese district, which lies outside the old walls, are built in a distinctive coastal shop style, with two-story yellow stucco buildings ornamented with flat yellow stucco pilasters worked in pseudo-classical patterns. The houses in the wealthier Cantonese district near the center of the city conform more closely to the classic Kunming style, combining white stucco ornamentation with wooden construction, but they are fancier than other Kunming houses, with second floors overhanging the street by about 2 ft. (a design that required a substantial use of costly lumber). There is also a district inhabited by people whose Jiangxi, Hunan, and Guangzhou forebears probably came to Kunming during the nineteenth and twentieth centuries. Their neighborhoods contain some houses built in distinctive canal-fronting styles, with elements such as elaborate window boxes not found in other areas.

Islamic districts are typically areas of dense housing, with mosques and markets scattered throughout. Hui houses are not usually outwardly different from Chinese houses, but it is easy enough to spot a Hui neighborhood if it has signs in Arabic, extensive markets for meat and other animal products, or Muslim restaurants. Most Kunming Hui neighborhoods have all these elements. In this form they are not incompatible with some of the ideals, or at least the norms, for Islamic districts in other parts of the world. The Islamic peoples of China's frontier cities tend to live in separate districts, just as their counterparts are wont to do in the cities of Southwest Asia. However, whereas in those cities Islamic groups of differing origins tend to live in separate districts, the mixed Islamic populations of cities like Urumqi, Lanzhou, and Xining were walled off only from the Chinese. Hui and Uygur lived within the same walled area in Urumqi, for example. Nonetheless the Islamic peoples were (and remain) socially

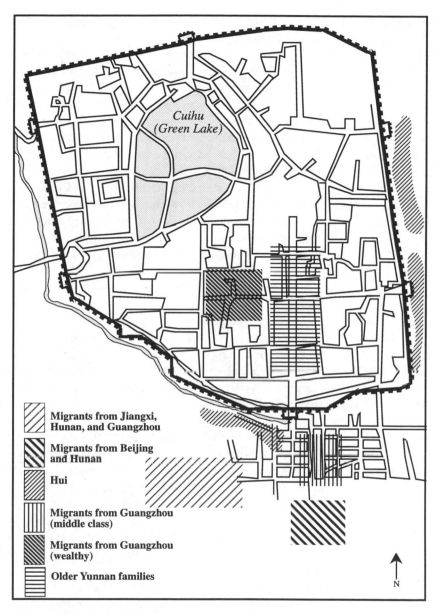

Map 20. Residential districts in Kunming in relation to former city walls. The "older Yunnan families" are descendants of the Nanjing residents who were sent to Kunming by the first Ming emperor. The class designations on the Guangzhou groups refer to their pre-1949 status.

differentiated by place of origin and nationality, maintaining separate mosques and living in clustered communities around them.

Class differentiation as well as ethnicity influenced the establishment and location of districts in the traditional Chinese city. Spatial differentiation within the Chinese city was expressed not only in the relatively simple status hierarchy between residents inside and outside the walls, but also in the economic differentiation of districts within and immediately outside of the city. Typically the poor lived within and just outside the east gate, the rich lived within the west gate (and perhaps outside of it), and the poorest class lived near the southern gate. There is an old Chinese saying: "The poor at the east gate, the rich at the west gate, and the beggars live at the south" (Wu Liangyong 1986: 123). This class-based district structure may have some relevance for the cultural segregation of the frontier cities. Islamic peoples, regardless of their wealth, were relegated to lower-class districts. The Islamic districts of Urumqi, Xining, Lanzhou,[17] and Kunming were located on the east and/or the south side of the city.

The traditional distinctions between Chinese and non-Chinese persist in the core areas of most frontier cities. In Urumqi Han Chinese still occupy much of the old central walled area, which has few non-Chinese residents. Uygur, Hui, and other non–Han Chinese peoples are concentrated in what was once the walled southern suburb. There is a smaller concentration of Uygur and Hui living northwest of the old city proper. And Uygur and Hui continue to live in outlying villages, growing fruit and vegetables for sale to city dwellers.

In Xining, too, the formerly walled central area is still occupied primarily by Han Chinese, and the formerly walled eastern suburb remains a primarily Muslim district. There are, however, several more recently settled Muslim districts. Just west of the river that parallels the path of the former western wall, there is a Muslim settlement on the south bank of the Huangshui River and another adjacent to and south of the former west gate (also across the river from the old city proper). Two other settlements lie north of the Huangshui: one across from the old walled Muslim suburb (east of old Xining) and one northwest of the train station, in the new village established for railway workers.

Tibetans who are integrated into the economies of the cities have tended to live apart from the walled areas. In Xining, for example, Tibetans live in villages scattered among the foothills of the valley in which the city is located, separated by as much as several miles from the densely settled city proper. This separation is not exclusion on the part of the Tibetans—some Hui and Chinese share their villages—but the separation from the Chinese city does allow for compact, mostly Tibetan settlements to function away from the immediate control of the city. These villagers are nevertheless economically tied to the city, supplying vegetables and fruits for Xining's markets, as well as a relatively large share of wool and other pastoral products.

Lanzhou's old central walled area also remains an area of primarily Chinese residence. Some Islamic people still live in the former outer walled suburbs, the traditional home of the city's Muslims. But the bulk of the Hui and other Islamic peoples now dwells west of the city, particularly in the twentieth-century developments of the Qili District, and just across the Yellow River, west and east of Baita Shan. There are also Hui and Dong-xiang villages outside of Lanzhou that are integrated into the urban system through the sale of agricultural products to city residents.

Hohhot, perhaps as a continuing legacy of its founding by the Man-chu, is an exception to the ethnic districting found in other frontier cities. It no longer has a Manchu population large enough to sustain the distinc-tion between the old Manchu city and the old Mongolian/Chinese city. Both areas are now occupied primarily by Han Chinese. But the city's substantial Hui population does live in its own enclaves, as it has done since long before 1949. The largest concentration is in the district north of the old Mongolian/Chinese city that bears their name—Huiminqu (Hui People's District). By contrast, the city's numerous Mongolians are scat-tered throughout the city. Many are recent migrants who live in modern factory-associated apartment blocks typical of post-1949 development (Jankowiak 1993: 31).

Efforts to build cities in the manner of those of eastern China clearly dominated the siting, construction, and management of the frontier cities in traditional times. Yet the prevalence of double-walled and twin forms is evidence of compromise in the multicultural environments of the fron-tier. The cohesion and cosmological integrity of cities were allowed to lapse in non-Chinese sections, enabling residents to follow some of their own traditions in land use and architecture. Thus a frontier form emerged in which the inner walled areas of the city were structured by ortho-dox Chinese practice while the outer walled and unwalled areas, though still controlled by the Chinese, were structured by their multicultural populations.

7

Monumental Architecture in Multicultural Contexts

Peoples with very different cultures meet on the Chinese frontier. At the least, this multicultural interaction might be expected to lead to innovation and borrowing in the realm of material lifestyle, and this is certainly true in the case of architecture. Given the constraints placed on overall city form by Chinese beliefs about city building, it is not surprising that from early on, the most active arena for the expression of multiculturalism was in the construction and decoration of individual structures. This chapter will survey the monumental architecture of both Chinese and non-Chinese peoples in each city as artifacts of the social, cultural, political, and economic processes that shaped it.

Monumental architectural style on the frontier ranges from a strict adherence to Chinese norms in administrative complexes to an eclectic mixture of cultural styles in Tibetan Buddhist temples and Hui mosques. The vernacular architecture also varies widely and is far more influenced by the availability of building materials in differing environments. Taken together, the assemblage of monumental and vernacular architecture is relatively more varied than in China's core area. Chinese and non-Chinese peoples alike have gone to some lengths to produce culturally distinct architectures under sometimes difficult conditions. The persistence of these distinctions to the present day is testimony to continued cultural identity separate and apart from identity with the State and the majority culture, even as the borrowing of styles represents the diffusion of ideas and techniques between neighbors.

Differentiating monumental from vernacular architecture in frontier regions is essentially a matter of perspective. Just as in the United States, for example, some would label the frontier forts, county courthouses, and churches of the American West monumental, while treating the whole of

Native American, Spanish, and Creole architecture as vernacular, so, on the Chinese frontiers, some have tended to limit monumental architecture to works carried out and controlled by the Chinese state. This perspective, however, gives little value to the monumental functions and designs of non-Chinese built landscapes. In this chapter I will discuss both Chinese and non-Chinese monumental architecture.

Chinese Monumental Architecture

Monumental architecture embodies the ideals and expresses the social position of its builders. The design and construction of monumental structures, as well as their placement within the urban landscape, is a deliberate expression. Nonetheless the designers and builders of monumental architecture must respond to the constraints of site-specific conditions. These constraints include not only limitations on building in terms of available sites, building materials, expertise and labor, but social and cultural constraints as well, particularly those constraints placed on minority peoples by a majority group.

Traditional Chinese monumental architecture was primarily either administrative or religious in function. There is little to distinguish the basic architecture, form, and site planning of administrative and religious structures and complexes. Monumental Chinese architecture was so standardized that even the houses and palaces of the elite bore a strong physical resemblance to Buddhist, Daoist, Confucian, and popular temples, and to administrative complexes. Variations in style were more a product of regional and historical differences than of functional variation. Government buildings in frontier regions under Chinese control tended to be archetypically Chinese in style and plan. Religious structures demonstrated far more variation and intermixing of styles and plans.

In contrast to the construction of government buildings, the blending of styles involved in the construction of religious structures in multicultural settings was rarely a specific attempt to convey a sociopolitical message.[1] Rather, more often than not, the blended styles of these structures were the contributions of local craftsmen who made use of the materials at hand. Whereas builders of government-sponsored structures were usually able to produce eastern Chinese-style structures even when the proper materials and skilled labor were locally scarce or nonexistent, the builders of non-Chinese religious structures often lacked the authority and social position to overcome such constraints and thus adapted to local natural and human resources.

Chinese monumental architecture is best seen not as an array of individual structures, but rather as complexes of buildings and landscaping. Generally speaking, each structure within an architectural complex functions as a single "room," and its courtyards and paths serve as "hallways" or "circulation space." Thus a traditional Chinese architectural complex may appear physically as an assemblage of structures but functions much as a single building. The main buildings are arranged along a succession of courtyards (usually two or three) set out on a north-south axis. Side courtyards flank the north-south median axis as well. In such arrangements, the main courtyard at the southern end of the axis serves as the main entrance to the public areas of the complex while the side courtyards are usually private residences and offices. Inside the southernmost courtyard a bell tower and a drum tower often flank the main entrance. In a temple, in the usual sequence of structures, one moves successively through an entrance hall to a courtyard, to a hall with a shrine, to a second courtyard, to a hall with a more important shrine, to an inner courtyard, and finally to a building that is slightly larger than the others, which contains the temple's most sacred shrine. This same hierarchical progression from south to north is found in administrative (yamen) complexes, with the chambers of officials ranging from lesser to greater importance taking the place of the shrines, and with a progression from public access areas at the south toward successively more private space to the north.

Every building in a complex is built on the same model. Though the buildings at the rear tend to be grander, with more roof levels, than the buildings at the front, all share certain features: a terrace with balustrades, pillars, a timbered structural framework, and one or more tile roofs. The terrace is a rectangular pedestal that stands high above ground level and forms the foundation of the building. It is usually constructed of rammed earth faced with brick or stone. Sometimes the terrace is built of several successively smaller tiers. Both the terrace and the stairway leading into the temple are bordered by balustrades. Wooden pillars placed in a grid pattern on top of the terrace support the heavy timbered structure of the building itself. The pillars are built in a variety of shapes and proportions. Tang dynasty pillars, for example, were quite sturdy, while Ming and Qing pillars were far more delicate. Buildings always have an even number of pillars (at least four). The pillars are augmented by load-bearing walls on the east and west.

The roof is supported by a structural framework that has been described as "perhaps the most original feature of Chinese architecture" (Pirazzoli-T'serstevens 1971: 88). This structure, composed of wood joined by mortise and tenon, is always rectangular, even if the outer walls are round or polygonal. It is constructed as a series of rectangular frames atop each other, each level with successively shorter beams on all four sides. When this structure is covered with roof tiles, the tiles rest in an inward curve, creating the sweeping curves that are the hallmark of the Chinese-style roof.[2] Since the entrance to the building is in the center of the long side of the rectangle, not in the gable end, as in many Christian churches, the roof is an important element of facade design. By Ming and especially Qing times, roof design had become so elaborate that the rank of buildings in the administrative hierarchy was displayed in roof design. The highest status was accorded to a hipped double roof, followed by a half-hipped double roof, a simple hipped roof, a simple half-hipped roof, and a gabled roof (Pirazzoli-T'serstevens 1971). But the most elaborate element of structure and roof design was the bracket system for supporting the eaves. This complex system involved stacked clusters of wooden brackets, which by Ming and especially by Qing times were less functional than ornamental and created extremely elaborate cornices.

Chinese temple and palace architecture is often quite colorful. Many of the structural elements, such as wooden pillars and roof beams, are usually painted red. The series of wooden latticed doors that make up the front facade of temples are also often red. The bracket systems supporting the roof are usually decorated in elaborate polychrome designs of red, blue, white, green, and gold. The round ends of eaves, projecting slightly from the roof itself, are usually painted with symbolic designs (such as swastikas, a Buddhist symbol, or peacock feathers, a symbol of administration).

Administrative Complexes in Frontier Cities

As one of the primary physical expressions of the power of empire on the frontier, administrative complexes were usually built in archetypical Chinese style, with little or no condescension to local customs or styles or compromise if the customary materials were not readily available. Because, as mentioned earlier, these structures do not differ significantly in their basic forms from Chinese temples, I will let the discussion of temple architecture serve for both.

Classic yamen were built in all the frontier cities with which I am familiar, and all were built in Chinese style, with a series of courtyards and pillared buildings with grand "flying" roofs (see Fig. 9). A number of these complexes were enlarged during the Republican era, but even the plainest concrete-block additions were ornamented with elaborate Chinese roofs to make them blend in with the old ones. The provincial administration

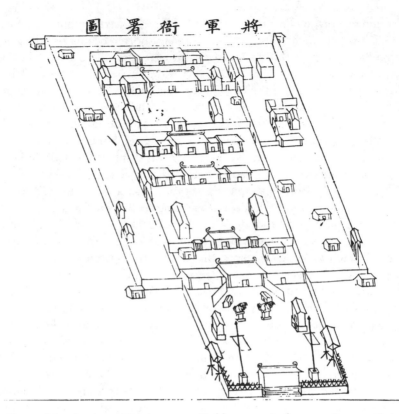

圖 署 衙 軍 將

Fig. 9. Manchu Army Headquarters, Hohhot, a typical yamen. Source: *Guisui xianzhi* ca. 1946.

complexes in both Xining and Lanzhou are good examples of enlarged yamen that have been maintained to the present day. (The preservation of such traditional governmental structures will be discussed further in Chapter Nine.)

Chinese Temples on the Frontier

There are many diverse types of Chinese temples, and there are different styles of temple within each of the three main Chinese religions—Buddhism, Confucianism, and Daoism—and within shrines and temples devoted to spirits in the pantheon of Chinese popular religion. Yet there has also been considerable consistency in architectural style. The main variations are usually found in the painted decoration and the ornamentation or embellishment of the buildings. Rarely is there any departure in the structure or design of the temple complex itself. There have of course been some variations in style over time, and there are geographic variations as well. Both kinds of variations are far more significant than those between temples belonging to different religions.

The majority of Chinese temples within the walled area of cities are devoted to Buddhism, Confucianism, or Chinese popular religion. Typically a city had numerous Buddhist temples, including temples to the Maitreya Buddha (Milefo) and the Great Buddha (Dafo), and many others centered on such figures as Guanyin (the Goddess of Mercy), Guandi (the God of War), and Chenghuang (the City God). It also had ancestral halls and other religious structures, all built in temple style.[3]

Chinese temples in the frontier cities are, for the most part, not remarkable in either form or function in comparison to Chinese temples in the east of China. This high degree of similarity is in and of itself interesting. Chinese living on the frontier went to great lengths to replicate Chinese temple forms in spite of environmental obstacles such as scarce supplies of wood and other building materials.

The history of Buddhist temples in the Kunming area predates the Mongol conquest and Yunnan's incorporation into the empire. But once the diverse cultures of the Mongol empire were established in Kunming, a panoply of religious structures were built, including mosques as well as temples devoted to Buddhism, Daoism, and Confucianism. Several important temples and pilgrimage sites were also established within a 15 kilometer radius of the city. Unfortunately, because of damage wrought during the insurrections of the nineteenth century, many of the structures one sees today are relatively recent (late nineteenth or early twentieth century) reconstructions.

According to a local gazetteer (*Kunmingshi zhi*), most of the 32 major temples in the Kunming area in the 1920s were Buddhist institutions. The Yuantong Temple is Kunming's largest and oldest surviving Buddhist temple. Its roots go back to the Nan Zhao period (about A.D. 800), and to the small Butuo Buddhist temple that once stood on Yuantong Hill, behind the present site (Wang Xuepei et al. 1987: 26; Yu Xixian 1962: 29). From 1314 to 1320, the temple was rebuilt and relocated to its present site at the base of the hill (*Yunnan — keai de difang* 1984: 388). The Ming historian Li Yuanyang wrote that the grounds of the temple included a fruit orchard, a vegetable garden, an arbor, and a bamboo grove. Yuantong Temple was rebuilt several times during the Ming and Qing (1686) dynasties (Yu Xixian 1962: 28).

According to the *Kunmingshi zhi*, the grounds were refurbished and opened as the Yuantong Public Park in 1921. Thus the temple had apparently fallen on ill times in the early twentieth century and been taken over by the local government.⁴ After 1949 the temple was used as the headquarters of the Yunnan Buddhist Association (Wang Xuepei et al. 1987: 26) and as a branch of the Yunnan Provincial Museum (*Yunnan — keai de difang* 1984: 388). It currently serves both as the headquarters of the Yunnan Buddhist Association and as an active, functioning temple. The main hall was restored in 1979, and during the mid-1980s another major restoration of both the buildings and the statuary was carried out.

One of the more notable of Kunming's other temples is the Wuhua Temple on Wuhua Hill, a Confucian institution dedicated to the God of Literature constructed at the beginning of the Yuan dynasty. Though much of the complex was destroyed during the uprisings of the late nineteenth century, the main hall was preserved into the Republican era. Other temples once stood on these slopes as well, including a Dragon King temple right at the top of the hill (*Kunming xianzhi* 1902: 18). None have survived.

Urban expansion has brought some temples that were previously outside the walls into the city. A photograph of Kunming's east and west pagodas taken around 1930 shows them standing in fields surrounded by only a few one- or two-story buildings. Both were spectacular in their early surroundings. The east pagoda, 50 m high, with 11 stories, was built between 1465 and 1488. The west pagoda, 42 m high, with 12 stories, was built in 1410 (Boerschmann 1931: 104). Today these pagodas are surrounded by tall buildings and can only be seen by pedestrians standing directly in front of them or glimpsed from a few high vantage points, such as the fourteenth floor of the Kunming Hotel.

There were also many temples nestled among the numerous low hills that surround Kunming on the west, north, and east sides. Southwest of the city, bluffs rise from the shores of Lake Dian to form a dramatic set of relatively high hills that are also the site of several famous temples.

Lanzhou had three great temples. Two stood outside the walled city: the Great Buddha Temple (Dafo Si), rising on the hills to the south, and the White Pagoda Temple (Baita Si), rising on the hills to the north. The Great Buddha Temple, known today as Five Springs Park (Wuquan Gongyuan), dates from a Buddhist temple complex first built in 1372 with a Great Buddha hall (Dafo Dian) and a Diamond Sutra hall (Jinwang Dian). It grew to encompass another 30 buildings, but most were burned down during uprisings in 1781 and 1861. Some of the structures were rebuilt in 1875, and others in 1907. More extensive renovation took place in 1919, when several new buildings and an elaborate *bailou* (memorial arch) gate were added. After 1949 the complex was taken over by the local government, which opened it as a public park in 1954. In 1988 the park offered an array of summer fair activities, tea shops, sports, and exhibitions. The Great Buddha Hall was undergoing restoration, and some Chinese Buddhists had begun to burn incense to the Buddha there.

North of the old city center, across the Yellow River, the White Pagoda Temple stands out against the steep cliffs. This Ming dynasty Buddhist temple is particularly interesting because the heritage of the Silk Routes is evident in its architectural decoration. Several of the halls are embellished with elaborate carvings of exotic beasts like camels and elephants. The white pagoda that gives it its name stands at the highest point in the complex, flanked by a bell tower and a drum tower (containing a drum that was apparently imported from India during the Ming dynasty). This complex also became a public park in 1958. Today it attracts both young and old to sip tea and play board games in the shady courtyards of the lower levels, and, on the rare clear day, to hike the winding paths to the pagoda for the best view of Lanzhou around.

The largest and most well known of Lanzhou's temples was the Puzhao Si, a Great Buddha temple established during the Tang dynasty near the center of the walled city. The complex ultimately came to have seven great halls, as well as bell and drum towers. All were built in Tang architectural style, and all save one were devoted to Chinese Buddhist practices. This interesting exception, the Hall of the Wheel of the Laws (Falun Dian), was built specifically for Tibetan Buddhist ceremonies and devotions during the Yuan dynasty. The wooden mani (Tibetan prayer wheel) inside the hall was approximately 10 m tall, with eight sides and six levels. Each face at each level was decorated with a Buddha. The four pillars surrounding the wheel were decorated with dragons in the Chinese style. Thus Lamaist tradition was incorporated into one of Lanzhou's three great temples. In 1928 the temple was converted to use as the Sun Yatsen Market. The entire complex was destroyed by Japanese bombs in 1939. Lanyuan Park now stands on the site (Cheng Taosheng 1987: 63–64; *Lanzhou fenglai* 1987: 59–60).

Another of Lanzhou's Buddhist temples, the White Lotus Temple (Baiyi Si) at 110 Jingyang Road, still stands on what would have been the southeast corner of the central walled area. It dates from the Ming dynasty (1631) and has a fairly typical main hall, with pillared structure supporting a grand roof of gray tile with a large diamond-shaped pattern of solid green tile at the center. The ridge of the roof is ornamented with dragons and phoenixes, and green ceramic elephants perch on the center of the ridgepole. The hall was empty when I saw it, but building materials assembled on the floor suggested that restoration would soon begin. On the northwest corner of the site, there is a baita-style pagoda (see discussion later in the chapter) 30 m tall, with a 2.8 m base. Each of its successively smaller stories has eight sides, with a niche for a Buddha on each side.

Like Lanzhou, Xining was dominated in traditional times by two temple complexes facing each other across the valley in which the city is located. The Temple of the Northern Spirit (Beishen Si) commanded the north bank of the Huangshui River, while the southern temple (now closed) occupied the top of a hill south of the city proper adjacent to the main road leading out of the city. Xining had 25 Chinese Buddhist temples, with about 60 monks in residence in the first half of the twentieth century; today it has fewer than 10 temples, and that number includes some Daoist institutions (*Qinghai shengqing* 1986: 585). The most prominent is the Temple of the Northern Spirit, which occupies a series of caves high in the cliffs north of the city. It is said to be shared by Buddhists and Daoists, but the Daoists are apparently more numerous and have the controlling interest in the temple today. A number of the caves in the cliff face have Daoist figures, incense, and wall hangings inside. The superstructural catwalks that connect the caves are built in Chinese style, with covered walkways paved in stone. Above the temple, at the crest of the hill, there is a pagoda on a square base. The temple has a long history. The caves were first occupied by Buddhists sometime between 516 and 528, when local monks painted religious paintings inside the caves. But the pagoda at the top of the hill, Ningshouta, was built only in 1915 (*Xiningshi* [map] 1984).

Hohhot's collection of temples reflects the multicultural nature of the city. The many temples within Xincheng, the walled Manchu garrison-city, were devoted to the Chinese/Manchu deities most revered by the Manchu military, such as the horse spirit and Guandi, the God of War. The God of War was also well-represented in the old Mongolian-Chinese city, perhaps attesting to the generally militaristic nature of life on the northern frontier. According to the county gazetteer, in the early twentieth century five of Hohhot's six God of War temples were in the Jiucheng area (*Guisui xianzhi* 1909: 222–28). Jiucheng also housed the city's two God of Literature temples. Each city had its own temple of the city god. Xincheng's (built ca. 1766) lay within the walls, near the south gate on the east side of the main north-south street, but Jiucheng's (built ca. 1730) was located just outside the north gate of the small walled administrative area. The existence of two separate city gods in "Hohhot" attests to the spiritual separation of the two cities. Among Jiucheng's other temples were two to the Dragon King and one to the God of Wealth, located just southeast of the Dazhao Lama temple.[5]

All of Hohhot's 56 Chinese temples (Buddhist, Daoist, Confucian, and popular) were destroyed or abandoned during the Cultural Revolution. Reconstruction on some of them began in the mid-1980s. In 1987–89 the city government undertook the reconstruction of the Goddess of Mercy (Guanyin) temple in the Old City district. That temple, built in the Qing era, is set in a single small courtyard surrounded by old housing. The entrance to the courtyard, the main hall, and the statues are all oriented toward the north, a clear violation of the Chinese ideal that so far begs explanation. When I was there, two stone lions stood guard outside the large red door and gate, the two side buildings inside were being used as offices and sleeping quarters for the construction workers, and the five statues in the main hall had been primed with a white basecoat. A table had been set up in the southwest corner of the main hall as a makeshift altar to the Amitabha Buddha. Oil lamps were burning on the table, which was covered with ornamental cloths, and there were pillows for worshippers to kneel on in front of it. The statues in the hall are flanked by two pillars with dragons wrapped around them; the decoration under the eaves at the top of the pillars includes diamond-shaped fengshui mirrors pointing north.

The first Chinese temple in the vicinity of Urumqi was a God of War temple built by the Qing troops after they conquered the area in 1755. It stood at the crest of Pingding Mountain, overlooking the city. Though it no longer stands, its vermillion walls earned the region an enduring nickname. Some people even today refer to Urumqi as "Old Red Temple" (Zan Yulin 1983: 8). The densest cluster of Chinese temples in the area was located at the base, sides, and summit of Hongshan, the rocky outcrop just northwest of Dihua, the Chinese city.

Though there were Chinese temples in both cities, it appears that Dihua had never had the numbers of temples that once operated in the Manchu city (Gongning Cheng), which was burned down in 1864. The conflagration destroyed at least 14 temples, including a Long Life temple, a God of War temple, and two Confucian temples (Zan Yulin 1983: 24).

Lamaist Monumental Architecture

Lamaist temples vary widely in style, and major contrasts can be seen between regions. They also vary tremendously in size and composition, from small village temples to temples large enough to be cities in their own right. Most of the larger temples to be addressed in this section serve as monastic communities formed by a number of buildings, including temples, academies (which always have shrines in them) for the instruction of monks, living quarters, and buildings devoted to administration, food preparation, and storage. Apart from those modeled directly on Chinese architectural layout, Tibetan temples are not aligned on a single linear axis as Chinese temples are.

It is common for Tibetan temple complexes to incorporate several different architectural styles. Some have several styles of buildings within the complex; others incorporate different stylistic elements within individual buildings. According to R. A. Stein, the combination of "Tibetan" styles with other styles was in no way considered a cultural compromise by Tibetans in traditional Tibet. On the contrary, they sometimes made concerted efforts to borrow styles from neighboring countries. For example, Samye Temple, one of the most famous and holy temples of Tibetan Buddhism, was built in three styles: the lower part in Tibetan style, the middle part with a Chinese roof, and the upper part with an Indian roof. Similar syncretic buildings and complexes were constructed throughout the Tibetan culture region, including even the Chinese-shaped roofs atop the purely Tibetan architecture of the Potala Palace and the Jokhang Temple in Lhasa. Foreign craftsmen were often commissioned to carry out the formation of temple complexes (Stein 1972: 283–84). Given this multiplicity of style in Central Tibet, then, it is perhaps not surprising that styles have been mixed in Tibetan structures on the frontiers as well. But whereas in most of central Tibet, Indian, Nepalese, Chinese, and other foreign borrowings are largely superficial, limited to ornamentation and roofs (Snellgrove & Richardson 1986: 140), the Lamaist architecture of the frontier incorporates these elements even in the basic structure of temple buildings and complexes.

The architectural diversity of Lamaist monasteries may also reflect the diversity of the Lamaist communities themselves. Many of the larger monasteries in Tibet and Mongolia were home to monks of widely varying origin. For example, on a visit to Kumbum Jampa Ling Monastery outside Xining in 1956, Rewi Alley observed that although most of the monks were Tibetan, there were also Mongolian monks and some Chinese monks. And, in addition to living in a monastery whose architecture combined elements of all three communities, the monks combined Chinese and Tibetan traditions by sleeping on Chinese-style beds within the Tibetan-style courtyard housing (Alley 1957: 33).

Two architectural forms derived from Tibetan Buddhist tradition have diffused relatively widely across both China proper and the frontiers: the *baita* and the *wutasi*. The baita is a shrine or pagoda that is usually incorporated into a Buddhist temple complex or placed on a hill or other auspicious site. The wutasi may either be a similar shrine-like structure or be as large as a building.

Baita (White Dagobas)

The baita is a shrine similar to a pagoda in function. It is usually made of brick or adobe painted white, and has a layered structure: a square pedestal, topped by a dome, topped by a series of successively smaller square or round layers that form a tower mounted on the relatively squat dome. At the top there is usually a spherical ornament. The baita, which usually contains sacred objects, is derived from the Indian stupa, which originated in Sanchi, India, in the second century B.C. and gradually diffused throughout the Buddhist world in variant styles. The Tibetan version, the chorten, is the one that diffused into Mongolia and China, particularly after the founding of the Yuan dynasty. The Mongols adopted the chorten as part of Tibetan Buddhism. It was well matched to their traditional piled-rock shrine, the obo (Chinese: *aobao*), with its dome shape and prayer flags mounted at the top (but unlike the chorten, the obo was not filled with sacred objects). Chorten were a particularly prominent feature of the Tibetan Buddhist temples of Inner Mongolia. Photographs of the Wushen Monastery from the late Qing, for example, indicate that it had at least 5 large and 17 small chorten; the actual number was probably at least double that figure (*Neimenggu gujianzhu* 1959: 49). The northern pagoda at Mount Fang, in Hebei Province, with its eight-sided Chinese-style base topped by a conical Tibetan-style structure, is one of many examples of this Yuan-era development (Sickman & Soper 1984: 447).

Like the Tibetan chorten, the Chinese form that emerged, the baita (referred to in English as a white pagoda or sometimes white dagoba), is filled with holy relics and riches, and it may serve as a funerary memorial in the fashion of the chorten commemorating the Dalai Lamas in Lhasa's Potala Palace. The most famous white dagoba in all of China is on an island in Beijing's Beihai Park, formerly on the grounds of the Imperial Palace (Forbidden City). It was built in 1651 to commemorate the first visit of the Dalai Lama. Its form is typical: a square platform supporting a square base (rectangular in some cases) topped by a nearly onion-shaped structure capped by a metal spire-like ornament. The whole of the structure is plastered over in white. The lines are simple, and the surface unmarred by decoration—a striking contrast to the richly painted and complex imperial buildings in the surrounding area. Beijing's other surviving baita, at the nearby White Dagoba Temple (Baita Si), was built even earlier. The temple itself, with its famous Buddhist halls, was constructed during the reign of Khubilai Khan by the Nepalese architect Aniko, and features a number of elements typical of Nepal's Newar Buddhist temple architecture in its interiors. The success of this building led to the construction of other structures incorporating Nepalese and Tibetan forms during the period (Rossabi 1988: 171).

The baita is an example of the diffusion of an architectural form from the frontier into China proper. There are only a few white dagobas widely scattered in eastern China, but they are significant to the extent that they represent a completely different architectural regime and conceptualization, and their form is so distinctive that it stands out amidst traditional Chinese architectural groupings. The construction of such forms indicates attempts at the imperial level to accommodate the religious tastes of foreign guests of the state and, at other levels, either similar gestures of goodwill toward non-Chinese populations, or, in places where the non-Chinese built their own temples, adherence to sacred tradition.

Baita were constructed throughout the Lamaist regions of the Chinese frontier, including some within the cities under study. For example, there were once two baita in Kunming. One, constructed during the Yuan dynasty as the focal point of Zhongjing Cheng (the eastern city established in 1254), stood at what is today the intersection of Baita and Tuodong roads. It was removed to facilitate the flow of traffic during urban improvement projects after 1949. The other, called Golden Net Pagoda (Jinwangta), still stands in Gongdu village, east of Kunming proper. Built in 1458, it is fashioned in the Tibetan-stupa style of the white dagoba in Beijing's Beihai Park. The pagoda proper, 14.5 m tall, is mounted on a high (10.3 m) square base. There is an arched passageway for pedestrians through the center (*Zhongguo lishi wenhua mingcheng zidian* 1985: 743).

Both the pagoda at Lanzhou's White Lotus Sect temple and the pagoda at the top of Baita Mountain, across the Yellow River, are built in a "sinified" baita style. Their dome sections are considerably narrower than in the typical baita, so that the whole structure is nearly conical in shape, not bulging in the dome section. Each is topped by a narrow tower, as is common in Lamaist shrines.

The Xilituzhao Lamaist temple in Hohhot has quite an ostentatious baita, which stands to the east of the main succession of courtyards in the complex. Its base is especially elaborate, quite tall and decorated with bas-relief images of Garuda and other religious figures, all painted in color for added contrast with the white background.

Wutasi (Five-Pagoda Temples)

A wutasi has five "pagodas," each a tapered tower constructed of successively smaller square layers atop a square pedestal of one or more stories. Four of the pagodas (all the same size) sit at the corners of the pedestal; the other, much larger, is at the center. This style, in which (to use Boyle Huang's description) the five pagodas stand "like a palm flower on a roof deck of a square temple" (Huang 1975: 615), appeared in China in Ming times. Chinese architectural historians, such as Liu Dunzhen, ascribe the five-pagoda temples to the influences of Lamaism and Lamaist styles during the Ming dynasty (Liu Dunzhen 1987: 365).

The Temple of the Diamond Sutra (Mahabodhi Temple) in Bodhgaya, India, seems to be the origin of the wutasi, but exactly how the style got to China is unclear. Some ascribe its introduction to the descriptions of the monk Xuan Zang, who visited Bodhgaya during the Tang dynasty, and others suggest it was adopted after a model of the Mahabodhi Temple was presented to the Ming court by the Indian monk Pandida. The Mahabodhi Temple is similar in form to the five-pagoda temples in China; however, the central pagoda on the pedestal is far larger in comparison to the four corner pagodas in Bodhgaya than it is in the Chinese versions.[6]

Five examples of this distinctive style are still to be seen in China today: at Beijing's Zhenjue Si, Biyun Si, and Xihuang Si, at Hohhot's Wuta Si, and at Kunming's Miaokan Si (Guan Xiaoxian et al. 1987: 271). The wutasi in Hohhot was built in 1727 and is believed to be directly or indirectly modeled after the temple at Bodhgaya. It is said to have been built by the Qing governor at the request of the lama of the Xiaozhao Temple, upon the occasion of his trip to Beijing. It may be that the lama saw one or more of the five-pagoda-style temples in Beijing and wanted one for Hohhot. The temple was popularly known as the Five Pagoda Temple (Wutasi Zhao), but the formal name the Qing governor gave it in 1732 was the Loving Light Temple (Cideng Si). The temple was originally constructed as a complex with three main halls (ibid., p. 269). The original structure deteriorated long ago and was replaced by the present one, officially renamed the Precious Pagoda of the Buddhist Relics of the Diamond Throne (Jingangzuo Sheli Baota; Gao Yinbiao & Wang Jizhou 1987: 12–13). Its base, three stories tall, is inscribed in four languages, Sanskrit, Tibetan, Mongolian, and Chinese, and is richly decorated with relief images of the Buddha, as are the five pagodas above. One of the most important features of the wutasi is its *zhaobi*, or spirit wall, protecting the northern side of the complex. The southern face of this wall is decorated with a map of the heavenly cosmos, with inscriptions in Mongolian.

Kunming's wutasi, the Diamond Sutra Pagoda, is located about ten km south of the city, in Gongdu district. It was built in 1457 (Wang Xuepei et al. 1987: 43–44) and is reputed to have been the only one of its type in Yunnan Province. It was declared a protected cultural relic in the Kunming city plan of 1980.

Lamaist Temples and Monastery Complexes

One striking feature of Lamaist temples in the Chinese-Tibetan-Mongolian frontier areas is the extent to which Chinese architectural elements were incorporated into them. This phenomenon indicates significant cultural borrowing in the realm of material culture and the built environment. Cultural borrowing has been much more significant in this case in material culture than in spiritual culture. The borrowing of elements of Chinese material culture may reflect respect and admiration for Chinese styles and arts. However, in many cases, borrowing may reflect more practical concerns such as the availability and limitations of craftsmen and resources.

Chinese influence is particularly evident in Labrang Monastery (Chinese: Labulangsi; Tibetan: bKra-shis-sgo-mang), located in the southwest of Gansu Province, 25 km east of the Qinghai border and about 150 km north of the Sichuan border, in a region traditionally at the edge of both the eastern Tibetan region of Kham and the northeastern Tibetan region of Amdo. Labrang is one of the great monasteries built on the instructions of the Fifth Dalai Lama. Several incarnations of the Dalai Lama have visited Labrang, including the current one, who stopped there in 1955 as part of a tour of important Lamaist sites on the route from Beijing to Lhasa.

Labrang is the seat of several reincarnate lamas, the most important of which is the Jiamuyang Lama. The first incarnation of the Jiamuyang was a monk trained in Lhasa in the early eighteenth century. In 1710 he built a small temple (at Xiahe), which became the site of Labrang Monastery. By 1716 Labrang had grown to a small community of 20 monks with its own school of medicine and an institute for the study of the Wheel of Life. The monastery continued to expand until 1949, by which time it had six great *lacang*,[7] 48 Buddha halls, and more than 500 courtyards for housing monks (Miao Sishu et al. 1987: 2–3). The seven-story Great Gold-tiled-roof Hall is the tallest building in the complex. Within the hall there is a golden statue of the Buddha (standing over 30 m tall) that was designed and built by craftsmen brought from Nepal (Wu Yue et al. 1985: 89). The Chinese influence is pervasive in the architecture, though it is thoroughly mixed with Tibetan (and even some Mongolian) elements that reflect the cultural diversity of the Sino-Tibetan borderlands. For example, the lower building of the Great Hall of the Sutras (Wensi Academy) has a Tibetan-style gold-plated roof, but the upper building has a Chinese green-glaze tile roof. Many buildings have gilt or colored tile roofs in Chinese style, and there are also Chinese-style gateways to the temple buildings.

To the west of Labrang, just outside of Xining, lies Kumbum Jampa Ling, also known by its Chinese name, Ta'er Si.[8] It is one of the six largest monasteries of Tibetan Buddhism's Gelukpa, or Yellow Hat sect. It was built in 1560 at the birthplace of the founder of the sect, Tsong Khapa, one of the most revered figures in Tibetan Buddhism. At its height the monastery had more than 3,600 monks, 20 public buildings, and over 7,000 dwellings. The monastery complex is situated on the bottom and sloping sides of a narrow stream valley, varying from 2,661 m to 2,786 m in elevation, surrounded by hills and mountains in each of the cardinal directions (Chen Meihe 1986: 1, 8).

The monastery was built in three stages. The first stage, from the mid-sixteenth to the early seventeenth century, saw the number of resident monks grow from 10 to more than 30 and the addition of several temple halls: the Maitreya Buddha Hall (Milefo Dian), the Great Summons Hall (Da Zhao Dian), the Joyous Gold Hall (Xijingang Dian), the Little Scripture Hall (Xiao Jing Tang), and the Third Reincarnate Buddha Hall (San-shifo Tang). All these early halls were built in Ming dynasty Chinese styles, and this was done, the Chinese architectural historian Chen Meihe argues, for two reasons: because the pastoralists of the area lacked the requisite skills in arts and construction, and so had to employ Chinese artisans; and because communications and trade were better between this area and China than between this area and Tibet. Nevertheless, though the temples were built using Chinese craftsmen, the details such as religious paintings were executed in Tibetan styles. The same tendencies toward a mix of Chinese and Tibetan styles can be seen in four other Lamaist temples built in eastern Qinghai during this period (Chen Meihe 1986: 9–10).

In 1629 the Mongolian king began building a 36-pillared Chinese-style structure, the Scriptures Hall (Jing Tang), initiating a second period of building activity. From the mid-seventeenth to the late eighteenth century, 52 new architectural projects were undertaken. In 1689 a new Scriptures Hall was constructed, this time in Tibetan style, with 80 pillars; the

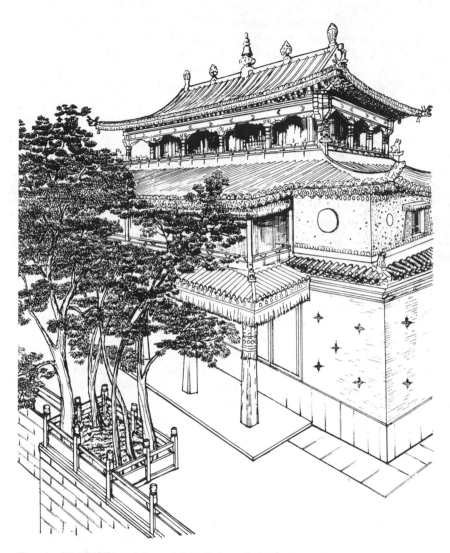

Fig. 10. Tsong Khapa Memorial Hall (Zongkaba Jinian Tadian), Kumbum Jampa Ling Monastery, outside Xining. Source: Chen Meihe 1986: 140.

hall was expanded to 160 pillars in 1776. The eight pagodas at the entrance to the complex—the hallmark of the monastery—were also built in 1776. The new building in this period centered around the Tsong Khapa Memorial Hall (see Fig. 10).

During this period there was relatively good communication between Kumbum Jampa Ling and Tibet and Mongolia, so that the influence of Tibetan architecture and arts became stronger. At the same time, according to Chen Meihe, local craftsmen became skilled enough in the building arts to combine Chinese, Tibetan, and local styles freely. The Tibetan style arrived in the area with artisan-monks from Tibet, who taught the local people their craft (Chen Meihe 1986: 10–12).

The third period, beginning around the mid-nineteenth century, was a time of decline for Kumbum Jampa Ling. Communications with both the Chinese regions and Tibet deteriorated. In 1868 three halls were burned down during local insurrections connected with Islamic uprisings throughout the northwest. These halls were rebuilt in 1874, 1886, and 1913, respectively, and some existing buildings were refurbished. In 1884 a new layer of gold-plating was laid on the roof of the Tsong Khapa Memorial Hall, and in 1906 the old colored glazed tiles on the roof of the Manjusri Hall (Hufashen Dian) were replaced by a gold-plated covering (Chen Meihe 1986: 12–13).

In the course of the centuries, according to Chen Meihe, two local styles of architectural ornamentation were absorbed into the style at Kumbum Jampa Ling: the *wutun* (five accumulations) style of Qinghai, and the *hezhou zhuandiao* (riverbank brick/tile carving) style of Gansu. Qinghai's wutun style is to be seen in the monastery's wood carvings, statuary, and especially paintings. Gansu's hezhou zhuandiao style, the decorative style of the Hui people, is found especially as decoration around the doors. This style particularly makes use of fired tiles with a top glaze. These are often fashioned in flower patterns and decorate corridors as well as doorways (Chen Meihe 1986: 14).

In Xining itself there was a smaller monastic complex, the Great Buddha Temple (Dafo Si). Little historical information is available on this Lamaist temple, which was located on the Great West Street, near the center of the old walled city. The temple was constructed during the Yuan dynasty, and the Xining Tibetans' rights to it were reaffirmed by the Ming dynasty sometime between 1368 and 1399 (*Xiningfu xinzhi* 1930s: 494). An old photograph of the main hall (in *Qinghai lishi jiyao* 1987) shows a Chinese-style rectangular structure of three stories, stepped inward from bottom to top. The first two stories were surrounded by covered, colonnaded arcades. The third story had a flat facade. Bells hung off the eaves, as they do in most Tibetan temples, to attract the attention of the gods, and there was a single ornament in the center of the ridge of the highest roof—an abstracted conical series of rounded forms common to Tibetan temples. Immediately in front of the building, there appears to be a sacred tree carefully preserved by a surrounding wall. Thus, though the form of this Tibetan temple within the Chinese city was basically Chinese, its ornamentation and embellishment were distinctly Tibetan. So was the placement of the tree adjacent to the main entrance—a placement that was anathema to Chinese geomantic beliefs. The temple site is obscured today, and I was unable to determine whether or not any building from the temple might remain hidden behind the modern structures that now line the Great West Street.

Mongolian Lamaist temples incorporate a mixture of elements of Mongolian, Chinese, and Tibetan architectural design (a notable exception is the completely Tibetan-style Wudang Temple at Baotou). The establishment of Lamaist temples in Hohhot began with the Great Temple (Dazhao Si), established with the founding of the city in the sixteenth century. Both the Ming and the Qing dynasty encouraged Lamaism and the construction and repair of Lamaist temples in Inner Mongolia (Dai Xueji 1981: 60).

By the middle of the Qianlong era (1736–96), the Hohhot area had 40 Mongolian Lamaist temples (*zhaomiao*), with some 3,000 resident monks. Seven of these were relatively large complexes, populated by several hundred monks each (Dai Xueji 1980: 60–61). At least 14 were still operating within the Jiucheng area on the eve of the 1911 revolution (*Guisui xianzhi* 1909: 222–23). Five are still standing today: the Xilitu Temple, the Great Temple, the Lesser Temple, the Wusutu Temple, and the Five Pagoda Temple.

The Great Temple (Dazhao) was one of two temples—the other was the Lesser Temple (Xiaozhao)—Altan Khan built at Hohhot in 1579. Originally called the Grand Kindness Temple (Hongci Si), the Great Temple was also known as the Silver Buddha Temple (Yinfo Si), in honor of a silver Buddha housed there, which was a gift from the Third Dalai Lama to Altan Khan on the occasion of Altan Khan's 1578 trip to Qinghai. In 1586 the Third Dalai Lama traveled to Hohhot and stayed at the Great Temple, thus ensuring its fame in the annals of Tibetan Buddhism (Wu En 1987: 393).

The Great Temple well exemplifies the fusion of Tibetan and Chinese styles in the Mongolian temples of Hohhot. It is built in temple courtyard style, but the main (Silver Buddha) hall at the north of the complex has a gray brick facade in Tibetan form, though there is only a small amount of the red-twig surface that adorns so many of the temples of Central Tibet. The center section of the facade juts out to form a veranda. On either side of this there are frescoes depicting the cosmic order in Tibetan style. On the southeastern corner of the roof, there is a temple ornament like those found in the Lhasa area and at Kumbum Jampa Ling, although it is silver rather than gold. The roof is a Chinese-style flying roof with extremely ornate blue rafters.

In 1987, when I conducted research in Hohhot, all the interior buildings, with the exception of the northernmost hall (the Buddha hall), appeared to have been completely stripped at one time (probably during the Cultural Revolution) and only recently restored. The main prayer hall was nearly barren and looked newly redecorated. But the farthest hall, onto which it opens, was filled with golden statues. The central statue, a silver (covered with gold-plate) Sakyamuni, and the two pillars wrapped with golden dragons playing with a pearl that flanked it, clearly testify to Chinese influence. This hall had old paint and decoration, as if it was not dismantled when the rest of the temple was in recent history.

In the design of both the Xiao Temple and the Xilitu Temple, there are strong elements of Tibetan style, including some elements borrowed directly from the Jokhang Temple in Lhasa (Jin Qi 1987: 271). Chinese elements were also applied in these temples, and fused with Tibetan elements to create buildings neither wholly Chinese nor wholly Tibetan in style.

The Xilitu Temple is also built in the Chinese temple style, with bell and drum towers (still containing the bell and drum) flanking the first courtyard. At the northern end of the complex, the main Buddha hall is covered with peacock blue glazed bricks. This blue color is favored in Mongolian architecture. There are small panels of Tibetan-style red-twig surface on either side of the facade. There is a juxtaposition of Tibetan and Chinese styles in the roof. The front part of the prayer hall has a Tibetan-style flat roof, with gold wheel-of-life and deer symbols on the southern edge. The rear part, a room that houses the temple's Buddha statues, is covered by a Chinese roof of blue tiles inset with a gold diamond pattern at the center. The other buildings all have Chinese-style flying tile roofs.

There is another striking example here of the mixing of styles, in a shrine that stands on the eastern side of the complex. It is a chorten, white and shaped like a Tibetan dagoba, but the "chorten" sits on a square marble pedestal with lion pillars and dragon-shaped drains (which collect rain runoff and expel it through their mouths), similar to the pedestals in the Forbidden City in Beijing. The walls are decorated with reliefs of Chinese-style dragons.

Let me emphasize once again, before moving on to the discussion of Islamic architecture on the frontier, that however syncretic these monastic complexes are in physical form, they remain wholly orthodox in religious practice and function. Here there is a clear distinction between the adoption of aspects of material culture and the adoption of aspects of spiritual culture. For the Lamaists of the frontier, material culture as it is expressed in architectural design is not directly tied to identity to the extent that the incorporation of Chinese and other non-Lamaist architectural elements does not compromise the holy nature of Lamaist shrines and temples.

Islamic Monumental Architecture

In much of the Islamic world and especially in Southwest and Central Asia, the mosque is associated with distinctive architectural elements, such as the dome and the minaret. In China there is considerable variation in mosque style reflecting regional characteristics, cultural factors, and frontier phenomena. During my first fieldwork in the frontier cities of China, I soon observed the striking regional variation in mosque styles. Mosques in Kunming, Hohhot, Lhasa, and Dali, for example, were at first glance remarkably similar to Chinese Buddhist, Confucian, and Daoist temples, yet in Xining and Lanzhou, there appeared to be a mixture of styles, even within individual mosques, between traditional Chinese and Central/Southwest Asian forms.[9] Mosques in Urumqi were also mixed, but most were Central/Southwest Asian in style. Mosques in Turfan were all Central/Southwest Asian in style.

This regional character, however, proved to reflect only the contemporary era of mosque construction and reconstruction in China. Twenty-five years ago, nearly all the mosques in these frontier areas, with the exception of those in Xinjiang, were primarily Chinese style. Photographs of mosques in the early 1960s from Beijing to Guangzhou, Kunming, Lhasa, Hohhot, and points in between (and even one in Turfan; Liu Zhiping 1985) indicate that, at that time, 33 of 45 mosques (better than 73 percent) were Chinese in style, against just six in Central/Southwest Asian style (six were built in various other styles). The trend toward the Central/Southwest Asian style is in fact a recent phenomenon associated with the post–Cultural Revolution recovery of Islam.[10] By the end of the Cultural Revolution, many of the mosques were in bad repair, closed, or turned over to factory production. Some casual observers in the 1980s, just ten years later, have mistaken recently rebuilt mosques for much older structures. This reflects the fact that the hasty construction and sometimes poor quality of building materials in mosques constructed during the 1980s has led to their rapid deterioration to conditions that Westerners have incorrectly attributed to age.

Mosques on China's interior frontiers in the twentieth century are indigenous architectural creations: the products of the architectural styles and techniques of each region of the frontier. This is a striking difference from the great mosques of the Chinese coast, where there has been considerably more "foreign" influence in Islam and Islamic design. The mosques of Guangzhou, Quanzhou, and Shanghai were all influenced by frequent trade contacts with non-Chinese Muslims and, in fact, during the early period of Islam in China, were established by these foreign traders.

Mosques in Imperial China

Islamic architectural practices must naturally differ from Chinese practice, since the fundamental nature of the mosque is different from that of the Chinese temple, with its collection of images and more individualistic acts of worship. Liu Zhiping identifies three periods of significance for the history of Islam and Islamic architecture in China. In the first period, from 651 to 1367, as Islam entered China, first from the coastal regions, and later over the Central Asian land routes, Islamic architecture and urban forms were primarily built by foreigners or by converts in non-Chinese styles, mimicking foreign styles. In the second period, from 1368 to the Opium Wars of the 1840s, Islam developed in China and became integrated into the Chinese milieu. In the far northwest ten different peoples had embraced Islam. And throughout China the Hui developed their own forms of mosque construction, relying heavily on Chinese temple styles. The third period, from the 1840s to the 1949 revolution, was a time of great unrest in all of China and included a series of rebellions in which Islamic people participated. The Chinese retaliated during these rebellions, and, as a general result, many mosques throughout China were destroyed. In Xinjiang Islam became stronger as Islamic groups united to form new alliances, and new mosques were constructed (Liu Zhiping 1985: 109). This divergent experience during the nineteenth century illustrates the significant distinction in China between those Islamic peoples closely linked to the Chinese in heritage and cultural features, and those more closely linked to Central Asian Islamic tradition.

The practice of mosque construction in China dates to the seventh century. There were two early traditions of mosque building corresponding to the two paths of Islam into China: one tradition on the southeastern coast of China and one in the Chinese Central Asian region. The first four mosques are said to have been built by the first Islamic emissary to China, sent by the prophet Mohammed to Guangdong toward the end of the seventh century (Chang & Blaser 1987: 171). According to Liu Zhiping, in the lengthy period of the introduction of Islam into China (651–1367), most mosques in China were built in what he terms an "Arabian" style, of brick and stone. These were constructed by traders in their ports of entry into China. The earliest mosques in eastern China were built in Guangzhou, Quanzhou, and Hangzhou; all were constructed with stone arch entrances and minarets characteristic of Islamic architecture elsewhere in the world at the time.

From the eighth to the tenth century, Islamic traders also entered overland from the west, establishing mosques first at Kashgar, and later throughout the Xinjiang region. These Central Asian mosques probably differed from those on the Southeast coast, particularly in the application of tile ornament to the mosque facade. An eleventh-century description of a mosque/tomb at Kashgar, for example, describes a building covered with glazed tiles, with a half-dome roof (Liu Zhiping 1985: 1–4). During the Five Dynasties and Song periods, however, there was unrest in the northwest, and the land route decreased in importance for trade.

Subsequently, the sea trade flourished, and the eastern seaports developed. Communities of "Arab" traders, who occupied districts in a number of eastern port cities, such as Guangzhou, Quanzhou, Hangzhou, Mingzhou (Ningbo), Mizhou, Banqiao, Hunzhou, and Jiangyang, contributed to the development of these places. There was Arab funding for the rebuilding of Guangzhou between 1068 and 1077, and financial support for the rebuilding of Quanzhou in 1211. Song dynasty annalists have written that mosques were built in "foreign" styles under the guidance of these foreign traders. The Quanzhou mosque is one of the few still displaying this Song style: built of stone and brick, with an "Arabian" style main gate, consisting of a tall rectangular block of brick construction with a high pointed-arch tunnel as the main entrance. Moreover, and significant to the Chinese, the Great Front gate is at the "side" of the main prayer hall rather than directly opposite (that is, the mosque is not oriented north-south as a Chinese temple would be; Liu Zhiping 1985: 1–4).

In the rest of China, change in mosque architecture took place in two main phases. During the Yuan dynasty, China was a relatively unified state, and travelers were able to move great distances through the region under Mongol control. This was the period in which Marco Polo was able to make his famous journeys through the empire. Islam spread easily under these conditions, both through the wide dispersal of Islamic mercenaries for the Mongol army and through the high numbers of Central Asian and Arabian traders permitted to travel in China. As a result, there were a number of Chinese and Mongolian converts to Islam during this time, and

Chinese architectural forms began to take hold in the Chinese Islamic world. In 1340 Ibn Battuta wrote that in every city he visited in eastern China between Quanzhou and Beijing there were Hui people, who had in each case built mosques. Nevertheless, despite the gradual introduction of the Chinese to Islam, mosque styles remained primarily Arabian in style during the Yuan dynasty (Liu Zhiping 1985: 3–5).

In the years between 1368 and 1840, a Chinese style of Islamic architecture developed among the growing population of Muslims. This was encouraged by imperial sponsorship of mosques. For example, the Ming emperor Taizu commanded mosques to be constructed in both Nanjing and Xi'an in the style of the grandest Buddhist temples of the period to impress visitors and appease the many highly placed Islamic officials at the Ming court. Later Ming emperors followed his lead, with the result that Chinese styles came to be widely applied in new mosque design and construction. During the early Ming, Muslim advisers to the court had connections with the southeast coastal Islamic community. Later, however, when the court was moved from Nanjing to Beijing, the Islamic community most involved in court life became the northern and northwestern Hui, further contributing to the sinicization of Islamic styles in the country (Liu Zhiping 1985: 4–6).

In the sixteenth century a Hui named Hu Dengzhou (1522–97) made the pilgrimage to Mecca and returned with scriptures and ideas from the cradle of Islam. He encouraged the construction of lecture halls in conjunction with mosques where people could assemble to learn from his teachings. From this start in Shaanxi, a new mosque form coupling a lecture/teaching hall with a building for worship spread throughout much of China. More and more mosques came to be built in an elaborated Chinese temple style, with a worship hall and a lecture hall forming the primary focus of the architectural group.

This new style did not entirely displace the earlier Arabian styles in eastern China or in Chinese Central Asia. A few mosques, restorations of Yuan structures, retained elements of the old styles, and in Xinjiang all but the Hui people maintained the more traditional mosque styles through the nineteenth century. But even these structures exhibited some distinct local styles through the integration of locally available materials with traditional Islamic styles (Liu Zhiping 1985: 8).

During the Ming and Qing periods, Islam grew and developed in China, where it was particularly prominent in the cities. By 1781, for example, there were said to be at least a thousand families of Hui in Xi'an, with seven mosques. And in the Daoguang period (1821–51), there were

48 mosques in Nanjing and more than 10 in Chengdu (Liu Zhiping 1985: 6–8). At the same time there was growth in the rural population of the Hui as well.

Many of these mosques, including a number of famous ones in the east, were damaged or destroyed during and after the Opium Wars, notably those at Guilin, Changsha, and Hefei. They were all rebuilt in the Qing style. Many others were damaged in the Taiping rebellion of the nineteenth century. Many of these were not rebuilt. For example, at the time of the rebellion, Nanjing still had 24 functioning mosques; by the end of the Qing dynasty, the number had dwindled to 7. In the northwest, by contrast, the Islamic population continued to grow, and mosque complexes called *daotang* were constructed in great numbers, incorporating guest rooms, coat rooms, washing rooms, and other structures in addition to the worship hall and the lecture hall. Islam particularly flourished in Xinjiang. At the end of the Qing, a census revealed more than 13,000 mosques in southern Xinjiang. Hetian county alone (Khotan) had 36 mosques serving 575 households (Liu Zhiping 1985: 9).

During the Cultural Revolution most mosques in China were either destroyed or converted to secular uses (some as antithetical to Islam as places to keep pigs, but most were used for social institutions such as libraries, schools, gymnasiums, or factories). In the years following the death of Mao Zedong, and particularly after 1980, many Islamic communities throughout China were able to reclaim these buildings or the land on which they stood, and to rebuild, renovate, and reopen them. Two distinct types of mosques are developing simultaneously as a result of these activities: mosques built in the Chinese temple style and mosques with a "Central/Southwest Asian" style. The Chinese-style mosques tend to be renovations of existing structures, while the Central/Southwest Asian–style mosques are usually completely new structures.

Frontier City Mosques

In the following sections I will describe and discuss a number of the mosques in the frontier cities addressed in this study. This discussion will differ from the previous discussion of Chinese and Lamaist temples to the extent that it will be concerned primarily with detailing the present characteristics of the mosques rather than their developmental history. There is little written history available on the mosques, and most are not mentioned in Chinese gazetteers and historical works or even marked on the maps in those works.[11]

The subject of contemporary mosques is worth examining because so little has been written on the revival of mosque building after the Cultural Revolution. During the period of my fieldwork, 1986–88, the frontier mosques were in an interesting state of revitalization not only because of their reopening or rebuilding, but also because of changing attitudes toward Islam and ethnic identity in China. What makes this transition period all the more interesting is that mosques were being rebuilt at a much faster rate than Chinese temples. Thus, while in the traditional period Chinese temples usually far outnumbered mosques in Chinese cities, during the present era there is an unusual situation in which functioning mosques far outnumber functioning Chinese temples in frontier cities.

As in eastern China, most of the pre-1949 mosques on the frontier (particularly Hui mosques) were built in the Chinese style. In general Chinese-style mosques on the frontier tended to be relatively simplified in their overall plan. Although the ideal Chinese temple structure incorporates a series of courtyards defined by buildings, most of the frontier mosques have only one courtyard. Combined data from my own observations and plans published by Liu Zhiping indicate that in the frontier provinces of Yunnan, Qinghai, Xinjiang, Gansu, and Inner Mongolia, 17 of 21 Chinese-style mosques have only a single courtyard. By contrast, there is an almost even balance in the rest of China: 12 mosques with multiple courtyards versus 13 with single courtyards. The high incidence of single courtyards on the frontier was probably due as much to economic factors as anything else. In fact, there is no symbolism for Islam in a progression of courtyards, as there is for the Chinese religions; most mosques throughout the Islamic world are built around single courtyards. In practical terms, then, extra courtyards would simply add expense to the construction project. Just as many Chinese temples in poor regions are constructed with only a single courtyard, so too it was perhaps expedient for the builders of mosques to resist expenditures on unnecessary courtyards. The most prominent use of multiple courtyards for mosques in China is found in the relatively elaborate mosques in the east, such as the Xi'an mosque, which were initially constructed with financial assistance from the Chinese government. What is significant about the predominance of single-courtyard mosques in China is that it illustrates the relatively superficial nature of the replication of Chinese forms by the Hui.

Kunming mosques seem to have survived the ravages of the Cultural Revolution more or less physically intact. Thus Kunming has not experienced the same rate of new mosque construction that other frontier cities have. Nonetheless, the Hui community in Kunming was active in renovating and reopening their mosques while I was carrying out my fieldwork in the mid-1980s. There are six mosques in central Kunming, located in areas of traditional concentration of Muslim population. The mosques serve as the foci for these neighborhoods. All of the mosques are built in Chinese style, with a single courtyard aligned along an east-west axis.

The Following the Wall (Shuncheng) Street Mosque (no. 1, Map 21) lies just outside the old walls in one of the city's two main Muslim districts, on a street lined with Muslim restaurants and shops. It stands near the

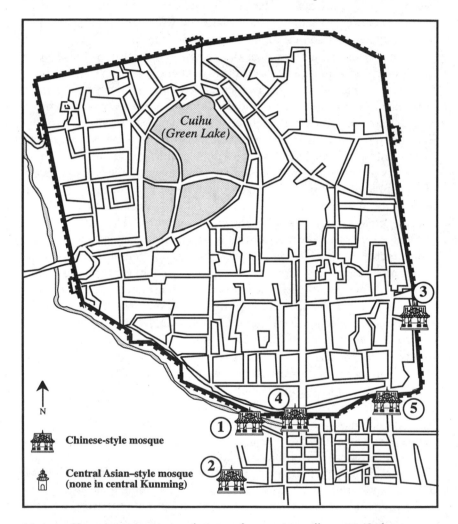

Map 21. Kunming mosques in relation to former city walls, 1988. Only mosques in the immediate area of the old walled city are shown.

western end of the street, slightly removed from the concentration of Muslim shops and restaurants at the other end, near the former south gate of the city. The mosque itself cannot be seen from the street, but an entrance arch inscribed with its name signals its presence 15 meters down a small alley. Just inside the gate there is a pool of water and an arrangement of stones in the Chinese-garden style, along with a plaque indicating that the mosque was designated as a historic relic in 1983. The courtyard is flanked on the north and south by two-story structures. The structure on the north houses the Yunnan Islamic Institute; the structure on the south houses a bath for worshippers to perform their ablutions in preparation for prayer. The main worship hall has a sloping roof of gray tile with a green diamond pattern. The roof is supported by elaborately painted red pillars that form a long porchlike entrance raised several steps above ground level. The interior of the hall is spacious with a high ceiling. Clocks mounted on the pillars and walls indicate the time in Mecca to ensure proper prayer practice. Several people indicated that the mosque dates from the Ming dynasty, but the gatekeeper said that it is about 200 years old. He may have been referring to the existing buildings, and the others to the site. There is no minaret.

Like the Following the Wall Street Mosque, the mosque at 153 Gold and Jade (Jinbi) Street (no. 2, Map 21) is oriented on an east-west axis. It is located on the south side of the street, about a half block east of the Number One Provincial People's Hospital. This mosque has an arched entrance with the name Eternal Peace Mosque (Yongning Qingzhen Si) inscribed in stone above the arch. This arch opens onto the northeast corner of the courtyard. On the east is a dormitory for young men who live at the mosque. The building on the south is low and unremarkable, and bears a sign reading Women's Worship Hall. The main hall has a tiled roof and red pillars. Paintings of Mecca and Medina decorate the facade adjacent to the wooden lattice doors. In 1988 I observed men dressed in white skull caps and dark blue "Sun Yatsen" (Zhongshanyi)–style suits facing due west as they prayed in this hall. Inside, the western wall is quite elaborately decorated with Islamic script, but there is no mihrab visible. The carved wooden *minbar* (pulpit) is movable. And like the Following the Wall Street mosque, this one has no minaret.

At 41 Golden Ox (Jinniu) Street, between the old eastern wall and the Panlong River (no. 3, Map 21), there is a mosque bearing the name Old Mosque (Qingzhen Gu Si).[12] Golden Ox Street, which follows the path of the former eastern wall of the city, is another area of Muslim concentration. The mosque is entered on the southern side of the courtyard, but as with other Kunming mosques, the main hall is oriented on an east-west axis, and there is no minaret. Above the main doors to the prayer hall, there is an inscription "Zhuzai Yuzhou" (God's Cosmos). The crescent moon seems to be missing from the ridgepole on the roof. There is a plaque indicating that the mosque was built in 1947.

In an interesting departure from tradition, the mosque at Sun-approaching Park (Jinri Gongyuan; no. 4, Map 21) is located within the old city walls, just inside the old south gate.[13] It has a very small courtyard (about 6 m by 12 m) and is oriented east-west, with the main prayer hall at the west. The qibla and the mihrab (about 0.6 m deep and 2.5 m wide) are on the west wall. There are many clocks in the mosque, both on pillars inside the hall and on the outside facade. On the north side of the hall, there are racks of robes for the men to wear over their street clothes. On the south side a screen of suspended sheets divides the women's prayer area from the men's. The carved wooded minbar is movable.

The mosque at the bend in Celebrating the Clouds (Qingyun) Street (no. 5, Map 21), another complex of buildings surrounding a central courtyard, with its entrance on the south side, has three bays along the front facade of the main hall, each 3.62 m wide. There are paintings of Mecca and Medina adjacent to the doors at both ends of the front covered gallery. The interior is quite simple. There are many clocks scattered around the complex, including two on pillars inside the prayer hall. The south section of the hall is divided off with suspended sheets to provide a place for women to pray. The mosque was built in the 1920s.

Lanzhou has perhaps the most prominent mosques of all the frontier cities. Recently constructed Central/Southwest Asian–style mosques so dominate the skylines of the north bank of the Yellow River and the Qilihe district west of the city center that contemporary visitors might well imagine Lanzhou as a cosmopolitan trading center on the ancient Silk Routes. There are more than 20 mosques in the old central area alone, and more than 30 in the whole of contemporary Lanzhou (nine are indicated on Map 22). The main mosque, the Great Mosque of the New Suburb (Xinguan Qingzhen Da Si), is on Huating Street in what was the walled eastern suburb (no. 1 on the map). Thus this mosque was located outside the walls of the Chinese administrators but inside the walls built to protect the Muslims. This is the oldest mosque site in Lanzhou, though the present structures were built only in 1984–85. According to the caretakers, a large Chinese temple–style building stood here before the Cultural Revolution. Today one wall remains from that era: the eastern outer wall of the courtyard, opposite the entrance to the main prayer hall. This wall is ornately

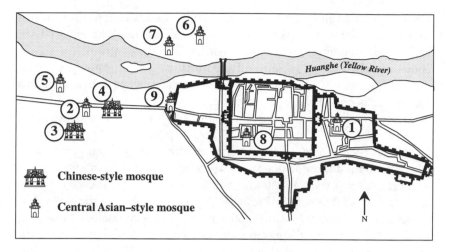

Map 22. Lanzhou mosques in relation to former city walls, 1988.

carved and topped with a spectacular, and distinctly Chinese, green tile roof. The main mosque building, built in 1985, has a large green dome in the center of the roof of the front veranda (the dome does not cover the prayer hall itself). On the northeast corner of the roof, there is a narrow, green-domed minaret. (Green is a significant color for Islam; most of the new style mosques are green.) The facade is decorated with Hui stone flower carvings and pink and green marblelike stone.[14] The interior is similar to many contemporary Hui mosques, with a fine polished wood floor and thick carpets, a plain niche on the west wall, a rack for clothing, and clocks. There is no separate section for women in the prayer hall itself. Approximately 3,000 worshippers came to this site for daily prayers before the Cultural Revolution; today the average is about 500.

The East Western Ferry Crossing Road Mosque (Xijin Donglu Qingzhen Si) across from Little West Lake (Xiaoxihu) Park (no. 2, Map 22) also has a green-domed minaret. This structure, which stands atop a two-story shop building on the corner, is formed by four pillars capped by the dome. There are filigree ornaments of carved wood painted gold where the pillars meet the dome. The dome is topped by a miniature Chinese-style pavilion, crowned with three orbs and a crescent moon, mounted on a spire. The shop on the first floor sells snack foods and spices but also seems to serve as a gathering place for elderly Hui men in the neighborhood. The mosque itself is entered through an arch and a stairway several shops to the east. A ramp leads up to the second-story level—there is a steep slope up from the street—to an open plaza adjacent to the mosque. The minaret forms the northwest corner of this plaza. The main prayer hall is quite modern in style: the facade is covered in green and yellow conglomerate; the roof is flat; and the north wall is almost entirely window, as is the east wall, which consists of a series of glass doors. The qibla wall inside is on the west. Five rugs depicting Mecca are mounted on the wall, surrounding its rather plain niche. The mosque was constructed in 1984.

About 50 m down a side street from the East Western Ferry Road Mosque stands a mosque that was built four years earlier, in 1980 (no. 3, Map 22). It has a very tall minaret, made up of several stories of Chinese-style pavilions, each with elaborately carved flowers under the eaves. The dome of the minaret is a rather narrow and high Chinese pavilion–style tiled roof. The minaret is mounted on a two-story building fronting the alley on the west side of the mosque. The building itself is unremarkable: a concrete box with a passageway on the first floor that leads past the south side of the prayer hall (oriented east-west) into the courtyard. Numerous mats strewn on a deep covered veranda attached to the eastern face of the prayer hall indicate that there is not enough space inside for all worshippers at peak weekly prayer times. At the edge of the veranda, facing the courtyard, there are elaborate metal screens with a three-dimensional cast flower design. There is only one clock displayed at this mosque.

A new mosque was under construction in 1988 (no. 4, Map 22) one block east of the East Western Ferry Road Mosque, one building in from the street itself. Remnants of housing and older remnants of temple walls and gates still visible on the site indicate that this mosque is being constructed on the site of a former temple that had been largely dismantled and replaced with housing. One building, identified by workers as a Sect Hall (Paisha), was nearly complete. This building, at the north end of the site, was several stories high, with a narrow and tall "inverted lotus" tile roof and other Chinese architectural elements such as painted wooden beams and Chinese-style roof ornaments. A sign at the entrance read "Zhengben Qingyuan" (The Pure Source of the Original Text). Unusual as this structure is on the grounds of a mosque, the people at the site seemed to accept it as quite normal. Work on the prayer hall, which is to lie southwest of the Sect Hall and be oriented east-west, rather than north-south, was to begin late that year. According to the site manager, the entire project has been funded by local Hui people. One family alone donated more than 10,000 yuan (U.S. $2,702). Almost all of the workers on the site were Hui, though some of the detailed painting was contracted out to a Chinese, and the roof tiles were purchased from a Chinese craftsman.

Not far away, off an alley one block north of the Qilihe bus stop, is another mosque that was built in 1984 (no. 5, Map 22). The prayer hall, made of green cement composite and tile, is oriented east-west. It has three onion domes, a large one in the center of the roof, and two small ones over the turrets that flank the eastern facade. Its qibla wall, on the west, is decorated with a rug woven with a Mecca design. South of the prayer hall is a two-story building with a small bath on the first floor for ablutions (it is about 2.5 m by 1 m and no more than 1 m deep). The mosque has very little courtyard space, and the prayer hall is small too; there is probably only room for about 50 people. According to the caretaker, this mosque is a replacement for a much more modest tamped-earth or brick-and-mud building that was destroyed during the Cultural Revolution.

There are two mosques west of White Pagoda Mountain (Baita Shan) across the Yellow River from Lanzhou proper. Both are oriented along an east-west axis, with the prayer hall opening onto a courtyard on the east. The larger of the two (no. 6, Map 22) has a large green onion dome that was badly in need of paint when I saw it. The other mosque, to the west, sits on the banks of the river (no. 7). It also has a green dome and seems to be a school for young men.

Two other mosques were under construction in 1988. One, northwest of the intersection of Zhongshan and Yongchang streets (no. 8, Map 22), is of some interest as a replacement for a mosque that was sited inside the old inner wall. But that mosque had itself been relatively recent, having been built some time after 1926. The new mosque is designed with a green dome at the center, flanked by green domed spires on the corners.

The other mosque under construction, at Liberation Gate (Jiefangmen), the western gate of the old city (no. 9, Map 22), stands on a very old site. The original mosque, a Chinese-style structure, with a round minaret constructed in the shape of an elaborate pagoda, was built in 1687 (substantially rebuilt sometime later). During the Nationalist period a second building was added on the west for ablutions and other religious functions. This new building was quite different from the body of the mosque—a combination of the "Western" style (in brick and stucco) and the old Central/Southwest Asian style, with tall pillars, hexagonal windows, and a tower at the east and west (Liu Zhiping 1985: 145–48). Both the Chinese-style mosque, with its pagoda/minaret, and the Central/Southwest Asian–style addition were dismantled during the Cultural Revolution.

In 1988 work had been completed on the main prayer hall, a round building with arched windows and a large dome. According to posters on the construction site, the entire complex will be built in Central/Southwest Asian style, on a similar plan to the old Chinese-style mosque. The new structure features a very prominent minaret styled as an elaborate dome.

The mosques of Xining represent a wide range of styles, from relatively conservative Chinese temple–like survivals of the Cultural Revolution to somewhat fanciful hybrids combining the onion domes of Central/Southwest Asia with newly invented "pagoda-style" minarets. Xining has long had a substantial Muslim population. Its mosques reportedly still had some 20,000 congregants in the late 1950s (Alley 1957: 34). There may have been 20 mosques.

The Great Mosque of the Eastern Suburb (Dongguan Qingzhen Da Si; no. 1, Map 23) is touted as a must-see for both Chinese and Western visitors (but this is due in part to the relative paucity of tourist sites within the city). The largest mosque in Qinghai Province, it accommodates more than 3,000 people on important occasions and serves as the Friday mosque for the entire city of Xining. The original mosque was built in 1380, at a time when the Ming government had appointed Hui to several high-level posts in Xining and was extremely interested in fostering trade in the area. That building survived for nearly 500 years; it was almost wholly destroyed by Qing troops in 1877 during their suppression of

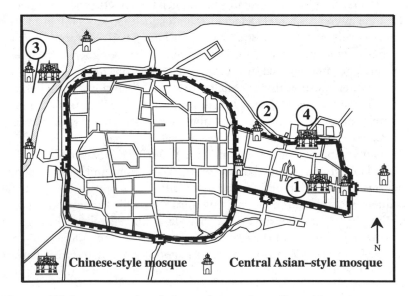

Map 23. Xining mosques in relation to former city walls, 1988.

Muslim revolts in the city. The mosque was rebuilt in 1895. In 1916 a Hui named Ma Wanfu, who was well versed in Islamic culture (having consulted with pilgrims returned from Mecca), came to Xining and persuaded the local elders that the building was not correctly oriented to Mecca. After some deliberation, they decided to raze the mosque and construct a new one according to Ma Wanfu's instructions. The new mosque was turned 45 degrees from the old one (La Bingde & Kong Xianglu 1985). Unfortunately, none of the references I consulted indicate what the old mosque's orientation was. Today it is oriented toward the west. This is, nonetheless, at once a striking example of how important proper orientation is to the Hui and clear evidence that they were quite capable of making a mistake in that respect.

In 1926 the mosque was expanded, with the construction of two large buildings flanking the single courtyard in front of the main prayer hall. Between 1926 and 1946 double minarets and an arched entrance were added on the east side of the courtyard. A bathhouse was also constructed, as well as 80 rooms of housing and cooking facilities. The mosque was closed in 1966 as a result of the Cultural Revolution. At the start of the 1970s, the buildings were reopened as the Laborers' Culture Palace (Laodong Renmin Wenhuagong). A movie theater, ball courts, and other public recreational facilities were installed in the old structures. The mosque was returned to the Hui in 1979. Families who had moved into the buildings during the Cultural Revolution were relocated, and restoration commenced on the structures themselves (La Bingde & Kong Xianglu 1985).

The Great Mosque is a spectacular example of the blending of styles in frontier mosque construction. It incorporates elements of Chinese, Central Asian, and Tibetan architecture. The compound is centered on a large stone-paved courtyard, with spaces marked off to allow worshippers to kneel in an orderly fashion. The main prayer hall, at the western side of the courtyard, is built in Chinese style; it has a glassed-in veranda/forecourt, with the main space beyond behind folding doors, and a gray tile roof ornamented with a large green-tile diamond. But the three golden spires on the ridgepole (a tall one flanked by two smaller ones) are distinctly non-Chinese. They are Tibetan temple ornaments that the mosque received as a gift, many years ago, from the abbot of nearby Kumbum Jampa Ling Monastery. The front of the glassed-in veranda section is protected by a fence of green and yellow metal pickets, each topped by a crescent moon. On the north and south sides of the courtyard, there are long two-story buildings housing offices, classrooms, a library, and other elements of the mosque.

The entrance to the courtyard is on the east, via an elaborate gate/wall of Central/Southwest Asian design, with a pointed arch in the center, flanked by two smaller arched entrances, the whole topped by a narrow walkway with a railing. This wall/gate is bordered on both sides by three-story-high hexagonal minarets of brick painted green. The third story of these towers is an open cupola-like structure: six pillars positioned at the points of the hexagon supporting a six-sided Chinese-style tile roof. The roof is adorned with a Tibetan-style ornament, topped by a crescent moon. This entryway has been renovated since the Cultural Revolution. When Rewi Alley saw the mosque in the 1950s, it had a minaret "of blue brick . . . half Chinese, half Central Asian in architecture" (Alley 1957: 34). A pre–Cultural Revolution photograph shows metal swastikas affixed to the sides of the minarets, three over each window in each face of the first and second floors (Liu Zhiping 1985: 335). These Buddhist symbols, further evidence of the syncretism in Hui mosque construction, have since been removed. The 1916 reconstruction of the mosque, as well as other construction projects in the years before 1946, was carried out with the assistance of architects and craftsmen who had been attached to Labrang Monastery in Gansu. Tu and Chinese architects and craftsmen were also employed from time to time. This is the source of at least some of the Lamaist and Chinese architectural elements in the complex, notably the six-sided minarets with the flying roofs and the swastika ornamentation (La Bingde & Kong Xianglu 1985).

Xining's Water Wall Gate Mosque (Xuechengmen Qingzhen Si), at the southeast corner of the intersection of Beixiao and Qiyi roads (no. 2, Map 23), was built over the years 1981–86. An earlier mosque of Chinese style was destroyed during the Cultural Revolution. The new buildings, with their green onion domes, are primarily Central/Southwest Asian in style, though a fengshui screen flanked by two moon gates stands at the entrance. The prayer hall is oriented east-west; the other buildings surrounding the central courtyard are not.

The Ocean of Prosperity Road Mosque (Xinghailu Qingzhen Si) is located at the northwest bend of Huangan Alley (no. 3, Map 23). According to the caretakers, it was built in the 1920s, but it has clearly been renovated. The main building is in Chinese temple–style, with a Chinese tile roof. But the facade has been renovated in a more Central Asian style, with a covering of tile. There are other Central Asian features that may be new additions as well. For example, the tower at the gate, which serves as a minaret, has a green-tile onion dome. This is possibly true also of the three pillars, each consisting of three green orbs topped by a crescent moon, that stand at the apex of the roof.

On Beiguan Street, just west of Renyi Alley, there is an old mosque in the Chinese style (no. 4, Map 23). Built in 1787, it is quite ornate, with wood- and stone-carved flowers and a tile roof. The paint on the facade is much faded. At some point the veranda entrance on the east side was glassed in. The mosque was used as a school during the Cultural Revolution, and though the main building is in use again as a prayer hall, an elementary school still shares the courtyard.

Many foreign visitors to Urumqi never see the Islamic district in the southern part of the city. Those who do, however, cannot but be amazed at the color and variety of the mosques there. Urumqi more than any of the other frontier cities has quite distinctive mosques, thanks to a mix of such disparate Islamic groups as the Uygur, the Hui, the Tatar, and the Sala. Here the flavor of the Islamic community is Central Asian, rather than Chinese.

After Dihua (Urumqi) was founded by the Qing government, Hui people from throughout northwestern China migrated to the new city to establish businesses in the southern suburb. Hui and other Islamic people from the east established communities based on place of origin, each with its own mosque. In the region of Ningxiawan, the first Islamic settlement (which was established by Hui migrants from Ningxia), there were separate mosques for groups of Muslims from Suiyuan (Hohhot), Xining (today's Qinghai Mosque), Suzhou, Lanzhou, and many other places, as well as mosques for groups of Islamic peoples like the Sala (Ma Zhengming 1984: 150). Today there are more than 30 mosques in the city proper, most of them located in the traditionally Islamic district south of the former south gate of Dihua. Map 24 shows 20 of the mosques in that area; all the references in this discussion are to that map.

The Great Shaanxi Mosque (Shaanxi Da Si; no. 1 on the map) is one of the city's most renowned mosques. The original Shaanxi Mosque, built by Hui migrants from that region soon after the founding of Dihua in 1755, was located north of the city, near today's Number One Middle School. In 1876, unhappy at the extent of power exercised by its imam, the Qing government closed the mosque, converted it to a God of Literature shrine, and forced the Shaanxi Hui to build a new mosque in the southern walled suburb (later, in 1927, the shrine was made a Confucian temple). It was 1906 before that mosque, the largest in all Urumqi, with a capacity of 500, was completed (Wulumuqi Wenshi Ciliao Liaoshi 1984).

The Great Shaanxi Mosque is built in Chinese temple style, of elaborately painted and carved wood. At the rear of the building, there is a squat eight-side pagoda that serves as a minaret. Inside the mosque

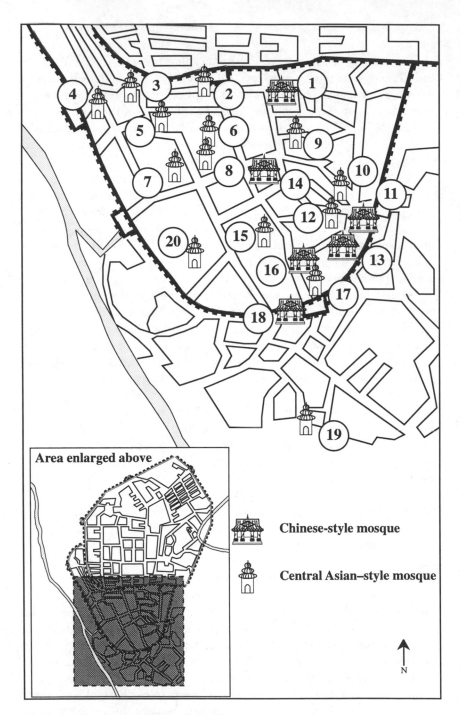

Map 24. Urumqi mosques in relation to former city walls, 1988.

this tower forms the back wall of the main prayer hall, where the qibla is located, oriented due west. There is only one courtyard. The mosque has unusual roof brackets arranged in the shape of an inverted triangle.[15] Though the mosque was declared a protected relic in 1957, it was severely damaged during the Cultural Revolution (Wulumuqi Wenshi Ciliao Liaoshi 1984: 148). Today the mosque has been declared protected again, and is undergoing reconstruction.

A new building of gleaming white tile near the site of the old (south) gate between the Chinese city and the Islamic suburb at Dihua (no. 2) houses a department store on the ground level and a mosque with gold-topped pillars and a large central onion dome on the second. The store is run by and caters to Uygur, with stalls of independent Uygur merchants selling Uygur clothes, hats, and cloth. In front of the building, there is a small plaza (15–21 m by 21–30 m) flanked by stalls selling fruit, Uygur clothes and cloth, and Arabic books. Just south of the plaza is an extremely narrow lane, also filled with shops. There seems to be no conflict between the functions of the mosque on the second floor and the department store below.

Jiefang Nanlu, the old suburb's main thoroughfare running south from the south gate, has no mosques for the first quarter mile or so. But the neighborhood one block west of the gate is a Uygur neighborhood that contains six mosques. The northernmost, the Binzhou Si (no. 3), is a small mosque that was founded and frequented in its early days by Hui migrants from Shaanxi. (The Binzhou that gave it its name was an ancient state in western Shaanxi Province that came under Chinese control in the year 725.) When I saw the mosque in 1988, it appeared to have served quite recently as a factory but had a pleasant and well-tended garden in the courtyard. Like its neighbor to the south and west (no. 4), it incorporates a green dome in its design. To the south of this pair is a Uygur mosque of recent cement construction (no. 5). The main building is of conventional form, with a green dome flanked by spires, but the overall plan of the compound is a bit unusual in that the outer gate faces west. The mosque to the east (no. 6) had clearly been taken over as a factory: the inside courtyard and prayer hall were still in the process of being converted back to religious use in 1988. The outer gate is topped by a small onion dome, but the main hall itself is (or at least was) low with a flat roof. Farther south is a mosque (no. 7) right on a street filled with a busy goldfish and pigeon market with a gateway decorated with a green onion dome, called the Old Market Mosque (Laofang Si). Immediately east is a mosque with a green onion dome flanked by four turrets (no. 8). This mosque is taller and older looking than the others in the neighborhood and exceptional in having all its signs in Arabic only.[16]

To the east of this cluster, a block off of South Jiefang Road, is a mosque of mixed architectural style (no. 9). It seems at first glance clearly Central/Southwest Asian in style (and is so shown on the map) because the gate is topped by a blue onion dome flanked by turrets. But the gate appears to have been a recent addition. The prayer hall itself is a dilapidated structure in the Chinese tile-roofed temple style.

The bulk of the other mosques in the old suburb are concentrated on the east side of Jiefang Nanlu south of Shanxi Xiang, the first major cross street south of the south gate area. The Qinghai Mosque, which was first established as the Xining Mosque by Hui migrants from that locale (no. 10), stands one block east of Jiefang Nanlu on Shanxi Xiang. It too had clearly been used as a factory and was undergoing reconstruction. The main gate, opening east onto Heping Lu, is topped by a white fluted onion dome. Atop the prayer hall is an oddly shaped (nearly conical) aluminum dome painted green, topped with a crescent moon. From remnants it is plain that this has replaced a Chinese-style tile roof. Chinese temple–style painted wooden pillars remain on the front porch of the structure, but most of the facade has been rebuilt in brick. On the north side of the front courtyard, a white-and-green tile arch was under construction. Farther east on Shanxi Xiang there is a small mosque similar in style to the Great Shaanxi Mosque, with a Chinese-style octagonal pavilion/pagoda on the west side (no. 11). There is a rather simple new entrance on the north side, topped with a vaselike ornament. The main prayer hall, which opens onto a small inner court, is very plain, and was clearly converted for other uses and partially destroyed. Movable objects within the prayer hall are almost sumptuous in the frontier context: good carpets on the ground, and rich paintings of Koranic scriptures in both Arabic and Chinese on the walls. The qibla niche is inside the eight-sided pavilion section of the hall.

The Sala Mosque farther south on Heping Lu (no. 12) was founded and maintained by the Sala people. Its unusual architecture combines Chinese and Central/Southwest Asian features. The roof is gray tile, in the Chinese temple style, but the roof is of such low pitch as to be nearly flat. There is a new gate, with a green dome topped by a vase-shaped ornament. (There is a mosque built in similar style near Kashgar in the far west.) The prayer hall showed signs of recent use as a factory. Just south across the intersection is the Balishen Mosque. This mosque (no. 13) is named after the hometown of its founders and congregation, just north of the city of Hami in eastern Xinjiang. The mosque has a brand new green gate opening onto Heping Nanlu, but the prayer hall is dilapidated, with a brown Chinese-style tile roof.

There are six mosques south of Shanxi Xiang on Jiefang Nanlu itself. Closest to the intersection, on the east side of the street, stands a Hui mosque built with Chinese architectural features (no. 14). Its gateway leads to a building with a passage through the first floor, opening onto a courtyard. The prayer hall and other mosque facilities are on the floor above. Farther south, on the west side of the street, stands the Yanghang Mosque (no. 15), which was established by Tatar migrants in 1897 (Liu Jian 1987: 18).[17] The gate, a spectacular and quite elaborate building, four stories tall, with a white fluted dome and pink-and-green decoration on the facade, was constructed in 1984, according to a date on the entrance arch. Inside, however, the mosque itself is a rather humble flat-roofed factory building that has been converted for religious use. The architecture of the gate building is Central/Southwest Asian style.

Farther south, on the east side of the street, the Ninggu Si, a Hui mosque, lies on a back alley just off the main street (no. 16). This structure is built in the Chinese style, with a pagoda-like minaret. The prayer hall shows signs of past conversion to factory use, but the Chinese-style bracketed tile roof remains intact. Just south of this mosque is an extremely small mosque that one could easily miss were its dilapidated domed minaret not visible from the street (no. 17). And farther south still, on the west side of the street, stands the Great South Mosque (Nan Da Si; no. 18), another Hui mosque that was being rebuilt in the 1980s in Chinese temple style. The building on the street side is two stories high, with an arched entrance in the center beneath a dome. On either side are rows of shops, including an Islamic bookstore. The buildings inside look as though they were nearly destroyed during the Cultural Revolution. But a careful restoration project was under way in 1988, though the roofs were being covered with bright green aluminum sheeting, rather than tile. The large new prayer hall is an elaborate structure with three tiers of roofs.

Another quarter-mile south on Jiefang Nanlu (no. 19), there is a Uygur mosque built in Central/Southwest Asian style, with much of the prayer space consisting of a porch covered with a flat roof supported by numerous rows of columns. On the top of the prayer building itself, there is a green aluminum church-steeple-shaped "dome" topped with a crescent moon.

The area's newest mosque (no. 20) was still under construction when I carried out fieldwork in the city. The completed part consists of a large two-story building faced in white tile and capped by a comparatively small dome. The windows are arched.

Hohhot has far fewer mosques than the other frontier cities in this study. Nonetheless, its mosques contribute to the unique character of the neighborhood directly north of the north gate of the old city district. The contrast between the elaborate Chinese-style architecture of the Great Mosque and the Central/Southwest Asian flavor of a new mosque under construction in 1988 just half a block away is particularly striking. Before 1949 there were seven mosques in Hohhot, four within the old city, one just north of the old city, one just outside the new city, and a new one constructed in 1924 at the bus station (between the old city and the new city). The four mosques inside the old city were called the East Mosque (built between 1796 and 1821), the North Mosque, the South Mosque, and the West Mosque, and were located accordingly. The mosque outside Xincheng was called the Northeast Mosque. The main Friday mosque, the Great Mosque, was located just north of the north gate of the old city (along with the Temple of the Town Gods and, in the twentieth century, a Catholic church). It was built in 1790, in a quite elaborate Chinese style (*Suiyuan xianzhi* 1909: 225–26) that was adhered to in its reconstruction in 1923. The twentieth-century version, like the original, has four pavilion-like structures placed on the roof in an eclectic manner. In 1941 a minaret was added to the compound (Liu Zhiping 1985: 124–25). Both this minaret, a six-sided, three-story structure of brick, topped by a six-sided wooden Chinese-style pavilion, and the pavilions mounted on the roof of the prayer hall have ornaments similar to those on Tibetan or Mongolian temples, but they are topped with crescent moons. Today there are also crescent moons and stars painted on the ends of each of the eaves supporting the roof: a surface usually painted with a swastika or peacock-feather design on a Chinese temple.

The new mosque under construction just down the street from the Great Mosque is several stories high and of Central/Southwest Asian style, with domes and turrets on all four corners and white and green stucco ornamentation. The smooth plaster walls seem an odd contrast to the varied surfaces of the Chinese-style Great Mosque. Nowhere did I see a clearer statement of the contrast between the traditional approach to mosque construction in the Chinese style and the recent emphasis on Central/Southwest Asian styles.

Monumental architecture is one of the most formal material expressions of culture available. In a multicultural situation such as the Chinese frontier, it is possible for many of the social and cultural relations between peoples to be played out through the medium of monumental architecture. In Chinese frontier cities the monumental architecture of the Chinese people largely reflects the efforts of the Chinese to deliberately express monolithic, pure, and carefully preserved culture. Chinese monumental architecture on the frontier also served, and continues to serve, as a physical expression of the near-absolute power held or desired by the far-flung emissaries of the Chinese empire. Just as the Spanish built great cathedrals and other structures around their plazas, or the British established colonnaded halls of justice in South Asia, so, too, the Chinese expressed the power of empire in their frontier constructions.

And what of the non-Chinese peoples and their monumental structures? Here there was greater complexity of purpose, as well as opportunity. Non-Chinese people were rarely able to affect the fundamental layout of Chinese frontier cities.[18] Rather, the non-Chinese peoples on the frontiers participated in a process of exchange with both their Chinese and their non-Chinese neighbors, and this process was clearly expressed in their architectural creations. Even the Hui, who were (and remain) culturally and socially close to the Chinese, showed some flexibility in the styles they adopted on the frontier. At the same time all of the non-Chinese peoples building within close proximity to the frontier cities incorporated many of the principles of Chinese monumental architecture, and even made much use of Chinese craftsmen and architects in their productions. Today the Hui in particular, as well as other non–Han Chinese peoples, are increasingly building monumental structures in distinctly non-Chinese styles, attempting through this medium to distance themselves from the Han Chinese and express a separate identity.

8

Environment, Regionalism, and Vernacular Architecture

In spite of the best efforts of both the Chinese and the non-Chinese peoples to reproduce their cultures and societies on the frontiers, the sometimes harsh conditions of frontier life, together with the influences of multicultural interaction, contributed to the development of distinct urban forms and ways of life. In daily life on the frontier, and in the construction of vernacular architecture by both the Chinese and the non-Chinese peoples, there was far more intercultural adaptation of architectural forms. At the same time the cosmopolitan nature of frontier cities is reflected both in the development of distinct forms of architecture indigenous to the regions where the cities are located and in the existence in many frontier cities of transplanted regional forms from a wide variety of distant locales. Here the great richness of the regional variation in both Chinese and non-Chinese culture is displayed side by side, as migrants to frontier cities contend with simultaneously maintaining ties to their home places and coping with quite different environmental and social resources.

Most cities in China have at one time or another included in their populations migrants from several different regions of China, but nowhere was the diversity so great as on the frontiers. Each new settlement attracted migrants from several core Chinese areas who brought characteristic regional features with them that were incorporated into the form of the frontier cities. These influenced the cultural, social, and built environments of the city. Practices developed in different environments and under different historical circumstances came to be commonplace on the frontier and remain so to the present day.

Environmental, Economic, and Social Contexts

Idealized Chinese urban plans did not differentiate city types by terrain or climate. There was no "desert" city, or "mountain" city, or "tropical" city—just the Chinese city. The local environment had influence on city forms primarily in terms of their geomantic siting. But once the site was selected, city founders attempted to precisely replicate the ideal Chinese city regardless of environmental factors.[1] In practice, however, the environment and the local landscape did have a significant impact on the layout of cities. This was particularly true when cities sprawled beyond their original walls. When possible, cities on the frontier were sited in places where there was good or reasonable fengshui and enough flat land to accommodate a square walled city.[2] Where subsequent growth enlarged cities far beyond early sites, the city form often confronted topographical and environmental limitations to the continuation of the ideal traditional form. Population growth led to compromises and, in some cases, abandonment of the principles of Chinese urban morphology. The succession of cities at Lanzhou, for example, were all located on the narrow plain between the Yellow River and the hills to the south; temples alone occupied the hillslopes.[3] Urban expansion led to early-twentieth-century settlement of the series of loess bluffs between the downtown area and the Qilihe district. These bluff settlements, inhabited by Han Chinese and some Hui, are composed of relatively simple flat-roofed mud or brick courtyard housing. These settlements, of course, do not conform to ideal fengshui prescriptions for site selection, and their layout does not reflect ideal Chinese principles of urban design. They are primarily residential, with just a few shops and restaurants on the main streets, and side streets too narrow for automobile transport. Similarly, in Xining, new development has taken place in a narrow and somewhat hilly region between the Huangshui River and the steep northern bluffs formerly used primarily for temples. Here there are relatively steep streets that curve with the contours of the hills, in contrast to the flat streets and sharp angled turns of Xining proper.

Both Urumqi and Hohhot are located on wide flat plains: local terrain has had little impact on the form of these cities. Although both have expanded onto the surrounding plains in the twentieth century, neither has yet reached the point where there is necessity for much building on the surrounding hillslopes. In the case of Urumqi, however, the striking natural outcrop, Hongshan (Red Mountain), that rises abruptly from the plain has affected the overall form of expansion in the twentieth century. Since the slopes are too steep for settlement, the hill marks a break in grid from the traditional city (orthogonal on the cardinal directions): the new development northwest of the city is aligned along a northwest axis paralleling the river. Kunming's twentieth-century expansion has also been across flat terrain, including lands reclaimed from Lake Dian.

Environment can affect elements of the layout of streets and houses within a city. For example, some neighborhoods in Kunming are organized along the edges of canals, a form nonexistent in the far drier cities of the northwest. When topographic features such as these water channels or the bluffs at Xining lent themselves to preconceived notions of city form, city builders were quick to take advantage of them. Once the defensive possibilities of the Panlong River were seen, it was used as a moat, which was completed with man-made channels. From at least the Qing dynasty, a small Muslim community across the river from Kunming was connected only by a bridge to the east gate. In the new China there is no need for moats, and the bulk of recent Kunming development is taking place to the east of the river. As a result this former natural barrier/defense has been bridged at a number of key thoroughfares so as to overcome its function as a dividing line. Kunming, like many of China's southern and coastal cities, has incorporated waterways into the structure of the city as well. The southern reaches of the city, which as late as the Yuan dynasty were either under water or right on the shores of Lake Dian, are traversed by several canals that once fed into the moat surrounding the city and connected it with the lake. These canals have meandering courses, giving the surrounding streets and housing a similarly meandering path.

Local environment had a significant impact on construction materials, thus placing design and building constraints on local architecture. Wood was the preferred building material in China, and, where it was scarce, it often became a decorative element in which the amount and elaboration of wooden ornament was correlated with social and economic status. Wood was culturally significant as a means of maintaining the continuity and connection with the past that was fundamental to Chinese culture and society in traditional times.

The development of wood as a prestige building material had a decided effect on the cities of the arid northwest, where its scarcity is evidenced in a sharp dichotomization of architectural forms: monumental structures relied heavily on the incorporation of wood, whereas vernacular structures, with few exceptions, made little use of it. The visual result—in Urumqi, Lanzhou, Xining, and to a lesser extent, Hohhot—is striking. Traditional vernacular buildings of mud brick and rammed earth rise out of the dust in clay shades ranging from yellow to gray in stark contrast to the traditional monumental buildings, with their bright red wooden pillars and elaborate wooden ornaments painted in vivid polychrome designs. The extensive use of wood in the construction of monumental structures in the form of temples, guild halls, government buildings, and the residences of the elite represented a strict adherence to Chinese tradition and Chinese style with neither compromise nor acknowledgment of local conditions. It was an expression of both the continuity of the Chinese empire and culture and the wealth of the Chinese elites and their local institutions. These structures typically have some mud-brick or rammed-earth load-bearing walls, but also incorporate non-load-bearing wooden walls, walls composed entirely of latticed doors, and wooden frames and roof supports. The cultural preference for monumental wooden structures was strong among the Hui as well, who constructed their mosques in the same wooden style as the Chinese built their temples.

The Lamaist peoples seem to have paid much less heed to the Chinese preference for monumental wooden structures, even where the architecture exhibits a strong Chinese influence. Lamaist monasteries in Hohhot, in Xiahe, and outside of Xining all have a number of Chinese-style buildings. In these structures, as in many Tibetan buildings, much wood is used, particularly for the beams and pillars that form the internal structure. Both the Chinese- and the Tibetan-style buildings in Lamaist monasteries, however, are constructed primarily of brick, rammed earth, or mud brick. More wood is incorporated in the facade in deference to Chinese tradition in Chinese-style buildings, while in the same complex there might be other buildings in the Tibetan style in which there is much less use of wood. However, significantly more wood is invariably used in Chinese-style buildings than in Tibetan-style buildings.

In Urumqi the Chinese tradition of wooden building meets with Central Asian traditions of monumental architecture built of mud brick. In this tradition color is introduced into the facade ornamentation via fired tiles in brilliant mosaic patterns of geometric designs. It is noteworthy that the Chinese did not seem to adopt this style even though wood to construct Chinese-style buildings was not plentiful in the immediate environs.

There is still a preference for wood in all types of construction, vernacular as well as monumental, among the Han Chinese. However, economic and resource limitations on the frontier have led the Chinese to make adaptations to more limited use of wood in house and shop buildings.[4] As a result, in Xining and Lanzhou, where wood has been relatively scarce for some time, doorway ornamentation in wood is preserved as a valued element of houses otherwise constructed of rammed earth, mud brick, or brick. In Xining, in particular, great care is taken to assure that the elaborate wooden decorative doorframes are saved and reused through successive rebuildings of the family home. The wooden doorframe becomes both a family heirloom and an element of both the Han Chinese and Hui traditional reverence for ancestors and generational continuity.

In Hohhot, where wood was somewhat less scarce, shops were built in brick on three sides, with a wooden facade and roof brackets. The more elaborate the wooden latticework and decoration on the facade, the wealthier the shop. This concept traveled beyond the city walls to the nearby steppe, where some Mongolians had elaborate Chinese wooden doorframes fashioned for their yurts, complete with elaborately arranged roof brackets for a miniature roof over the doorway.

Forms transplanted from other environmental regions are sometimes seen on the frontier, especially in elite neighborhoods. Though Lanzhou is largely a city of traditional mud-brick courtyard housing, there are a number of old two-story wooden buildings similar to southern and eastern Chinese structures clustered around the area that once housed the regional administrative complex, near the center of the city. Both their location and their wooden construction suggest that they were once the homes of the city's elite.

In contrast to the examples from the northwest, the majority of the traditional buildings in Kunming, as in other southern cities, are constructed of wood. The lower floors of houses and shops combine wood with brick; the upper stories are completely wooden. For this reason, a city like Kunming has a substantially more vertical aspect than northern cities. Its streets are lined with two-, three-, and four-story traditional buildings, whereas in Xining, for example, even two-story structures were rare until recent years. Kunming houses influenced by Bai styles incorporate stonework in their designs as well.

What is significant about the use of wood for housing in Kunming and other southern cities, however, is that despite the general difference in house form, the city form adheres closely to the traditions of the north. The variation in building materials and the height of housing do not lead to variation in street layout or the siting of monumental structures. The same can be said, moreover, of cities throughout China, including cities on the frontier. The availability of local building materials may have a strong impact on subelements such as house form, and thus it does play a role in the different regional characteristics of frontier cities. But local building materials rarely had an impact on the overall form of the city.

And although vernacular architecture was often constrained or influenced by local natural conditions, monumental architecture demonstrates relatively less variation across environmental zones in China (as well as in many other parts of the world). Roof shapes varied north to south, and building materials varied with location, but the basic elements of monumental architecture, in contrast to vernacular architecture, remained similar at any given time across the empire. For example, the roofs of monumental buildings were not built flat in arid conditions, as the roofs of vernacular buildings tended to be.

While the physical context affected the composition of vernacular architecture in frontier cities, the social and economic contexts of the frontier came to affect basic living patterns in the cities. Cities in regions based on nomadic and/or subsistence economics are anomalies to begin with: places that are important for political, economic, or religious reasons but that are fundamentally different from the mainstream culture of the area. Cities in nomadic areas are detached from the daily life and practice of the majority of the people in the regions in which they are located. Many of these people may visit a city only once or twice in a lifetime, and even those who live by trade may confine their trips to a few times each year.

In areas of local agriculturally based subsistence economies, the trade and frontier defense cities established by the Chinese were tied primarily to long-distance trade and only secondarily to local economies. Many were founded as self-sufficient forts and were thus disassociated from the local economies. It was possible for the cities to exist in relative isolation from their setting, with cultural practices and social organization differing from and relatively little affected by the surrounding milieu. The empire's defensive strategy was based in nonreliance on local trade for food and other necessities. Chinese cities on the frontier were expected to fend for themselves in terms of food and shelter provision. Those that did not, perished. Early forms of trade with people in the region tended to be in the form of trade for nonsubsistence items (in Chinese terms) such as the tea-and-horse trade with Tibetans and Mongolians. However, after the regions were relatively stable, the cities tended to engage in regular exchange for subsistence produce with people in the regions in which they were located. And the local social environment was of vital interest to the cities whenever they were under threat from the outside. Thus the cities maintained relations with local leaders as much as possible, and took steps to defend against invasion from local peoples.

Neighborhoods

Though the superstructure of the Chinese city, including roads, walls, and the placement of monumental structures, was relatively rigid, there was some opportunity for variant expressions of distinct cultural features within this structure. This was especially true among the regionally mixed Chinese populations of the frontier cities. It was not uncommon in traditional times for the neighborhoods of the walled city to be differentiated, in at least subtle ways, by architecture that reflected the place of origin of their residents. As noted, Chinese migrants when they could tended to replicate the styles of the home place rather than to adopt local styles. But allowances had to be made for the lack of wood and other materials and of building expertise, and many neighborhoods ended up blending native-place traditions with whatever the practicalities of frontier living ordained. In time the adoption of ornamentation and even structural elements from non-Chinese architecture worked to further modify traditional vernacular styles.

As in the rest of China, Chinese neighborhoods in frontier cities contained a number of functional elements such as housing, shops, temples and shrines. Neighborhood temples and shrines were often dedicated to deities associated with the primary defining features of the neighborhood, such as those associated with specific places or trades.

Non-Chinese people living within walled suburbs of frontier cities also had some opportunities to shape their neighborhoods with distinct cultural features. The Hui and other Islamic groups tended to form neighborhoods focused on both mosques and the gathering places—open squares and markets—associated with them. Mongolian and Tibetan neighborhoods also focused on religious institutions, with houses forming rings around monasteries and temples.

Local Associations

Like migrants to cities in China's core area, migrants to the frontier cities often established native-place and trade associations in their new homes. Maintaining a link to the native place was particularly important to the Chinese. William T. Rowe, in his thorough study of associations based on attachments to native place in late imperial Hankow, uses frequency of return "home" to the native place from the city as a measure of the strength of these ties. He found that though city dwellers varied in their practices, a high number of them made seasonal or at least occasional trips to their native places (Rowe 1984:234). But most migrants to Hankow came from regions within relatively easy reach of the city, such as Ningbo, Guangzhou, Shanxi, Shaanxi, and Anhui. Yearly "vacations," pilgrimages, or business trips to these places were well within the realm of possibility in late imperial times. The situation was quite different on the far frontiers. Chinese migrants to cities like Urumqi and Kunming most likely shared the cultural values of migrants to Hankow, to the extent that they would have believed in the importance of regular trips to their native place and eventual burial there. This, however, was rarely possible, given the great distances, hardships, and travel time separating them from their native places (though some got a "free ride" home courtesy of the government; witness William Rockhill's example of criminals being transported from Xinjiang all the way back to Shanxi, a journey of four months, so that they could be beheaded in their native province; Rockhill 1891: 14).

Guilds (*huiguan*) based on native place and/or occupation provided a means for Chinese on the frontier and throughout China to maintain the customs and connections of their home places.[5] These guilds, which developed in eastern China as early as the beginning of the fifteenth century, became significant elements of urban society in the mid to late sixteenth century; by the end of the century, they had become quite widely distributed and relatively standardized. According to Yung-cheng Kao, the development of trade guilds was concomitant with the clustering of trades into districts that followed reforms in the internal structure of cities at the end of the Tang dynasty, when street commerce became a characteristic feature of Chinese cities (Kao 1981: 55). The craft or trade guild was closely related to the place-associated guild, since migrants from a particular region commonly monopolized a specific craft or trade.

Both native-place and trade guilds maintained halls where members gathered for meetings and banquets and for the worship of patron deities. There were, for example, patrons for house builders, tailors, and printers, and also for trades such as booksellers and furniture merchants.[6] Some of the professions (e.g., performers and white-collar workers) also had guilds, halls, and patrons (Guo Licheng 1984).

Guilds served social functions by uniting people of a native place and sponsoring their interests vis-à-vis local administration, and served economic functions through their collection of monies from members and subsequent sponsorship of public works or trade fairs (or appropriate bribes of officials), or loans to members. And they fulfilled an important social role by helping to maintain linkages between peoples of the same place, though they were no substitute for actual pilgrimage to the ancestral home. In frontier cities, places so far removed from the eastern core areas, maintaining the native-place associations and guilds was perhaps given special attention.

On the frontiers, where all Chinese were migrants or descendants of migrants, guilds developed as one of the most powerful organizational forces behind both society and city space. Guilds often owned property that they rented or sold to their members, creating regional enclaves within the cities. Schools and temples operated by guilds ensured the continuity of regional beliefs and practice. Guilds sponsored public works projects, controlled markets and trade, and served as powerful lobbies with the local government.

The guilds of Urumqi are an excellent example of how these groups functioned on the frontier. The city came to have a number of neighborhoods or districts based on place of origin—such as Ningxia Wan, Shanxi Xiang, Henan Zhuangzi, and Hezhou Gong—as new migrants sought out and settled with older ones from their native regions. Congregation by place began with Chinese military occupation, when the army maintained separate garrisons for soldiers from Sichuan, Hubei and Hunan, Anhui, Henan, Shaanxi, and Gansu provinces. After Xinjiang was made a province in 1884, many of these soldiers were demobilized and settled in Urumqi, where they established place-associated communities and guilds along with other migrants from their provinces. The Hunan and Hubei Huiguan stood on the south side of today's Tianshan Building, and the Gansu Huiguan stood across from today's North Gate Hospital. The Zhongzhou Huiguan was located on the west side of today's People's Square, the Sichuan-Yunnan-Guizhou Huiguan was established on the site of today's Minzhulu Department Store, the Jiangxi-Zhejiang Huiguan was situated just inside the Little East Gate, and the Jin-Shaan Huiguan was established just outside the Great West Gate, inside the God of War Temple. The Jin-Shaan Huiguan split into two separate huiguan in 1917, and a new Shaanxi Huiguan was established next to the site of today's Number One Muslim Cafeteria on Zhongshan Road East. There were also several smaller huiguan, referred to as *gongsuo*, such as the Hebei Gongsuo and the Shandong Gongsuo (Zan Yulin 1984: 80–81).

According to Zan Yulin, all the great guild halls of Urumqi were constructed as large temple-like complexes, with imposing front gates, side buildings, and a great hall. They were elaborately decorated with paintings and flying roofs in the classic Chinese style. The most magnificent was the Hubei-Hunan Huiguan (Zan Yulin 1984: 81).[7]

Many guild halls also served as complete temples, such as the God of War (Guandi) Temple/Shandong Huiguan and the Confucian Temple

(Wenchangguan)/Sichuan-Yunnan-Guizhou Huiguan. All of the guilds held yearly temple fairs, at which trade and entertainments took place. The Hubei-Hunan Huiguan held its temple fair annually at the beginning of the sixth month, the Gansu Huiguan held its temple fair at the beginning of the ninth month, and the Shaanxi Huiguan held its temple fair at the beginning of the second month. Each temple fair lasted for three days to one week (ibid., p. 82).

The guilds had their own wealth and property, primarily derived from legacies of members without surviving relatives, contributions from the members, and rents. All of the large Urumqi guilds owned enough property to provide a significant proportion of their operating budgets. For example, the Gansu Huiguan owned agricultural lands, as well as a block of about 30 houses that it rented out. The Hubei-Hunan Huiguan owned a high percentage of the street-fronting shops in the city, for which they collected rents commensurate with the prestigious locations of the shops (Zan Yulin 1984: 83). Like guilds elsewhere, the Urumqi guilds provided some social services, particularly for their own members. Both the Gansu and the Hubei-Hunan Huiguan, for example, ran elementary schools for their members' children during the Nationalist era (ibid., p. 84).

The first guild in Lanzhou—the Shan-Shaan Huiguan, an association for migrants from Shanxi and Shaanxi—was founded in 1708 (on Shanzishi Road). Between 1821 and 1851 the Jiangxi, Jiangnan, and Zhejiang guilds were established (on Jinta Alley; however, the Jiangnan Huiguan relocated to Shanzishi Road in 1879). In 1856 a separate Shaanxi guild was built on Gongyuan Alley. The Hubei, Hunan, Sichuan, and Yuzhang guilds were all established (on Xihou Street) between 1862 and 1874.[8] The Guangdong, Yudong, and Yunnan-Guizhou guilds were established (on Jinta Alley and Yongchang Street) between 1875 and 1908. The early Nationalist period saw the founding of the last large guild—the Shandong guild—on Muta Alley, as well as a number of small guilds on Huiguan Alley in the east of the city (Gong Chang 1987). The building burned down in 1896, and the guild hall was rebuilt in 1901 in a new location behind the tea market. A separate Shaanxi Huiguan was formed in 1929. Its hall, in the northeast part of the city, also served as the God of Wealth (Caishen) Temple (*Qinghai fangzhi ciliao leipian* 1987: 290).

There were also a number of guilds in Hohhot. Most of these were in Jiucheng (the Chinese/Mongolian city). In 1921 a guild named after Suiyuan (the Manchu city) was built in Jiucheng. The Liangcheng Huiguan, for people originating in a region southeast of Hohhot, was also located in Jiucheng, as was a guild established by migrants from Hebei (*Guisui xianzhi* ca. 1946: 177). There were also a number of trade guilds in Hohhot (33 during the early twentieth century), including the Xinjiang Association for Industry and Trade (Xinjiangye Gonghui). Several of these associations were housed within the grounds of the God of Wealth Temple in Jiucheng, such as the tailors' guild, the papermakers' guild, and the woolen goods guild.

Landscape Gardens

Chinese gardens are carefully orchestrated groups of buildings, pathways, waterways, pools, and green areas, designed to create scenes that can be experienced with all the senses, to establish moods, and to appeal to a particular aesthetic sense and background in the literary classics and history. The Chinese garden is a programmed experience, in which scenes of natural beauty are presented in a planned sequence and carefully framed in a variety of window and building placements and vista points. Historically there have been a number of regional variations in garden-styles, but all share similar characteristics. The most famous and often emulated gardens are those of Suzhou, in Jiangsu Province.

Classical Chinese gardens are based upon resources available in fairly humid climates, where large quantities of water are available and much use is made of ponds, slow-moving streams and lush vegetation. Many classical gardens imitate, in miniature, the humid weathered karst landscapes of southern China. The most famous stones to use for the rockery sections of Chinese gardens are specially weathered into fantastic shapes in the waters of Lake Tai, near Suzhou. In the gardens of eastern China, these elaborate rock formations, ponds, and a variety of vegetation types are combined with architectural elements to produce a synthesis of man and nature in the microcosm of the garden.

Elite Chinese on the frontier went to extraordinary lengths to recreate such gardens on the frontier, and the effort continues strong even today. A number of the public parks in frontier cities are former temple gardens that have been opened to the public. The Jincheng public garden in Lanzhou represents one recent attempt to recreate a complete Suzhou-style garden in the arid loesslands of the northwest. Pathways, walls, pools, and bridges are formed in modern concrete. There are wooden and concrete pavilions built in the classic Chinese style. The landscape is densely planted, though the plants seem to be struggling to gain a hold, and ubiquitous yellow loess dust has dulled what in Suzhou might be brilliant green effusions of leaves dripping with morning dew.[9]

In traditional Kunming, where the climate is more suited to gardening, there were more careful attempts to emulate styles borrowed from the cultural heartland of the Chinese. Several temples in Kunming have gardens in typical Chinese style (though with local variations). The garden most resembling the Suzhou style is probably the assembly of plants, water, structures, and pathways at Black Dragon Pool (Heilongtan), north of Kunming proper. This Ming dynasty Daoist complex, arranged around two pools, is designed with pavilions capturing views, and water and pathways binding the whole site.[10]

Hohhot's Manduhai Park, with its interconnected pools, bridges, and pavilions, is another attempt to build a Chinese-style garden on the frontier. The total effect of the park, however, with willow trees and grassy lawns as the primary vegetation, is not in the Suzhou style. Though the park makes stylistic reference to classical garden styles, it is more park than garden and lacks the careful orchestration of views of the Chinese tradition. The same sort of effort to capture something of the classical style can be seen in a pool with Taihu-like stone formations at its center in the entrance courtyard of Inner Mongolia University. There is a display of Taihu-like stones in front (south) of the memorial archway leading into the Xiazhao Lama Temple as well.

Such attempts to replicate the elite iconography of the Chinese garden in remote or even climatically inhospitable settings illustrates a desire to make cultural linkages to the core area as well as political and economic linkages. Like the design and construction of monumental architecture, garden design is costly and requires materials difficult to obtain in the frontier environment.

Vernacular Architecture

In China, as in most of the world, housing in particular demonstrates wide regional variations. These are influenced by regional variations in resources, climate, and culture. Until the 1980s, however, little study had been carried out on this topic.[11] During the 1980s and 1990s, there has been a growing literature on vernacular architecture in China. China's Building Industry Press (Zhongguo Jianzhu Gongye Chubanshe) has produced a series of books on housing in the provinces. Volumes completed during the 1980s cover Yunnan, Fujian, and Jilin provinces, as well as cave housing. Some Western researchers have also published material on vernacular architecture in China. Before 1949 the most notable work was that of Joseph Spencer on housing. In the 1980s, Ronald Knapp, a geographer, published two books on vernacular architecture in China: a general survey, based on information obtained at a conference on vernacular architecture held in Beijing in the mid-1980s, as well as information culled from Chinese sources and several field trips, followed by an in-depth study of vernacular architecture in Fujian Province (Knapp 1986, 1989). Knapp's work is the most comprehensive survey of Chinese vernacular architecture published to date. Chao-kay Chang and Werner Blaser also survey eastern Chinese vernacular architecture in *China: Tao in Architecture* (1987).

Chinese urban vernacular architecture contrasts with that in much of the rest of the world to the extent that it has long been influenced or controlled by the state. At the most basic level government involvement in overall urban planning and structure meant that all housing was limited by the structure of the city as a whole. Ronald Knapp observes, moreover, that common houses from the Tang dynasty onward were limited to three bays in width by imperial law (Knapp 1986: 19). In fact, even the use of certain types of building materials and levels of craftsmanship (degree of ornamentation) were officially controlled and assigned by social status in traditional China (Chang & Blaser 1987: 49). Thus in North China "the use of colour, decoration and also the height and proportions of the buildings and the depths of the roof trusses were regulated, with the humble courtyard house of the commoner being limited to buff grey roofing tiles and low, non-axial gateways. The use of *dougong* [roofbrackets] and colour ornamentation was forbidden [to commoners]" (Chang & Blaser 1987: 50). Despite the state's efforts to regulate architecture, some of its strictures were not rigidly enforced outside the capital cities even in the core areas (ibid., pp. 50–51), much less on the frontier. Neighborhoods of Kunming show a variety of different styles, ranging from wooden shophouses to the elaborate decorated houses of the Bai; traditional houses in Hohhot vary widely from mud brick to wooden construction; and Ugyur houses in Urumqi incorporate grape arbors.

There are several basic regional contrasts in Chinese vernacular architecture. Particularly in North China vernacular architecture differs significantly from monumental architecture in structure. Monumental architecture is based on a massive wooden frame, closed in with wooden curtain walls and movable door panels. Vernacular architecture is usually structured around thick load-bearing walls of brick, mud brick, or rammed earth. The incorporation of wood into the Chinese house in the north has become a symbol of prosperity. Wood has long been associated with wealth and prestige in China—a fact probably closely tied to the scarcity of wood in the deforested regions of North China. Similarly, in both Tibet

and Xinjiang, combinations of load-bearing walls with columns the same
height as the walls (supporting flat roofs) are common. In the south, in
contrast, there is considerably more use of wood in vernacular construction. Two-story houses are thus more common, as are pitched roofs. However, like northern houses, southern houses are likely to be formed around
courtyards. Houses and shops in the south also tend to be much more
open to the street than the houses in the north. For example, shop facades
are open during the day and boarded over at night. In the north there is
far more likely to be a door system to shield the shop interior from cold
weather.

House Forms

Frontier cities exhibit both distinctive vernacular styles built by local
groups and unique forms developed as a synthesis of two or more architectural traditions. The diffusion of vernacular architectural practices between groups reflects both aesthetic appreciation and practical application. As Joseph Spencer has observed in regard to wooden houses on the
western frontiers, patterns of adoption and borrowing of styles by various
groups are extremely complex. Spencer illustrates this with a particularly
striking example from one of the frontier areas:

Wooden houses present an interesting problem in distribution and relationship.
They are found throughout the Chinese-Tibetan border country, from Yunnan
northward in Kansu [Gansu]. . . . There seems to be a pattern of all-wooden construction employing logs, hewn timber and planks. . . . Within this belt of country
live Chinese, non-Chinese of various racial and ethnic relationships, and Tibetans.
All patterns of houses seem to be occupied today by all kinds of people. . . . The
Chinese readily adopt non-Chinese architecture when infiltrating into the Tibetan
border county. . . . Although in their own environment the Chinese, as has been
indicated, do use wood in various ways, they do not seem to possess their own all-
log-and-hewn timber house pattern. [Gerald Reitlinger] attributes the wooden
houses to the peoples of Tibeto-Burman racial stock. (Spencer 1947: 269)

Similarly, Robert Ekvall, writing about southern Gansu, noted that Tibetans made more use of relatively sophisticated construction in wood
than the Chinese did. He also suggests, however, that many of the Chinese in the region adopted Tibetan architectural practices, and lived in
Tibetan-style houses, including the Tibetan two-story house form (Ekvall
1939: 45).[12]

Hui houses in the five cities in this study tend to be more or less identical to Chinese houses. In the pre–Cultural Revolution era, however, it
was apparently common for a Hui house to be marked with a sign (in

Arabic or Chinese) identifying it as an Islamic household. This was partly a means of discouraging non-Muslims from bringing pork into the house (Gladney 1987: 229). The practice has largely been abandoned in the cities in which I worked. Traditional Hui housing reflects the same types of regional variations in style as Chinese housing.

In some cases vernacular forms vary even within regions. For example, the traditional housing of Xining and Lanzhou differs considerably, even though these cities had access to similar building materials in traditional times. There are two main types of traditional housing in Lanzhou. In poorer neighborhoods (and on the relatively recently settled hills surrounding the city), people live in courtyard houses constructed of mud brick or other brick coated with a mixture of mud and straw. Each house has a covered veranda, formed by the wooden eaves of the roof without any supporting columns. The roof, tar paper held down with rocks, is stretched across these beams and one to three lateral beams inserted into the end walls, and slopes gently up from front to back. There are also some newer houses on the bluffs. Most are of the same scale and style of the others but are constructed of red brick and tile. Some have modern elements such as second stories or iron railings. Octagonal windows are quite popular today in brick housing.

The houses inside Lanzhou's old city walls are altogether different. They have two stories and are constructed of brick or stone and wood. Many are built on a "C"-shaped plan, with a rectangular back section of three rooms and two-roomed wings on each side. This plan is similar to that of the characteristic *keyin* (bean-shape) housing of Kunming. The second floors of the houses are lined with wooden balconies on the courtyard side, and wooden columns extend from ground level all the way to the second-story roof. The roofs are "chop" style, sloping down fairly steeply, with a slight inward curve, from back to front.

Chinese houses in Xining are constructed of mud bricks or rammed earth, covered with a coating of mud and straw. The mud-straw roofs, raised on wooden rafters, are often grown over with grass and wildflowers, and are either flat or very gently pitched, sloping slightly downward from the back of the house to the front. According to Chow Dinzu, Tibetans in the area usually reside in flat-roofed mud-brick houses, with the exception of the Hwari, a Tibetan group in the Datong area, who live in wooden houses (Chow Dinzu 1949: 122). At nearby Kumbum Jampa Ling Monastery, the monks' quarters are built in a local style called the *zhuangke* (village nest) that Chen Meihe identifies as common among the Chinese, Hui, Sala, and Tu of eastern Qinghai. By his description, houses built in this style are single-family dwellings with rectangular facades and courtyards enclosed by a rammed-earth wall approximately 1 m thick and 4–5 m high. On each side of the courtyard are three or four rooms whose entrances onto the courtyard stand beneath covered verandas. One of the center rooms is a shrine room, with sleeping rooms on either side. In the four corners, there are a kitchen, a storehouse, a fodder-storage area, and an all-purpose room. The walls and roof are covered with mud and grass. Flowers and shrubs grow inside the courtyard (Chen Meihe 1986: 14).

The traditional Chinese houses of Hohhot are primarily of the North Chinese courtyard style, constructed of mud bricks and/or rammed earth. There is no such thing as a unique Mongolian house style, since most Mongolians in traditional times lived in yurts. Street-front vernacular buildings in the area of the Dazhao Temple in Hohhot's Old City District (Jiucheng) are relatively elaborate in construction, with a significant use of wood. Several are two stories high. The typical traditional building is one story tall and three times as deep as it is wide, with a shop at the front and living quarters behind. The gray tile roof slopes up from the front of the house to a ridgepole at the center of the building (at a height of nearly two stories on one-story buildings), then slopes down to the back wall. It is supported by a structure of large wooden columns spaced about 1.5 m apart, linked by crossbeams. This street-fronting building stands at one end of a courtyard, with additional structures arranged on the other sides.

Most of the houses that line the streets of this district today, however, are simple one-story structures with brick load-bearing walls on the sides, wooden lattice facades, and tile roofs. In many cases (particularly on the eastern side of the Old City District), these structures appear to have been courtyard houses at one time. The courtyards and original street-fronting structures seem to have been removed during street-widening projects, leaving the "back" structures to front on the now-wider streets. Residents have created small "courtyards" of their own by erecting brick walls (1–2 m high) to enclose a little space in front of their homes. These small forecourts, about 2 m deep, contain houseplants, the stove, and some storage.

The traditional houses of the New City (Xincheng) and Huimin districts differ considerably from these old Chinese-Mongolian houses. The Manchu residents of Xincheng and the Muslims of Huimin were more likely to build houses in what is referred to as "Shanxi style," a mud-covered brick or rammed-earth affair with a roof that slants downward from back to front. Wood tends to be used particularly sparingly in the houses of the Huimin District. Some Hui also occupy "Ningxia-style" houses, which incorporate quite elaborate wooden lattice facades and courtyards.

According to scholars at Hohhot's Institute of Mongolian History (personal communication, 1988), before the 1949 revolution the majority of the ethnic Mongolians in the area lived in monastery housing, and most of the others preferred their yurts to houses. (By one estimate, fewer than 2,000 Mongolians all told lived in Hohhot before 1954; Jankowiak 1993: 16). Apparently, many of the wealthier Mongolians had Chinese houses built for prestige, then lived in their yurts in the courtyards or next to the houses. Others erected an elaborate Chinese-style gate, with a small tile roof, double doors, and a front step, at the entrance to their yurts. When Mongolians lived in Chinese-style houses, they hired Chinese to design and build them. Conversely, though no such structures are to be seen today, some of the Chinese in Inner Mongolia during Qing times apparently lived in round mud-brick houses patterned after Mongolian yurts. These were initially supported by a central pillar, and later, by thickened load-bearing walls. The houses were oriented, in accordance with geomantic principles, with doors facing south (Pirazolli-T'serstevens 1971: 173).

The classic "Yunnan" house is built in a completely different style from the houses of Hohhot, two stories tall and painted red or green. The first story is built of mud brick; the second is constructed of wood, with over-hanging eaves and latticed windows. In Kunming many (if not all) such houses have a street-front shop on the first floor and a courtyard behind that is accessed either directly from the street through a simple door next to the shop or through the shop itself. Some of the rear structures in these courtyard arrangements are two stories tall, like the front structure, and have balconies running around the second floor. In wealthier neighborhoods there is a white stucco coating on the first floor of the houses. The houses in the Guangdong residents' district, by contrast, are completely covered in stucco. On the second floors of most houses there are windows with both latticed and solid shutters to allow for a range of ventilation and protection from the elements. Many residents lower the latticed shutters to form a shelf for their potted plants.

The majority of houses in Kunming are built in *keyin* (bean-shape) style, a reference to the distinctive "C" or "U" shape of the courtyard structure. In actuality the rooms are all quite perpendicular to each other, and the curves suggested by the term "bean shape" are not really in evidence. It is a house form that is also typical of the housing of the Bai people. This form has *sanjiansier* (three rooms and four ears), where there are three rooms across the back of the courtyard (on each floor) and two rooms on each wing flanking the courtyard. The flanking wings tend to be only one story tall, while the rear building is two stories. The flanking rooms serve as animal pens and kitchens on the first floor. There may be attic space for storage (*Zhongguo jianzhushi* 1986: 124). There are windows only on the courtyard sides of buildings.

Kunming provides clear evidence for the transplanted regional character of vernacular architecture. The Cantonese merchants living and operating shops on Jinbi Road, and particularly on Tongren Street, have gone to great lengths to reproduce the stuccoed-brick buildings of their home region. This neighborhood may date only from the early twentieth century, when southern Chinese were drawn to Kunming by the prospect of lucrative trade with the French (Schinz 1989: 293). Its yellow row-buildings, covered arcades on the ground-floor storefronts, and pilasters rising the full two-story height of the buildings are a striking contrast to the red-and-green wooden structures in the surrounding neighborhoods.

In Urumqi both Chinese and Uygur people traditionally occupied courtyard housing. The Uygur house was perhaps far more focused on the courtyard as a room than the Chinese house. In Xinjiang Uygur spend much of the hot summer under the comparatively cool shade of grape (or other vine) arbors in their courtyards. Residents sometimes move their beds out onto the arbor-covered patio for use as both day and night furniture. Today even televisions are placed out under the shade of the arbors.

In Urumqi there are a number of high-rise apartment buildings that are at least partially occupied by Uygur, in which similar arbors have been cultivated out over the tiny backyards of the bottom-floor units. Here the Uygur are making use of traditional and vernacular landscape design even in the context of a modern concrete structure. As for traditional Chinese housing in Urumqi, what remains today (near the base of Hongshan) is simple mud-and-brick courtyard housing, with roofs that slope slightly downward from back to front.

Certain individual elements of houses of the frontier are particularly distinctive or interesting as geographic phenomena because of their distinctive distributions, which in some cases are extremely limited and ethnically specific, and in others are relatively widespread and cross-culturally adopted on the frontier.

Doorframes

In 1957 Rewi Alley, observing that some of Xining's traditional houses were to be demolished and rebuilt, hoped that "the carved tiles and the old carved lintels of doors [would] be transferred to the new buildings" (Alley 1957: 32). Houses in Xining are, for the most part, simple in appearance, with high mud-coated walls on the street facades sheltering the courtyards within. However, the city's houses do have quite distinctive frames on the doors leading into the courtyards. These frames are wooden, with elaborate carving, particularly on the top cross-piece. The carvings are usually patterns of flowers. Relatively plain doorframes are primarily composed of brick tiles, with only a lintel of carved wood in the inner passage of the door. Such a doorframe might have only a few flowers carved on it. More ornate doorframes are constructed with elaborately carved wooden pieces and brick or stone; in a few cases the doorframe is composed primarily of carved wood. A typical doorframe, at the widest span at the top, measures about 2 m across (nearly 7 ft.).

These doorframes are family heirlooms, preserved despite any reconstruction of the houses themselves. For example, a house on Fayuan Street has a carved doorway that residents date to 1909. And on Beiguan Street, residents claim that though their houses are only about 30 years old, the doorframes are about 80 years old. Several residents there told me stories of how their doorframes survived Japanese bombings during the Second World War when the rest of the house was demolished. Even some of the new brick houses in old Xining have old carved wooden doorframes inserted into the new brick.

Xining houses usually have a short passage or wall beyond the front doorway, so that the passerby cannot see into the courtyard even when the outer door is open. Within the courtyards the houses have wooden verandas that are similarly carved with flowers. These may also be family heirlooms. The verandas are typically supported by four columns that create three bays. The wooden decoration at the top of the bays is arched in addition to being highly carved.

Though very little new ornamental doorway construction is being done in the city today, the art has not been entirely lost. Both floors of an elaborate new two-story building in downtown Xining, for example, are decorated with new carved wooden veranda ornaments. But I saw very few examples of new carved doors in the city.

Decorative doorframes are found elsewhere, particularly in the northwestern region, but Xining's tradition remains uniquely its own. Courtyard doorframes in Lanzhou, for instance, are more often stone than wood, and though the stone is sometimes carved, the carving tends to be relatively simple. Wooden doorframes in Lanzhou are more commonly decorated with wooden lattices than with carved designs.

Kang

The *kang*, the traditional bed and sitting surface of the northern Chinese, is a raised brick platform with a hollow center in which hot coals are inserted. This massive raised structure is a permanent element of house construction. Long ubiquitous in traditional housing in northern China proper, it has diffused widely to some of the non-Chinese groups on the northwestern frontier. According to a professor at the Qinghai Nationalities Institute (personal communication, 1988), for example, many Tibetans living in the region of Xining have adopted this Chinese-style structure. In this area Tibetans, Han Chinese, and Hui live in mixed villages in houses that are said to be virtually identical, although the houses of the Tibetans are easily identifiable from the outside by the Tibetan prayer flags mounted on the roofs. Robert Ekvall also reported Tibetan adoption of the kang, in the 1930s in southern Gansu Province. He observed that "most significant of all the material borrowing [was] the adoption among the Tibetans of the kang—the heated platform or masonry bed of the Chinese which is the most important part of the Chinese house" (Ekvall 1939: 44).

Mongolians in Inner Mongolia make use of the kang today, though this is possibly a late development, found primarily in houses built relatively recently for settling nomads. It is unclear whether or not Mongolians used the kang traditionally. The Hui have also adopted the kang. In general, however, in traditional times the kang may have been less prevalent on the frontier than they were in North China proper, in spite of the severe weather conditions. In the late nineteenth century, William Rockhill noted:

In the inns at Hsi-ning [Xining] one finds little comfort. . . . The rooms are frequently without *kangs*, having only copper fire-pans in which they burned bricks made of coal and chopped straw. On the broad, flat rim of the fire-pan stands usually a pot of tea and milk. When there is a *kang* it is often only a wooden box without any chimney or firing hole. The planks on top are removed when it is necessary to light it. (Rockhill 1891: 55)

The striking environmental and cultural differences between the Chinese core area and the frontier created conditions for the development of adaptation and variation in the physical and social construction of cities in frontier regions. These differences are most clearly evident in the realm of vernacular architecture, though differences also exist in the monumental constructions of the cities. At the same time cultural continuity in these multicultural regions created cities with cosmopolitan aspects that were paralleled only in some of China's east coast ports [13] and imperial capitals such as Tang Chang'an.

9

The Persistence of Traditional Forms in the Contemporary City

Don't be in any great hurry to see the historic vestiges of [Hohhot]. They are either in bad shape, uninteresting, or inaccessible.
——Alan Samagalski et al., *China, a Travel Survival Kit*, 1988

During the twentieth century there have been rapid and far-reaching changes in the nature of urbanism in China. Some cities have grown as much as ten times in size. Old cities have been engulfed by new streets, new housing, new architectural styles, new industrialization, and new ways of life. Political ideology, as well as national urban development policies, have changed the character and morphology of all of China's cities. It is not surprising that Chinese urbanization since 1949 is most often discussed in terms of urban growth and development, and that many visitors to contemporary Chinese frontier cities are struck by the recent development and, like the guidebook authors quoted above, miss their deep historical character. Not only have many more aspects of the traditional city survived than is often realized; its very structure has played an important role in shaping the contemporary city. Chinese cities today have weathered centuries of transformation, and, as has been demonstrated earlier in this book, the complete destruction and rebuilding or the massive growth and decline of cities have been commonplace features of urban evolution in China. But the pace of this change has been particularly rapid in the twentieth century both as a result of modernization and social change during the Republican era and, especially, as a result of concerted efforts to change China after 1949. During the rapid processes of transformation that continue to shape and reshape Chinese cities since 1949, many vestiges of the past have survived despite sometimes concerted efforts to remove all traces of them. I will open this chapter with a discussion of elements of traditional Chinese urban form that have been destroyed. Then, beginning with the lingering imprint on the landscape of those elements that have been destroyed or nearly destroyed, I will continue with a discussion of ways in which fragments of traditional Chinese urban form and structure survive in the much transformed cities of new China. In the last pages of this chapter, I will discuss official efforts to designate cities, neighborhoods, and individual structures for preservation.

The Decay and Destruction of Urban Features

There are some who argue that the very nature of the Chinese city works against the persistence of city forms. Yung-cheng Kao, for one, asserts that "the assumption that the physical form of a city persists after it is built may not be applicable to Chinese cities, where most of the buildings were built of wood, and the whole city was quite possibly demolished by frequent civil wars and rebuilt afterwards" (Y.-c. Kao 1981: 16). Though I do not agree with Kao's assertion that the entire city and its form are usually completely lost between one "generation" of the city and the next, it is true that some elements are relatively impermanent and subject to decay and destruction. This is most true for vernacular buildings and notably so in the case of common housing, which was built of quickly deteriorating rammed earth and mud-brick in the north and of highly inflammable wood in the south. Nonetheless, it is clear from the preceding discussion that street patterns, large acts of monumental architecture, and city walls do persist.

There is also a common misperception that most of the destruction of China's traditional urban forms and architecture took place during the Cultural Revolution. It is undeniably true that a great deal of destruction occurred in those years.[1] But it is also true that city walls and gates were torn down in many places well before the Communist era, and that in fact traditional houses and temples succumbed to progress and the ravages of time throughout history. The deliberate and symbolic destruction of urban elements is by no means a new invention. To cite only one example, the first Ming emperor destroyed much of the Mongol Yuan city of Dadu (Beijing) at the start of the Ming dynasty in order to rebuild it as his capital.

War and Rebellion

War has probably taken the greatest toll on Chinese cities over the centuries. Damage was inflicted by invading armies throughout Chinese history, and cities have been built and rebuilt as a result. For example, the Xiongnu, attacking from the north, sacked the city of Yeh in A.D. 307, and burned the city of Luoyang (Saragh) to the ground in 311. But whereas Luoyang was destroyed and rebuilt several times in the subsequent centuries (Sinor 1969: 93–94), the Manchu city at Urumqi, Gongning Cheng, is one example of a city that was completely abandoned after it was raided by a local insurrection. The city was built in 1771 and immediately occupied by the Qing bureaucrats and troops in the area. In 1805, just 34 years later, it already had four gates, 6,500 rooms of barracks, a drum tower, and at least 13 temples, including a God of War (Guandi) temple, a God of Literature (Wencheng) temple, a Temple of the Town Gods, and a Confucian temple. Ninety-two years after its founding, however, the entire city of Gongning Cheng was burned to the ground by local peasants in a Hui rebellion. The site was abandoned, and the residents moved to the Chinese city, Dihua. During the 1930s a normal school was built over the ruins. Today the campus serves as an agricultural college. Only part of the south wall of Gongning Cheng remains (Zan Yulin 1983: 8–26). Although the wall has been much eroded over time, the remaining core of the earth wall is still much taller than a person and 1–1.5 m thick.

Rebellions by local people are always a potential threat to cities and occupying populations on the frontier. Rebellion may or may not lead to the destruction of the city. For example, when the Tibetans attacked the city of Xining in the ninth century, they occupied the city and made it their headquarters for the next three hundred years of their control of the region, rather than destroy the city completely. Some frontier rebellions have been destructive, however. One of the most destructive frontier-wide rebellions was that of the late nineteenth century. Kunming, for example, lost nearly all its Chinese temples in the course of a revolt of Muslims and other non-Chinese peoples against oppressive labor and social conditions. Retaliations against these rebellions worked their own havoc, resulting among other things in the razing of the Great Mosque in Xining and the destruction of some buildings at Kumbum Jampa Ling Monastery.[2] A Western account of the battle over Xining captures the ethnic hostilities and the ways in which they resulted in the destruction of local cultural sites:

[The Chinese] kept thousands of soldiers on the city walls, being especially vigilant on the side overlooking the Mohammedan quarter. The double gates had been barricaded, and all the houses near the walls had been destroyed, lest they might be used for protection in the case of an attack. . . . The Mohammedans in the suburb began to attack the city, and their cannon played with great precision on the troops stationed on the wall. . . . Nothing incensed the Chinese more than the willful destruction of the beautiful Nan Hsi Xi temple on a hill just beside the city walls. (Rijnhardt 1901: 89–90)

The Demise of Monumental Structures

The pace of urban change in China, and particularly the pace of the abandonment and destruction of city structures, increased dramatically at the close of the nineteenth century. From that time forward, the traditional structure of cities was eroded by two main forces: the abandonment of traditional institutions that accompanied the decline and fall of the Qing dynasty and the turbulent period that followed, and the rapid introduction of foreign ideas and methods of building and city planning, as well as the need for urban change to accommodate the implementation of modern transportation systems such as automobile and rail transport.

Throughout Chinese history temples have been abandoned or neglected when their caretakers transferred their loyalties to other beliefs or were themselves persecuted in times of religious purges and fervor. But the twentieth century has seen the demise of all forms of temple in China. Beginning in the late nineteenth century, there was a general secularization of some aspects of Chinese society. Temples were increasingly abandoned or neglected. Support for Confucian temples, for example, faltered with the fall of the imperial dynasty that sponsored and legitimated the Confucian hierarchy. And the failing economy and chaotic social conditions of the times often precluded the reconstruction of temples destroyed during the era's violent conflicts, such as the Muslim revolts, the Taiping rebellion, and the Sino-Japanese war. In Lanzhou, for example, the Great Buddha Temple and the Zhuangyan Temple both were abandoned and fell into disrepair during this period (the Zhuangyan Temple buildings were converted for use as the Gansu Provincial Education Association in 1926).

After 1949 many temple structures were either converted for secular use, hidden away within newly built institutional compounds, or destroyed to make way for new development. Kunming fared better than some of the cities in terms of temple preservation.[3] There were at least 32 temples before 1949 (*Kunming shizhi* 1920s: 337–64), and about one-third of them still stand today. But Xining, which had at least 18 temples in the 1930s, now has only four; Lanzhou, which had at least 37 in the pre-1949 period, now has only six; and Hohhot, which had 56 in the waning Qing years, now has only two (*Xiningfu xuzhi* 1937: 123–44; Cheng Taosheng 1987: 62–63; *Guisui xianzhi* 1909: 222–28).

City walls have also suffered during the twentieth century. Neglect, lack of maintenance funds, dismantling to make way for new development, and dismantling to remove symbolic reference to the past imperial order have all contributed to the demise of most of China's once-fabled city walls. City walls have been built and rebuilt throughout most of Chinese history. Most cities have passed alternately through eras in which great attention and resources were given to the maintenance and construction of walls, and eras in which walls were either deliberately destroyed or allowed to decay. In the most general sense, periods of wall construction and maintenance tended to coincide with periods of consolidation and strength of the dynasties, while the decline of city wall integrity tended to coincide with the decline of the dynasties themselves or the importance of particular cities.

The end of the Manchu Qing dynasty in the nineteenth century was a time of relatively little wall maintenance and construction, and the Republican era in the first part of the twentieth century was marked by substantial modifications to, and in some cases removal of, walls to allow for development.[4] This process began with the widening of city gates to facilitate automobile and truck traffic. But although, for example, Kunming's south wall was removed in the 1940s to make room for a wide "Shanghai-style" boulevard (Schinz 1989: 294), its remaining walls were dismantled only after the PRC came to power. In the People's Republic of China, walls have been removed rather than repaired. The wall surrounding the Manchu city (Suiyuan) at Hohhot was torn down between 1954 and 1957 to "facilitate the needs of development" (Guan Xiaoxian 1987: 227).[5] Lanzhou's walls still stood in 1949, although gates had already been altered at that time to facilitate traffic. The removal of most of Lanzhou's walls has taken place in a piecemeal fashion and much of it during the late 1970s and 1980s in order to expand the construction area in the congested downtown (*Neimenggu gujianzhu* 1959: 86). And the walls of Xining and Urumqi, which appeared in photographs and descriptions through the 1940s, have also been dismantled.[6]

Lingering Imprints in the Urban Landscape

In spite of the many forces for the decay and destruction of elements of China's urban landscapes, many elements—particularly fragments of city walls and buildings—have survived, buried behind modern structures during the course of recent development. And even where the physical structures have been completely destroyed, there remain lingering imprints of past urban forms in the contemporary urban landscape.

City Walls

The fate of city walls has been the subject of considerable discussion and debate throughout the twentieth century in China. As late as the

1920s, Eric Teichman remarked that "[t]he walls of Lanchou are well built and kept in good repair, and the whole city has an air of compact strength, comparative cleanliness, and prosperity" (Teichman 1921: 115). Many walls remained in place on the eve of the 1949 revolution. Since the revolution, although there has been a continued demand that walls be dismantled to make way for modern development, the main philosophical debate in regard to city walls has been over whether they are the ultimate expression of the feudal tendencies of the past, and therefore an abomination to be torn down for the good of all citizens, or whether they are a symbol of China's proud cultural and engineering traditions, and thus worthy of preservation. In Beijing the debate remained heated until it was rumored that Mao Zedong wanted the city's walls removed. On the frontiers, however, the costly and time-consuming job of wall removal has often been avoided by constructing new buildings "in front of" the old walls. For example, large sections of the primary central wall of Lanzhou still remain, but in the late 1980s, they were only rarely visible from the street through occasional construction site–created gaps in an otherwise solid line of buildings (see Map 25). From an elevated vantage point such as the top of the Victory Hotel downtown, several long sections of wall were visible, including the southwest corner of the inner wall. Most of the wall appeared as a regular but severely eroded yellow loess ridge of earth running between apartment blocks and interrupted by streets. Much of the west and south sides of the inner wall remained, as well as a couple of

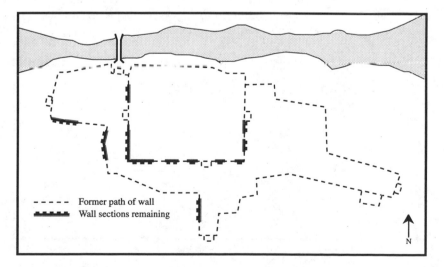

Former path of wall
Wall sections remaining

N

Map 25. Remaining walls at Lanzhou, 1988.

sections of the east side. There were also short sections of the outer wall near the Western Walled Suburb Intersection (Xiguan Shizi) bus stop and along Winespring (Jiuquan) Road. Most of the surviving wall segments were overgrown with trees, bushes, and grass, and nearly all the bricks that once faced them have long since been removed, exposing the rammed-earth core to the elements. The one spectacular exception was the southwest corner, which retained most of its brick facing and graceful curved form. These wall segments may soon disappear. In 1988 there were a number of active construction projects clearly engaged in removing sections of wall to make way for new building foundations. No preservation efforts were under way.

By all accounts Xining's walls were memorable. In the description of one nineteenth-century traveler, "Its walls, which are higher than those of Khotan and which look dignified with a dark colour which the years have given them, form a quadrilateral of four thousand by two thousand feet" (Grenard 1891: 204). A substantial portion of the north wall was still standing when I visited the city, as were short sections of the west and east walls (see Map 26). Xining is a special case, for its walls were partially formed from bluffs; thus it is the bluffs as much as the walls that still define the shape of the old walled city. The sections of wall on the north side, for

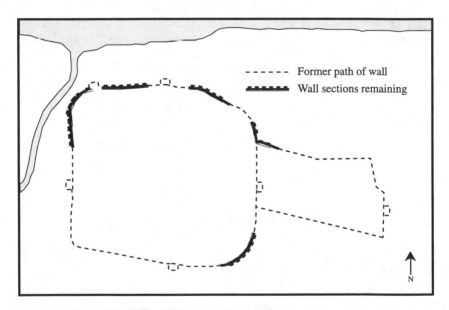

Map 26. Remaining walls at Xining, 1988.

example, by and large stand between the cliff, which was in fact an element of wall in itself, and closely built modern apartment buildings. Most of the eastern and western segments are also screened by apartment buildings. The south wall has been completely destroyed.

In both Kunming and Hohhot, the majority of the city walls were removed during the twentieth century, and what sections remain are hidden within compounds of other structures. In Kunming a short vegetation-covered section remains on the northern rim of Yuantong Hill in the city zoo. The other walls that survived to 1949 have since been removed and replaced by road. The northeastern corner of the New City (Xincheng) wall at Hohhot was still standing in 1988, but it was contained within the compound of the Inner Mongolian Autonomous Region Party Headquarters, where it was no longer a very visible or readily identifiable element of the urban landscape.

Street Patterns

Street patterns can both recall old urban forms and obscure their remnants. In many Chinese cities the former location of the walls tends to shape the street pattern still in the city core, with only a few main roads entering and exiting the former walled area, usually at the places where gates once stood. Sometimes modern ring roads are built along the route of the former walls as well, tracing the shape of the old city. And often, as in the past, the main roads clearly meet near the center of the former walled area.

The relatively small number of streets entering the old urban core reflects the fact that before city walls were removed, main roads were built through their gates, which were often widened to accommodate them. These arteries became major thoroughfares through downtown areas and remained so even after the removal of the walls. While the walls were still in place, long solid stretches of buildings were constructed along their inside edges, broken only by a few alleys. Developing new crossroads through these areas would have entailed the costly demolition of these structures and was not often done even after the walls were removed.

Once walls were removed, new rights-of-way following the paths of the walls were created through what were by now often densely settled neighborhoods. Planners saw this as an opportunity to create wide ring roads. These preserved the shape of the city walls in cities throughout China, such as Beijing, Lanzhou, and Kunming.

Nonetheless, some post-1949 road patterns have obscured the former paths of the city walls. In Xining the modern roads that now form a square around the downtown area run parallel or perpendicular to the Huang-shui River. But recent maps of Xining are printed so that these roads, which form the basis for a series of new roads that lead away from them, are square with the page, as if, as on a conventional map, they are aligned with the cardinal directions. Although the orthogonal pattern of these roads seems to suggest the former location of the walls, in fact the modern map is printed with northeast, rather than north, at the top. The former walls were aligned with the cardinal directions and thus the main axial roads, which run northeast-southwest and northwest-southeast, are not square with the former shape of the city. Consequently, the new roads do not accurately preserve the former path of the walls.

Similarly, modern roads in Urumqi might suggest walls far more square than the relatively irregularly shaped walls that surrounded the city of Dihua. The modern orthogonal street pattern obscures a more complex reality. And in Hohhot there has been a deliberate emphasis on construct-ing new streets in the space between the two old walled cities so as to obscure the separate identity of each. Neither of the old cities is completely surrounded by new roads, so that the outer edges of the walls (those op-posite the new city center) are difficult to follow.

Old Neighborhoods

The tendency in recent Chinese urban development to build new struc-tures along street frontages often obscures more traditional sections be-hind a modern facade two or three stories high and one building deep. This tendency is quite dramatic in Urumqi, for example, where shops along the major arteries of the city, such as Shengli Road leading to the south and Youhao Road leading to the northwest, obscure large sections of traditional housing immediately behind the street-fronting shops. Ur-ban development has left large areas of traditional housing behind the main roads of Hohhot's Xincheng district, the main north-south and east-west routes through old Xining, the main road leading out of Lanzhou to the west, and south of Kunming's busy Jinbi Street.

This curtain of development is one of the features of the modern Chi-nese city that leads foreign visitors to claim that "all Chinese cities look alike." It is a characteristic not only of frontier cities, but of cities of the heartland, such as Xi'an, Beijing, and Guangzhou, as well. These new structures are in part a natural outgrowth of the traditional city, where after about the time of the Tang dynasty, the main streets were lined with shops that masked the dwellings behind. It also reflects the importance of appearances and facades in post-1949 Chinese development.

Names on the Map

Through the centuries, place-names have been key indicators of power and position in China. Each dynasty proclaimed its own set of names for elements in the landscape ranging from provinces and cities to rivers and mountains, and even temples and streets. The national and local governments of the People's Republic of China have been no exception: a broad-scale naming and renaming of urban elements has been the rule throughout the post-revolution era. The preservation or, in many cases, reinstatement of place-names is in a very real sense the acknowledgment of the legitimacy of those places in Chinese history and culture.

Past features are particularly well represented in the names of streets and bus stops.[7] Both serve as points of reference for Chinese who still navigate their cities by traditional landmarks that have long since disappeared. Many of these names were not officially used during the Cultural Revolution but have since been reinstated. They are now commonly printed on Chinese city maps.

In Kunming place-names commemorate a host of former landmarks: Milesi Xincun (Maitreya Buddha Temple New Village), which is also preserved in a bus-stop name, Milesi (Maitreya Buddha Temple); Wenmiao Xixiang (Confucian Temple West Alley); Wenmiao Zhijie (Confucian Temple Forestreet); the Dong Damen (Great East Gate) and Xiao Ximen (Little West Gate) bus stops; Beimenjie (North Gate Street); Baita Lu (White Pagoda Road); and the district names Baima Si (White Horse Temple, also used for the local bus stop) and Jinma Si (Golden Horse Temple).

Likewise Lanzhou has Baiyun Guan (White Cloud Temple), Jiefangmen (Liberation Gate), Andingmen (Stability Gate), Guangwumen (Vast and Powerful Gate), and Shuangchengmen (Double Wall Gate) bus stops; Yingmenjie (Valor Gate Street); Xiaoshaomenwai (Outside the Little Little Gate Street); Jinta Xiang (Golden Pagoda Alley); and Muta Xiang (Wooden Pagoda Alley).[8]

Several Hohhot place-names mark sites in the old Chinese/Mongolian city: Jiucheng Beimen Qichezhan (Old City North Gate Bus Station); Gonzhufu Jie (Princess Palace Road); Guanyin (Goddess of Mercy) Temple Road; and Wenmiao (Confucian Temple) Road.

Xining has Ximen (West Gate) and Dongshaomen (Little East Gate) bus stops, Guanmen Jie (Watch Gate Street), Cangmen Jie (Granary Gate Street, which marks the former entrance to a city grain storage facility), Chongshangsi Jie (Devotion Reward Temple Street), and Leimingsi Jie (Thunderous Sound of Birds Temple Street).

Urumqi examples are Nanmen Tiyuchang (South Gate Sports Stadium; the reference is to the south gate of Dihua city); and the Daximen (Great West Gate), Xiaoximen (Little West Gate), Beimen (North Gate), and Dongmen (East Gate) bus stops. The district that lies in the former site of Gongning Cheng is called Laomancheng (Old Manchu City).

The persistence of old names like these in all the cities and their frequent association with transportation linkages indicate the continued importance of the form of the old city and its lasting imprint on the modern Chinese city. Major roads follow the routes of old walls, and people still rely on the walls for spatial reference.

Preservation Through Conversion

One of the most common ways in which older structures in Chinese cities have persisted in spite of redevelopment is through their conversion to alternative uses. Conversion is a form of urban preservation to the extent that the structure itself is preserved, although the use and sociocultural meaning of the structure is usually not maintained. Motivations for conversion range from the concrete practicality of reuse to the abstract symbolic transformation of an institution. Portions of religious structures and other examples of prerevolution architecture have been preserved through their incorporation into compounds designed for other purposes. Nearly all the monuments that have survived have been used for purposes other than the ones they were designed for. Some have now been rehabilitated to their original purposes; many remain inside factory walls. But it is important to note that only the shells of the structures were preserved in this manner. Internal furnishings and religious objects have been lost in most cases, as was the religious function of the structures. Government offices, factories, and social centers are typical of the kinds of conversions of older structures that have taken place in China in recent years.

Conversions for Government Use

Preserving a structure while changing its use is a traditional Chinese practice. The similarity in design between elite private residences, temples, and administrative compounds has long facilitated such conversions. Thus many temples of the nineteenth century were private dwellings during the eighteenth century and became public offices in the twentieth. One famous example is the Lama Temple in Beijing, which was converted from an elite private mansion when its owner became the emperor to Beijing's Lamaist monastery, the Yonghe Gong. Similarly, the Houfu Zhai, or Marquis' Palace, in Lanzhou began as a residence in the seventeenth century, became a Confucian temple in the eighteenth century, and was turned into a kindergarten after 1949.

During the twentieth century many temples, administrative buildings, and homes of the wealthy have been converted for government uses such as schools, courts, and public offices. But most traditional complexes, though they may have occupied large areas, had too little actual built space for these operations. The result, as noted earlier, is a thorough mix of modern buildings that occupy previously open areas at the entrance of the compound and historic structures occupying the space at the rear. There are a number of examples of this type of conversion in Hohhot and Lanzhou.

The Governor's Mansion (Jiangjun Fu) in Hohhot was converted several times. This large complex, covering some 30,000 m^2 in all, was constructed between 1737 and 1739 at the center of the Manchu city (at the northwestern corner of the main crossroads today). To the south of the complex, opposite the main gate, there was a massive spirit wall. The complex had small gates on the east and west sides, in addition to the main (south) gate, and five great halls, progressing from south to north, from public to private, with 130 rooms in all. The fifth and most private hall had flower gardens on either side. The complex served as the governor's residence until 1921, as the regional government's headquarters until 1954 (under both the Nationalists and the Communists), and as the Supreme Court of the Inner Mongolian Autonomous Region from 1956 until the mid-1980s (*Huhehaote shi* 1985). In 1988 it was undergoing extensive renovation. The court itself had been moved to a modern structure closer to the center of government between the two old cities. Despite all these changes, relatively few modifications were made to the buildings of the compound as a whole.

In contrast, a Chinese princess's palace that became part of the normal university in Hohhot in the 1920s has been considerably transformed, with a number of new classroom buildings filling in the courtyards and surrounding the older structures of the complex. The palace was built for the sixth daughter of the Qing Kangxi Emperor, Princess Seaclam (Haibang), who came to Hohhot to marry a Mongolian prince in 1697. Called the Princess's Mansion (Gongzhu Fu), it was completed in 1706 on a site northwest of the Manchu city, with six courtyards facing the Daqing Mountains on the north and the Mongolian city on the south. There were three great gates beyond the vermilion front gate, as well as side gates on the east and west. The living quarters were also located east and west of the main axis. The complex included a flower garden, complete with a small mountain, a fish pond, and a pavilion. A white tower stood at the rear of the complex. The entire palace consisted of 69 rooms. The garden and the white tower were destroyed in 1921, when the complex was converted into a normal university (Gao Yinbiao & Wang Jizhou 1987: 25). By the late 1980s the site had been transformed by the addition of several classroom buildings, but the palace buildings were still standing at the south end of the campus. Though they were dilapidated and badly in need of repair, and the courtyards were unkempt with weeds coming up through the flagstones, the complex still conveyed a sense of both grandeur and grace, with courtyards delicately screened by moon gates. Several of the buildings appeared to be in use. One looked as if it might have served as a gymnasium at one time, and another, one of the side living quarters, had been made into a library. Several rooms were apparently being used for classes. Nonetheless, the buildings were by and large intact and still possible to restore.

There is little outward evidence of the old complex that is now the Lanzhou Newspaper Office (Lanzhou Baoshe) on Long March Street. This structure too has been converted more than once. It was originally the home of an official of the Sui dynasty who was appointed to Lanzhou from Shanxi Province. He abandoned it during peasant uprisings and, with the fall of the dynasty in 618, the residence was converted to a Buddhist temple. In 1926, after centuries of operation as one of Lanzhou's three great temples (the Zhuangyan Si), it became the headquarters of the Gansu Province Education Association. According to Cheng Taosheng, no one made an attempt to preserve the temple's Buddha images. By the time the new authorities took it over after the revolution and converted it into the newspaper office, three empty halls and a few scrolls and paintings were all that remained (Cheng Taosheng 1987: 63).

In the center of the South Garden (Nanyuan) area just outside the southern gates of Lanzhou, near the Xiaoshao Gate, there was once a Buddhist temple called the Indigo Garden Temple (Dianyuan Si).[9] This temple, which was devoted to Guanyin, the Goddess of Mercy, and last renovated as a temple in 1847, is used today as the Drumtower Alley Elementary School (*Lanzhou fenglai* 1987: 75). The Marquis' Palace (Houfu Zhai) in Lanzhou was first constructed in 1675 for a Qing official from Shaanxi Province and then converted in 1740 into the Gaolan County Confucian Temple (Gaolanxian Wenmiao). After the revolution the complex became the Yanshou Alley Kindergarten (ibid., p. 82). The Dacheng Dian, one of the great halls of the Ming-era Lanzhou Prefecture Confucian

Temple (Lanzhoufu Wenmiao) at 81 Wudu Road, is still standing. It has been a middle school since 1939, when at the instigation of several famous Lanzhou authors and scholars, the Lanzhou Zhike Zhongxue (also known as Xingwen Zhongxue) was established on the site. It became the Lanzhou Building the Nation Middle School (Lanzhou Jianguo Zhongxue) in 1950 and the Number Two Middle School in 1953. Another of the city's temples, the Golden Flower Temple (Jinhua Miao) on the west end of Jinger Street, has been converted into the Jiuquan Street United Hospital (ibid., p. 108).

Factory Grounds

The simplicity of traditional Chinese monumental architecture lent itself to factory conversion. The great barnlike structures of traditional temples and houses could be converted to other uses without structural alteration, and the large courtyards between buildings were easily filled with buildings or used as workyards. This ease of conversion was particularly important on the impoverished and fast-developing frontier, where conversion of existing structures might mean substantial savings over new construction or expensive demolition projects. This fact is no doubt largely responsible for the preservation of many examples of traditional architecture to the present day.

In Xining, for instance, an old-style temple lies inside the grounds of a cloth dyeing factory that occupies the block bounded by Xinlong Alley, Yinma Alley, Xinmin Street, and Daxin Street. It was established in 1929 by people from Shaanxi Province. An inscription on a bricked-over gate just west of the entrance to the complex identifies it as the God of Wealth Temple (Caishen Dian). Neighborhood residents referred to it as the God of Wealth Huiguan, or local association. The complex served both as the Shaanxi guild hall and the temple to its patron, the God of Wealth. The entrance on the south leads into a small gate hall, followed by a courtyard, followed by a larger main hall on the northern edge of the complex. The main hall has a deep overhang at the entrance, and the doors (which are normally kept tightly locked) are of wood lattice with a wooden backing. The walls flanking the front veranda bear partially plastered-over relief scenes of flowers in vases. The roofs are typical gray tile, sloping up to a ridgepole decorated with elaborate carved (or cast) flowers. Today the temple buildings are used only for storage. The courtyard has been filled with several one-story buildings, and one must walk through these factory buildings and dodge many lines hung with multicolored cloth to reach the locked main hall at the rear of the complex.

Several examples of classical Chinese architecture can also be found within the confines of Hohhot's factories. At least three of the compounds clustered near Inner and Outer Qiaoerqi Temple (Qiaoerqi Zhao) streets in the southeastern quadrant of the old Chinese/Mongolian city contain old temples. These factories contain several different temples besides the Qiaoerqi Temple (a Lamaist temple) itself. All these compounds follow a similar pattern, as does the one in the old Manchu city at Dongfeng Street: the temple buildings, somewhat dilapidated, stand at the center of the compound toward the rear (north) surrounded by modern buildings at the front and sides.

This type of conversion has gone on in all of the cities in this study. The old structures are often not visible from the street and can be identified only from some high vantage point by their incongruous traditional roofs. In all the cases I saw, there had been substantial construction of supplementary modern structures both surrounding the temple and within the temple courtyards. In most cases the decorative elements of the traditional structure had been left to decay. A notable example can be seen at the foot of Hongshan, in Urumqi, where a temple building with its once grand roof nearly collapsed stands within a modern factory complex.

In some instances traditional structures formerly used as factories have been returned to their original owners. Such is the case with a number of mosques in Urumqi, which were clearly used as factories and were being restored for religious use in 1988. The Qinghai Mosque is a particularly good example of this phenomenon. And in at least one case that I am aware of, compensation has been paid to allow former owners to put up new buildings. A Christian church on the main north-south street in the Manchu city area of Hohhot was constructed with funds provided by the factory that now occupies the old church buildings. The manufacturing unit apparently decided that it was cheaper to pay for the construction of a new church than to move the factory off the church grounds. Given the cost of reclaiming the converted buildings for the church, the Christian organization agreed and constructed a new church on a new site.

Workers' Cultural Palaces

A workers' cultural palace (*gongren wenhua gong*) is an essential post-1949 element of most large Chinese cities. It functions as a social and political center for a number of varied activities. The one in Kunming, for example, has art, music, film, and dance studios, an audiovisual center, several large public auditoriums and exhibition halls, and a host of other educational and recreational facilities (Wang Xuepei et al. 1987: 53). Although Kunming built a whole new complex expressly for this purpose (complete with an impressive 18-story skyscraper), many cities have converted former temples to this use, particularly on the economically hard-pressed frontier. The Temple of the Town Gods (Chenghuang Miao) at 198 Zhangye Street in Lanzhou, for example, was made into the Number One Workers' Club (Diyi Gongren Julebu) in 1956. The club was closed in 1968 and remained closed for the duration of the Cultural Revolution, reopening again only in 1979. No doubt the shutdown helped protect the temple buildings from destruction at the hands of the Red Guards, although they had clearly lost their religious function by 1956 (and perhaps even before 1949; the record is unclear). In the fall of 1987, the temple complex was operating as a senior citizens' college/center, with the buildings somewhat dilapidated and little used. By the summer of 1988, however, the Workers' Club had reopened, and the compound was lively with young people playing pool and older men playing board games, drinking tea, and gossiping. One of the buildings served as a library, another as an art exhibition hall, and still another as a bookshop. On some summer evenings disco dances with live bands were held in what had once been the temple's most important halls. Black-and-white photographs of prominent citizens hung on many of the interior walls. The garden was well tended, though the grass was worn near the pool tables. The senior citizens' college had been moved to the rear of the complex, into buildings that had not been restored and were quite dilapidated.

Approximately 1 km to the west of the Workers' Club is the Lanzhou Workers' Cultural Palace. This complex of classical Chinese architecture lies just outside the old west gate of the city, across a bridge and stream from the central city. It dates back to the Tang, when it was called Cloud-peak Temple (Yunfeng Si). But like its name, which was changed under both the Song and Ming dynasties,[10] it has been altered over the centuries. The temple was rebuilt (presumably in response to either dilapidation or fire damage) in 1552, 1734, and 1809, and then expanded in 1823 and again in 1841. With grounds spreading across 3 li, it was the largest Daoist temple in the city. After substantial damage in 1942 during Japanese air raids, the temple complex was rebuilt in the early 1950s at a cost of 2.5 million yuan (approximately U.S. $1,000,000 at the time) to serve as the Lanzhou Workers' Cultural Palace. Though some small factory workshops were subsequently built at the perimeters of the complex, the primary buildings continue to serve in that capacity today (*Gansusheng lanzhoushi chengguanqu* 1983).

Xining's Workers' Cultural Palace is a complex of relatively modern buildings built on the site of the former Confucian temple, whose main hall still occupies the center of the complex. This temple dates to at least

1747, from records of contribution for ceremonies to be held there. In contrast to Lanzhou's Workers' Cultural Palace, with its many original temple buildings, only the main hall has been preserved. All the other old structures have given way to new ones (*Xiningfu xuzhi* 1937: 126).

A Cultural Palace (Wenhua Gong) on Qiyi Road on the north side of old Xining stands directly opposite the Qinghai Province Central Hospital against Xining's northern cliff/wall. This structure was formerly a temple, but today it is rather dilapidated. There is a yard in front with no ornamentation or garden, and one small modern building on the west side.

Kunming, as noted, built a wholly new workers' palace. One of its other facilities, however, the Kunming City Arts Center for the Masses (Kunmingshi Qunzhong Yishuguan), downtown, off Zhengyi Street, occupies the former site and some of the former buildings of an old Confucian Temple (Wenmiao) complex, established in 1690 (*Kunming diqu de mingsheng guji* 1962: 27). The temple was damaged during the Second World War and taken over in 1949, to become in turn the Masses' Art Garden (Dazhong Youyiyuan), the City Cultural Palace (Shi Wenhuaguan), and, from 1981, the City Arts Center. It was closed during the Cultural Revolution (Wang Xuepei et al. 1987: 54).

The end result in all of these conversions was similar: in each case a temple complex was converted for use as a community center. This conversion took place regardless of the past religious use of the complex—be it a temple of the town gods or a Daoist or Confucian shrine. I have yet to locate, however, a surviving workers' cultural palace that was formerly a non-Chinese edifice, even though several of the mosques and Lamaist temples in the five cities were built in Chinese temple style. The Great Mosque in Xining is an interesting exception, in that it was used for this purpose during the Cultural Revolution, at a time when most of these facilities were shut down. But it was returned to the Hui people afterward, as were a number of other mosques throughout the frontier that had been turned into schools and libraries in that period. Though none of the Chinese edifices taken over to this end have been returned fully to religious use, several shrine rooms have been opened in the Lanzhou Workers' Cultural Palace, and local residents wishing to worship the Daoist gods there can purchase printed prayers and incense from elderly women who stand outside the front gate.

Public Parks

Though temple complexes and other elements of the traditional landscape in China were occasionally converted into public parks in the late

Qing and Nationalist eras, the conversion of temples into public parks has become common since 1949. Like the conversion of old temple grounds into workers' cultural palaces, conversion into public parks opens formerly closed areas to the public. Unlike the workers' cultural palace, however, the public park tends to be a relatively unprogrammed use of the site. Though some of the old structures may be used as tea houses or for historical displays, and some areas may be set aside for organized sports, most of the temple grounds are left for patrons to use as they please. In many cases the structures themselves are closed to the public and serve as offices, residences, and storage facilities for the maintenance staff. The use of old temple complexes as parks, more than the other kinds of uses, has helped to preserve their open areas. Often the grounds are developed as hiking trails or gardens. Some of these "trails," on rather steep sites, resemble the stairstepped pilgrimage routes that wind their way up Tai Shan, Emei Shan, and other sacred peaks.

Lanzhou's Five Springs Park, as noted earlier, was a Buddhist temple complex dating back to 1372 that was turned into a public park in 1954 (*Gansusheng lanzhoushi chengguanqu* 1983: 135). Most of the temple buildings have been converted to secular amusements: art galleries, side shows, photograph booths, and snack bars. There are, however, vestiges of the earlier spirit of the place. One building houses a 2.8-m-high bell dating from 1202, which originally hung in the Puzhao Temple (Lanyuan) in central Lanzhou, and several other buildings at the rear and highest point in the park are being restored for religious use. Some adjacent ones, in fact, are already functioning as Buddhist temple halls; local people burn incense there before the Great Reclining Buddha. Parkland surrounding the temple buildings is developed, with some pathways and benches for strolls on the hillside.

Unlike Five Springs Park, White Pagoda Mountain (Baita Shan) Park, a converted Ming dynasty temple complex on the north bank of the Yellow River opposite Lanzhou, has no religious function today. It was made into a public park in 1958. The buildings on the lower slopes serve as tea and soft drink gardens, catering to young and old alike, and those at the mid-level are devoted to exhibition halls. For people who hike all the way to the top, there are soft drinks for sale, benches on which to rest and enjoy the view, and some of China's ubiquitous tourist-site photographers eager to provide souvenir photographs of visitors at the most scenic spots. The hike up to the white pagoda is difficult once one leaves the lower-level temple complex. Several stairways climb circuitously through trees and past small pavilions to the summit. A ridge trail makes the steep climb worthwhile, providing ample photo opportunities and a panoramic view of Lanzhou sprawled out along the south bank of the Yellow River.

Urumqi's People's Park (Renmin Gongyuan) was once the site of a lake-front temple outside the city walls. In 1884, when Xinjiang Province was established, a Temple to the Dragon King (Longwang) was built beside the lake in order to demonstrate the goodwill of the new provincial government. One pavilion has been constructed at the center of the lake, and others have been built on the park grounds to accommodate park functions (*Wulumuqi luyou* 1987: 11). The complex's elaborate front gate, a memorial to the Qing poet and scholar Zhang Jingchou, has been preserved.[11] The temple itself was closed after the founding of the People's Republic. However, the temple buildings are preserved as the venue of a cultural palace.

Kunming's temple-parks rank among the city's foremost tourist attractions. Daguan Park, 2 km west of the city proper near the lake, contains Daguanlou, a Guanyin (Goddess of Mercy) temple that was built in the Qing Kangxi era (1662–1723). It was made into a public park in 1923, during the Nationalist era (Wang Xuepei et al. 1987: 20–22). The Western Hills Forest Park (Xishan Senlin Gongyuan), just west of Kunming proper, on the north bank of Lake Dian, contains a number of small temples, as well as two large and renowned temples—the Magnificent Pavilion Temple (Huating Si) and the Greatest Magnificence Temple (Taihua Si). Former pilgrimage routes up the slopes of these temples have been developed as hiking trails and staircases, and a favorite weekend pastime is to ride the bus to the top of the mountain, then spend the day hiking down, with stops at the temples-cum-snackbars on the way.

Hohhot's People's Park (Renmin Gongyuan) was first established on Reclining Dragon Hill (Wolong Gang) as Dragon Spring Park (Longquan Gongyuan) in 1931. Though the hill was not a complete temple complex, it was a sacred site with some shrines connected with it. The government of the People's Republic of China renewed the area as a park in 1950 and changed its name to People's Park in the process (Gao Yinbiao & Wang Jizhou 1987: 32). In contrast to the other cities in this study, there are no public parks in Xining that were originally temples, though like Hohhot, it has a public park, at Tiger Hill, associated with a formerly sacred hill site.

None of the five frontier cities in this study have parks that were formerly non-Chinese temples or residences. In Lhasa, however, the Norbulingka (the Dalai Lama's summer palace) has been converted into a public park and museum. Most of the non-Chinese monumental structures on the frontier have either been destroyed, transformed beyond recognition, or returned (in the case of mosques) to religious use. Kunming has a tea shop in a public park near the Workers' Cultural Palace that is designed to look like a Bai house or temple, but it is of recent construction.

District Preservation

The recent history of the preservation, change, and reconstruction of elements of frontier cities in China is inextricably linked with twentieth-century Chinese policies toward minority nationalities and minority nationalities' regions. To some degree urban preservation efforts reflect political climates and periods of greater tolerance and acceptance of multi-cultural traditions and diversity. And the ways in which urban preservation has been accomplished reflect a history of constantly shifting power balances on the frontier. Though the experience of urban preservation on the frontier is not strikingly different from that in the core area, the multi-cultural aspect of the frontier lends a level of complexity to the issue of preservation. On the frontier preservation affects the extent to which the physical manifestations of cultural diversity can or cannot be maintained. Thus the following discussion will address preservation movements and policies as they have been formulated on a nationwide scale, as well as examples of specific acts of preservation, obscuring, or destruction as they have occurred in frontier cities.

The preservation of whole cities or entire urban districts is a relatively new concept in China that has gained some prominence in Chinese architectural journals in recent years. More common, but still rare in the Chinese context, is the preservation of individual structures within the city, rather than larger areas. The theoretical ideas behind the Chinese movement for the preservation of urban landscapes are partially derived from Western sources, with Venice, Rome, Paris, and Washington, D.C., held as models. The rationale given for overall urban preservation in China includes a number of factors, ranging from cultural preservation to tourism development. The economic benefit to be achieved from tourism development is one of the most commonly cited reasons for preservation.

Preservation has been the focus of several national conferences in China, such as the conference on "Investigations of Questions Regarding the Economic and Social Development of Famous Historical Cities," held in Changzhou in May 1986. From the remarks of participants in these meetings, it is clear that the greatest difficulties facing Chinese preservationists today are the potential conflicts between future development and preservation efforts and the fact that many cities already have been developed to the point that there is little to preserve.[12] Not much has been done even in the east to preserve large areas of the cities intact. With the exception of some substantially rebuilt districts (to be discussed in Chapter Ten), preservation is limited to a few particularly significant urban areas, such as the imperial hill station at Chengde and the home of Confucius at Qufu. Neither of these is a typical settlement in any sense. Otherwise the "preservation" of large areas is primarily restricted to height and scale restrictions in a few cities.

Still less attention has been focused on preserving districts in frontier cities. Nevertheless, two cities are the targets of major efforts in this direction. These are the Bai city of Dali, in northwestern Yunnan Province, and Lhasa, the capital of the Tibetan Autonomous Region. Dali is one of the few cities in China in which the old city area has been designated for preservation more or less in its entirety. Officials in Yunnan Province hope to preserve the old city of Dali both for historical research and for tourism. This project has been relatively successful in terms of maintaining the city's traditional appearance; most new development in the region has taken place a few miles away, in Xiaguan, the county seat. However, despite a plan to have all tourists stay in Xiaguan, rather than Dali (Peng Yongan & Li Chongguo 1985: 1–14), a new hotel has been constructed in Dali, and tourists continue to overnight there.

Dali is a Chinese-style walled city, built in a rectangular form with multistory (rebuilt) gates opening onto the north and south ends of the main thoroughfare. This street, the only major street and the only long, straight street within the city walls, is lined with traditional one- and two-story shops and houses. Many examples of traditional vernacular architecture can be found along the side streets as well. In addition, several of the area's old monumental structures have been rebuilt and preserved in the area, including a mosque and two Christian churches inside the city walls and a Daoist temple just outside the south gate. The Bai have left their distinctive mark on Dali as well. Both old homes inside the walls and new homes outside the walls display large slabs of marble and granite, evidence of the quarrying activities that have long given fame to the region. Many local shops specialize in marble products, particularly grave markers, which are carved to order for Chinese, Islamic, and Christian customers. Bai women in traditional dress are still a common sight on the streets. Their dark blue costumes, accented by brightly colored aprons and headgear, clearly distinguish them from Chinese women.

There is also a plan to preserve the old city neighborhoods of Lhasa.[13]

For Lhasa's old city area, the State Statistical Bureau reported in the late 1980s that "historical and cultural sites and parks will be protected and new structures will be integrated with existing ones so as to preserve the character of the ancient city" (PRC, State Statistical Bureau 1987: 90). Efforts have been made to protect the old city center surrounding the Jokhang Temple. There has been little infilling with modern buildings, and those that have been constructed there have been built in a modified Tibetan style. Perhaps the most high-profile new construction in old Lhasa is the large public square adjacent to the entrance to the Jokhang Temple that was built in 1984 to commemorate the twenty-fifth anniversary of Tibet's "liberation." Although the square has no local cultural roots, it is heavily used by both pilgrims circumambulating the Jokhang and people going to and from the temple and adjacent market areas.

The Preservation of Monumental Architecture

The preservation of individual historic monumental structures is primarily a twentieth-century concept in China. In past centuries buildings such as temples and palaces were maintained and rebuilt for as long as people continued to value and use them. When they were abandoned or destroyed beyond repair, there were no governmental or local attempts to preserve them as cultural artifacts.

During the twentieth century, however, there have been efforts to preserve China's cultural heritage as embodied in monumental architectural structures. These deliberate efforts have been primarily directed toward designated cultural heritage sites, which are designated at many scales, from individual stelae and statues to entire cities, and by government agencies ranging from town committees to the national government. At the largest scale, the national government has designated entire cities as "Noted State Historic and Cultural Cities." In 1982, and again in 1987, the State Council released lists of cities designated by the national and provincial governments for preservation (Qin Fengxia & Shen Bingrong 1987: 65). In general this type of designation enables the implementation of some protective legislation, such as height restrictions on buildings in historic districts, but does not necessarily provide for active preservation or reclamation. Individual sites have been identified for preservation by the Bureau of Management of Cultural Relics, an organization under the State Council. The first list issued by this agency, in 1961, identified 179 sites. These designations were implemented under considerable public debate over whether to preserve (*shou*) or liberate (*fang*) old structures.

A second list, issued in 1982, added 70 sites. The sites are identified in six categories: "Revolutionary Sites and Memorial Buildings," "Stone Caves," "Ancient Architecture and Historic Memorial Buildings," "Stone Inscriptions and Carvings," "Archaeological Sites," and "Historic Tombs" (Cady 1982: 48). The identification of "Ancient Architecture and Historic Memorial Buildings" is of course the most relevant category for urban preservation. Of the 77 architectural sites designated in 1961, 37 are located in urban areas. And 14 of the 28 designated in 1982 are in urban areas (ibid., pp. 48–61). Despite the predominantly rural demographic and spatial character of China, the emphasis is clearly on urban preservation. But in fact this national designation of sites is fairly limited. More than half of these 51 sites are in just four cities, namely, Beijing (29 percent), Chengde, near Beijing (9 percent), Suzhou (9 percent), and Lhasa (9 percent). Moreover, the 20 cities in which the rest are distributed are almost all in eastern China.

The 1961 designation of preservation sites did not guarantee preservation during the ravages of the Cultural Revolution, which had substantial impact on urban landscapes from the mid-1960s to the mid-1970s. Sites listed in 1961 such as the Ganden Monastery in Tibet and the Guangxiao Temple in Guangzhou, for example, did not survive the Cultural Revolution unscathed. Ganden, one of the three great monasteries of the Lhasa area (located 45 km east of Lhasa), was founded in 1409, and at its peak was the residence of about 3,300 monks (*Zhongguo mingsheng cidian* 1987: 995). The monastery was completely destroyed (it is now undergoing reconstruction). Guangxiao Temple is considered to have been one of the earliest temples in Guangzhou, founded in the fourth century before the city was established (ibid., pp. 800–802). Though the complex was by no means completely destroyed, it did suffer some damage during the Cultural Revolution when it was converted to use as a school.

There has been considerable unevenness in the designation of preservation sites. One of the fundamental difficulties with preservation in the PRC is that many types of traditional architecture and urban construction in China, such as courtyard houses and city walls, have been held up as symbols of the undesirable aspects of traditional Chinese culture and thus more often than not have been targets for destruction rather than preservation. The designation of preservation sites has been rare in China's politically and ideologically charged post-1949 years. For example, only the Xi'an city wall was designated for preservation in 1961 (Cady 1982: 54) at a time when there were still numerous other city walls in relatively good condition, including the Beijing wall. Its preservation reflects an extraor-

dinary act of local advocacy in the face of national pressure for the elimi-
nation of city walls and the stratified society they were widely considered
to symbolize.

Preservation is an issue that has largely been left to local governments
to decide, and considerably more sites have been designated for preservation by local agencies than by the national government. Xi'an, for example, has many historic structures that have been included in the city's
"Plan for the Conservation of Historic Monuments," which has provided
for the protection of the wall and other structures such as the bell and
drum towers since 1953 (Han Ji et al. 1982). Thus the city maintained
much of its wall while other cities, like Beijing, removed theirs during
the 1960s.

Preservation is particularly interesting in the frontier context, where
the vicissitudes of the status of minority groups have been played out in
the field of preservation. The minority nationalities' monumental architecture is primarily religious; thus official attitudes toward religion also affect
building preservation in frontier regions. Often preservation in these areas
has been contingent on whether or not the physical structure is still intact,
regardless of function. Nearly all the social or cultural practices associated
with such monumental architecture have been either curtailed for the fore-
seeable future or suspended for a significant length of time at least once
during the post-1949 era.

Direct government[14] preservation of monumental architecture on the
frontiers targets both buildings designated for protection and preservation
as historic or cultural relics that are protected and are actively used today,
and those that are protected and serve as monuments only. There is little
preservation "for preservation's sake" in the five cities. Though each has
a museum for the display of small artifacts, the same care is not, in general, applied to larger cultural artifacts.

The city of Kunming has designated 40 preservation sites, in both the
city center and the surrounding districts (rural districts within the city limits): nine points of revolutionary interest (1911 and 1949), three cave
temples, fifteen buildings of architectural or historical significance, eight
stone historical markers (stelae and other monuments) and five archaeological sites. Fifteen of the 40 are in the central city area, namely, the site
of organization for the 1911 revolution, on the west bank of Green Lake;
the former home of Comrade Zhu De (Chu Te; 1886–1976), one of the
key figures in the history of the Chinese Communist Party (though it is
now Kunming's Number Six Kindergarten and a factory dormitory); the
place where the Yunnan branch of the CCP was established in 1926; two

sites on and near Kunming Normal University related to an uprising on December 1, 1945; the North Gate Bookstore, which published and sold materials in support of the Communist Revolution between 1944 and 1946; Yuantong Temple; Ziwei Temple (a Daoist temple at the outlet of Baita Road); Qingzhen Gusi, a mosque near the former south gate; the Eastern and Western pagodas, located in the south of the central city area); the Dade Temple pagoda, on Huashan Street; a stele commemorating the Dali kingdom; a stele at Kunming Normal University commemorating the founding of the Southwest United University by migrants from the north in 1946; and a section of the Ming wall in Yuantong Park.

The Urumqi Cultural Preservation Office is working on two preservation projects: the renovation of the six halls of the Confucian Temple, which are to become a museum of city history (in the tradition, perhaps, of the Palace Museum of Beijing and other museums created from former cultural sites), and the renovation of the Shaanxi Great Mosque, which is to be restored to religious use.

Three sites in the vicinity of Lanzhou have been designated for preservation. The Great Buddha Temple (Dafo Si) in Red Wall Village north of Lanzhou, a Lamaist temple established in 1492, was severely damaged during the Cultural Revolution. Only one of the original buildings survived relatively intact. Named a provincial cultural preservation unit in October 1981, it is under reconstruction (*Lanzhou fenglai* 1987: 120; Cheng Taosheng 1987: 65). So is the White Lotus Sect Buddhist Temple. This city-sponsored project was several years away from completion in 1988. The exterior of the structure was still under repair, and the interior had not yet been touched. The third site, the Binglingsi Buddhist caves and carvings outside the city, have been preserved and are displayed intact as a tourist attraction.

Although Labrang Monastery, in southern Gansu, was designated a provincial cultural preservation unit in 1961, most of the buildings were either destroyed or severely damaged during the Cultural Revolution (Miao Sishu et al. 1987: 176). The monastery was reopened in 1979, and about 500,000 yuan (approximately U.S. $300,000) of national funds were provided for renovation. Nevertheless, from a 1958 photograph purchased in Xiahe, the complex appears to have been reduced to about a third or a half its former size. The main losses seem to be monks' housing, converted to factory and other uses, but also include a large sacred grove and several temple buildings. Since its reopening, the Panchen Lama has visited the monastery (1980), the Great Scriptures Hall (Dajing Tang) has been rebuilt (also in 1980), and Labrang has been added to the State

Council's list of national cultural preservation sites (1982). (Ibid.; Cady 1982: 61).

The Inner Mongolia Autonomous Region is in the process of renovating the former Manchu governor's mansion (as discussed below) and has designated it for preservation. Other designated preservation sites in the city of Hohhot are the Xilituzhao and Dazhao Lamaist temples in the old Mongolian/Chinese city. Xining's Great Mosque and nearby Kumbum Jampa Ling Monastery are designated historic monuments and cultural museums whose personnel are officially listed as museum employees. When Rewi Alley visited Kumbum Jampa Ling in 1956, it had nearly 2,000 monks in residence (Alley 1957: 33). In recent years they have numbered only in the hundreds.

The Preservation of Vernacular Architecture

The preservation of vernacular architecture is a quite recent and still not fully accepted concept in Chinese urban planning. Vernacular architecture has posed both spatial and ideological barriers to preservation. Since large private houses were socially unacceptable after the 1949 revolution, many were converted into multiple-family dwellings. Other traditional forms like courtyard housing have been perceived as substandard and as a barrier to modern development. Throughout most of the twentieth century, and particularly during the post-1949 era, the tendency has been to replace these structures with modern housing as quickly as possible. From the social standpoint, this has not been an unreasonable movement. The PRC has markedly improved the living conditions of many city dwellers by providing compact, affordable (heavily, and sometimes completely, subsidized) apartment block housing (see, e.g., Sit 1985). Nonetheless, in a few areas the Chinese are now recognizing that, while it is impractical and, in fact, impossible for all or even most of China's urban population to live in traditional housing, it is worthwhile to preserve some traditional neighborhoods in the interests of cultural preservation.

Beijing is an excellent example of both the problems surrounding the preservation of vernacular architecture and government attitudes toward it. Many of Beijing's traditional courtyard houses were razed to make room for modern highrises after 1949, and many of the remaining ones are scheduled for destruction in the 1990s. But the neighborhood immediately west of the Lama Temple and several other districts have been designated for preservation. The difficulty is that by the time this decision was made, these onetime single-family houses had been divided into multi-family units, so that their internal structure, as well as other elements, had been substantially altered. The same situation faces preservationists throughout China.

The city government of Urumqi, like the government of Beijing, is targeting individual vernacular structures for preservation. The Urumqi Preservation Department is in the process of identifying representative examples of traditional housing in Urumqi, including houses of the Mongolian, Hui, Uygur, and Manchu peoples. Unfortunately, as planning personnel observe, this is not so easily done because there are few genuinely traditional houses left. Most houses have either been replaced by apartment blocks or substantially renovated and subdivided.[15]

Throughout China there has been an emphasis on the preservation of individual buildings, particularly monumental architecture and very occasionally vernacular structures. Such preservation efforts have relatively little impact on the overall landscapes of the cities. But there are also some recent attempts to preserve and/or renovate complete neighborhoods within Chinese cities. Belated as these efforts are, there are still neighborhoods in the frontier cities that retain a good deal of their old character.

The busy Daguan Street market area near the center of old Kunming was designated as a preservation site in the 1980 city plan, although no city funds seem to have been set aside for restoring the many old picturesque wooden shop/dwellings. Preserving them has proved difficult, in part because of conflicting government regulations, and in part because of the residents' desire to modernize. The old structures are all two to three stories tall. Many of these wooden structures are unsalvageable and in need of replacement. Unfortunately, there is a regulation that new buildings containing housing units must be at least six stories high in central Kunming. Thus it is impossible under the law to replace an old building with a newer building that conforms to the architectural character of the neighborhood. Moreover, where renovation is possible, the high cost and scarcity of traditional building materials—particularly wood—put the job out of reach for the average household or enterprise. A lack of expertise in the traditional crafts is another hindrance. Consequently, many structures are being renovated with aluminum and glass facades that substantially alter the character of the neighborhood.[16] Local residents argue that the wooden buildings are badly deteriorated and traditional building materials and expertise are too expensive. The growing ranks of successful businesspeople, moreover, assert that a modern facelift for a building will be better for business than preservation.

The neighborhood of the Dazhao Temple in the old Chinese/Mongolian city in Hohhot has received special funds from the national government to restore shops and houses to their 1920s appearance as a result of the city's 1987 designation as one of China's "Noted State Historic and Cultural Cities" (Qin Fengxia & Shan Bingrong 1987: 65–66). This interesting preservation project was off to a good beginning in 1988. Many of the shops had been given new gray brick and wood facades, as well as brightly painted decoration. The shops that have been restored, moreover, represent different styles of building. Though most have wooden lattice windows and sloping tile roofs, with elaborately painted wooden eaves, a few are flat-roofed, with arched facades and wooden ornaments hanging down under the eaves. Several of the shops have signs indicating they are run by or cater to Muslims. In contrast to other restored streets in China built as tourist attractions, the shops here still serve local purposes, as butcher shops, hardware stores, and general stores, and the street peddlers are mainly farmers come to sell their produce out of carts. Though the emphasis so far has been on restoring the buildings on the east-west street running in front of the Dazhao Temple, some work has been done down the side streets, including Tongxuntan and Dazhaoqian streets. Since targeted projects encompass not only all the area's street-fronting buildings, but some courtyards as well, the housing above and behind the shops and courtyards is included in the preservation efforts.

This example contrasts with Beijing's Liulichang (Glazed Tile Factory) Cultural Street, a neighborhood that has been renovated to its appearance in Qing times. Fifty-four shops in Liulichang were renovated in 1979 in order to boost tourist business. The shops in the area are devoted to selling books, antiques, curios, and souvenirs. Tour buses full of foreign visitors make daily stops at the neighborhood's restaurants and shops.

Some Chinese lament the fact that Liulichang shops sell "manufactured antiques and bric-a-brac" and describe it as a "new street in fancy dress having no relevance with the life of inhabitants in the back streets" (Chen Zhanxiang 1985: 15). Indeed the adjacent housing is ordinary, even somewhat dilapidated, and appears to have derived little benefit from being near the project. Chen Zhanxiang's criticism of the planners for developing a mere facade only seems apt.

Many Chinese urbanists, however, agree with Qian Li, who praises Liulichang as a classic preservation project. To Qian, the reconstruction of an area that can be traced from its first effective settlement as a village in the Liao dynasty (915–1125), to the establishment of kilns to produce glazed tiles in the Yuan dynasty, to its development as a market for books and antiques and a haven for imperial examinees in the Ming and Qing periods represents the preservation of Chinese social history itself (Qian Li 1987: 36).

Liulichang and Hohhot's Dazhao neighborhood are only two of an increasing number of street areas that are being restored in China. For example, a 357-m-long east-west street in the southern part of the imperial hill station at Chengde is being restored in the Qing style at a cost of about 4,000,000 yuan (about U.S. $1,000,000 in the late 1980s). The street was originally built up by traders from Inner Mongolia, Shanxi, and elsewhere, who came to the area in 1803 and set up shops specifically to cater to the imperial entourage. It was a typical market street of its time, lined on both sides with 46 shops constructed of wood, tile, and rammed earth. Today's reconstruction includes a number of changes to meet contemporary needs, and particularly the needs of tourists. The hope is to encourage foreign tourism in Chengde. It is already a major domestic tourist destination, with over 1,000,000 Chinese visitors in 1985 (and about 9,000 foreign visitors). The project is somewhat controversial because new shops have been constructed on top of a filled-in canal that used to run behind the traditional shops for flood control (Wu Tianzhu 1987). Critics contend that the developers have thereby not only created something that did not exist in the past, but also destroyed a good example of sound traditional civil engineering.

Another notable restored street is Kaifeng's Song Capital Street (formerly Sun Yatsen Street).[17] This 400-m-long street runs south from Longting Park, site of the Longting (Dragon Pavilion), where the imperial palace was located during the Song dynasty. Lined with two-story wood-and-tile replicas of Song buildings, it has separate lanes for bicycle and motor traffic, as well as wide sidewalks—a change that even purists find acceptable because of the legendary width of the Imperial Way, which included a separate lane down the center for the emperor, covered arcades, and narrow canals planted in lotuses and bordered by flowering trees (Gernet 1962: 41–42; Tan Manni 1981: 14). Other streets have been reconstructed in Tianjin and in Tunxi (Anhui Province; Xiao Lianwang 1987; Qinghua daxue 1987).

These reconstructions of traditional neighborhoods in China—which are primarily shopping districts—are similar to attempts in the United States to revitalize cities by building ports and marketplaces in "upscale" but nostalgic forms. Like the Chinese projects, Boston's Quincy Market, Seattle's Pike Street, San Francisco's Pier 39, and Baltimore's Harbor (to name just a few) are commercial ventures as well as preservation projects.

Another form of vernacular preservation—the attempt to capture something of the essence of a vernacular style in new construction—will be discussed at some length in the next chapter. One example of this process, in Lanzhou, was initiated by the Architectural Institute of China Cave Dwelling/Earth Architecture Research Institute (Zhongguo Jianzhu Xuehui Yaodong Ji Shengtu Jianzhu Yanjiuhui). Originally founded in 1963 to find a solution to the "problem" of cave housing in the North China loess plateau, the institute shifted its efforts in 1980 from trying to find a substitute for cave houses to trying to preserve cave architecture as an alternative housing form.[18] Ronald Knapp notes that there have been two national conferences in China on earth-sheltered dwellings, and there was an international conference on earth-sheltered housing in Beijing in fall 1985 (Knapp 1986: 31, 39). These indicate an interest in earth dwellings among Chinese planners and architects. The institute's current demonstration project in Lanzhou (on the north side of the Yellow River, opposite the old walled city) is an entire community of cave dwellings built in tiers into the loess cliff face in the *kaoshan yaodong*, or cliffside cave dwelling–style. The goal of the project is to provide 2,000 homes in a planned community that will include a community center and shops as well as housing. The homes so far constructed make extensive use of prefabricated material, and average 10 m deep by 5 m wide, with vaulted ceilings of various heights. All face south and take advantage of both passive solar heat and earth insulation. Each group of houses is to consist of three to five tiers of caves, with about 10 cave bays per tier. The planners claim that those dwellings are safer and more durable than traditional cave dwellings, and that the design will control slope erosion.

Chinese cities have been fundamentally transformed since 1949, and a great deal of their architecture and form have been destroyed. What is most significant for the study of urban morphology on the frontier, however, is that many fine examples of traditional architecture and urban elements survived. The most common pattern for expansion on the frontier was, first, to make use of existing structures instead of razing them, and, second, to build new structures on land not previously built upon. A second significant fact, from the standpoint of preservation, is that the Islamic and Lamaist peoples on the frontier have been, with government tolerance and sometimes encouragement, restoring buildings to return them to traditional use, as mosques and temples. These reconstructions can never capture the full impact of the historic buildings, of course, but they do represent a renewal of traditions momentarily lost in the tides of politics. Moreover, as the following chapter will demonstrate, there is renewed government interest in maintaining and even creating a cultural heritage in other ways in frontier cities.

Contemporary Transformations and Restructuring

All Chinese cities have undergone fundamental and far-reaching changes since 1949. These changes have affected every aspect of city life and landscapes, from the location of districts to the style of housing developments. Though there have been a number of distinct periods of targeted regional urban development, the cumulative effects of urban development policies since 1949 have been national in scope. Thus urban development and planning policies forged in the industrial cities of the east have been implemented in the west, along with enough industrialization to create what approaches a standardized urban form throughout China. Nonetheless, a reemerging regionalism in the frontier cities is manifesting itself in the attempt to use local styles in government and other buildings. This chapter will focus first on the impact of national urban development practices on the frontier cities, with an emphasis on developments during the 1980s, and then on the trend toward regionalism.

Growth and State Control

Urban growth has been a major concern in the formulation of urban development policy in contemporary China. The national priorities, when generalized over the post-1949 era, have been to limit the growth of large cities and encourage the growth and development of medium-sized and small ones. Growth-oriented urban development programs such as those instituted during the 1950s under Soviet influence have generally targeted medium and small-scale cities in peripheral regions for development while discouraging growth in large well-established cities in eastern China. There has been little control of the growth of cities in the west of China, perhaps in part because the cities of the frontier have all been classed as medium- and small-sized cities, and in part because state policies have emphasized the large-scale migration of people from eastern China to the west. In fact, some cities in the frontier regions, such as Lanzhou, were directly targeted for growth during the Maoist era. Consequently, these cities have increased in size two to sixteen times since 1949.[1] Urban population growth on the frontier has not only resulted in a substantial expansion in the built area and infrastructure, but radically changed the ratio of Han Chinese to non–Han Chinese peoples. Once proportionately large non–Han Chinese urban populations have been overwhelmed by Han Chinese in-migrants. In addition, planned urban growth has redirected urban activities away from traditional markets and business districts.

As Table 8 indicates, the built area of the frontier cities has grown phenomenally since 1949: from over 300 percent in Kunming to more than 1,600 percent in Xining. Maps 27–31 illustrate the extent of urban growth outside the area originally enclosed by city walls for all five cities. In the mid-1980s the total newly built floorspace for the entire country since 1949 was 1,052,100,000 m² (Kirkby 1985), while the total newly built floorspace in the five frontier cities was 228,470,000 m². These figures indicate that those five cities alone accounted for as much as 21 percent of the national total. (But this is likely to be an overestimate; see, e.g., Kirkby 1985 on the reliability of the national data.)

The rate of population growth has been no less phenomenal, with increases of as much as 1,100 percent for Urumqi and 940 percent for Xi-

TABLE 8
Growth of Population and Built Area (Floor Space) in Frontier Cities, 1949–1980s

City	Population (000)			Floor space (000 m²)		
	1949	1980s[a]	Pct. gain	1949	1980s[a]	Pct. gain
Kunming[b]	267	626	234%	1,290	5,840	352%
Xining	50	470	940	3,000+	50,000	1,666
Lanzhou	195	1,000+	510	16,000	146,000	910
Urumqi	100	1,100	1,100	1,730	16,730	960
Hohhot	110	523	475	1,407	12,670	900

SOURCES: *Qinghai sanshiwunian* 1985: 90; Liu Man 1986: 424; *Yunnan dizhou shixian gaikuang* 1987: 11; *Tuanjie jianshezhong de neimenggu* 1987: 231–33; *Huhehaote gaikuang* 1987: 14–18, 230; *Xinjiang weiwuer zizhiqu gaikuang* 1985: 190.

NOTE: Values reported in this table are not necessarily reliable for fine comparisons and should be taken only for the general representation they give of rapid growth since 1949. The total gain in new floor space between the 1940s and the 1980s was 207,813,000 m².

[a]For varying years, 1984–87.

[b]Population figures are for city center districts only, and floor space figures are for housing area only.

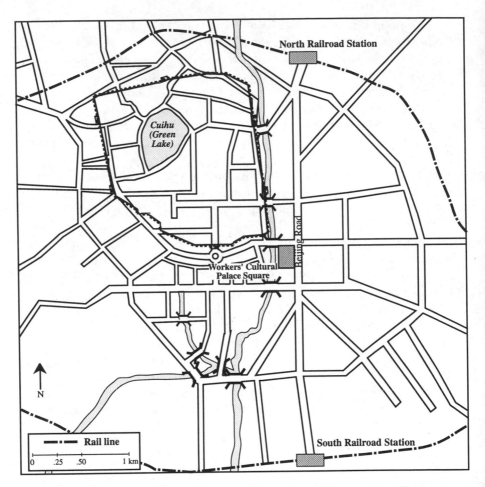

Map 27. Contemporary Kunming (1988) in relation to former city walls.
Source: adapted from PRC, State Statistical Bureau 1987: 79.

ning (Table 8). The in-migration of Han Chinese workers to support the growing industry in the frontier regions clearly accounts for much of this growth. The growth rate is difficult to chart, however, since some of the migration has not been permanent (there have been substantial reverse migrations at times). X. Yan notes that the primary component of this migration to the frontier has been members of the "labouring class," and that they do not perceive themselves as permanent migrants (X. Yan 1990: 15). This perception of impermanence was no doubt particularly widespread when the migration was the result of political policies, such as the "send-

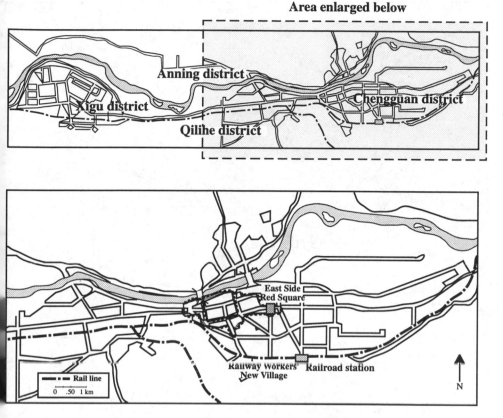

Map 28. Contemporary Lanzhou (1988) in relation to former city walls. Source: adapted from PRC, State Statistical Bureau 1987: 84. Old walls have been rotated 10° to match the distortion in the contemporary base map.

ing down" of Chinese to the frontier during the Cultural Revolution. Nonetheless, there has been substantial net population growth on the frontier, which has had a profound effect on its cultural composition. By 1975, for example, fully 38 percent of Xinjiang's population was Han Chinese, as against just over 8 percent in 1949 and about 6 percent as late as 1953 (Heberer 1989: 94).

Statistics for the pre-1949 period are extremely unreliable and difficult to come by. Table 9 pieces together what information is available on the frontier cities to chart the population trends. Data so sketchy as these do not lend themselves to generalization, but the figures on Xining, Hohhot, and Kunming's city center show clearly enough that the local peoples have

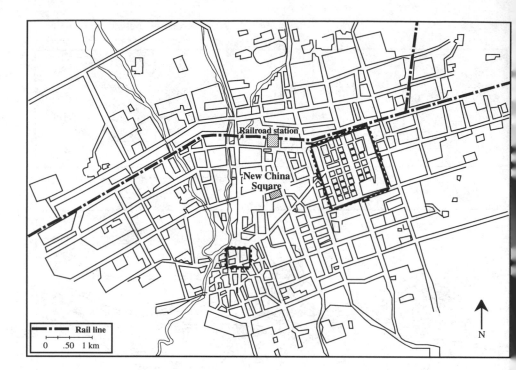

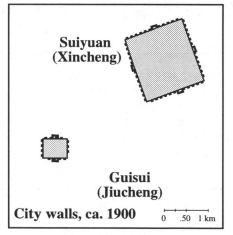

Map 29. Contemporary Hohhot (1988) in relation to former city walls. Source: adapted from PRC, State Statistical Bureau 1986: 68.

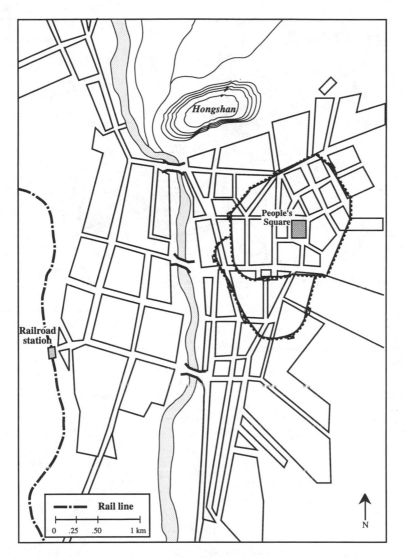

Map 30. Contemporary Urumqi (1988) in relation to former city walls. Source: adapted from PRC, State Statistical Bureau 1986: 149.

lost considerable ground to a faster-growing Han Chinese population. Still, Hohhot is something of a special case, for though its non-Han share has dropped overall, the proportion of Mongolians may actually be higher than in 1949, since many Mongolians were moved into the city during the 1950s. By Rong Yang's data for 1956, Mongolians accounted for 6 per-

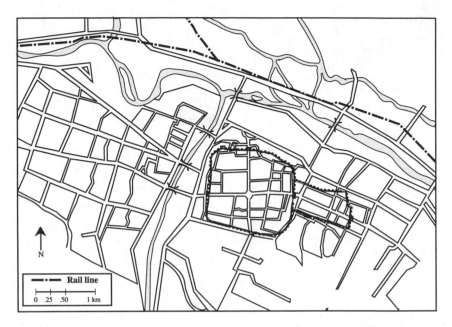

Map 31. Contemporary Xining (1988) in relation to former city walls. Source: adapted from PRC, State Statistical Bureau 1987: 170.

TABLE 9
*Non–Han Chinese as Percent of Total Population
in Frontier Cities, 1949 and 1980s*

| | 1949 population | | | 1980s population | | |
| | | Non-Han | | | Non-Han | |
City	Total	Number	Pct. of total	Total	Number	Pct. of total
Kunming[a]	—	—	—	3,268,172	359,498	11%
Xining	50,000	20,000[b]	40%	979,000	225,170	23
Lanzhou	195,000	—	—	1,000,000	68,906	7
Urumqi	100,000	—	—	1,100,000	253,000	23
Hohhot	110,000	25,285	23	1,247,706	136,000	11–12

SOURCES: Ding Shuiren 1987: 35–40; *Kunming shiqing* 1987: 84; Grenard 1891: 204; *Qinghai shengqing* 1986: 460; Yang Guangrong 1987: 181–82; *Huhehaote gaikuang* 1987: 20.

NOTE: The population estimates vary greatly by source, and accordingly these data are presented only to illustrate a general trend. Percentages are rounded to the nearest decimal.

[a]The 1980s figures are for the entire administrative area. Parallel figures for 1949 are unavailable, but data on the city center alone indicate a significant fall-off in the non-Han population. Its total population in 1949 was 267,000. There were 30,945 non-Han residents in 1964, so even assuming no population growth at all, non-Han peoples accounted for almost 12% of the total. By the 1980s the figure had declined to 5% (30,615 in a total population of 624,967).

[b]Extrapolated from Grenard's 1891 estimate of 15,000 Chinese inside the walls and 10,000 Muslims in the suburbs.

cent of the Hohhot population (14,907 in a total of 268,211), whereas Jankowiak puts their share at 11 percent in 1982 (Rong Yang 1979: 235; Jankowiak 1993: 10, 16).[2]

The frontier cities discussed in this study have long been predominantly Chinese cities with an attached, but always minority, non-Chinese population. But substantial population growth in the Han Chinese populations of the cities has led to a decrease in the significance of the non–Han Chinese populations in recent years. This demographic "sinification" of the frontier is of course just one generation old—a very short time in the lengthy context of Chinese urban history. Whether and to what extent the second generation of Han Chinese industrial migrants to the frontiers will stay there remains to be seen. Views on this subject vary widely among the second-generation frontier Han Chinese I have spoken with. Some consider the frontier their home; others cannot wait for an opportunity to go east. Many Han Chinese did return to the east when it became possible to do so, after spending time on the frontiers during the Cultural Revolution.

Standardization and the Impact of Industrialization

Despite the efforts of China's architects to create regional styles in recent years, the single most outstanding development for the urban landscape in the post-1949 era is the standardization of urban form and the establishment of nationally distributed standards and patterns for the organization of urban space. Similar phenomena have, of course, taken place throughout the world during the twentieth century, but they are perhaps more extreme in countries like China that have extremely centralized state control. New structures have been standardized for both industry and housing. The most common type of new (post-1949) building for both purposes is a multi-story (three- to eight-story) concrete structure with a uniform facade and plan based on simple rectangular units. Standardization has also occurred in urban morphology. Extremely wide boulevards, with separate side-lanes for bicycle traffic, divide new districts in nearly every Chinese city into uniform rectangular modules. The urban communalization movement's emphasis on combining workplace and living quarters (within the same compound) has affected neighborhood development not only in these districts but throughout the city. In the standardized new development of Chinese cities, districts have been created in which residential buildings and industrial buildings are interspersed, leaving few purely industrial or residential districts. The role of older urban forms in this process has been to adapt to and make way for new development, rather than the reverse.

These uniform urban patterns have been applied as much, if not more, on the frontier as in the Chinese core. The "boomtown" nature of the frontier cities has contributed to a dogged adherence to plans and designs originating in Beijing and other eastern cities. This standardization is clear in virtually all new construction, from ceremonial centers to housing.

New Ceremonial Centers

The most prominent of all the urban features developed in the post-1949 era is the new ceremonial center. Victor Sit identifies this trend as a direct application of Soviet practices: "In imitation of some cities in the USSR, some large Chinese cities acquired Stalinesque central ceremonial squares as an explicit expression of new forms of social interaction and national pride" (Sit 1985: 9). The archetype of such centers is Tian'anmen Square in Beijing. In many cities smaller squares have been made, each with a large, paved plaza, surrounded by monumental buildings and space for viewing stands on at least one side. The initial intent of these squares was to hold mass meetings and demonstrations. Today they serve primarily as urban parks and as sites for elaborate floral displays commemorating holidays such as National Day. To some Chinese urban planners, the creation of Tian'anmen Square was a key point in the establishment of Chinese-style socialist urban planning. The establishment of the square provided a symbolic center for Chinese socialism. At the same time the Forbidden City and other elements of traditional architecture and urban space in downtown Beijing were retained, after long controversy with Soviet advisers, who preferred the complete rebuilding of the central city area.

Outside of Beijing there is less symbolic value placed on locating the square in the center of the traditional city. Rather, the square is often placed in some position that was not formerly a city center, in an attempt to either unify separated older centers, or connect the old city areas with recent development. This is particularly true in several of the frontier cities. For example, Kunming's planners decided to develop the area east of the old walled city into the city core and built the Workers' Cultural Palace Square (Gongren Wenhuagong Guangchang) to serve as the new heart of the city (see Map 27). The 10,000-m² plaza, with a large pool and fountain, benches, and planter boxes, stands at the northern entrance of the Workers' Cultural Palace (Wang Xuepei et al. 1987: 53–54).

Hohhot: typical courtyard house. See Chapter Eight.

Lanzhou: remnant of the southwest corner of the inner city wall stands above courtyard housing (Map 25). This remnant is not visible from street level. See Chapter Nine.

Detail of wall remnant at Lanzhou, showing remains of Ming dynasty brickwork.

Exposed rammed-earth core of the Lanzhou city wall at a construction site. The wall had been dismantled here to make room for new buildings.

Hohhot: restored 1930s-style shop (selling Muslim food) in the preservation district at the heart of the Old City District. The shop name is in both Mongolian and Chinese. See Chapter Nine.

Kunming: typical shops, Second World War era. (Photo courtesy of the National Archives, Washington, D.C.) See Chapter Nine.

Kunming: typical shop conversion, 1988. Preservation efforts compete with the shopowners' attempts to modernize.

Contemporary Kunming: modern work-unit compounds predominate outside the old city core (Map 27). See Chapter Ten.

Contemporary Lanzhou: the low area on the banks of the Yellow River is the old city, which is now surrounded on three sides by modern development (Map 28). See Chapter Ten.

Contemporary Hohhot (Map 29). See Chapter Ten.

Contemporary Urumqi (Map 30). See Chapter Ten.

Contemporary Xining: new development now fills the valley from the Huangshui
River to the hills to the south (Map 31). See Chapter Ten.

Hohhot: New China Square.

Xining: the intersection of the old city's main axes continues to serve as a central square for the contemporary city.

Hohhot: the Standing Committee of the National People's Congress of the Inner Mongolia Autonomous Region is housed in this structure, which is ornamented with a Mongolian yurt-like dome.

Urumqi: a yurt-style dome ornaments a highrise on Heilongjiang Road.

Urumqi: the government of the Xinjiang Uygur Autonomous Region is housed in this building, which stands at the north end of People's Square and features mosque-like ornamentation.

Lanzhou's East Side Red Square (Dongfang Hongguangchang) is also designed to unite old and new development. It lies between the old walled city and the primary post-1949 development area (see Map 28).[3] The north side of the square faces large red grandstands adorned with patriotic slogans in large white characters. The square is used both in the daytime and in the evening for children to ride electric cars, for popsicle stands, and for photo booths. Built in 1958–59, it originally covered 45,000 m^2, an area large enough for 100,000 people to assemble at one time. In 1983 the southern end was made into flower gardens with high raised beds. Soon after that, the 14-story United Office Building and the 15-story Science Building were also built in the southern portion of the square (Zhao Shiying 1987: 139). These construction projects reduced the total area of the square by one-third to one-half.[4]

Hohhot's New China Square (Xinhua Guangchang), located on the southwest corner of the intersection of Xinhua and Xilingol roads (see Map 29), serves a different purpose. In this position it lies approximately halfway between the old Manchu city and the old Chinese/Mongolian city. The square is an active place on summer evenings, filled with families treating their children to rides in miniature cars, watermelon, and popsicles, young people playing pool, and older people playing board games until 11:00 P.M. or midnight. During the day the square is clear of such activities and is used mainly as a shortcut by rush-hour bicycle commuters.

Urumqi's People's Square (Renmin Guangchang), though slightly removed from the main downtown area, is nonetheless referred to as the city center (see Map 30). The square stands to the south of the Xinjiang Uygur Autonomous Region's administrative headquarters, several blocks east of the center of the old walled Chinese city (Dihua). This site has an interesting history. The square sits at the former site of a ceremonial complex constructed around a spring-fed lake, which, after 1886, was developed into a lotus pool surrounded by temples and local association halls. Near the pool area there were an eight-sided pavilion and a long covered corridor, in traditional Chinese garden style. In the late nineteenth century, a market also grew up near the pool, specializing in clothing and small metalwork. But the area slid into decline in the early twentieth century. The pool dried up after roads were built on all four sides of it, and in 1933 the site became the city garbage dump. It was said to be a rough neighborhood. During the next years several of the houses adjacent to the dump were abandoned, creating a larger unoccupied area. According to

one story, in the late 1930s a scholar living near the site saw people shoot-
ing out the windows of a neighboring house and persuaded the police to
tear it down. Soon other houses were torn down, so that by 1944 there
was quite a large open space. By another account the dismantling of the
houses was connected with some suspicions related to the earth god. In
any case the open area was used in 1949 for a rally marking the founding
of the People's Republic and was later paved over in cement (Zan Yulin
1983: 40–42; Ma Shaoxin 1985: 61–63). The square is bordered by
planter boxes. A large office building for Party and government use stands
on the north side.

Lhasa's public square is adjacent to the Jokhang Temple, despite Chinese city plans that called for the development of the area near the Potala
Palace as the city center (Bo Guangzhang & Re Bi 1983: 36). Built in 1984
for the twenty-fifth anniversary of the Tibetan Autonomous Region, this
relatively small square contains large planter boxes that both Tibetans and
foreign tourists use as substitutes for park benches. It is flanked on two
sides by new apartment complexes built in a pseudo-Tibetan style.

Xining has not built a public square as such, but the much-widened
intersection at the junction of Bei, Nan, Xi, and Dong roads serves much
the same purpose (see Map 31). For important events, such as the Lantern
Festival (Yuanxiao), the streets are closed for the day, and the intersection
becomes a public plaza. The wide sidewalks at the four corners also serve
as gathering and meeting places. The area outside the main post office on
the southwestern side of the intersection is especially popular as a spot
where young and old alike stop to chat and sit on the steps.

New Axes and Economic Centers

Large-scale urban planning in China after 1949, like citywide planning in much of the world, has sought to impose spatial rationalism on
the city with an overlay of transportation infrastructure and economic development on both the existing urbanized area and expansion zones.
Strategies for such planning include, for example, the construction of ring
roads and major access roads with linkages to targeted development
zones. In Beijing the ring roads provide the framework for urban planning
to the extent that they are used to designate boundaries between different
zones for height restriction and types of land use. In cities where the traditional areas are too cramped to handle rapid and widespread new development, the new superstructure has often been used to create a new
"center" for the city, as is the case in all but one of the cities in this study.
The rationale behind the creation of new centers is both practical and

ideological: to improve traffic flow and make room for new development, and to replace the old center with a new heart wholly representative of the new China.

Xining is the only city in this study where the government designated the old city center as the new city center. The old walled area is to continue as the center of the vastly larger developing city, with development on all four sides (Chen Jun et al. 1985: 406). In spite of this plan, the bulk of contiguous development has taken place to the west of the former walled city. The Nanchuan River, which follows the path of the old western wall, serves as an axis that not only divides the older city site from new development but also divides the urbanized area more or less in half.[5] The primary new road axis is the east-west road, which is a widening and straightening of the old east-west axis that passed through the east and west gates of the walled city. The bulk of Xining's commercial establishments lie along its route, as do the provincial government offices, the main post office, the sports stadium, the airline office, and the Great Mosque.

Kunming planners have designated Beijing Road, which parallels the former route of the eastern wall, as the axis for new development. The center will lie between the old area to the west of Beijing Road and the new area to the east. The public square and the Workers' Cultural Palace anchor this city core. Beijing Road runs directly north from the train station and thus serves as a main artery into the city. Between the train station (which is near the southern limit of development for the city proper) and Dongfeng Road (the primary east-west artery), Beijing Road is already quite well developed, with a combination of hotels, restaurants, department stores, and public buildings. This development includes some structures specifically oriented toward foreign tourists, such as the ultra-modern Golden Dragon Hotel, a Hong Kong joint venture opened in early 1988, and, at the other end of the scale of accommodations for foreign tourists, the Three Leaves and Kunhu hotels, which offer dormitory accommodations for budget travelers, and the Lala Cafe, which offers coffee and "Western" food, along with bicycle rentals and travel information. The development on the southern end of Beijing Road, between the train station and the ring road (Huancheng Nanlu), is quite recent: 1985 maps still show this stretch of Beijing Road flanked by fields, with only the bus station and one hotel built along it. North of the Dongfeng Road intersection, however, there was very little completed development on Beijing Road itself in the late 1980s. A few large buildings were under construction, and a row of old-style shops on Renmin Road was clearly scheduled for demolition in the near future. The area to the east of Beijing Road is also much less developed north of Renmin Road. Thus the whole north-eastern quadrant of the city is relatively underdeveloped, with old housing and agricultural land only occasionally broken by small factories. The old sections of town, the walled area and the streets that ran just along the southern and eastern sides of the wall, remain the primary shopping and commercial areas. The area southeast and east of Beijing Road is devoted primarily to large compound-style factories and institutions, such as hospitals, sports arenas, and the library.

Development in Urumqi has been focused along the primary thoroughfare, which enters the old walled city area from the south, exits the "north gate," and then veers sharply to the northwest. This northwestern spur is where the bulk of Urumqi's newest department stores, government buildings, and apartment blocks have gone up. But this development, northwest of Hongshan, is only one or two buildings deep: complexes line the main road, but the land behind remains in either agricultural land or housing. The city's secondary areas of development are north of the route of the former north wall of Dihua and along all roads leading to and from the city proper.

In Lanzhou development has taken place primarily on the east and southeast sides of the old city, and secondarily in a satellite area several miles to the west (Xigu District). Here development has not taken place along a single identifiable axis the way it has in the other cities. Rather, there are several different axial systems in the newly developed areas of the city. The pre-1949 north-south axis, Winespring (Jiuquan) Road, which runs from the Sun Yatsen Forest (Zhongshanlin) area, the former site of a park constructed in 1926 to commemorate Sun Yatsen (Zhao Shiying 1987: 42–43), to the Provincial Administration complex,[6] remains the center of commercial activity.

To the east of the old city, there is a ceremonial axis running north-south from the New Railroad Village (Tielu Xincun) area, former agricultural and brick-kiln land that was built up to house railway workers after the Shanghai-Qinghai (Longhai) rail line reached Lanzhou in 1952 (Zhao Shiying 1987: 137). This axis, Gaolan Road, runs into the East Side Red Square (Dongfang Hongguangchang) and then splits into two roads skirting the east and west sides of the square. The street pattern on either side is a maze of diagonal and twisting streets with no relation to the road's north-south orientation.

The second axial system in Lanzhou's new development is the radial system emanating from the railway station. This consists of two major roads, Pingliang Road and Tianshui Road. Pingliang Road runs northwest until it crosses Donggang Road, then continues north to the bank of the Yellow River. Tianshui Road runs due north to the agricultural and village lands outside the city. Both streets are well developed, with apartment-and-work-unit compounds and commercial buildings.

These north-south axes are connected by three arteries that run approximately east-west parallel to the Yellow River along the length of eastern Lanzhou. All three change names several times before they merge into a single road at Jiefangmen, the former west gate of the outer wall. That road continues on west several miles as a link to the Xigu District.

In recent years there have been increasing efforts throughout China to create industrial and development zones targeted toward improving access to foreign markets. These have primarily been concentrated in the eastern cities. However, in 1992 there were two such zones under construction, for completion in 1993, on the outskirts of Lanzhou: the Lanzhou New and High Technology Zone and the Lianhai Economic Development Zone. The Lianhai zone will contain industries specializing in silica, carbon, and aluminum products. Plans were also under way in 1992 to open up an "ethnic economic development zone" in Linxia, south of Lanzhou, to foreign investment.

Hohhot's new development is aimed at filling in the space between the two old cities and creating a new center in that space. To accomplish this, two major axes have been developed: Sun Yatsen West Road–Sun Yatsen East Road, linking the west gate of Xincheng to the north gate of Jiucheng; and Xilingol North Road–Xilingol South Road, linking the train station to a textile factory district in the south. The first, despite its name, actually runs southwest-northeast. Yet another new road, which runs due west from the former west gate of Xincheng, is relatively wide but dwindles down quickly after it crosses the Zhadagai River. New blocks of streets between the two old cities more or less correspond perpendicularly to these new axes, though a diagonal road (Zhongshan) breaks the grid somewhat. According to city plans, the two intersections formed where the east-west and north-south axes cross are the administrative and cultural centers of the city. The northern intersection is the site of the Science Building (Kezhi Dalou) and New China Square. The southern intersection is the site of the municipal government offices. The triangle formed by these three roads contains the administrative offices for the Inner Mongolia Autonomous Region, and the Museum of the Autonomous Region. Some development has taken place within the old and new cities as well.

For example, the old city's main north-south street has been widened, and the traditional courtyard housing replaced with shops topped by several stories of apartments (Guan Xiaoxian et al. 1987: 230).

New Trends in Housing

The Chinese have built extensive high-rise apartment complexes in order to relieve the problems of overcrowding and overpopulation in cities. Any visitor to Beijing will be struck by the number of 5- to 15-story apartment complexes, each incorporating several tall buildings. There, as in many other cities, these new complexes have largely replaced traditional courtyard houses. The construction of high-rise apartment buildings has had an impact on cities on the frontier, as well as cities in eastern China. In general, however, it seems that in multiethnic cities there has been less emphasis on replacing minority (particularly Muslim) traditional housing with highrises than there has been on providing highrises for Chinese in-migrants. This is largely due to the high demand for new housing for recent in-migrants, in contrast to the fact that older residents of the cities already had housing of some sort.

Xining, for example, added more than 7,000,000 m² of housing between 1949 and the mid-1980s (for a reported increase of about 320 percent),[7] in a period when the population in the city center alone increased tenfold (*Qinghai shengqing* 1986: 460). There has been phenomenal housing development in Urumqi as well, with the addition of more than 8,000,000 m² of housing by the early 1980s, an increase of nearly 900 percent. This increase was still less, however, than the 1,100 percent increase in population over the same period (*Xinjiang weiwuer zizhiqu gaikuang* 1985: 190–91). Only Kunming has succeeded in outpacing the rate of population growth: it added 4,550,000 m² of housing between 1949 and 1984, for an increase of 352 percent, while the population increased 234 percent (*Yunnan dizhou shixian gaikuang* 1987: 11–12). Yet Kunming's city center is still more densely populated than the core areas of the other frontier cities.

Housing development has taken place both through the construction of new structures on previously vacant or agricultural land and through the destruction and replacement of existing structures. For example, in 1965 nearly 5,000 m² of traditional courtyard housing around Hohhot's rail station was destroyed and replaced with nearly 19,000 m² of new multi-story housing (*Dangdai zhongguo de chengshi jianshe* 1990: 552).

As the Chinese government embarks on its new economic policies, more and more cities are allowing and encouraging private homeownership and building. This "new situation" will undoubtedly bring about some rebuilding of private homes in traditional styles. So far the most notable example might be the Bai "suburbs" outside Dali. The situation does raise interesting questions for the Han Chinese people relocated within the last generations to frontier areas. Given the choice, will they build traditional Chinese homes, traditional homes of the local area, modern homes, or a hybrid of these styles? And will the non-Han people who have been relocated to modern highrises return to more traditional housing if given the opportunity?

Another trend that may have an impact on the structure of frontier cities is the breakdown of the work-unit housing system in the post-Mao era. Once urban communes were established at the end of the 1950s, many if not most urban Chinese resided in housing both legally and spatially tied to their workplace. As the children of workers assigned to work-unit-based housing mature and seek work, however, there are neither the jobs nor the housing spaces available for them to similarly occupy work-unit housing in all cases. The work-unit housing system did not account for the fact that one generation would mature before the previous generation was ready to relinquish its housing and its jobs. Consequently, many young adults live with their parents and commute to their place of work. At the same time the new opportunities for employment outside the work-unit system also have led to increased detachment of workplace and living place in Chinese cities. In many cities neighborhood committees based on residence rather than on workplace have been formed to take over social services once provided by the workplace. It is as yet unclear what if any effect this changing structure will have in frontier cities. But it is likely that these changes will enable a strengthening of ethnic enclaves based on combined spatial and organizational-administrative separatism within the city.

Many Western observers find the new China's cities rather stark, particularly on the arid northwestern frontiers. To Paul Theroux, the Lanzhou of the late 1980s "still looked like a city on the frontier, with the patched and botched appearance of all Chinese cities—no trees to speak of but plenty of tall factory chimneys and power-lines" (1988: 181). This observation is perhaps unfair. There are plenty of street trees in many districts of Lanzhou, just as there are in other Chinese cities, thanks in part to beautification efforts after 1949. I often sought their shelter from the heat of the midday sun. Che Muqi well appreciated the change when he returned to the city in 1974, after an interval of 20 years: "Through the window I saw flower beds. The bright colours were a sharp contrast to the old impression of the loess plateau. Later I walked on several boulevards lined with towering white aspens. . . . I had seen old Lanzhou and comprehended how precious the colour green was to the city" (Che Muqi 1989: 55).

Xining has had the least successful planting program of China's frontier cities. Relatively few street trees are to be seen along the redeveloped main arteries, and there are only a few parks. Government statistics bear out the impression that it lags far behind the other cities in this respect, with only about 8 percent of its area in green space, compared with more than 22 percent in Hohhot, almost 18 percent in Lanzhou, and 15 percent in Urumqi (PRC, State Statistical Bureau 1986).[8]

Foci of Community Life

Community life in the traditional Chinese city was focused around a number of institutions: the guild or clan hall, local temples, and the marketplace for the Chinese; the mosque and the marketplace for the Muslims; and (in the urban milieu) the monastery for Mongolians and Tibetans. Most of these institutions have changed substantially in the post-1949 era, and, consequently, ways of urban life have changed dramatically as well. Guild and clan halls have been abolished, and there is no indication they will return. These institutions have to a great extent been replaced by the *danwei* (work unit), which provides social as well as economic services for its members. This system, too, is changing, with the legitimization of *geti* (private or independent) enterprises. It is not clear who or what will provide social and community services for families who choose to engage in private enterprise. Local temples ceased to function as the foci for community activity at least as early as the mid-1960s (and earlier in many places). Some local temples have been rebuilt, but they function on a relatively limited scale, with significantly reduced activities and participants.

Ironically, institutions replacing the temples as the focus of Han Chinese community life are sometimes housed in former temples. The Temple of the Town Gods in Lanzhou, the Confucian Temple in Kunming, and the Confucian Temple in Xining, as mentioned earlier, have all been transformed into Workers' Cultural Palaces or the equivalent. Here elderly men may still gather to play board games, and the young gather to play pool and dance, but religious activities are rarely carried out in them. Similar institutions housed in new buildings serve the same functions but tend to cater to a wide constituency—the city as a whole or large districts within the city—and so are even less likely replacements for the local neighbor-hood temples.

The closure of most mosques in the 1960s, combined with some relo-cation of Islamic peoples, forced China's Muslims to find other venues of community focus. Dru Gladney contends that, in the absence of mosques, urban Hui communities shifted to using Muslim restaurants as gathering places, and that the practice has continued even with the reintroduction of mosques today, in light of the fact that many functions traditionally carried out by mosques are now primarily the responsibility of the state (such as marriage; Gladney 1987b: 209). I would contend that in areas of high concentration of Islamic peoples, such as the northwestern frontiers of China, the focus of community life may yet shift back to the mosques, which are being rebuilt in large numbers. That these are financed solely with the pooled donated savings and labor of the local Islamic communi-ties suggests that those communities place great importance on reestab-lishing their own mosques regardless of the cost and possible political risks. In Lanzhou, Urumqi, and Xining, moreover, the sheer number of mosques that are being rebuilt in relatively compact areas, with five or six mosques located within five to ten minutes' walk of one another, suggests that neighborhood rather than simply sectarian concerns are involved. This profusion of mosques is apparently greater than would be required by local differences in belief and affiliation with Islamic sects. They may represent decisions by many different micro communities within urban Muslim populations to rebuild, at great expense, mosques that identify them as distinct communities.

Urban Mongolian and Tibetan populations were traditionally socially centered on monastic communities. The closure of monasteries, therefore, was extraordinarily disruptive to these groups. Today, where urban mon-asteries have been reopened, as in Hohhot, life is refocused on them, even reduced as they are, to skeleton crews of monks and staff.

What is evident on the frontier, then, is that non-Han communities are tending to coalesce around traditional institutions, whereas the Han Chi-nese are much more likely to use recently established institutions than to reinstate traditional institutions. As these differentiated social ties are ex-pressed in the physical and spatial organization of the city through the rebuilding of mosques and other structures, life on the frontier may be-come increasingly pluralistic. Non–Han Chinese peoples are establishing a more distinct and visible identity within these Chinese cities than they have had in the past 30 or 40 years.

The Development and Application of Local Styles

The introduction of Chinese architectural elements has always been a concrete expression of the Chinese presence in the frontier regions. As previous chapters have demonstrated, in the past there has been considerable intermixing of architectural styles on the frontier. Within the cities, however, Chinese styles have dominated.

The Soviet Influence

Throughout most of the post-1949 era, local styles in frontier cities have been overshadowed by the new rulers' drive for a uniform socialist style, drawing heavily on the 1930s Soviet model. Soviet-influenced construction practices and building styles far outlasted the regime's early political ties with the USSR. Soviet-style buildings were constructed in concrete and concrete-block modular forms, three to five stories high, assembled around a central courtyard or parking lot within a walled compound. This modular building style has been nearly all-pervasive in much of urban China, including cities on the frontier. There the influx of Han Chinese migrants in large numbers to the cities has precipitated phenomenal growth, which has been accommodated through the fast construction of concrete compound-style housing as described above. Most of this new housing has been built on previously agricultural land or unused sites surrounding the cities; however, in many cases districts of traditional housing have also been razed to make way for higher density modern structures.

This modular building style served both functional and ideological ends. The buildings were fast and inexpensive to construct, and capable of housing a high population density in low-rise buildings surrounded, in the ideal, with open space. At the same time the Soviet-style concrete blocks symbolized the new socialism: consistent, modern, and efficient. This style became widely used in the 1950s and remained common into the 1980s. In fact, the bulk of new construction has actually taken place since the mid-1970s. Construction styles began to change significantly only in the mid-1980s, with a new trend toward high-rise development and the application of regional styles.

The New Chinese Styles

One of the reforms that have been taking place in China since the mid-1980s is the official sanction and encouragement of architecture based on regional styles, rather than international or socialist styles.[9] In some cases the earlier periods of strict adherence to Soviet models are being criticized by Chinese architects and architectural historians. For example, Wang Shiren describes Chinese architectural theory and style in the 1950s and 1960s as "the mistake of studying the Soviets, and taking the 1930s Soviet critical retrogressive architecture and transforming it into the model of regional form, with the result of going along an even more evil road" (Wang Shiren 1987a: 59). Wang's statement is characteristic of the attitude of many contemporary Chinese planners and architects toward the recent past.

This attitude began to be given public expression in the 1980s, which saw a movement for the "sinification" of buildings to correct past "mistakes." This sinification has been carried out through the modification of Soviet-style buildings dating from the 1950s and 1960s, and through the design of new buildings with stylistic reference to traditional elements. The construction of "cultural streets" (as discussed in Chapter Nine), such as Liulichang in Beijing, is an example of the sinification of districts within Chinese cities. In many cases individual structures have been modified as well. Most of these structures, however, have been government buildings or, in some cases, hotels. New housing continues to be constructed in modern compound form.[10]

One of the prime examples of a new structure embodying the concept of traditional decoration in state architecture is the National Library in Beijing (opened in 1988). Though its large blocklike multi-story white buildings are thoroughly modern, their blue tile roof ornaments and pillars project an unmistakably "Chinese" appearance. The buildings themselves are in no way traditionally Chinese, but the ornamentation attached to them makes convincing reference to the graceful curves of the traditional style.

There has been relatively little sinification of buildings in the frontier cities, but there have been attempts to carry out similar procedures using architectural reference to the traditional forms of the frontier regions. The creation and application of local styles in frontier areas is an interesting and sometimes problematic architectural design and application problem, for in contrast to the Chinese architectural tradition, which has been documented and practiced for several thousand years as a state architectural style, many of the frontier peoples do not have traditions of permanent, nonreligious public structures. Nonetheless, traditional architectural elements are being transformed to ornament just such structures. Ironically, the result of the demand for local-style architecture by central architectural agencies has been to encourage local architects to "create" local styles suitable to large-scale monumental architecture.

The process by which movements in architectural style begin and diffuse through China is still highly centralized. In the People's Republic architectural style, like all creative endeavors, is perceived as an expression of the state's ideology, and is thus mandated by state policy. Even movements encouraging individualism are ultimately derived from state practices tolerating, allowing, or encouraging individual expression in the arts. Moreover, style is always a secondary consideration to functional requirements. State ideology has continuously advocated maximum speed and efficiency in new construction. Paradoxically, the ideological imperative also lends extreme importance to style.

Architectural planning agencies under state control attempt to translate state ideology into appropriate concrete form in architecture. In order to coordinate architectural practice, including style applications, throughout the country, they publish articles outlining the "Party line," and hold periodic conferences on the latest guidelines. Local agencies then work to replicate these nationwide ideals as closely as possible within the constraints of each local situation.

There have been a number of articles and conferences on architecture in China that have included examples of foreign architecture. The infusion of foreign ideas has led to increased variety in contemporary Chinese architecture. Nonetheless the infusion of new styles in recent years has been limited to "modern" forms, to abstracted classical Chinese forms, and to the creation of forms for the expression of regional character.

The Taiwanese architectural historian Fu Chaoching (Fu Zhaojing) traces the start of the regionalist trend in Chinese architecture particularly to activities of the Chinese Architectural Association in 1981: its First Conference on Cave Housing and Earth Dwellings, held in Yan'an in June and its meetings with the committee for the Aga Khan Award for Architecture, in October (Fu Chaoching 1988: 67). Regional architectural styles were given further legitimation with the publication, under the association's auspices, of a series of books on the vernacular housing of each province, such as *Jilin minzhu* (Vernacular Housing of Jilin; 1985), *Yunnan minzhu* (Vernacular Housing of Yunnan; 1986), and *Fujian minzhu* (Vernacular Housing of Fujian; 1987).

A number of Chinese scholars also published on the subject. Guo Rirui, for example, wrote quite eloquently on the need to research and apply local styles in a journal article of 1987. He argued that the root of architectural style in non–Han Chinese regions was deeply buried, and that it was time to seek this root, to research, study, apply, and develop it (Guo Rirui 1987: 15). These sentiments were echoed by Wang Shiren, who stated that "the tools of architecture include nationality forms; this is a basic law of architecture" (Wang Shiren 1987a: 60).

Wang Shiren provided guidelines for the study of such "nationality forms" with two admonitions to researchers. First, that it is necessary to limit the practice of taking Han Chinese architectural systems as a standard in order to understand non–Han Chinese architecture. Non-Han architecture must be understood in its own temporal and spatial contexts. Second, that it is particularly important in the study of non–Han Chinese architecture to make a distinction between monumental and vernacular architecture, and not to judge the two by the same set of standards (Wang Shiren 1987a: 61). Statements like these represented a complete change in architectural theory from the earlier socialist models, with their emphasis on national criteria for architectural design based primarily on functional and construction requirements.

Fu Chaoching has identified three ways in which regional styles have been applied: the restoration or complete replication of old forms, compromises between old and new, and the application of local motifs as ornaments (Fu Chaoching 1988).

Zhang Qinnan, writing as the director of the Planning Office of the Construction Ministry, offered a possible explanation for these varying levels of application of regional styles when he set forth some of the basic considerations for the development of local styles that were recurring themes in Chinese architectural design conferences in 1985–86, namely, that the foremost priority in terms of the overall project was suitability (applicability or functionalism), followed by economics, and finally, artistic merit. Priorities for the aesthetic design itself included, first, modernity (contemporaneity), followed by ethnicity (people's character) and, finally, local character (place character; Zhang Qinnan 1987: 13).

Of the priorities for the project itself, only the lowest of the three, that of artistic merit, is applicable to the development of place-specific styles. Of the priorities for aesthetic considerations in design, the second and third specifically address the desirability of creating place- and people-specific styles. The current situation reflects these priorities well: in most new buildings the foremost considerations are function and expense; and a majority seem to be built in modern, "international" styles.

Frontier Motifs

The issue of "local" styles takes on new dimensions in multicultural frontier cities. There is clearly a movement to employ regional and *minzu* (nationality) styles in both Han Chinese and non–Han Chinese China.[11]

Architects are earnestly attempting to create styles that both represent regional character and serve modern functions in frontier cities. There are three conditions on the frontier that make this a difficult process. First, it is often more difficult to replicate non–Han Chinese forms for use as civic buildings or multifamily housing than it is to replicate traditional Han Chinese forms for these purposes. Whereas Han Chinese architectural forms lend themselves easily to new applications, since similar forms were traditionally used for housing, administrative complexes, and religious structures, and Chinese-style buildings can be built quite large, non–Han Chinese architectural forms have been far more use-specific than traditional Chinese structures, and are thus less easily adapted to these kinds of modern uses. Many of the frontier peoples have completely dissociated housing and temple forms, and may have no traditional secular architecture for the accommodation of state functions. The new buildings designated to incorporate regional styles include administrative buildings for large numbers of office workers, factories and other production facilities, mass housing projects, and social services institutions such as schools. Particularly in formerly nomadic regions where structures such as yurts typify the secular architecture, the application of traditional style to modern uses requires quite an act of imagination and creation. The noninterchangeability of religious and secular architecture in non–Han Chinese culture also causes problems for the application of regional styles. It may be controversial to borrow mosque, temple, and tomb styles for the adornment of secular structures.

Second, in multicultural situations it may be difficult to adequately or accurately produce a single representative regional style. In the Xining region, for example, several different groups of Tibetan Buddhist peoples and several different groups of Islamic peoples are represented in significant numbers. What, then, is the appropriate regional style for a new provincial capital building? In some cases styles have been abstracted and fused into "generic" minorities' styles. The most prominent example of this is the development of a structure designed to mimic both the dome shape of the yurt and the mosque dome.

Third, Chinese architects may not have the training to understand and use the full range of local styles. Ironically, though the forms of non–Han Chinese architecture are being abstracted and applied as ornamentation, few of the actual traditional decorative motifs of non–Han Chinese architecture are being employed. In Inner Mongolia the only decorative motif applied from Mongolian design is the upside-down three-leaf clover design placed on "yurt"-styled ornaments. And though the non-Han peoples of Qinghai have numerous indigenous decorative motifs, none have been incorporated into buildings designed to capture local styles.[12]

Many of the theoretical and practical ideas about regional styles were formulated in Inner Mongolia, where there was considerable experimentation with building monumental structures in local styles as early as the 1940s and 1950s. One solution to the design problems inherent in creating regional styles is simply to enlarge the traditional forms to suit the space requirements demanded by contemporary use. Though this is a relatively rare solution, since few forms, as noted, can stand this kind of change, it was the one chosen by the architects of the Nationalities Arts Auditorium in Hohhot. This building, a "yurt," constructed of concrete block and blue tile, is large enough to house exhibits on Mongolian culture, as well as an auditorium with a 200-m² stage. It was built in 1957, long before the contemporary architectural movements discussed here.

Another, even earlier attempt to capture the yurt form is the Chinggis Khan Memorial, built in the grasslands about 70 miles southwest of Hohhot in 1956.[13] This monument provides an interesting example of the blending of Chinese and Mongolian architectural styles. Its three large yurt-shaped halls have brown tile domes decorated with blue tile patterns and brown knob top ornaments. But the buildings themselves are eight-sided, with flying Chinese-style eight-sided roofs fringing the domes. The central hall, which is larger than the others, has two levels of Chinese roof, separated by a row of windows below the dome.

The Inner Mongolia Horse Racing Track in Hohhot is also a good example of yurt-style monumental architecture. The grandstand is covered by five large domes built in 1959. The central dome is massive, with a two-story glassed enclosure forming its base. The flanking domes are much smaller. All of the domes are white ornamented with blue outlines of the traditional patterns commonly placed on ceremonial yurts that produce something of an Escher-like interlocking effect. The grandstand is relatively plain, with an extruding center section. Three sides of the five-story octagonal tower that supports the central dome stand out from the facade to form a grand entrance.

Rather than build large yurts for all public buildings, however, the latest trend is to build an ordinary building and then to attach a yurt-shaped structure to the roof. In effect and function, these structures are not unlike the spires that adorned the Soviet-style monumental structures of the 1950s and 1960s. The most prominent example of this style is the headquarters of the Standing Committee of the National People's Congress of the Inner Mongolia Autonomous Region. What is an otherwise unremarkable building (a five-story rectangular block of office space, stepped into a two-story square block) is surmounted by a tall yurt, with windows all around its first level and a white tile dome with brown tile patterns similar to those stitched in felt on yurts and a decorative brown knob on the top. The yurt at the top of the structure is the only element that represents the "regional" style created by state architects for Hohhot. Nonetheless, because this "yurt" is the only part of the building visible from afar, it does serve as a landmark and a hallmark of the city. The dome is a central feature of the cover photographs of no fewer than four books about Hohhot (see Yun Fen 1987; Guan Xiaoxian et al. 1987; Gao Yinbiao & Wang Jizhou 1987; and *Neimenggu luyou* 1987).

In Lanzhou, Xining, and Urumqi, the most prevalent contemporary "local" style is found in the placement of large onion domes reminiscent of the domes of Central/Southwest Asian mosques on the tops of modern high-rise buildings. This style is particularly ironic in Xining and Lanzhou, where there is no traditional Central/Southwest Asian architectural style. The majority of Muslims in both cities are, and were in the past, Hui, who built in modified Chinese architectural styles.

Architects have put a dome on prominent display atop the Lanzhou Youth Palace by elevating it well above the roof on a series of columns. The Science Palace across from Red Square is also reminiscent of mosque styling, with a narrow white-domed observation tower that looks more like a minaret than any of the ones on the city's mosques. The tower, a pole surrounded by a spiral staircase leading several stories up to the balconied dome, is similar to one in the Kashgar Civic Marketplace (Kashi, Xinjiang) that was clearly intended, according to the Chinese architects, as an abstraction of a minaret (Li Lixin 1987).

The most prominent Central/Southwest Asian feature of Xining is the green onion dome on top of the Huangzhong Building, an office and shop complex at the corner of South Huayuan Road and Dongguan Street built in 1986–87.[14] A Muslim restaurant refurbished in the mid-1980s at the Xining Hotel is also built in the form of a mosque, complete with domed turrets and Central/Southwest Asian arches leading into the western entrance.

The main gate to the Qinghai Nationalities Academy in Xining is an attempt to combine a number of architectural styles with modern design. The tops of the short walls on either side of the gate are made to look like the red-branches-and-medallions pattern at the top of a Tibetan temple. Brackets on the columns of the gateway are abstracted to the point that they could be interpreted as either Tibetan or Han Chinese style. The entire gateway is built in the classical three-arch style of Chinese monumental architecture. Students now pass freely through what would once have been separate entrances for the gods, the emperor, and the populace. As for the campus, though one writer describes it as a "grouping of architecture in nationalities style" (Li Shengcai 1985: 433), apart from some ornamentation on the roof overhangs that is somewhat reminiscent of the Central/Southwest Asian pointed-arch style, the modern block buildings are unremarkable. It is interesting that Tibetan styles have not been used much in Xining, given both its proximity to the Tibetan culture region and the relative adaptability of Tibetan architecture to contemporary uses.

Urumqi is the only city on the frontier to employ two minority styles, though the abstracted Central/Southwest Asian mosque is clearly the design of choice. To the Chinese architects who attended a national seminar on contemporary Chinese architectural design in Urumqi in 1987, Xinjiang's many buildings with Central/Southwest Asian motifs demonstrated a "relatively enlightened incorporation of *minzu* characteristics, the spirit of the times and local color" (Zhou Ganshi 1987: 16). Still, though the use of dome styles on public buildings may be increasing in step with architectural and political trends, it is not a new development in Urumqi. Both the 1953 Xinjiang Uygur Autonomous Region Museum and the 1956 People's Theater are capped by ribbed domes reminiscent of the Central/Southwest Asian style. However, these older domes are plated in copper/bronze-colored metal and "flattened," so that they are wider at the base than at the top, rather than in the onion-dome style, which is narrow at the base, wide in the mid-section, and narrow again at the top. This style is probably Soviet in origin and resembles that used in state buildings constructed by the USSR in Central Asia.

Urumqi has a number of new domed government buildings, such as the Party and government office building on the north end of People's Square. This 11-story building is a simple rectangular office building with several "local" features added. A large onion dome about five stories high, topped with a spire, in the center of the roof and two towers, three stories high with taller pillars at each of their four corners, at the far ends contrive to give the building a mosque-complex look. The facade is also designed to capture the flavor of Central/Southwest Asian Islamic design. To achieve the effect of a colonnaded arched facade, each column of windows (26 columns in all) is surmounted by a pointed arch. Such arches, called *jiangong*, are specifically identified by the Urumqi architect Gao Qinglin as an element of the Xinjiang nationalities style that is "pleasing" to non–Han Chinese comrades (Gao Qinglin 1987). Pointed arches are a prominent feature in Gao Qinglin's design of the Xinjiang Guesthouse. The train station, the Sun Yatsen Road Trade Center, the new wing of the Kunlun Hotel (though here the arches are somewhat rounded), the Xinjiang Science and Technology Center, the Friendship Guesthouse, and many other buildings have arched facades as their primary architectural reference to local style.

The Xinjiang People's Assembly Hall combines both the abstracted pointed-arch style on the facade (with eight arched bays on either side of three wide window panels over the front entrance) and domed turrets at each of the four corners of the building in a style reminiscent of Islamic tombs or mosques. A smaller structure on the east side of the main assembly hall contains individual meeting rooms for each of the province's regions decorated in the style of the peoples represented (Liu Jian 1987: 5).

The pointed arches on the front of the Uygur Medicine Hospital on Yan'an Street extend all the way up to the top of the building's fourth story. A tall rectangular tower extrudes from the facade. This tower is topped with a ribbed onion dome and spire. The author Liang Feng describes the hospital's design as "possessing the richness of Uygur architectural style, glimmering and splendid among Urumqi's architectural works" (Liang Feng 1987: 41).

The 17-story new wing of the Xinjiang Overseas Chinese Hotel (Xinjiang Huaqiao Binguan) has an almost post-modern reference to the pointed-arch style. Here the architect has added vertical slots in the concrete just above the four bays of arches at the sixteenth-floor level on each side of the structure to create a light and latticelike effect. These concrete lattices stand out slightly from the building facade but are recessed in comparison to the pillars of the arched bays, which in traditional design should lead up to them. These pillars rise all the way to the top (seventeenth-floor) level.

A few buildings in Urumqi make reference to the yurt, including the highrise at the end of Heilongjiang Road, which has a yurt-shaped ornament at the top. Considering the numbers of Kazakh, Mongolian, and other nomadic peoples in Xinjiang, it is interesting to note that most of the "national styles" applied in Urumqi have been references to mosques and not to other indigenous architectural forms such as the yurt.

Kunming has relatively little in the way of new buildings in regional architectural styles, with one notable exception: a tea shop/public garden in the center of town reminiscent of the Dai architecture of southern Yunnan Province. The Dai house typically has a long sloping roof (accounting for about two-thirds of the total height from the floor level) and is elevated above the ground on stilts. It is curious that Yunnan, the most culturally diverse of the provinces, has the fewest examples of regional styles in its capital city. Architects have not yet developed some decorative motif that is at once apt and easily added to new buildings in Kunming, as has been done in all the other capitals of minority areas. That may come about soon, however, for Kunming is attempting to boost its non-Chinese image in order to promote tourism. In 1992 the White Pagoda, a famous landmark of the Dai community in Xishuangbanna, Yunnan, was moved to Kunming as part of the development of an Ethnic Culture Tourist Zone, a Dai village and a Bai village constructed next to each other on the shores of Lake Dian (*Beijing Review*, April 6–12, 1992: 36). This development is similar to such projects in the United States as the Polynesian Cultural Center in Hawaii and Colonial Williamsburg in Virginia. Yet in one sense Kunming has more architectural reference to tradition than any of the other frontier cities, for it alone still has several large districts of traditional buildings in their distinctive forms.

The attempts to create and apply local styles discussed above all involve large-scale government-sponsored projects. Yet their impact may ultimately reach well beyond state-run department stores and government office complexes. Already their presence has enabled a new movement toward architectural expression in some smaller-scale projects. Certainly the bold new architectural statements embodied in the Central/Southwest Asian–style mosques that are being constructed throughout the frontier cities by local Islamic groups are fueled, in part, by the government's new flexibility in the matter of cultural expression. At the same time these new styles as they are stated in large architectural projects make the multicultural nature of the frontier cities more visible than it has been in decades. This, too, might have greater implications as Han Chinese, non–Han Chinese, and foreign visitors alike become increasingly aware of the heterogeneous nature of the frontier. In a society in which actions have often spoken far louder than words, deliberate modifications of the landscape carry a powerful message.

Since 1949 there have thus been substantial changes in urban form throughout China. These changes have, in some ways, brought the frontier much closer to the core area as uniform programs were implemented throughout China. Similar buildings, or traffic circles, or district structures can be seen throughout China today, whether one looks for them in Beijing and Shanghai or in Xining and Urumqi.

Yet many of these changes are superficial, reaching the form but not the substance of cities on the frontier. Many frontier cities maintain their traditional structure behind a one-building-wide facade of new structures lining the boulevards. And while the new architecture may strive for uniformity, the frontier cities remain the most multicultural places in China.

Moreover, in recent years there has been a conscious effort among China's planners and architects to renew the physical expression of multiculturalism on the Chinese frontiers. Though the articulation of this effort is far from complete, and far from ideal in its completed form, it does represent a return to a more visibly multicultural frontier urban form. At the same time the government's recent tolerance of "grass-roots" multicultural expressions, such as the reconstruction of mosques and temples, is also contributing to a more varied urban landscape on the frontiers.

Conclusion

The Great Wall, holding for a score of centuries as the most colossal tide mark of the human race, stands as the symbol of [the sometimes abrupt boundary of the Chinese Empire in] Chinese history. In recurrent periods, however, the inland border of China has not been a sharp edge, defined by the Great Wall, but a series of frontier zones, varying in depth from south to north (and in Tibet from east to west) and stretching away indefinitely into the plains and mountains and forests of Siberia, the vague depths of Central Asia, and the wastes of Tibet.

— Owen Lattimore, *Inner Asian Frontiers of China*, 1940

As the Great Wall long stood as a symbol of the boundaries between the Chinese empire and the rest of the world, so, too, the walls of China's frontier cities symbolized the same ethnic boundaries, reproducing the political and socioeconomic relations of the empire in miniature. Each frontier city replicated the structure of the empire, from the elite confines and inner chambers of the Chinese rulers, through a hierarchical and tightly controlled occupation of space based on status and ethnicity, to a hinterland bound by economy, contract, and coercion to the central walled area. Indeed, urban forms on the frontier often approached Chinese ideals for spatial organization more closely, in their much simplified expressions, than the more complex forms of the Chinese heartland.

Unlike the Great Wall, which in many periods and along much of its length did not mark the actual frontier between Chinese and non-Chinese, city walls on the frontiers were often enduring demarcations of ethnic boundaries. But there was at times great flexibility of social interaction and cultural expression, despite these rigid walled boundaries, which contributed to the development of unique multicultural settlements. Until the twentieth century the Chinese constituted a majority only within the confines of the walled realms they defined.

Chinese Frontiers, Frontier Cities, and Frontier Dynamics

The Chinese frontiers are distinctive among the world's frontier regions in their persistence over more than 2,000 years, the great and historically dynamic cultural diversity of the inhabitants, and the broad variation of their settlement and subsistence patterns, ranging from rural agricultural villages and pastoral nomadism to highly developed indigenous urban civilizations. Another fundamental characteristic of the Chinese frontier is the degree of cultural continuity on all sides of the frontier. Just as non-Chinese populations have withstood centuries of Chinese influence, and long political and economic domination, without becoming wholly Chinese—although they often adopted many facets of Chinese culture—so despite millennia of contact with the peoples of the frontier and even the adoption of new ideas and cultural forms as a result, the Chinese steadfastly maintained their own traditions.

Chinese control of the western frontiers was often rather light and sometimes tenuous, and even in periods of tight control, the empire's military and administrative presence was confined in most areas to a far-flung network of walled cities, towns, and forts. The far western frontiers were fundamentally urban—oases of Chinese settlements in what must have often seemed inhospitable arid lands sparsely populated by alien peoples. Before the nineteenth century, Chinese rural settlement rarely extended beyond the immediate hinterland of these urban outposts. And even the security of the urban settlements was sometimes fragile, for there were more than a few occasions when non-Chinese peoples seized control of or destroyed Chinese military outposts and frontier cities.

The history of Chinese rule over the outer frontier regions is one of recurrent expansion and contraction of political control beyond the inner frontier of Chinese agrarian settlement. As Chinese administration of the far regions in the west, north, and southwest waxed and waned, with it went the fortunes of the empire's frontier settlements. During times when the Chinese extended their power and authority into these reaches, they established and reestablished their forts and cities in them. During times when Chinese administration fell back to the inner line of Chinese settlement, these forts and frontier cities were often abandoned to fall into ruin or to be occupied by non-Chinese.

Frontiers are places of cultural affirmation and persistence, as well as cultural change. In the history of the United States, for example, there are countless examples of the reproduction of heartland forms, or modified versions of them, on the frontier, from the colonnaded portico of the county courthouse to eastern table manners. But what was reproduced on or transplanted to the frontier was only a small part of the larger culture of the core areas. The Chinese frontier experience similarly presented a challenge to the replication of eastern Chinese ways of life and especially eastern Chinese urban form and architectural styles. The degree to which the Chinese maintained cultural traditions on the frontier, in spite of the difficulties of frontier life, is striking. The reproduction of traditions from the heartland may often represent what was felt important enough to preserve, if at all possible, even on the frontier. The Chinese went to considerable effort in frontier cities to reproduce large-scale urban form and the sociospatial structures it represented, as well as monumental architecture, in spite of the great costs involved. In the sphere of the physical representation of culture in the landscape, great imperial expense was deemed justified to ensure the successful replication of Chinese monumental forms on the frontiers. Vernacular forms, however, were by and large left to the scant resources of their builders, who often had to adapt to local building materials.

For the average Chinese on the frontier, far removed from those resources that might allow him or her to comfortably reproduce the lifestyles of eastern China, the most important tradition to maintain was probably the vestige of continued ties to the homeplace. Frontier cities were rich in organizations and edifices dedicated to that end. For the non-Chinese migrant to the alien Chinese urban world, both a community and a sense of cultural distinctiveness may have been equally important. The persistence of the Chinese frontiers as frontiers was rooted in perceptions of cultural differences on the part of all concerned. In Chinese cities, where people of different culture came into daily contact, these perceptions were constantly reinforced.

The Morphology of Chinese Frontier Settlements

The social, cultural and economic histories of peoples on the Chinese frontiers have been inextricably linked for centuries. Over the course of 2,000 years or more, distinctive ways of life and settlement patterns developed in the frontier regions as balances of power shifted back and forth between peoples. These dynamic regions remain to this day the most culturally diverse regions of China.

Cities were built and rebuilt in these regions by many peoples, but only the Chinese built and occupied cities in all of the regions of the Chinese frontier. The pattern of Chinese occupation of frontier areas usually emphasized the construction of new cities and rarely, if ever, involved the wholesale takeover and reuse of existing cities. Nonetheless, new Chinese cities on the frontier were often built adjacent to indigenous ones, and most also attracted non-Chinese settlement outside their walls almost from the start. As a result city forms on the frontier developed as conglomerate forms, incorporating indigenous settlements into predominantly Chinese designs.

In all aspects of urban form, from architecture to city form as a whole, Chinese ideals served as structural frameworks that could be filled in by controlled expressions of cultural identity, wealth, or individualism. In many cases these concepts regarding cosmology, geomancy, social hierarchy, and land use constrained the ability of both Chinese and non-Chinese peoples to influence their surroundings. City form and landscape developed within sets of regulations that ranged from the control of land assignment within the walls and the orthogonal layout of streets to limitations on the number of roof levels and the height and size of a structure. Yet in some places and times, variations were permitted or negotiated, both in the inner cities and in their suburbs, and Chinese cities on the frontiers did reflect a degree of cultural pluralism.

Cultural pluralism was expressed in the form of Chinese cities in three ways: twin cities, in which the walled city stood adjacent to an indigenous city; double-walled cities, in which a walled non-Chinese settlement was attached to the walled city; and walled Chinese cities in which non-Chinese peoples clustered in unwalled neighborhoods just outside the city walls. The overall structure of these cities was usually, in the broadest sense, faithful to the accepted ideals for the construction of Chinese cities. City walls, the placement and design of monumental structures, and the overall layout of streets conformed to the Chinese model. These forms became thoroughly regulated throughout the empire, and particularly on the frontier, during the Ming dynasty, which saw a massive rebuilding of city walls throughout China to intensify distinctions between the Chinese and non-Chinese peoples.

Though the Chinese were in the minority in the frontier regions, they usually maintained majority populations within the cities themselves. In areas of high cultural diversity on the frontiers, exclusively Chinese (or Manchu) walled citadels contained and disseminated most elements of Chinese culture. The cities were intentionally maintained as bastions of core culture. But that core culture, be it Chinese or Manchu, was relatively basic. Many cultural and social practices were distilled to their elemental forms when practiced by military men and exiles. In such conditions it is reasonable to assume that the most characteristic, central, and valued aspects of identity and lifestyles were affirmed and maintained in the form of frontier cities. This contrasts with the assertions of Owen Lattimore and others that the frontier contains the "least typical" aspects of the core culture. Frontier cities are among the "most typical" in China in terms of their initial core settlement area.

This is evident at many scales of urban form and landscape in the preponderance on the frontier of square inner-walled city forms and the auspicious placement of monumental structures and city gates. The builders of the frontier cities took great care to reproduce the archetypical Chinese city. Frontier cities differ from classic Chinese cities not in the central walled area, but rather in the suburbs and districts outside it.

Both social and spatial differentiation and hierarchies were maintained within the frontier cities. Spatial differentiation was complex and highly stratified among Chinese of different clans, classes, and trades, between the Chinese and the non-Chinese peoples, and within the non-Chinese population. Chinese immigrants grouped themselves by occupation and place of origin in neighborhoods within the walled enclave; non-Chinese peoples lived outside the walls in their own neighborhoods based on ethnicity, religion, occupation, and place of origin. In addition, some non-Chinese peoples maintained ties with the cities from villages at some remove, as did the Xiningfan (Xining Tibetans), the Bai of the Lake Dian region, and the Hui and Dongxiang who farmed the land just outside of Lanzhou.

This spatial differentiation, as evident in districting patterns, did allow for some flexibility within the variant districts of the city. There was limited opportunity for non-Chinese peoples to build sections of the cities in their own styles, or in some modified forms of those styles. Thus, for example, the Muslim quarters of frontier cities often lacked a geomantic alignment of streets and houses, and mosques and marketplaces served as community focal points.

Different non-Chinese groups on the frontier demonstrated basic differences and approaches to living within the orbit of the Chinese frontier cities. Broad contrasts are evident, for example, between Islamic and Lamaist peoples. Islamic peoples succeeded to a great extent in finding a social, economic, and spatial niche in the Chinese frontier city. Their occupations were distinct from those of the Chinese, but played an important role in the urban economy. Within the separate quarters they occupied outside the walled cores of the cities, they were able to exercise a degree of influence on the built environment and to construct and operate their own cultural institutions such as mosques and tea shops.

In contrast, Lamaist people were far less socially, economically, and spatially integrated into the structure of the Chinese frontier city. Lamaist peoples tended to be either sojourners or traders within the cities. Those who lived in urban areas generally resided in a village or monastery somewhat removed from the city. Only occasionally, as in the case of Hohhot's small Lamaist population, was there any significant participation of Lamaist peoples in a predominantly Chinese urban milieu before 1949.

The preference of different non-Chinese peoples for congregating in their own neighborhoods and settlements in the cities, and the Chinese beliefs and practices that at the same time excluded them from living within the central walled area, may have kept their residences spatially segregated, but considerable economic and cultural exchange did take place across those boundaries. The movement and interchange of cultural ideas can be seen, for example, in the diffusion of architectural styles and decorative forms. There was considerable intermixing of Chinese and non-Chinese architectural styles on the frontier prior to 1949, particularly in the non-Chinese architectural endeavors. The non-Chinese peoples tended to maintain their own distinctive styles in the vernacular but to borrow considerably from both Chinese characteristic designs and elements of other non-Chinese people's architecture for their mosques and temples. This was at least partially attributable to a lack of non-Chinese carpenters with the skills required for monumental architecture, but it also had to do with the dictates of the Chinese, as in the case of the removal or restrictions on the building of minarets for geomantic reasons. Some Chinese styles were adopted out of appreciation or fashion as well and might be still further blended with another group's forms. Tibetans adopted Hui motifs in some temple embellishments; the Hui oramented some mosques with Lamaist decorations. As a result the landscape of frontier cities became relatively cosmopolitan and multicultural in the Chinese context. Through successions of borrowing, some patterns developed that were unique to the frontier realm.

The Chinese city on the frontier was thus at once a striking replica of a standardized Chinese urban ideal and a multicultural settlement with distinctive characteristics of its own. It is a duality that to a great extent continues to mark the frontier cities today.

Contemporary Frontier Cities

Chinese cities have changed more in the past half-century than they did in the previous 2,000 years. These changes are sometimes criticized for having virtually eliminated the unique cultural heritage of Chinese urban life and landscape. But in fact some traditional forms are still to be found in many cities, and it is still possible to read much of their past morphology in the present-day landscape. This is nowhere more true than on the frontier, where there has been persistence in both spatial and cultural patterns despite the rapid growth and development that has intensified Chinese settlement, promoted new forms of residential, functional, and neighborhood organization, and disavowed many of the spatial patterns characteristic of Chinese walled city forms.

Cities on the frontier have to a great extent retained such features as ethnic districting, housing and street patterns, and market areas. They have also retained some temples and other examples of monumental architecture and not least, their city walls, for fragmentary as these may be, their routes are still clearly visible in the spatial distribution of social and economic activities. Development has come later and in some ways less comprehensively to the frontier than to the cities of the east, leaving more of the earlier landscapes intact. But in these multicultural places there may also be more concern with maintaining and even reestablishing cultural identity in architecture and urban space.

In the post–Cultural Revolution era, frontier cities are experiencing a restoration of traditional and regional landscapes more rapidly than cities in eastern China. One key factor in this phenomenon is that the non-Han Chinese peoples, particularly where they live in relatively high concentrations, have initiated the process of restoration more quickly than have the Han Chinese and are building bold statements of identity. Many Muslim and Lamaist people are rebuilding religious structures throughout the frontier regions, using bright colors and, in the case of mosques, tall minarets to significantly alter the landscapes in which they live. Mosques were reopened and rebuilt by local Muslims so rapidly in the 1980s that some districts in the cities now have a high concentration of them. Lamaist temple complexes, though much reduced in staff compared with the traditional era, have also been reopened and restored with donations of labor and money from the faithful. Lamaist temples are again functioning throughout the Tibetan and Mongolian culture regions, and many that were damaged or destroyed are being rebuilt. In contrast, only a few Chinese temples in each city have been restored, and more often than not, that has been done by the state for the purposes of tourism or as museums, rather than by people who wish to worship at them. Those Chinese temples that are being restored seem relatively inactive, with little religious activity taking place in them.

The new state architecture on the frontier, which borrows on non-

Chinese themes, is placing a stronger imprint of multiculturalism on these cities than there ever was before. This emphasis is part of a general rejection by contemporary urban planners of the attempts to standardize the form and appearance of Chinese cities that marked the Mao era. The stress today is on creating unique images for the cities that reflect the culturally diverse nature of the regions they occupy. This policy is applied at many different levels, from the preservation of vernacular houses to the construction of government buildings with elements of local styles. Contemporary urban planning for many of these cities now includes the active preservation and maintenance of their frontier character.

The application of local styles is sometimes contrived and not necessarily a true representation or preservation of local culture. The styles applied in this program are highly abstracted and limited to the decorative, rather than structural, elements of buildings, and are typically applied out of context and out of scale: yurts are elevated several stories above the ground to decorate the roofs of government offices, and the grand domes of Central Asian mosques and mausoleums adorn modern high-rise department stores. There even seems to be a certain standardization in the formal creation of these symbols for some kinds of uses. The abstracted "mosque" and the abstracted "yurt" can be quite similar in both form and function. The relative uniformity of these "national styles" on the frontier can conceal a relatively high level of cultural diversity within the non–Han Chinese population. This is true particularly where a motif from only one of several cultures in a region has been chosen as a symbol for all of them.

Historical patterns of alternate expansion and contraction of Chinese control of the frontiers have been fundamentally altered during the past half-century by the new and very different political, economic, and social policies of the PRC. The PRC has to some degree worked to end the frontier both by significantly changing its ethnic composition and by striving to integrate it politically, economically, socially, and culturally with the eastern core. But China has not yet witnessed the "end of the frontier" in the sense that Frederick Jackson Turner proclaimed the end of the American frontier in 1890. The Chinese frontiers continue to exist as cultural frontiers even if they are not—as of 1995 at least—dynamic political ones. The frontier regions are still inhabited by non–Han Chinese peoples who have maintained their distinct identities. Massive settlement of the frontiers by Han Chinese, including agrarian settlement as well as urban migration, and fuller integration of these regions into the political, economic, and social orbit of "China proper," are not likely to extinguish these ethnic frontiers, leaving open the possibility—as in the former Soviet Union—of nationalistic movements reasserting sovereignty. And in the vast regions of these persistent frontiers, from Inner Mongolia to Xinjiang, Tibet, and Yunnan, the Chinese cities will remain frontiers in microcosm, special areas of cultural interaction and potential confrontation, as they have been for centuries. The frontier cities of China will very likely continue to embody the interaction of cultural, social, and environmental factors with a degree of complexity that perhaps can be found only on dynamic frontiers where radically different peoples, ways of life, and urban traditions interact.

Reference Matter

Appendix

Survey of Pre-1949 City Shapes

The two tables below present the particulars on the 233 cities I classified by wall forms. As I noted in the discussion in Chapter Six, the classification is based on the shape of the inner city walls, not on the shape of the entire settlement, which could embrace one or more outer walled or unwalled suburbs. Table A.1 provides a city-by-city breakdown; Table A.2 presents a summary of the data.

In compiling the survey, I consulted the following sources: Chang Sendou 1961, 1963, 1970, 1977; *Changjiang* 1982; Chen Qiaoyi 1986; Cheng Guangsu 1953; Chihli River Commission 1924; Cressey 1955; Dyson 1927; Fukuda 1975; *Gansu tongzhi* 1966; Geil 1911; Great Britain 1927; Japan, Koka Rikugun 1939; *Jiangnan tongzhi* 1968; Mannerheim 1940, Mingcheng Shihua 1984; Pannell 1977; *Qingguo Shandongsheng* 1935; Richard 1908; *Rongxian zhi* 1936; *Ruchengxian zhi* 1932; Ryder n.d.; Schinz 1989; Skinner 1977; Steinhardt 1990; Wallacker et al. 1979; *Xinjiang dilizhi* 1914; Yaguang Geographical Society 1936; *Zhengning xianzhi* 1968; *Zhongguo lishi wenhua mingcheng zidian* 1985; *Zhongxiu Jingyuanwei zhi* 1968.

TABLE A.1

The Sample Cities by Shape and Orientation

Province & city	Lat.[a]	Long.[a]	Shape[b]	Orientation[c]	Province & city	Lat.[a]	Long.[a]	Shape[b]	Orientation[c]
Anhui					Hebei				
Anqing	30	117	irr	ncd	?	40	117	asq	cd
Boxian	34	115	sqd	cd	Baoding	39	115	irr	cd
Chuxian	32	118	irr	cd	Cangxian	38	117	irr	cd
Dangtu	31	118	asq	cd	Dexian	37	116	irr	cd
Fengyang	32	117	sqt	cd	Dingxian	38	115	irr	ncd
Hefei	31	117	asq	cd	Huolu	38	114	asq	acd
Jintan	31	119	rnd	ncd	Mancheng	39	115	asq	cd
Mengcheng	33	116	irr	ncd	Pingguxian	40	117	sq	cd
Shouxian	32	116	asq	cd	Sanhexian	40	117	sq	cd
Sixian	33	118	irr	cd	Shanhaiguan	40	119	irr	ncd
Xiaoxian	34	116	ard	acd	Xingtai	37	115	asq	cd
Xuancheng	30	118	irr	acd	Xuanhua	41	115	asq	cd
Zhengyangguan	32	116	ard	cd	Yutianxian	40	118	sq	cd
Beijing					Zhengding	38	114	asq	cd
Beijing	39	116	asq	cd	Henan				
Liangxiangzhen	39	116	sq	cd	Anlu	31	113	irr	acd
Tongxian	40	117	irr	cd	Handan	36	114	asq	cd
Fujian					Kaifeng	35	114	asq	cd
Fuzhou	26	119	irr	acd	Lingbao	35	111	sq	cd
Quanzhou	24	118	irr	acd	Luohe	34	114	irt	cd
Gansu					Luoyang	34	112	sq	cd
Anxi	40	95	sq	cd	Nanyang	33	112	asq	acd
Didaozhou	35	103	sqd	cd	Runing	33	114	irr	cd
Dunhuang	40	95	asd	cd	Suixian	34	115	ard	cd
Ganzhou	39	100	sq	cd	Weihui	35	114	irr	cd
Jiayuguan	39	98	sq	cd	Xuchang	34	113	sq	cd
Jingyuan	37	104	sqd	cd	Yancheng/				
Jinta	39	98	irr	acd	Dahezhen	34	114	asq	cd
Jiuquan	39	98	asd	cd	Zhangde	36	114	sq	cd
Lanzhou	36	104	asd	cd	Zhongmouxian	35	114	sq	cd
Liangzhou	38	102	sqd	cd	Zhoujiakou	34	115	irr	cd
Liutaofu	35	104	sqd	cd	Zhoukouzhen	33	115	sq	cd
Pingliang	35	106	ird	cd	Hubei				
Qinzhou	34	105	sqd	cd	Hanyang	30	114	irr	ncd
Wuwei	37	102	sqt	cd	Jiangling	30	112	irr	cd
Zhengningxian	35	109	asq	cd	Wuchang	30	114	irr	ncd
Guangdong					Xiangyang	32	112	irr	ncd
Guangzhou	23	113	ird	cd	Xinyang	31	112	irr	cd
Meixian	24	116	sq	cd	Yingcheng	30	113	irr	ncd
Nanxiong	25	114	ird	?	Yingshan	30	115	irr	acd
Zhaoqing	23	112	asq	cd	Hunan				
Guangxi					Changsha	28	112	asq	cd
Guilin	25	110	irr	cd	Chenzhou	25	113	asq	cd
Nanning	22	108	irr	ncd	Qiyang	36	117	sq	cd
Rongxian	23	111	asq	cd	Rucheng	26	114	asq	acd
Guizhou					Inner Mongolia				
Guiyang	26	106	asq	cd	Hohhot	42	112	sqt	cd
Zunyi	27	106	irr	acd					

TABLE A.1
Continued

Province & city	Lat.[a]	Long.[a]	Shape[b]	Orientation[c]	Province & city	Lat.[a]	Long.[a]	Shape[b]	Orientation[c]
Jiangsu					Boxingshan	37	118	sq	cd
Changshu	31	120	irr	cd	Changbaxian	37	119	sq	cd
Changzhou	31	119	irr	acd	Changlexian	35	119	sq	cd
Danyang	32	120	irr	ncd	Changqing	37	117	asq	ncd
Jurong	32	119	irr	acd	Changzhi	36	113	asq	ncd
Kunshang	31	120	irr	acd	Daming	36	115	sq	cd
Nanjing	32	118	irr	cd	Dengzhoufu	37	120	irr	acd
Nantong	32	121	asq	acd	Depingxian	37	117	sq	cd
Peixian	34	117	asq	acd	Dezhou	37	116	irr	cd
Suqian	34	118	ird	cd	Donghexian	36	116	asq	cd
Suzhou	31	120	asq	cd	Enxian	38	116	sq	ncd
Taicang	31	121	irr	ncd	Feichengxian	36	116	sq	cd
Wuxi	31	120	irr	acd	Fushanxian	37	121	sq	cd
Xuzhou	34	117	ird	cd	Gaoluanxian	36	119	sq	cd
Yangzhou	32	119	asq	cd	Gaotangzhou	37	116	rnd	cd
Yixing	31	119	irr	ncd	Guide	36	116	sq	cd
Zhenjiang	32	119	irr	acd	Haichangxian	36	121	sq	cd
Jiangxi					Haifengxian	37	117	sq	cd
Anyi	28	115	irr	ncd	Hanheng	36	119	sq	cd
Anyuan	25	116	rnd	cd	Huangxian	37	120	irr	cd
Huichang	26	116	rnd	cd	Jiaodengxian	37	123	sq	cd
Ji'an	27	115	irr	ncd	Jiaozhou	36	120	irr	cd
Jingdezhen	29	117	ard	cd	Jimoxian	36	120	sq	cd
Jingzhou	25	115	irr	cd	Jinan	37	117	ird	cd
Jiujiang	29	115	irr	ncd	Jinghaiwei	37	122	sq	cd
Longnan	25	115	ard	cd	Jingzhou	37	116	sq	cd
Nanchang	28	116	irr	cd	Jining	35	116	asq	cd
Pingxiang	28	114	ard	ncd	Jinxiang	35	116	irr	acd
Ruichang	29	115	irr	ncd	Le'anxian	37	118	sq	ncd
Xingguo	26	115	rnd	cd	Lelingxian	37	117	sq	ncd
Xingzi	29	116	ard	cd	Lijinxian	37	118	sq	acd
Liaoning					Linqing	37	115	asq	cd
Kaiyuan	42	124	sq	cd	Linyi	35	118	irr	cd
Liaoyang	41	123	sq	ncd	Linzixian	37	118	irr	cd
Shenyang	41	123	sq	cd	Louxiaxian	37	121	sq	cd
Ningxia					Mantaixian	37	118	sq	cd
Guyuan	36	106	sqd	acd	Ninghaixian	37	121	sq	cd
Yinchuan	38	106	sqt	acd	Ningyang	35	116	irr	cd
Qinghai					Pingduzhou	36	120	ird	cd
Xining	36	102	sqd	cd	Pingyuanxian	38	116	irr	cd
Shaanxi					Qidongxian	37	117	asq	cd
Xi'an	34	108	sq	cd	Qihe	36	116	sq	cd
Yulin	38	110	asq	acd	Qingcheng	37	118	sq	cd
Shandong					Qingyunxian	38	117	sq	cd
?	36	118	irr	acd	Qingzhou	37	118	sqt	cd
?	37	116	sq	cd	Qufu	35	116	ard	cd
?	37	120	sq	cd	Rizhaoxian	35	119	sq	cd
Binzhou	37	119	sq	acd	Rongchengxian	37	122	sq	cd
Boshan	36	118	irt	cd					

continues

TABLE A.I
Continued

Province & city	Lat.[a]	Long.[a]	Shape[b]	Orientation[c]	Province & city	Lat.[a]	Long.[a]	Shape[b]	Orientation[c]
Shanxian	34	116	sq	cd	Hanzhong	33	107	asq	cd
Shenxian	36	115	asq	cd	Mianyang	31	104	asq	?
Shouguangxian	37	118	sq	cd	Xinjiang				
Tai'anfu	36	117	sq	cd	Aksu	41	80	sq	cd
Tengxian	35	117	asq	ncd	Barkol	43	96	sqt	cd
Wacheng	37	119	irr	cd	Gucheng	44	89	asd	cd
Weifang	37	119	asq	cd	Hami	42	93	sqt	cd
Weihaiwei	37	123	sq	cd	Hetian/				
Weixian	36	119	irt	acd	Khotan	37	79	sq	cd
Wuchengxian	38	116	irr	cd	Kuerla/				
Wudingfu	37	117	sq	cd	Qarashahr	41	86	sq	cd
Yangxinxian	37	117	sq	cd	Shache/				
Yanzhou	35	116	asq	cd	Yarkand	38	77	sqt	cd
Yidu	37	118	ast	cd	Tulufan/Turfan	42	89	sqt	cd
Yixian	35	118	asq	cd	Wulumuqi/				
Zizhouxian	36	118	sq	cd	Urumqi	44	88	asq	cd
Zouxian	35	117	irr	cd	Wushi	41	79	sq	cd
Shanghai					Yining/Kuldja	43	81	sq	cd
Baoshan	31	121	sq	?	Yunnan				
Shanghai	32	122	ard	cd	Dali	25	100	asq	ncd
Songjiang	31	121	asq	cd	Kunming	25	103	asq	cd
Shanxi					Luliang	25	104	sq	cd
Datong	40	113	sq	cd	Zhejiang				
Fencheng	35	111	sq	cd	De'an	29	115	irr	ncd
Fenyang	37	111	sq	ncd	Duchang	29	116	ard	acd
Houmazhen	36	111	asq	cd	Hangzhou	30	120	ird	cd
Jincheng	36	113	irr	cd	Jiading	31	121	ard	cd
Linfen	36	111	irr	ncd	Jiashan	30	120	asq	acd
Qinxian	36	112	asq	ncd	Jiaxing	30	120	asq	?
Taigu	37	113	sq	cd	Ningbo	30	121	irr	acd
Taiyuan	37	113	sq	cd	Shaoxing	30	120	asq	cd
Yuncheng	35	110	sq	ncd	Wenxi	28	120	asq	?
Sichuan					Wuxing	31	120	irr	acd
Chengdu	30	104	asq	ncd	Xinjiang	30	120	irr	cd
Chongqing	29	106	irr	ncd					

[a] Latitude and longitude are rounded to the nearest whole degree. Note that this slight imprecision matches the fact that the maps were produced "by hand" (on Macintosh and IBM-compatible computers using a drawing program, Aldus Freehand), without precise placement of the cities through a geographic information system.

[b] Shape abbreviations: sq = square, asq = almost square (these two categories, as with all other "almost" categories, were collapsed for analysis); rnd = round, ard = almost round; irr = irregular; sqd = square, double; sqt = square, twin; ird = irregular, double; irt = irregular, twin. There were no double or twin round cities.

[c] Orientation abbreviations: cd = aligned with the cardinal directions, acd = almost aligned with the cardinal directions, ncd = not aligned with the cardinal directions, ? = alignment not indicated on source maps.

TABLE A.2
Summary of City Survey

Category	All cities (N = 233)		Cities west of 105° east long. (N = 30 [13%])		Cities west of 110° east long. (N = 41 [18%])		Cities west of Aihui-Tengchong line[a] (N = 29 [12%])	
	No.	Pct.	No.	Pct.	No.	Pct.	No.	Pct.
Shape								
Square	142	61%	29	97%	36	88%	28	97%
Irregular	75	32	1	3	5	12	1	3
Round	16	7	0	0	0	0	0	
Orientation								
Cardinal	195	84	27	90	36	88	28	97
Not cardinal	33	14	2	7	4	10	0	0
Not indicated	5	2	1	3	1	2	1	3
Double/twin	34	15	14	47	18	44	18	62

[a]See Map 2.

Notes

Introduction

1. In this book I use the term "Silk Routes" rather than "Silk Road" to emphasize the multiple trading routes in this vast network. The Silk Routes are discussed in greater detail in Chapter Three.

2. The PRC officially classifies and registers the ethnicity of its citizens. At present 56 peoples (which the Chinese call *minzu*) are recognized, including the majority Han Chinese. These 56 categories mask still greater cultural diversity. Even among those people who are classified as Han Chinese there is considerable regional variation in many aspects of culture. The term *minzu* is sometimes translated as peoples, nationalities, or ethnicities. The Chinese term for the non–Han Chinese peoples is *shaoshu minzu*, which is usually translated as "minority nationalities." This translation carries political undertones, however, and many Western scholars prefer to use the term *shaoshu minzu* rather than translate it.

3. Over the great span of history covered by this book, what is meant by modern ethnonyms such as "Han Chinese" and "Chinese" has varied greatly. For the 20th century I follow the PRC government's usage on terms like "Han," "Uygur," and "Hui," but I use "non–Han Chinese" rather than the common label "minorities," since in many cases nonethnic Chinese are in the majority in the frontier regions. There is some controversy among historians and anthropologists over when the term "Han" first came into currency, and for this reason, I prefer to use the simple terms "Chinese" and "non-Chinese" in discussing earlier centuries to establish a basic distinction between the representatives of the Chinese empire on the frontier, and both the indigenous peoples of the frontier regions and the other non-Chinese people who congregated in frontier cities.

4. David Buck (1978) noted this trend in connection with his decision to choose a research site that was neither a port city nor a former capital (Jinan, in Shandong Province).

5. I made relatively little use of Chinese geographical journals, which in general are either focused on physical geography or approach questions of urban ge-

ography in terms of statistical economic analysis, matters that, although interesting in themselves, had little bearing on my subject.

Chapter One

1. I have chosen to include Yunnan and Gansu in this study, although both provinces are sometimes treated as part of China proper, not as frontier regions. Both provinces do have substantial Chinese populations and are relatively well integrated with the core area. Yunnan nevertheless remains a border region with a high degree of cultural diversity, while much of Gansu, including the city of Lanzhou, still lies on the edge of the heartland of Chinese settlement. Yunnan is a special case. Much of it was part of a succession of non-Chinese kingdoms until the areas ruled by the Nan Zhao kingdom, including the Kunming region, were incorporated into the core region of China by the Mongols during the Yuan dynasty. They continued to be administered by subsequent dynasties until the end of the Qing. Yunnan thus was more clearly and irreversibly (to this day) integrated with the "core" regions of China than were Xinjiang, Gansu, Qinghai, Tibet, Inner Mongolia, and other regions that passed in and out of Chinese imperial control until ultimately becoming incorporated into the PRC. Both Kunming and Lanzhou have functioned as frontier settlements for most of their histories. Though neighboring Sichuan province might have qualified, too, since it has its share of frontier outposts, trading towns, and cities (the classic example being Dajianlu), I have excluded it on the grounds that its major city, Chengdu, is not really a frontier city but the center of a region that has long been a heavily settled Chinese homeland. For a fine account of the agrarian frontier in what is now southern Sichuan under the Song dynasty (960–1279), see Von Glahn 1987.

2. There are other areas that also might be considered Chinese frontier zones. Historical Chinese colonization and political, economic, and cultural influences have clearly had a major impact on historical urban development and form in Korea, Taiwan, and Vietnam—spectacularly, for example, in the case of the Vietnamese capital of Hue, which was built in the 19th century with Qing dynasty Beijing as a model (Keyes 1977). The adoption of Chinese urban planning and architectural styles in Japan, where several imperial capitals were modeled on Chang'an (Xi'an), the capital city of the Tang empire (618–907), and early urbanization in Thailand are also important aspects of this topic (Kornhauser 1976, 1983; Wheatley & See 1978; Yazaki 1968). I hope to explore these dimensions of Chinese frontier urbanism in future work.

3. The discussion of the Chinese frontiers as a cyclic process was initiated by Lattimore in the 1940s and continued by Gari Ledyard in 1983. Thomas Barfield draws on the work of both to present his interpretation of the cyclic nature of the Chinese frontier process, although he differs with Lattimore on the progression and length of the cycles and approaches the cycles from the perspective of the formation of nomad empires (Barfield 1989: 10). All three authors focus primarily on the political and economic relations between the Chinese empire and the peoples of the frontier.

4. Most if not all the Chinese would have surely found the idea of celebrating the frontier as a source of worthy cultural and social practices absurd. Chinese civilization was largely regarded as an achievement of the core area's centuries of development and not as something crystallized by the outcasts and "barbarians" of the frontiers.

5. Jonathan Spence notes that the first example of the Chinese empire dealing with a foreign nation as an equal sovereign state in late imperial times was the Qing dynasty's assignment of relations with the Russian empire to a special bureau, the Lifan Yuan (Spence 1990: 66–67).

6. Current thinking inclines instead to the view that the two groups are interdependent, at least to the extent that nomadic societies tend to rely on trade with sedentary peoples for some aspects of their subsistence, and sedentary people to benefit from that trade. See, for example, Barfield 1989.

7. Three notable exceptions are J. J. Van Nostrand, "The Problems of Cultural Frontiers" (1941); Werner J. Cahnman, "Frontiers Between East and West in Europe" (1949); and Paul L. Mackendrick, "Roman Colonization and the Frontier Hypothesis," in Wyman and Kroeber 1965, all of which address frontier issues in Greek and Roman times.

8. L. D. Barrier describes Lattimore's frontier discussions as a "geopolitical" approach to the cultural and political unity of China (Barrier 1977). By this he refers to Lattimore's emphasis on the geographical aspects of the political identity of a state such as China: an identity built through the frontier experience.

9. Lattimore's frontier feudal lords seem to resemble the Chinese compradors, who worked as intermediaries between European firms and Chinese traders in the treaty ports during the 19th and early 20th centuries.

10. John Bodley asserts that the process of frontier feudalism amounts to the creation of a debt peonage system where lack of regulation has afforded traders and colonizers opportunities to exploit indigenous peoples either directly or through agents (1982: 37).

11. Sichuan had been a part of the Chinese empire since the Qin dynasty, but there was a substantial migration into previously unsettled (by Chinese) areas of Sichuan during the Song period.

12. Kristof goes on to suggest that "this is what the Chinese frontier policy of keeping the Chinese in and the barbarians out aimed at," but the Chinese example does not really fit his argument, since it embraced not only the regions within such inner boundaries as the Great Wall, but also great stretches of maintained frontier area beyond.

13. When I refer to cycles in this context, I am speaking in terms of the spatial expansion and contraction of the Chinese empire's control of the far frontier regions. This is different from Barfield's (1989) frontier cycles, which refer to the periodic development of nomad confederacies in regions outside the area controlled by the Chinese empire.

14. Many Chinese agriculturalists did settle in Inner Mongolia during the 16th century. See, for example, Jagchid & Symons 1989: 173.

15. Though, as he also notes, the Chinese authorities did make attempts "to

supplant the 'profane cults' (*yinci*) of the natives with appropriate secular exemplars from the pantheon of Han civilization" (Von Glahn 1987: 15).

16. Moser stands out in his attempt to demonstrate the diversity of the Han Chinese in his 1985 book, *The Chinese Mosaic.*

17. According to Morris Rossabi, the Mongols under Khubilai Khan (with the encouragement of their Chinese advisers) established a tuntian system in Henan and Shaanxi (Rossabi 1988: 23).

18. Barfield is concerned, however, with nomads who lived on the northern frontiers of China and whose lands were not politically incorporated into the Chinese state. The inner Asia he discusses "was a zone of long-term interaction between two opposing cultures [Chinese and nomadic] with powerfully fixed ideas of themselves and others. For more than 2,000 years the nomadic peoples of the steppe confronted the world's largest agrarian state without being politically incorporated by it or adopting its culture" (Barfield 1989: 2).

19. The Qidan had made Beijing their southern capital by A.D. 1000, with their central capital north of the Great Wall and their western capital at Datong, just inside the wall (Fairbank 1992: 114). The Mongols and the Manchu both made Beijing their capital at various periods.

20. With the important difference that China's autonomous regions do not have a constitutional right to secede.

21. For detailed treatments of the issue of the state identification of minorities in China, see Gladney 1991: 81–98; and Gladney 1990. See also the works of Dreyer, Eberhard, Heberer, and Schwarz listed in the Bibliography.

22. I choose the religious categories "Islamic" and "Lamaist" here as a means of grouping otherwise quite distinct peoples. Clearly, these categories are mere conveniences and do not begin to address the wide cultural variation within the larger group. I prefer "Lamaist" to "Tibetan Buddhist" as a way to indicate that many followers of that religion are not Tibetans.

23. The origin of those peoples remains unclear, and there is increasing evidence for early cultures in other regions of China, such as the southeast coast.

24. Data on 20th-century pilgrimages by Muslims from China are evidence of these renewed ties. Eight hundred thirty-four Hui made the Hajj over the years 1923–34. Dru Gladney reports that 500 Uygur made the Hajj in 1988, and that between 1980 and 1987, a total of 6,500 Uygur made the Hajj (Gladney 1990: 18).

25. Thus the residents of Kashgar were known as Kashgarliks, the residents of Aksu as Aksuliks, and so forth.

26. Gladney questions the process by which the Sala and Dongxiang were identified as separate groups while other similarly sized Muslim groups are grouped together under the "Hui" category (Gladney 1991: 34).

27. Tsong Khapa was named after his birthplace near Tsong Kha in the Kokonor (Qinghai Lake) region of today's Qinghai Province, not far from Xining (Richardson 1984: 40).

28. Tsong Khapa's third successor was given the title Third Dalai Lama, while his first successor, Gedun Truppa, was retroactively named First Dalai Lama and

his second successor, Gedun Gyatso, was named Second Dalai Lama (Richardson 1984: 40–41).

29. The name Qiang is now applied to a group of people who migrated from the Tibetan area and live in Sichuan and Yunnan.

30. Members of the Manchu imperial family practiced Tibetan Buddhism and were educated by lamas in Beijing.

31. After the death of Gusri Khan, most of the actual power in Tibet was consolidated by the Dalai Lama, although the Mongols retained their titles as heads of state there until 1717 (Richardson 1984: 42).

32. George Moseley, Wolfram Eberhard, and Xin Jiguang are just a few of the many scholars who have attempted to classify these peoples by language. Though no two classifications are exactly alike, they are in general agreement on the broad groupings of people. Moseley (1973) identifies the Tibeto-Burman (Yi, Jingpo, Naxi, Lisu, Lahu, Bai, and Hani), Mon-Khmer (Va and Bulang), and Miao-Yao language groups. Eberhard (1982: 98) identifies several language groups: the Thai (e.g., Zhuang), Tibeto-Burman (e.g., Yi), Yao and Miao, and Austroasiatic (e.g., Va). Chinese sources (e.g., Xin Jiguang 1987) tend to categorize many of the southwestern minorities under the "Han-Tibetan" (Sino-Tibetan) language family, such as the Yi, Bai, Lisu, Lahu, Naxi, Achang, Pumi, Dulong, Nu (Achang, Pumi, Dulong, and Nu are classed as the "Tibeto-Burman branch of the Chinese-Tibetan Family"), the Mon-Khmer language group, including the Va, Dulong and Bulang, or the "Baiyue" group, including the Zhuang, Tong, Shui, Bouyei, and Lisu.

33. In the pre-1949 era, the Bai were often referred to as the Minjia or Min-chia.

Chapter Two

1. Though Guandi is often referred to as the God of War, the deity is sometimes taken to represent other strengths as well, such as wealth.

2. Jincheng can also be translated as Golden Walls.

3. The Xiongnu, a "far-flung tribal confederation" (Fairbank 1992: 61), occupied much of the Mongolian steppe from the Warring States era (476 B.C.–221 B.C.) to the end of the Han dynasty (A.D. 220). They fought numerous wars with the Chinese during that period, and it is believed that the Qin emperor built the first Great Wall as a defense against them. These repeated incursions were apparently for the purpose of obtaining grain, cloth, metals, and other items not commonly available to their nomadic community (Fitzgerald 1961: 162; Hyer 1982: 59).

4. The Xianbi were a nomadic people who originated in Mongolia and later established states from Gansu to Hebei and Shandong (Fairbank 1992: 73).

5. Gusiluo is a Chinese transliteration of a Tibetan name meaning "son of Buddha."

6. The walls roughly followed the path of the Ming walls, whose ruins are still visible.

7. The Xixia kingdom was founded by the Tangut in the north of China during the 11th century.

8. That there was some communication and interconnection between these far-flung Islamic communities is clear. For example, an Islamic leader from Yunnan who came to Xining in the late 13th century and died there was buried with honor just southwest of the walled city, by the order of the administrator of Xining. This holy grave became a pilgrimage site for Islamic peoples from far outside the region (*Qinghai lishi jiyao* 1987: 116–22).

9. The Mongol Khoshot Khanate, which was founded by Gusri Khan and successively presided over by Dayan Khan, Dalai Khan, and Lacang Khan, ruled the Qinghai Lake and Qaidam Basin region from 1636 to 1717 (Grousset 1970: 522–25). During the reign of Dayan Khan, the Mongols controlled the Ordos, Kokonor, and Amdo regions (Sinor 1969: 206), so that Xining was at the very edge of the area of Chinese control.

10. But the Chinese had probably been a majority in those earlier eras when they held the city and a substantial Hui and settled Tibetan population had not yet developed in the immediate area.

11. This historical account, except as otherwise noted, is based on Rong's unpublished manuscript.

12. The "*hu*" in their name, often translated as barbarians, was applied to most of the northern and western non-Chinese groups in ancient times.

13. The Wei, or Toba, were Tungusic people. They were apparently considerably sinified after contact with the Chinese (Fairbank 1992: 73). According to C. P. Fitzgerald, after they established their northern dynasty, they intermarried with local people, including Chinese, and assimilated many Chinese customs. Fitzgerald observes that "in A.D. 500 the Wei Emperor actually issued a decree prohibiting the use of the Tartar language, costume and customs in favour of those of China. The Wei dynasty was thus completely identified with the Chinese culture, and did much to preserve and restore the literature of the Han era" (Fitzgerald 1961: 261).

14. During the 6th century the Ruanruan were conquered by the Tujue (552–744), a Central Asian group that dominated Mongolia for two centuries (Hyer 1982: 60).

15. The Liao dynasty, established by the Qidan (Khitan) people, ruled parts of northern China from 916 to 1125. "A Mongolian people from whom North China got the medieval European name Cathay," (Fairbank 1992: 84), the semi-nomadic Qidan, who numbered about four million in all, straddled the frontier between the agricultural regions of northern China and the pasturelands of Mongolia and Manchuria (ibid., pp 84–85).

16. Liao Fengzhou should not be confused with the Sui-Tang prefecture of that name. The Fengzhou of Sui and Tang times was located on the north bank of the Yellow River, about 300 km due west of Hohhot, on a site first occupied during the Han dynasty. During the Liao and Jin dynasties, this site was part of the Western Xia state and the name Fengzhou was used to refer to the settlement in the Hohhot area (Rong Yang 1979: 30–31). During the Liao-Jin period, there was

also a place called Fengzhou in the Hedong area of the Song state, southwest of Hohhot in northern Shaanxi Province.

17. Marco Polo referred to Hohhot as the city "Tenduc."

18. These refugees also joined Altan Khan's armies in campaigns against China. Some of the Chinese who participated in the construction of Hohhot may have been earlier migrants to the area.

19. Wulumuqi is the Chinese pronunciation of the city name. Urumqi, or Urumchi, is the name commonly used by speakers of Western languages. Both are approximations of the Uygur name for the region.

20. Jiangnan is the term for the region south of the Yangzi in the Shanghai and Nanjing region, long considered one of China's most cultured and productive areas.

21. The graveyards for Jiangxi, Guangxi, and Fujian lay to the east of the city; those for Shandong and Shanxi to the north, for Zhejiang and Shaanxi to the west, and for Sichuan to the northwest.

22. There had been moats around some cities in earlier periods, but they were much more prevalent during and after the Ming.

23. French residence had another lasting effect: Kunming residents developed a taste for French bread, which is still produced in Kunming for the local market.

24. The American-built road, called the Stillwell Road in honor of the general, connected up with the Chinese-built Burma Road at Mu Se. It was built in 1944–45.

Chapter Three

1. Thomas Barfield does discuss cities to the extent that he claims the Ugyur fell in 840 in part because they weakened themselves by establishing a city to house their wealth, which made them an easy target for invasion (Barfield 1989: 159). But since that city, Karabalghasun, was nearly 100 years old at the time, this seems to me to ascribe too much blame to the city for the Ugyur's predicament.

2. A primate city, usually evaluated in a national context, is a city with well over twice the population of the next largest city in the country. Primate cities typically carry out by far the majority of urban functions for an entire country and contain the vast majority of the urban population as well. Bangkok and Manila are good examples in Asia. It is difficult to speak of primate cities in connection with China because it has so many very large cities.

3. It is always possible that a major influx of foreign investment could make a city like Xining the next Silicon Valley of Asia and spur the sort of population growth characteristic of Asia's primate cities, but this seems unlikely, given the abundance of areas with less harsh environments and better access to transport and other resources available to potential investors. Even Kunming, which is attracting a small amount of foreign interest, must wait for the many eastern cities with far better access to international markets to become saturated before experiencing this type of economic and population boom.

4. Wright is aware, however, that in some areas events did not fit this pattern,

for he notes that in the settlement of the Yangzi valley, military outposts that eventually became cities were the first to introduce Chinese-style agriculture (Wright 1977: 52).

5. It is common today to classify urban places and hierarchies of settlement forms (cities, towns, villages) in terms of population. While this is often a useful generalization, I prefer functional categorizations for frontier situations.

6. Although it should be noted that the cities included in this study were high-order administrative units that administered quite large areas in addition to serving military functions. Many smaller frontier cities can fittingly be said to have had a "narrow span of control."

7. Keith Buchanan asserts that for the far west, air transport has been the key integrating factor (Buchanan 1970: 260). But though air transport has added a wider possibility of destinations, it is rail transport that still moves the bulk of people and goods between the far west and eastern China.

8. Most Chinese trains are still pulled by coal-fueled steam engines. In 1982 electric or diesel engines were used on the Beijing-Guangzhou, Beijing-Shanghai, Beijing-Shenyang, Harbin-Dalian, Shanghai-Hangzhou, and Baoji-Chengdu lines, and electrification projects were under way on the Shijiazhuang-Taiyuan, Xiangfan-Chongqing, Lianyungang-Lanzhou, and Beijing-Baotou lines (Xue Muqiao 1982: 583, 585).

9. The Lanzhou-Lianyungang line (the line linking Lanzhou to Beijing, Shanghai, Xi'an, and other major cities) was so heavily used by the early 1980s that it was one of five lines in the nation identified as "strained" by official agencies (Xue Muqiao 1982: 588). It is even more heavily used today.

10. Disease and accidents reportedly took an average of 6,000 lives a year during the course of this difficult project. Two years after the first train ran the length of the line, the railway workers staged an uprising, in conjunction with the uprisings against the Qing government then taking place all over China (Yu Jiahua et al. 1986: 533–34).

11. Sichuan was the primary entrepot for tea into Tibet.

12. Two species of rhubarb are grown in China: *Rheum palmatum* (Bei Dahuang), which is grown in Hubei, Sichuan, and Yunnan provinces, and *R. tanguticum* (Jigua Dahuang), which is grown in Qinghai, Gansu, and Sichuan. The species traded in Central Asia was most likely *tanguticum,* a medicinal plant used particularly in treating bowel disorders (*Cihai* 1979: 1432).

13. Similar items are also now available near some reopened Buddhist temples in eastern China, such as the Temple of Six Banyan Trees in Guangzhou, but on a very small scale.

14. The site where it stood, Mingde Street, is now occupied by the People's Bank (Renmin Yinhang), Tianshan branch.

15. I did not include Kunming in this discussion of banking because I was unable to locate sources on the developments there.

16. The improvement of Lanzhou's varied industrial base continues. In 1987, for example, I met a retired European brewery master who was working as a consultant for a Lanzhou brewery. He had great hopes of turning a relatively unknown local product into a national brand-name beer in a class with the famous

Tsingtao (Qingdao) beer, produced on the coast with German methods and exported throughout the world.

Chapter Four

1. Mote does grant that the concentration of people and wealth in Chinese cities must have led to some urban-rural differentiation, but he considers the distinction relatively unimportant (Mote 1977: 117).

2. Though of course these walled features in and of themselves are not uniquely Chinese, the rigid adherence to the principle of the wall at all levels has been a notable, if not unique, feature of Chinese architecture and urban-planning practice.

3. The concept of building the city as a hierarchical order of similar forms was an ancient one but was perhaps best and most widely realized in the Ming and particularly the Qing period (see, e.g., Wu Liangyong 1986).

4. Discussions of architecture in the Chinese classics, usually found in the sections on "Rites and Deportment" or the "Five Elements" (of Confucianism), contain detailed descriptions of ground plan and layout, with no details about the appearance of the structures (Mote 1977: 112).

5. Numerology is also incorporated in architecture and city planning, for example, in beliefs about the number of rooms a building should have and how many buildings should be contained within a complex.

6. Thus, for example, the main temple at Heilongtan (Black Dragon Pool), just north of Kunming proper, lies on a southwest-facing slope, with the pool at the southwestern entrance to the complex. The small temple adjacent to the west bank of the pool is actually sited along a northwest-southeast axis. It is interesting to note, however, that the four tombs located near the temple site, but not close enough to the pool to have a direct relationship to it, *are* sited along a north-south axis.

7. The variation, from city to city, in the assignment of the most auspicious sites is perhaps indicative of the power and power structures at work. In some cities the Confucian temple was awarded the preeminent position; in others, it went to one or another of the administrative complexes.

8. Nonetheless, good fengshui is not proof against all calamities. The Jade Emperor Temple was burned down in 1933, reputedly by the local warload Jin Shuren. The temples at the base of the hill were also destroyed during the warlord era (Zan Yulin 1983: 11–13).

9. Although Kunming's site was chosen long before the Mongols arrived, they built the first truly substantial city there, and it is interesting to note that this good siting is consistent with many other cities founded during the Yuan dynasty.

10. The temple burned down in 1353 and was rebuilt in 1358.

11. This is a simplified generalization of the principles of this highly developed and complex siting system.

12. The south gate did provide access to the road to Lushaer and Kumbum Jampa Ling Monastery.

13. According to Taylor, the town god was most likely a development of the

Six Dynasties and Tang eras, with roots in an earlier worship of gods of the soil, or *she* (Taylor 1977: 34). A purely local deity, it was expected to intercede on the town's behalf in times of natural disaster. The town god was always identified with the spirit of some human being and was "neither violent nor dangerous, though very powerful and requiring to be approached with respect" (Johnson 1985: 424).

14. The yingbi and the zhaobi (also sometimes called *zhaoqiang*) serve the same purpose, but whereas the first can be either inside or outside a courtyard, the second is always on the outside. The term yingbi appears in the famous 18th-century novel *Hongloumeng* (Dream of the Red Chamber), vol. 3, which refers to a yingbi used to protect the northern side of a structure.

15. Similarly, spirit screens are common in Chinese restaurants in the United States, regardless of the direction the building is facing. Although some might be built out of true adherence to the principles of fengshui, in many cases these American spirit screens might simply be conforming to the expected decor.

16. Bagua literally refers to the set of eight trigrams in the Chinese divination system but is used for any kind of small mirror that serves the same purpose (warding off evil) as an actual set of eight trigrams would do if mounted in the same position.

17. I also saw a number of mirrors in Kunming that have been painted over or look to have been fairly recently scraped free of paint. This may indicate that their use is or was officially discouraged, yet residents are reluctant to remove them.

18. The most interesting of the Dali mirrors was an eight-sided white bagua plate, with one of the eight trigrams on each side and a yin-yang symbol in the center.

Chapter Five

1. I have chosen to discuss "Islamic" city forms here, for example, rather than Central Asian city forms, since the vast majority of China's Islamic people (the Hui) are not Central Asians.

2. Von Grunebaum cites this as analogous with the location of the cardo, decumanus, and forum in the Roman town.

3. Apart from the spatial relationship with the mosque, this market structure is not significantly different from that of the Chinese, which was also organized by product.

4. Fourteen other plans in the book either did not have a direction arrow or had one that was too blurry to read.

5. This district structure was, of course, substantially disrupted during the Cultural Revolution, when mosques were closed, destroyed, or appropriated for other uses.

6. The separation may be even more finely distinguished. In Urumqi, for example, one Hui mosque caters exclusively to migrants from Qinghai and another exclusively to migrants from Shaanxi.

7. Tall pagodas might have had a similar effect, but presumably their sites were carefully chosen to augment the local geomancy rather than disrupt it.

8. A medical college that once commanded the hill adjacent to the Potala was destroyed by the Chinese after 1949.

9. For example, in 1959 Drepung and Sera, outside of Lhasa, had some 7,000 and 5,000 monks, respectively, and Tashilunpo, in Xigaze, had about 4,000 (Dowman 1988: 63, 67, 273).

10. See Snodgrass 1985 for a detailed explanation of the symbolic and spatial character of stupas.

11. In Tibetan Buddhism holy relics, such as the bones of reincarnate lamas and other sacred objects, as well as holy books containing prayers, are commonly encased in a shrine inside a temple. Thus the temple itself is infused with the holiness enclosed within. Circumambulating an entire temple complex will gain believers merit for the next life in the same way that prostrating themselves before images of holy figures will.

12. Before its recent expansion, the city of Xiahe, Gansu, site of Labrang Monastery, was likewise encircled by a circumambulation route.

13. This system and the story of Songsten Gampo's founding of these temples are recorded in the Tibetan text *Mani Kabum*, believed to have been compiled into a single volume from a number of different sources in the 13th century (Dowman 1988: 284–86).

14. The Astronomical Academy, a relatively more "Lamaist"-style building than most at Kumbum Jampa Ling, is oriented along a northwest-southeast axis, with the entrance on the southeast. The School of Medicine is on a southwest-northeast axis, with the entrance on the southeast.

15. Another example of Lamaist geomancy can be found at Labrang Monastery (Labulangsi), south of Lanzhou in Gansu Province. The halls, which are built with many Chinese architectural features, are oriented in several different ways, none of which align with the cardinal directions. An analysis of published plans of the monastery (Liu Dunzhen 1987: 374–77) confirms my observations. The Academy (Wensi Xueyuan), for example, is oriented along a northwest-southeast axis (at an angle 10° north of west), and the Long Life and Happiness Temple (Shouxi Si) along a northwest-southeast axis (at an angle 60° north of west). As one of the first monasteries founded under the Fifth Dalai Lama's assertive architectural program, Labrang meets his requirement: it stands on a hillside that provides a commanding view of the narrow river valley below.

Chapter Six

1. Multicultural cities also developed in eastern China, particularly in port cities and imperial capitals. But the frontier cities were different. Although they usually maintained a Chinese majority (or even exclusive Chinese settlement) within their walls, the surrounding area was generally inhabited primarily by non-Chinese people.

2. Tibetans may have had more impact historically on the architecture and morphology of small cities, especially key trading centers on the Chinese-Tibetan frontiers in Gansu and in Sichuan, but this topic awaits further research.

3. The city has long had a substantial Mongolian population, but the Chinese are still in the majority, as they have been since relatively soon after Hohhot was established, despite a considerable rural-urban Mongolian migration soon after the PRC was founded.

4. For an abridged English translation of his book *Shina jokaku no gaiyo* (1940), see Wallacker & Knapp 1979.

5. The survey data and the sources consulted are provided in the Appendix, pp. 321-25.

6. To ensure that I had a fair representation of western cities, I counted all the cities in the *Atlas of the People's Republic of China* (1984) west of 105° east longitude. The atlas shows 104 cities in this area, ranging in size from less than 10,000 population to more than a million. My survey includes 30 cities for this region. They represent about 29% of the current total but probably a higher proportion of the pre-20th-century total, since some of the 104 are of recent vintage.

7. The Aihui-Tengchong definition of the west embraces parts of Inner Mongolia, Shaanxi, and Ningxia that are not included in the 105° definition.

8. She uses the term "double city" for a specific pattern, in which two walled enclosures shared at least one common wall and one of the enclosures was the palace city (Steinhardt 1990).

9. According to Steinhardt, the Liao (Qidan) were the first rulers to build imperial double cities expressly for the purpose of segregating the "ruling dynasty and its race from nonnative subjects" (Steinhardt 1990: 124).

10. Unlike "guo," which always refers to a walled suburb, "guanxiang" can be used also for unwalled areas.

11. A Chinese visitor to Urumqi in 1915 commented that the streets in the suburb were so muddy as to be nearly impassable for wheeled vehicles (Zan Yulin 1983: 37).

12. Wolfram Eberhard cites the example of a small town in Xinjiang (from an account by a Turk sometime during the Qing dynasty). In this case the Chinese and the Hui formed one unit, and the Uygur another. "There was an old town, in which the local Dungans [Hui] and the Chinese lived, and a new town, in which Turks [probably Uygur] lived. The Chinese operated ten shops, the Dungans three, the Turks four. The Chinese had only one temple, but the Muslim population [Dungans and Turks] had eight mosques, one religious seminar, and two schools" (Eberhard 1982: 63).

13. Chang notes several other types of multiple cities as well, including cities divided on either side of a river; cities where one level of administrative yamen was housed in a separate walled area; twin cities where one part was administrative, and commercial functions were carried out in a separate walled area; and cities that were "twinned" as a result of late site changes (S.-d. Chang 1977: 92–94).

14. The historical record is unclear on whether the areas were separate or adjoining.

15. And on such historical maps, prominent landmarks are often marked only by an oblong or rectangular marker filled with the name of the place, without any indication of its precise location or shape.

16. The location of the districts is based on information provided by faculty members of Beijing University and Yunnan Normal University.

17. Lanzhou also had an Islamic district on the west side.

Chapter Seven

1. But as one would expect, those religious structures most clearly tied to state administration, such as Confucian temples, tended to conform more to the Chinese model.

2. There is no structural reason why this curve need be very pronounced; the roofs of northern Chinese temples in fact tend to appear almost straight. But in southern China especially, the stylistic value placed on the curvature led to an exaggeration well beyond what was structurally required.

3. Guanyin is the Chinese version of the Buddhist incarnation of Avalokiteshvara (Padmapani). She is said to have been incarnated on Putuo island, near the central coast city of Ningbo. The cult of Guanyin was particularly popular in China during the Tang dynasty (Wright 1959: 82).

4. The main gate once bore the inscription "Yuantong Shengjin" (Accommodating Victory; *Kunmingshi zhi* 1920s: 338). The inscription was changed sometime in the 1960s to "Youhai Gongchang" (Children's Factory).

5. There were also several Christian churches in Hohhot by 1949: eight Protestant churches, five in Jiucheng and three in Xincheng, and two Catholic churches, one just north of the old city near its Temple of the Town Gods, and one just outside the west gate of the new city.

6. The Diamond Temple at Bodhgaya marks the place where the Buddha achieved illumination under the Bodhi tree, in about 530 B.C. The sutra after which it is named (known in India as the Prajnaparamita Sutra) is notable in Chinese history as the oldest known example of printing.

7. A lacang is an institute for the study of religious and philosophical subjects, laws, or medicine. Each lacang contains a hall for scriptures and religious texts (Jingtang, or Hall of Sutras), and a Buddha hall with images of the Buddha and other revered figures relevant to the specialty of the particular institute.

8. The Tibetan name, Kumbum, or "thousand images," refers to the belief that the sacred Bodhi tree that sprang up near the site of Tsong Khapa's birth bears thousands of leaves patterned with sacred images. The Chinese call the temple Ta'er Si (Temple of the Pagodas) for the row of chortens (white dagobas, baita) at the entrance to the monastery.

9. These Central/Southwest Asian–style mosques were primarily located in Chinese Central Asia. I use "Central/Southwest Asian" here as a broad term for mosques built with the use of such Central, Southwest, or South Asian features as domes, pointed arches, and tall, narrow minarets.

10. In Xinjiang, there have long been domed mosques. The Id Kah Mosque in Turfan is one of the few of these domed older mosques still intact.

11. With some exceptions in relatively recent gazetteers, which do sometimes list mosques along with other city temples.

12. There is some confusion surrounding this name. The Kunming City Planning book lists the Qingzhen Gu Si as Site 21—the mosque at Jinri Gongyuanko next to the department store. This mosque bears the Qinzhen Gu Si sign. But inside is another sign, Dongmen Qingzhen Si (East Gate Mosque), which seems the more likely name for a mosque in this location. Perhaps the sign was moved at some point and has yet to be returned to its original location.

13. The area where it is located was named after the south gate of Kunming, whose tower was called the Sun-approaching Tower. There is a traffic circle where the gate once stood.

14. The Hui of northwest China are known for their elaborate building decorations. These carvings and paintings usually feature patterns intertwining several different kinds of flowers, such as lilies in a tuliplike pattern in profile with the petals visible, daisies with 12 petals as seen from above, and daisies in profile with just five petals showing.

15. The pavilion in Urumqi's People's Park has similar brackets.

16. Most of the mosques in China today, including those in Xinjiang, have signs in Chinese characters on their outer facades, though they might also have signs in Arabic. Signs within the compounds are sometimes only in Arabic, particularly quotations from the Koran and other religious inscriptions on the walls inside prayer halls.

17. Yanghang, the foreign business district, was the place where businesses operated by nonresidents were located, as well as markets for trade in foreign goods. "Foreign" probably referred to Central Asian peoples from the Russian side of the Central Asian region.

18. Except, of course, when non-Chinese empires such as the Mongol and Manchu empires ruled China.

Chapter Eight

1. Exceptions were made, however, in riverine or particularly mountainous environments, where there was simply not enough flat land to have "straight" walls on all sides of the city. Cities of irregular shape were common in the mountainous regions of Fujian and Hunan, for example.

2. In eastern China more subtle interpretations of fengshui sometimes lead to the purposeful incorporation of nonlevel sites and other elements contrary to the simple form of the ideal.

3. With the exception of some Islamic village communities on the hilly terrain of the north bank of the Yellow River opposite Lanzhou.

4. Wood use is also limited in poorer and long deforested regions of North China, particularly on the loess plateau.

5. There are a number of Chinese terms for native-place, commercial, and craft associations, which I have combined into the English category "guilds." These terms had variant meanings in different places. Those in most common usage were *huiguan* (native-place association), *gongsuo* (public hall, usually asso-

ciated with a trade association), *bang* (association), and *hang* (company). A distinction was sometimes made between *shangbang* (commercial association) and *gongbang* (craft association). See Rowe 1984: 253–56 for a more complete discussion of these terms. To facilitate the presentation of this section, I will simplify the situation by using the term guild or huiguan to encompass all of these.

6. The Maitreya Buddha, for instance, was a patron of gold- and silversmiths, the White Lotus Guanyin a patron of jadeworkers, the God of Literature a patron of booksellers, and the Yellow Emperor a patron of tailors.

7. The group's patron was Xiayuwang, the spirit of Emperor Yu, who founded the reign of Xia: a spirit of virtue and enlightened leadership. The patron of the Gansu Huiguan was Fuxi, the legendary ruler to whom the introduction of farming, fishing, and animal husbandry in China is attributed.

8. Yuzhang, or Camphor Tree, is an old term for the Nanchang region of Jiangxi Province.

9. The most successful part of this new garden is the collection of miniatures (similar to Japanese bonsai) in one of the pavilions near the central pool. There are also other recent attempts to emulate the Suzhou style in Lanzhou. The Lanzhou Hotel has a Taihu stone group in the rear courtyard, but it is lost in its surrounding asphalt parking lot. This is a clear attempt to make reference to traditional landscape design borrowed from a completely different environmental regime.

10. In Kunming, as in Lanzhou, recent hotel landscaping incorporates Taihu stone designs. There is an elaborate formation in the pool at the front of the Kunming Hotel (a recent construction designed to attract both foreign tourists and Chinese conventioneers) in spite of the fact that the building is built in quite modern style, with no traditional elements in the design.

11. This lack of study of vernacular architecture was related, in part, to the official identification of much vernacular architecture as substandard and with the concurrent attempt to replace vernacular architecture with modern structures. The American Urban Planning and Historic Preservation Study Team, a group of architectural and planning professionals who made a professional tour of Chinese architectural preservation sites in 1982, experienced some frustration with the lack of attention to the vernacular by their Chinese counterparts (Cady 1982: ii, 32). My own experience also was that Chinese professionals prefer to concentrate on monumental structures. The issue of preservation will be dealt with thoroughly in Chapter Nine.

12. I will not discuss these forms in depth here because there are no examples of Tibetan houses within the cities under study. In brief, however, the traditional Tibetan urban house is usually two stories tall, constructed with either a wooden frame or stone walls overlaid in a mixture of dung, mud, and straw, all painted white, and the first floor, which is used mainly for animals and storage in rural areas, may be used instead as a shop.

13. In some eras of active maritime trade there were cosmopolitan non-Chinese communities in trading ports such as Quanzhou.

Chapter Nine

1. Though exactly which structures were torn down, and when, is hard to determine. Few are ever mentioned in contemporary city histories and descriptions.

2. Xining itself served as a refuge for many people fleeing the rebellion in its early stages. In Susie Rijnhardt's words, "Hundreds of homeless and wounded people seeking shelter were flocking into the already overcrowded city, where the temples were turned into temporary hospitals" (Rijnhardt 1901: 69).

3. I am referring only to Chinese temples in this discussion, not Lamaist structures.

4. There was also some destruction of walls associated with the Japanese bombing of Chinese cities during the 1940s.

5. The imposing drum tower of Hohhot's Manchu city (Suiyuan), a two-story structure similar to the tower that still stands in Xi'an today, survived into the late 1950s (*Neimenggu gu jianzhu* 1959: 86).

6. The Xining wall had been one of the oldest on the frontier—a Ming wall dating from 1386, which had been repaired in 1575, 1709, and 1773, as well as during the Qianlong period (1736–96) and the Tongzhi period (1862–75; Zhao Kai 1986: 76–77).

7. In Chinese cities bus stops are usually designated by names that are printed on both bus maps and bus stop signs.

8. The last street is named after a very ancient temple, built on the orders of the ruler of the Gaochang kingdom, based in the area of Turfan, during Tang times (*Lanzhou wenshi ciliao* 1987: 133).

9. The temple was surrounded by fields of Liaolan (*Polygonum tinctorium*), from which indigo dye and medicinal materials were extracted (*Lanzhou fenglai* 1987: 75).

10. It was called the Nine Suns Daoist Temple (Jiuyang Guan) in Song times, and from Ming days on, the Golden Heaven Daoist Temple (Jintian Guan).

11. Zhang Jingchou was "sent down" to Urumqi in 1768 and stayed in the area for two years. Though this assignment clearly indicates that Zhang was out of favor with the Qing court, local officials were delighted to have a scholar of note in their midst. Zhang repaid their warm welcome with poetry commemorating the area (Zan Yulin 1983: 14). Today the site of his cottage is a 20-hectare garden (established in 1918) within People's Park, consisting of pavilions and tea houses.

12. See Liu Yan 1988; Qian Li 1987: 36; Qin Fengxia & Shen Bingrong 1987; Wang Shiren 1987b; Xiao Tong 1986; Shu Maowei 1986; and Zhu Zixuan 1988.

13. Though there is a sizable new settlement adjacent to the old city of Lhasa, and the destruction of some areas of the city had already taken place (particularly during the 1960s and early 1970s).

14. Of course at many times during the post-Revolution era nearly everything could be argued to be under the auspices of the government. In order to narrow this category somewhat, I refer here only to projects that have been officially designated for preservation by the administrative branches of the government, either through use as government buildings or designation as cultural relics.

15. To ensure some authenticity, the museum of the Xinjiang Uygur Autonomous Region in the city has prepared a display of life-size models of several types of yurts and a Uygur house. It also includes small models of several mosques and tombs.

16. One hardware store I photographed in November 1987 had made this conversion by the time I returned the following April with the addition of an aluminum-and-glass facade. See photo, Kunming: typical shop conversion.

17. Kaifeng was the capital of China during the Wei dynasty (A.D. 220–65), and again from the Five Dynasties period through the Northern Song dynasty (907–1127).

18. According to the director of the Cave Dwelling Institute, there were about 6,000,000 cave dwellings in China in 1987 (personal communication, 1987). Though this figure seems slightly low if Ronald Knapp is right that approximately 40,000,000 Chinese then lived in earth-sheltered dwellings in the loess region (Knapp 1986: 31), the two figures confirm each other to some degree.

Chapter Ten

1. Even taking into account major changes in city boundaries and in the definition of "urban" for census purposes.

2. According to the absolute figures in Jankowiak's table (based on an unpublished report of the 1982 census), some 20% of the city's population was ethnically non-Han, a considerably higher share than the one in my Table 9. By his data Hohhot's New District was 83% Han, 13% Mongolian, 2% Hui, and 3% Other; the Hui District 45% Han, 15% Mongolian, 35% Hui, and 5% Other; and the Jade (old city) District 91% Han, 6% Mongolian, 2% Hui, and 1% Other. For the city as a whole, his figures work out to 80% Han, 11% Mongolian, 6% Hui, and 3% Other. But these statistics are problematic because his table shows a total of 380,927 residents as against his text figure of 492,011 (Jankowiak 1993: 10). In any event, the 11%–12% figure (from 1987) in my table is for the entire area Hohhot administers (i.e., is based on a population of more than a million, rather than the under 500,000 of the city center). Interestingly, Rong Yang comes up with 11% for the city proper in 1956. His breakdown is 238,366 Chinese (89%), 14,907 Mongolian (6%), 11,695 Hui (4%), 2,947 Manchu (1%), and Other, 296 (0.1%; Rong Yang 1975: 235).

3. This is the primary area of new downtown-style development. Other areas, particularly west of the old walled city, have seen major industrial growth since 1949.

4. The move was not without precedent. The construction of the Mao Zedong Mausoleum substantially reduced the size of Tian'anmen Square, perhaps unintentionally ensuring that no gathering there could ever be as large as the ones celebrating Mao and his policies had been.

5. The next-most-developed areas in Xining are the old walled city itself and an eastward and northern extension of the walled city that accommodates the train and bus stations at the northeastern edge of town.

6. The park was dismantled after 1949 to accommodate "the needs of development" (Zhao Shiying 1987: 42–43).

7. Sources differ over the built housing area of the city. Li Shengcai (1982: 406) reports a total built housing area of 6 million m², an increase of 700% over the housing area in 1949. This implies that the total housing area in Xining in 1949 was only 85,000 m². By contrast, the report in *Qinghai Shengqing* (1986) of a 320% increase in housing area since 1949 (to a total of 7 million m²) implies a total housing area in 1949 of 2,200,000 m².

8. These figures include the grounds of public parks, a substantial number of which, as we have seen, were established after 1949. A number of these parks were once the grounds of private estates and temples.

9. There are some divisions in the Chinese architectural community between proponents of a return to traditional styles, or at least the incorporation of traditional elements in modern buildings, and proponents of new international styles, such as Western post-modernism. Western styles are being applied far more widely than regional styles, particularly in industrial and business-oriented construction.

10. The most recent innovation in new housing is the increased use of prefabricated high-rise construction. There is virtually no new construction of single-family housing, nor has there been in the years since 1949. Isolated cases of single-family home construction in recent years have occurred primarily in outlying suburban or rural areas, where some of China's new economically successful farmers have begun to build homes for themselves, and where joint-venture entrepreneurs build for foreign businesspeople.

11. There are some nonstate applications or reassertions of local and/or cultural styles as well. The most notable phenomenon of this sort is the rebuilding of mosques in the Central/Southwest Asian style discussed earlier. The Central/Southwest Asian motif has been applied outside both the state context and the religious context, such as the Dongfeng Restaurant just off Wangfujing Street in the heart of downtown Beijing, the Turfan Hotel (Turfan Binguan), and the department store in downtown Turfan.

12. A 1986 publication, *Qinghai minzu tu'anji* (Nationalities' Patterns of Qinghai), includes 319 decorative patterns that are found in the paintings, carvings, or tent designs of five different nationalities in Qinghai. Many of these patterns do not have any religious significance (Zhang Weiyuan & Zhang Piyu 1986).

13. Though the memorial is sometimes referred to as Chinggis Khan's Mausoleum, the whereabouts of his grave, in line with Mongolian custom, are unknown.

14. The dome may or may not actually function as a mosque. I asked a number of people who either did not know or thought it was not a mosque. A few older men, however, believed that it was a mosque. In all probability it is not.

Bibliography

Sources in Western Languages

Akiner, Shirin, ed. 1991. *Cultural Change and Continuity in Central Asia*. New York: Kegan Paul International.

Alexeiev, Basil M. 1928. *The Chinese Gods of Wealth*. London: School of Oriental Studies.

Alley, Rewi. 1957. *Human China*. Christchurch: New Zealand Peace Council.

Allworth, Edward. 1990. *The Modern Uzbeks: From the Fourteenth Century to the Present, a Cultural History*. Stanford, Calif.: Hoover Institution.

Alonso, Mary Ellen. 1979. *China's Inner Asian Frontier*. Cambridge, Mass.: Harvard University Press.

Alsayyad, Nezar, and Guita Boostani. 1989. "Mosques," in J. A. Wilkes and R. T. Packard, eds., *Encyclopedia of Architecture: Design, Engineering, and Construction*. New York: Wiley.

Andrews, John, ed. 1966. *Frontiers and Men*. Melbourne: Cheshire.

Aris, Michael. 1980. *Bhutan: The Early History of a Himalayan Kingdom*. New Delhi: Vikas Publishing House.

Avedon, John F. 1984. *In Exile From the Land of Snows*. New York: Knopf.

Barfield, Thomas. 1989. *The Perilous Frontier: Nomadic Empires and China, 221 B.C. to A.D. 1757*. Cambridge, Mass.: Blackwell.

Barrier, L. D. 1977. "Concerning Theories on the Cultural and Political Unity of China." Paper presented at the Second New Zealand Conference on Asian Studies, University of Canterbury, Christchurch, May 11–14.

Barsh, Russell L. 1984. "The International Legal Status of Native Alaska," *Alaska Native News*, July.

Barthold, V. V. 1962. *Four Studies on the History of Central Asia*. Leiden: Brill.

Beauclair, Inez de. 1970. *Tribal Cultures of Southwest China*. Taibei: Orient Culture Service.

Bell, Charles. 1924. *Tibet: Past and Present*. Oxford: Clarendon Press.

Berger, R. 1979. "Economic Planning in China," in N. Maxwell, ed., *China's Road to Development*. New York: Pergamon Press.

Billington, Ray Allen. 1956. *The Far Western Frontier*. New York: Harper & Row.

Birrell, Anne. 1988. *Popular Songs and Ballads of Han China*. London: Unwin-Hyman.

Bodley, John H. 1982. *Victims of Progress*. Palo Alto, Calif.: Mayfield.

Boerschmann, Ernst. 1931. *Die Baukunst und Religiose Kultur der Chinesen* (The architecture and religious culture of the Chinese). Berlin: Walter de Gruyter.

Bonine, Michael. 1983. "Cities of the Middle East and North Africa," in S. D. Brunn and J. F. Williams, eds., *Cities of the World: World Regional Urban Development*. New York: Harper & Row.

———. 1987. "Islamic and Middle Eastern Cities: Some Myths and Realities." Paper presented at the Colloquium, Department of Geography, University of California, Berkeley.

Borodina, Iraida. 1987. *Central Asia—Gems of 9th–19th Century Architecture*. Moscow: Planeta Publishers.

Bradley, Neville. 1946. *The Old Burma Road: A Journey on Foot and Muleback*. London: Travel Book Club.

Broek, Jan. 1941. "The Problem of Natural Frontiers," in *Frontiers of the Future*. Los Angeles: University of California Press.

Brunn, Stanley D., and Jack F. Williams, eds. 1983. *Cities of the World: World Regional Urban Development*. New York: Harper & Row.

Buchanan, Keith. 1970. *The Transformation of the Chinese Earth*. New York: Praeger.

Buck, David. 1978. *Urban Change in China: Politics and Development in Tsinan, Shantung, 1890–1949*. Madison: University of Wisconsin Press.

———. 1984. "Changes in Chinese Urban Planning Since 1976," *Third World Planning Review*. 6.1: 5–26.

Budnick, Dan, Georg Gerster, Paul Lau, Wu Shouzhuang, and Jerry Young, photographers; Kevin Sinclair, text. 1988. *Over China*. Los Angeles: Knapp Press.

Burgess, J. Stewart. 1928. *The Guilds of Peking*. New York: Columbia University Press.

Bussagli, Mario. 1981. *Oriental Architecture, 2: China, Korea, Japan*, tr. John Shepley. New York: Electa/Rizzoli.

Cady, Janet, ed. 1982. *Historic Preservation in the People's Republic of China: Observations of the American Urban Planning and Historic Preservation Study Team, May 16–June 2, 1982*. New York: National Committee on U.S.-China Relations.

Cahnman, Werner J. 1949. "Frontiers Between East and West in Europe," *Geographical Review*, 39.4: 605–24.

Chandran, J. 1971. *The Burma-Yunnan Railway: Anglo-French Rivalry in Mainland Southeast Asia and South China, 1895–1902*. Athens: Ohio University Center for International Studies.

Chang, Chao-kang, and Werner Blaser. 1987. *China: Tao in Architecture*. Basel: Birkhauser Verlag.

Chang, Chih-yi. 1949. "Land Utilization and Settlement Possibilities in Sinkiang," *Geographical Review*, 39.1: 57–75.

Chang, Hajji Yusuf. 1984. "Muslim Encounter with the Mongols and Its Varied Consequences for Muslims in West Asia and China," *Journal of the Institute of Muslim Minority Affairs*, 5.2: 269–93.

Chang, Sen-dou. 1961. "The Chinese Hsien Capital: A Study in Historical Urban Geography." Ph.D. dissertation, University of Washington, Seattle.

———. 1963. "The Historical Trend of Chinese Urbanization," *Annals of the Association of American Geographers*, 53.2: 109–43.

———. 1970. "Some Observations on the Morphology of Chinese Walled Cities," *Annals of the Association of American Geographers*, 60.1: 63–91.

———. 1977. "The Morphology of Walled Capitals," in G. W. Skinner, ed., *The City in Late Imperial China*, Stanford, Calif.: Stanford University Press.

Che Muqi. 1989. *The Silk Road, Past and Present*. Beijing: Foreign Languages Press.

Chen Cheng-siang. 1984. *China: Essays in Geography*. Hong Kong: Joint Publishing Co.

Chen, Ching-lung. 1981. "Trading Activities of the Turkic Peoples in China," *Central Asiatic Journal*, 25.1–2: 38–53.

Chen, Zhanxiang. 1985. "Comments on the Rebuilding of Liulichang Street," *China City Planning Review*, 1.1: 14–17.

Cheuk, Lau Tak. N.d. *Sitting Up at Night and Other Chinese Poems*. Hong Kong: Chinese University of Hong Kong.

Chihli River Commission. 1924. Cartographic Collection, University of Washington Library, Seattle.

Chow, Din Zu. 1949. "Geographic and Historic Foundations of Present-Day Distribution of Peoples in the Nan Shan–Kokonor Area." M.A. thesis, University of California, Berkeley.

Chu, Wen Djang. 1966. *The Moslem Rebellion in Northwest China, 1862–1878: A Study of Government Minority Policy*. The Hague: Mouton.

Clark, Leonard. 1954. *The Marching Wind*. New York: Funk & Wagnalls.

Connor, Walker. 1984. *The National Question in Marxist-Leninist Theory and Strategy*. Princeton, N.J.: Princeton University Press.

Cressey, George B. 1955. *Land of the 500 Million: A Geography of China*. New York: McGraw-Hill.

Cressy-Marks, Violet. 1942. *Journey into China*. New York: Dutton.

Cui Gonghao. 1990. "The Process, Characteristics and Tendencies of Urban Development in China," *GeoJournal*, 21.1–2: 25–32.

Curzon, George Nathaniel. 1907. *Frontiers*. Oxford: Clarendon Press.

Dabbs, Jack. 1963. *History of the Discovery and Exploration of Chinese Turkestan*. The Hague: Mouton.

Das, Sarat Chandra. 1970 (1902). *Journey to Lhasa and Central Tibet*, ed. W. W. Rockhill. New Delhi: Manjusri Publishing House.

David-Neel, Alexandra. 1927. *My Journey to Lhasa: The Personal Story of the Only White Woman Who Succeeded in Entering the Forbidden City*. New York: Harper.

———. 1931. *With Mystics and Magicians in Tibet.* London: Bodley Head.

———. 1936. *Tibetan Journey.* London: Bodley Head.

———. 1979. *Le Tibet.* Paris: Plon.

Dowman, Keith. 1988. *The Power Places of Central Tibet.* New York: Routledge & Kegan Paul.

Drake, F. S., ed. 1967. *Symposium on Historical, Archaeological and Linguistic Studies on Southern China, South-East Asia and the Hong Kong Region.* Hong Kong: Hong Kong University Press.

Dreyer, June. 1968. "China's Minority Nationalities in the Cultural Revolution," *China Quarterly,* 35: 96–109.

———. 1972. "Traditional Minority Elites and the CPR Elite Engaged in Minority Nationalities Work," in R. A. Scalapino, ed., *Elites in the People's Republic of China.* Seattle: University of Washington Press.

———. 1976. *China's Forty Million: Minority Nationalities and National Integration in the People's Republic of China.* Cambridge, Mass.: Harvard University Press.

Dyson, Verne. 1927. "Cities, Provinces and Dominions of China." Manuscript. Hamilton Library, University of Hawaii.

Eberhard, Wolfram. 1971 (1950). *A History of China.* Berkeley: University of California Press.

———. 1982. *China's Minority Nationalities: Yesterday and Today.* Belmont, Calif.: Wadsworth.

Edmonds, Richard Louis. 1985. *Northern Frontiers of Qing China and Tokugawa Japan.* University of Chicago Department of Geography Research Paper No. 213.

Eitel, Ernest J. 1987 (1873). *Feng Shui.* Singapore: Graham Brash.

Ekvall, Robert. 1938. *Gateway to Tibet.* Harrisburg, Pa.: Christian Publications.

———. 1939. *Cultural Relations on the Kansu-Tibetan Border.* Chicago: University of Chicago Press.

Elvin, Mark. 1973. *The Pattern of the Chinese Past.* Stanford, Calif.: Stanford University Press.

Elvin, Mark, and G. William Skinner, eds. 1974. *The Chinese City Between Two Worlds.* Stanford, Calif.: Stanford University Press.

Epstein, Israel. 1983. *Tibet Transformed.* Beijing: New World Press.

Esposito, John, ed. 1987. *Islam in Asia: Religion, Politics, and Society.* New York: Oxford University Press.

Fairbank, John King. 1992. *China: A New History.* Cambridge, Mass.: Harvard University Press.

Fei, Hsiao-tung. 1981. *Toward a People's Anthropology.* Beijing: New World Press.

Feuchtwang, Stephan. 1977. "School-Temple and City God," in G. W. Skinner, ed., *The City in Late Imperial China.* Stanford, Calif.: Stanford University Press.

Feuchtwang, Stephan, Athar Hussain, and Thierry Pairault, eds. 1988. *Transforming China's Economy in the Eighties.* Boulder, Colo.: Westview Press.

Fitzgerald, C. P. 1941. *The Tower of Five Glories: A Study of the Min Chia of Ta Li, Yunnan.* London: Cresset Press.

———. 1942. "The Tali District of Western Yunnan," *Geographical Journal,* 91.1: 50–60.

———. 1965 (1961). *China: A Short Cultural History.* New York: Holt, Rinehart & Winston.

———. 1972. *The Southern Expansion of the Chinese People.* New York: Praeger.

Fleming, Peter. 1936. *News From Tartary: A Journey from Peking to Kashmir.* New York: Scribner's.

———. 1961. *Bayonets to Lhasa.* Hong Kong: Oxford University Press.

Franck, Irene M., and David M. Brownstone. 1986. *The Silk Road: A History.* New York: Facts on File.

Geil, William Edgar. 1909. *The Great Wall of China.* New York: Sturgis & Walton.

———. 1911. *Eighteen Capitals of China.* Philadelphia: Lippincott.

Gerhard, Dietrich. 1959. "The Frontier in Comparative View," *Comparative Studies in Society and History,* 1: 205–29.

Gernet, Jacques. 1962. *Daily Life in China on the Eve of the Mongol Invasion, 1250–1276,* tr. H. M. Wright. Stanford, Calif.: Stanford University Press.

———. 1985. *A History of Chinese Civilization,* tr. J. R. Foster. Cambridge: Cambridge University Press.

Gibb, H. A. R., and J. H. Kramer, eds. 1953. *Shorter Encyclopedia of Islam.* Ithaca, N.Y.: Cornell University Press.

Gladney, Dru. 1987a. "Muslim Tombs and Ethnic Folklore: Charters for Hui Identity," *Journal of Asian Studies,* 46.3: 495–532.

———. 1987b. "Qingzhen: A Study of Ethnoreligious Identity Among Hui Muslim Communities in China." Ph.D. dissertation, University of Washington, Seattle.

———. 1990. "The Ethnogenesis of the Uighur," *Central Asian Survey,* 9.1: 1–28.

———. 1991. *Muslim Chinese: Ethnic Nationalism in the People's Republic.* Cambridge, Mass.: Council on East Asian Studies, Harvard University.

Goodman, David, ed. 1989. *China's Regional Development.* New York: Routledge.

Great Britain, Ordnance Survey Office. 1927. Collection of British Army maps, Cartographic Collection, University of Washington Library, Seattle.

Grenard, F. 1974 (1891). *Tibet: The Country and Its Inhabitants.* Delhi: Cosmo Publications.

Grousset, René. 1970. *The Empire of the Steppes: A History of Central Asia,* tr. Naomi Walford. New Brunswick, N.J.: Rutgers University Press.

Grunfeld, A. Tom. 1987. *The Making of Modern Tibet.* New York: Sharpe.

Guibaut, André. 1944. "Exploration in the Upper Tung Basin, Chinese-Tibetan Borderland," *Geographical Review,* 34.3: 387–404.

———. 1987 (1947). *Tibetan Venture.* New York: Oxford University Press.

Harle, James C. 1986. *The Art and Architecture of the Indian Subcontinent.* London: Penguin Books.

Hedin, Sven. 1903. *Central Asia and Tibet*. New York: Scribner's.

Heberer, Thomas. 1989. *China and Its National Minorities: Autonomy or Assimilation?* London: Sharpe.

Hoag, John D. 1975. *Islamic Architecture*. New York: Rizzoli International.

Hourani, A. H., and S. M. Stern, eds. 1970. *The Islamic City*. Oxford: Bruno Cassirer.

Huang, Boyle. 1975. *Architecture, Building and Planning*. Taibei: Daliu Shudian.

Huc, Evariste-Regis, and Joseph Gabet. 1987 (1928). *Travels in Tartary, Thibet and China, 1844–1846*. New York: Dover.

Hyer, Paul. 1982. "An Historical Sketch of Koke-Khota City, Capital of Inner Mongolia," *Central Asiatic Journal*, 26.1–2: 56–77.

Imahori, Seizi. 1955. *Chinese Feudal Society: An Intensive Investigation of Social Groups in Kuei-Sui Since 1644*. Tokyo: Japan Society for the Promotion of Science.

———. 1978. *The Social Structure of Feudal China*. Tokyo: Japan Society for the Promotion of Science.

Israeli, Raphael. 1978. *Muslims in China: A Study in Cultural Confrontation*. London: Curzon Press.

Israeli, Raphael, and Anthony H. Johns, eds. 1984. *Islam in Asia, 2: Southeast and East Asia*. Boulder, Colo.: Westview.

Jagchid, Sechin, and Paul Hyer. 1979. *Mongolia's Culture and Society*. Boulder, Colo.: Westview.

Jagchid, Sechin, and Van Jay Symons. 1989. *Peace, War and Trade Along the Great Wall: Nomadic-Chinese Interaction through Two Millennia*. Bloomington: Indiana University Press.

Jankowiak, William R. 1993. *Sex, Death and Hierarchy in a Chinese City*. New York: Columbia University Press.

Jochim, Christian. 1986. *Chinese Religions: A Cultural Perspective*. Englewood Cliffs, N.J.: Prentice-Hall.

Johnson, David. 1985. "The City-God Cults of T'ang and Sung China," *Harvard Journal of Asiatic Studies*, 45.2: 363–457.

Jones, Stephen B. 1959. "Boundary Concepts in the Setting of Place and Time," *Annals of the Association of American Geographers*, 49.3: 241–55.

Kang Zhixin. 1980. "China's Capital Construction in 1980," in Xue Muqiao, ed., *Almanac of China's Economy, 1980*. Hong Kong: Modern Cultural Co.

Kao, Ting Tsz. 1980. *The Chinese Frontiers*. Aurora, Ill.: Chinese Scholarly Publishing Co.

Kao, Yung-cheng. 1981. "The Unit-of-Place in the Planning of Chinese Cities." M.A. thesis, University of California, Berkeley.

Karamisheff, W. 1925. *Mongolia and Western China, Social and Economic Study*. Tianjin: Librairie Française.

Keyes, Charles F. 1977. *The Golden Peninsula: Culture and Adaptation in Mainland Southeast Asia*. New York: Macmillan.

Kingdon-Ward, F. 1932. "Explorations on the Burma-Tibet Frontier," *Geographical Journal*, 80.6: 465–83.

———. 1947. "Tibet as a Grazing Land," *Geographical Journal*, 110.1–3: 60–75.

Kirkby, R. J. R. 1985. *Urbanization in China: Town and Country in a Developing Economy, 1949–2000 A.D.* New York: Columbia University Press.

Knapp, Ronald G., ed. 1980. *China's Island Frontier: Studies in the Historical Geography of Taiwan.* Honolulu: University of Hawaii Press.

———. 1986. *China's Traditional Rural Architecture: A Cultural Geography of the Common House.* Honolulu: University of Hawaii Press.

———. 1989. *China's Vernacular Architecture: House Form and Culture.* Honolulu: University of Hawaii Press.

Kornhauser, David. 1976. *Urban Japan: Its Foundations and Growth.* London: Longmans.

———. 1983. "Castle Town Complex to Urban System: The Origins and Growth of a Hierarchy of Cities in Japan," in Clifton W. Pannell, ed., *East Asia: Geographical and Historical Approaches to Foreign Area Studies.* Dubuque, Iowa: Kendall/Hunt.

Kristof, Ladis K. 1959. "The Nature of Frontiers and Boundaries," *Annals of the Association of American Geographers*, 49.3: 269–82.

Lai, Chuen-Yan David. 1974. "A *Feng Shui* Model as a Location Index," *Annals of the Association of American Geographers*, 64.4: 506–13.

Lamar, Howard, and Leonard Thompson, eds. 1981. *The Frontier in History: North America and Southern Africa Compared.* New Haven, Conn.: Yale University Press.

Lamb, Alastair. 1968. *Asian Frontiers: Studies in a Continuing Problem.* London: Pall Mall Press.

Landon, Perceval. 1905. *Lhasa: An Account of the Country and the People of Central Tibet and of the Progress of the Mission Sent There by the English Government in the Year 1903–4.* London: Hurst & Blackett.

Lattimore, Owen. 1932. "Chinese Colonization in Manchuria," *Geographical Review*, 22.2: 177–95.

———. 1940. *Inner Asian Frontiers of China.* London: Oxford University Press.

———. 1950. *Pivot of Asia: Sinkiang and the Inner Asian Frontiers of China and Russia.* Boston: Little, Brown.

———. 1962. *Studies in Frontier History: Collected Papers, 1928–1958.* Paris: Mouton.

Le Coq, Albert von. 1985 (1928). *Buried Treasures of Chinese Turkestan.* Hong Kong: Oxford University Press.

Ledyard, Gari. 1983. "Yin and Yang in the China-Manchuria-Korea Triangle," in Morris Rossabi, ed., *China Among Equals.* Berkeley: University of California Press.

Lee, Robert H. G. 1970. *The Manchurian Frontier in Ch'ing History.* Cambridge, Mass.: Harvard University Press.

Lee, Samuel. 1968 (1829). *The Travels of Ibn Batuta.* New York: Johnson Reprint.

Lesdain, Count de. 1908. *From Pekin to Sikkim: Through the Ordos, the Gobi Desert, and Tibet.* London: John Murray.

Lessing, Ferdinand D. 1942. *Yongho Kung: An Iconography of the Lamaist Ca-thedral in Peking with Notes on Lamaist Mythology and Cult*. Stockholm: n.p.
————. 1976. *Ritual and Symbol: Collected Essays on Lamaism and Chinese Symbolism*. Taibei: Orient Cultural Service.
Leung, C. K. 1980. *China: Railway Patterns and National Goals*. University of Chicago Department of Geography Research Paper No. 195.
Lewis, John W., ed. 1971. *The City in Communist China*. Stanford, Calif.: Stanford University Press.
Li, Chi. 1928. *The Formation of the Chinese People*. Cambridge, Mass.: Harvard University Press.
Li Xue Wei and Kevin Stuart. 1990. "The Xunhua Sala," *Asian Folklore Studies*, 49: 39–52.
Liang Ssu-ch'eng (Liang Sicheng). 1984. *A Pictorial History of Chinese Architecture: A Study of the Development of Its Structural System and the Evolution of Its Types*. Cambridge, Mass.: MIT Press.
Lip, Evelyn. 1979. *Chinese Geomancy*. Singapore: Times Books International.
Liu, James T. C., and Wei-ming Tu. 1970. *Traditional China*. Englewood Cliffs, N.J.: Prentice-Hall.
Lo, Chor-pang, Clifton W. Pannell, and Roy Welch. 1977. "Land Use Changes and City Planning in Shenyang and Canton," *Geographical Review*, 67.3: 268–83.
Lo Hsiang-lin. 1967. "Islam in Canton in the Sung Period," in F. S. Drake, ed., *Symposium on Historical, Archaeological and Linguistic Studies on Southern China, South-East Asia and the Hong Kong Region*. Hong Kong: Hong Kong University Press.
Loewe, Michael. 1965. *Imperial China*. New York: Praeger.
————. 1968. *Everyday Life in Early Imperial China*. New York: Putnam.
Ma, Laurence, and Edward Hanten, eds. 1981. *Urban Development in Modern China*. Boulder, Colo.: Westview.
MacGregor, John. 1972. *Tibet: A Chronicle of Exploration*. Delhi: Vikas Publishing House.
Mackerras, Colin, ed. 1972. *The Uighur Empire According to the T'ang Dynastic Histories*. Columbia: University of South Carolina Press.
————. 1988. "Aspects of Bai Culture: Change and Continuity in a Yunnan Nationality," *Modern China*, 14.1: 51–84.
McMillen, Donald H. 1982. *The Urumqi Military Region: Defence and Security in China's West*. Australian National University Strategic and Defence Studies Centre Working Paper No. 50.
McNeill, William H. 1983. *The Great Frontier: Freedom and Hierarchy in Modern Times*. Princeton, N.J.: Princeton University Press.
Mandel, William M. 1985. *Soviet But Not Russian: The "Other" Peoples of the Soviet Union*. Palo Alto, Calif.: Ramparts Press.
Mannerheim, C. G. 1940. *Across Asia, from West to East in 1906–1908*. Helsinki: Suomalais-Ugrilainen-seura, Société Finno-ougriene.
March, Andrew L. 1968. "An Appreciation of Chinese Geomancy," *Journal of Asian Studies*, 27.2: 253–68.

Maxwell, N., ed. 1979. *China's Road to Development*. New York: Pergamon Press.

Migot, André. 1955. *Tibetan Marches*. New York: Dutton.

Mikesell, Marvin. 1960. "Comparative Studies in Frontier History," *Annals of the Association of American Geographers*, 50.1: 62–74.

Miller, David Harry, and Jerome O. Steffen. 1977. *The Frontier: Comparative Studies*. Norman: University of Oklahoma Press.

Moseley, George. 1973. *The Consolidation of the South China Frontier*. Berkeley: University of California Press.

Moser, Leo J. 1985. *The Chinese Mosaic: The Peoples and Provinces of China*. Boulder, Colo.: Westview.

Mote, F. W. 1967. "Cities in North and South China," in F. S. Drake, ed., *Symposium on Historical, Archaeological and Linguistic Studies on Southern China, South-East Asia and the Hong Kong Region*. Hong Kong: Hong Kong University Press.

———. 1970. "The City in Traditional Chinese Civilization," in James T. C. Liu and Wei-ming Tu, eds., *Traditional China*. Englewood Cliffs, N.J.: Prentice-Hall.

———. 1977. "The Transformation of Nanking, 1350–1400," in G. W. Skinner, ed., *The City in Late Imperial China*. Stanford, Calif.: Stanford University Press.

Murphey, Rhoads. 1980. *The Fading of the Maoist Vision: City and Country in China's Development*. New York: Methuen.

Myrdal, Jan. 1979. *The Silk Road: A Journey from the High Pamirs and Ili Through Sinkiang and Kansu*. New York: Pantheon.

Nagel's Encyclopedia-Guide. 1982. *China*, tr. Anne L. Destenay. Geneva: Nagel.

Ni, Ernest In-hsin. 1948. "Social Characteristics of the Chinese Population: A Study of the Population Structure and Urbanism of a Metropolitan Community." Ph.D. dissertation, University of Chicago.

Norins, Martin R. 1944. *Gateway to Asia: Sinkiang*. New York: John Day.

Osgood, Cornelius. 1963. *Village Life in Old China*. New York: Ronald Press.

Paldan, Thupstan. 1982. *A Brief Guide to the Buddhist Monasteries and Royal Castles of Ladakh*. New Delhi: Golden Printers.

Pannell, Clifton W. 1977. "Past and Present City Structure in China," *Town Planning Review*, 48.2: 157–72.

———, ed. 1983. *East Asia: Geographical and Historical Approaches to Foreign Area Studies*. Dubuque, Iowa: Kendall/Hunt.

Pastner, Stephen L. 1979. "Lords of the Desert Border: Frontier Feudalism in Southern Baluchistan and Eastern Ethiopia," *International Journal of Middle East Studies*, 10: 93–106.

People's Republic of China, State Statistical Bureau. 1985. *China: A Statistics Survey in 1985*. Beijing.

———. 1986. *China Urban Statistics, 1985*. Hong Kong: Longman.

———. 1987. *China Urban Statistics, 1986*. Hong Kong: Longman.

Pirazzoli-T'serstevens, Michele. 1971. *Living Architecture: Chinese*. London: MacDonald.

Prescott, J. R. V. 1965. *The Geography of Frontiers and Boundaries*. Chicago: Aldine.

―――. 1978. *Boundaries and Frontiers*. Totowa, N.J.: Rowman & Littlefield.

Prescott, J. R. V., H. J. Collier, and D. F. Prescott. 1977. *Frontiers of Asia and Southeast Asia*. Carlton, Australia: Melbourne University Press.

Qinghua University, Department of Architecture. 1985. *Historic Chinese Architecture*. Beijing: Qinghua University Press.

Reps, John W. 1979. *Cities in the American West: A History of Frontier Planning*. Princeton, N.J.: Princeton University Press.

―――. 1981. *The Forgotten Frontier: Urban Planning in the American West Before 1890*. Columbia: University of Missouri Press.

Richard, L. 1908. *Comprehensive Geography of the Chinese Empire*, tr. M. Kennelly. Shanghai: T'usewei Press.

Richardson, Hugh E. 1984. *Tibet and Its History*. London: Shambala Press.

Richardson, Hugh E., and David Snellgrove. 1986. *A Cultural History of Tibet*. London: Shambala Press.

Rijnhart, Susie C. 1901. *With the Tibetans in Tent and Temple: Narrative of Four Years' Residence on the Tibetan Border, and of a Journey into the Far Interior*. Chicago: Fleming Revell Co.

Rock, Joseph. 1947. *The Ancient Nakhi Kingdom of Southwest China*. Cambridge, Mass.: Harvard University Press.

Rockhill, William Woodville. 1891. *The Land of the Lamas: Notes of a Journey Through China, Mongolia and Tibet*. London: Longmans Green.

―――. 1894. *Diary of a Journey Through Mongolia and Tibet*. Washington, D.C.: Smithsonian Institution.

Ronan, Colin. 1978. *The Shorter Science and Civilisation in China*, vol. 1. Cambridge: Cambridge University Press.

Rossabi, Morris. 1970. "The Tea and Horse Trade with Inner Asia During the Ming," *Journal of Asian History*, 42: 136–68.

―――. 1975. *China and Inner Asia: From 1368 to the Present Day*. New York: Pica Press.

―――, ed. 1983. *China Among Equals*. Berkeley: University of California Press.

―――. 1988. *Khubilai Khan: His Life and Times*. Berkeley: University of California Press.

Rossbach, Sarah. 1983. *Feng Shui: The Chinese Art of Placement*. New York: Dutton.

Rowe, William T. 1984. *Hankow: Commerce and Society in a Chinese City, 1796–1889*. Stanford, Calif.: Stanford University Press.

―――. 1989. *Hankow: Conflict and Community in a Chinese City, 1796–1895*. Stanford, Calif.: Stanford University Press.

Ryder, C. H. D. N.d. [1915?]. *Chinese Turkestan and Kansu. Maps from Surveys Made During the Explorations of Sir Aurel Stein K.C.I.E., 1900–01, 1906–08, 1913–15*. Dehra Dun: Survey of India Offices.

Salter, Christopher L. 1976. "Chinese Experiments in Urban Space: The Quest for an Agropolitan China," *Habitat*, 1.1: 19–35.

Samagalski, Alan, Robert Strauss, and Michael Buckley. 1988. *China, a Travel Survival Kit.* South Yarra, Australia: Lonely Planet.

Sauer, Carl O. 1930. "Historical Geography and the Western Frontier," in *Trans-Mississippi West.* Proceedings of a conference held at the University of Colorado. Boulder, Colo.: n.p.

Scalapino, R. A., ed. 1972. *Elites in the People's Republic of China.* Seattle: University of Washington Press.

Schafer, Edward H. 1963. *The Golden Peaches of Samarkand: A Study of T'ang Exotics.* Berkeley: University of California Press.

Schinz, Alfred. 1989. *Cities in China.* Berlin: Gebruder Borntraeger.

Schomberg, R. C. F. 1979 (1933). *Peaks and Plains of Central Asia.* Lahore, Pakistan: Al Biruni.

Schurmann, Franz. 1968. *Ideology and Organization in Communist China.* Berkeley: University of California Press.

Schwarz, Henry G. 1963. "Chinese Migration to Northwest China and Inner Mongolia, 1949–1959," *China Quarterly,* 16: 62–74.

——. 1984. *The Minorities of Northern China: A Survey.* Bellingham: Center for East Asian Studies, Western Washington University.

"The Second Official List of Noted State Historic and Cultural Cities." 1987. *China City Planning Review,* 3.3: 65–75.

Serruys, Henry. 1982. "Towers in the Northern Frontier Defenses of the Ming," *Ming Studies,* 14: 9–76.

Shabad, Theodore. 1972. *China's Changing Map: National and Regional Development, 1949–1971.* New York: Praeger.

Sickman, Laurence, and Alexander Soper. 1956. *The Art and Architecture of China.* Baltimore: Penguin Books.

Sinor, Dennis. 1969. *Inner Asia.* Bloomington: Indiana University Press.

Sit, Victor F. S., ed. 1985. *Chinese Cities: The Growth of the Metropolis Since 1949.* Hong Kong: Oxford University Press.

Skinner, G. William, ed. 1977. *The City in Late Imperial China.* Stanford, Calif.: Stanford University Press.

Skinner, Stephen. 1982. *The Living Earth Manual of Feng-Shui: Chinese Geomancy.* London: Routledge & Kegan Paul.

Smith, Nicol. 1940. *Burma Road.* New York: Garden City Publishing.

Snellgrove, David, and Hugh Richardson. 1986. *A Cultural History of Tibet.* Boston: Shambala Press.

Snodgrass, Adrian. 1985. *The Symbolism of the Stupa.* Ithaca, N.Y.: Cornell University Press.

Speiser, Werner. 1965. *Oriental Architecture in Colour.* London: Thames & Hudson.

Spence, Jonathan D. 1990. *The Search for Modern China.* New York: Norton.

Spencer, Joseph. 1947. "The Houses of the Chinese," *Geographical Review,* 37.3: 254–73.

Stein, Aurel. 1987 (1912). *Ruins of Desert Cathay: Personal Narrative of Explorations in Central Asia and Westernmost China.* New York: Dover.

————. 1983 (1921). *Serindia: Detailed Report of Explorations in Central Asia and Westernmost China*. Delhi: Motilal Banarsidass.

————. 1925. "Innermost Asia: Its Geography as a Factor in History," 2 parts, *Geographical Journal*, 65, May and June.

Stein, R. A. 1972. *Tibetan Civilization*. Stanford, Calif.: Stanford University Press.

Steinhardt, Nancy Schatzman. 1984. *Chinese Traditional Architecture*. New York: China Institute.

————. 1990. *Chinese Imperial City Planning*. Honolulu: University of Hawaii Press.

Stevens, Stan. 1992. "Tibet: Land of Snows," in *The Year of Tibet: Resilience of a Culture*. South Asia Working Paper No. 1, University of Hawaii at Manoa.

Stevenson, Paul Huston. 1932. "Notes on the Human Geography of the Chinese-Tibetan Borderland," *Geographical Review*, 22.4: 599–616.

Sun Jingzhi, ed. 1988. *The Economic Geography of China*. Hong Kong: Oxford University Press.

Swain, Margaret Byrne. 1990. "Commoditizing Ethnicity in Southwest China," *Cultural Survival Quarterly*, 14.1: 26–29.

Tan Manni. 1981. "Urumqi: Multinational City in China's Far West," *China Reconstructs*, 30.1 (Jan.): 32–39.

Tapp, Nicholas. 1986. "Geomancy as an Aspect of Upland-Lowland Relations," in *The Hmong in Transition*, ed. G. Hendrick, A. Deinard, and B. Downing. New York: Center for Migration Studies of New York, Inc., and the Southeast Asian Refugee Studies Project of the University of Minnesota.

Taylor, Romeyn. 1977. "Ming T'ai-Tsu and the Gods of the Walls and Moats," *Ming Studies*, 3: 31–49.

Teichman, Eric. 1921. *Travels of a Consular Officer in North-West China*. Cambridge: Cambridge University Press.

Theroux, Paul. 1988. *Riding the Iron Rooster: By Train Through China*. London: Penguin Books.

Thompson, Laurence G. 1989. *Chinese Religion*. Belmont, Calif.: Wadsworth.

Thubten Legshay Gyatsho. 1979. *Gateway to the Temple: A Manual of Tibetan Monastic Customs, Art, Building and Celebrations*, tr. David Paul Jackson. Kathmandu: Ratna Pustak Bhandar.

Tregear, T. R. 1965. *A Geography of China*. Chicago: Aldine.

Turner, Frederick Jackson. 1986 (1920). *The Frontier in American History*. Tucson: University of Arizona Press.

Twitchett, Denis. 1966. "The T'ang Market System," *Asia Major*, 12.2: 202–48.

————. 1968. "Merchant, Trade and Government in Late T'ang," *Asia Major*, 14.1: 63–95.

Van Nostrand, J. J. 1941. "The Problems of Cultural Frontiers," in *Frontiers of the Future*. Los Angeles: University of California Press.

Vasil'ev, Vasilij Pavlovich. 1960. *Islam in China*, tr. Rudolf Lowenthal. Washington, D.C.: Central Asian Collectanea.

Vogel, Ezra. 1969. *Canton Under Communism: Programs and Policies in a Provincial Capital, 1949–1968*. Cambridge, Mass.: Harvard University Press.

Von Glahn, Richard. 1987. *The Country of Streams and Grottoes: Expansion, Settlement, and the Civilizing of the Sichuan Frontier in Song Times.* Cambridge, Mass.: Council on East Asian Studies, Harvard University.

Von Grunebaum, G. E. 1961. *Islam: Essays in the Nature and Growth of a Cultural Tradition.* New York: Barnes & Noble.

Waardenburg, Jacques. 1991. "Islam in China: Western Studies," in Shirin Akiner, ed., *Cultural Change and Continuity in Central Asia.* New York: Kegan Paul International.

Waddell, L. Austine. 1988 (1905). *Lhasa and Its Mysteries, with a Record of the British Tibetan Expedition of 1903–1904.* New York: Dover.

Wade, Richard. 1959. *The Urban Frontier: The Rise of Western Cities, 1790–1830.* Cambridge, Mass.: Harvard University Press.

Waldron, Arthur. 1990. *The Great Wall of China, from History to Myth.* Cambridge: Cambridge University Press.

Wallacker, B. E., and R. G. Knapp. 1979. *Chinese Walled Cities: A Collection of Maps from Shina Jokaku no Gaiyo.* Hong Kong: Chinese University Press.

Watt, John R. 1977. "The Yamen and Urban Administration," in G. W. Skinner, ed., *The City in Late Imperial China.* Stanford, Calif.: Stanford University Press.

Webb, Walter Prescott. 1951. *The Great Frontier.* Austin: University of Texas Press.

Weber, Max. 1951. *The Religion of China: Confucianism and Taoism.* Glencoe, Ill.: Free Press.

Wheatley, Paul. 1971. *Pivot of the Four Quarters.* Chicago: Aldine.

Wheatley, Paul, and T. See. 1978. *From Court to Capital: A Tentative Interpretation of the Origins of the Japanese Urban Tradition.* Chicago: University of Chicago Press.

Wieczynski, Joseph L. 1976. *The Russian Frontier: The Impact of Borderlands Upon the Course of Early Russian History.* Charlottesville: University of Virginia Press.

Wiens, Harold. 1954. *China's March Toward the Tropics.* New Haven, Conn.: Shoestring Press.

———. 1963. "The Historical and Geographical Role of Urumchi, Capital of Chinese Central Asia," *Annals of the Association of American Geographers,* 53.4: 441–64.

Wilkes, Joseph A., and Robert T. Packard, eds. 1989. *Encyclopedia of Architecture: Design, Engineering, and Construction.* New York: Wiley.

Winters, Clyde. 1979. *Mao or Muhammed: Islam in the People's Republic of China.* Hong Kong: Asian Research Service.

Woodhead, H. G. W., ed. 1924. *The China Year Book, 1924–5.* Tientsin: Tientsin Press.

Wright, Arthur F. 1959. *Buddhism in Chinese History.* Stanford, Calif.: Stanford University Press.

———. 1977. "The Cosmology of the Chinese City," in G. W. Skinner, ed., *The City in Late Imperial China.* Stanford, Calif.: Stanford University Press.

Wu, Aitchen K. 1984 (1940). *Turkistan Tumult*. Hong Kong: Oxford University Press.

Wu Liangyong. 1986. "A Brief History of Ancient Chinese City Planning," *Urbs et Regio*, 38.

Wyman, Walker D., and Clifton B. Kroeber. 1965. *The Frontier in Perspective*. Madison: University of Wisconsin Press.

Xie Yichun and Ashok Dutt. 1990. "Perspectives on City-Size and Investment Effectiveness in China," *GeoJournal*, 21.1–2: 33–38.

Xin Jiguang, ed. 1987. *Minority Peoples in China*. Beijing: China Pictorial Publications.

Xue Muqiao, ed. 1982. *Almanac of China's Economy, 1981*. Hong Kong: Modern Cultural Co.

Yaguang Geographical Society. 1936. Maps of Shandong Province, Cartographic Collection, University of Washington Library, Seattle.

Yan, Xiaopei. 1990. "The Spatial Dimension of Chinese Urbanization," *GeoJournal*, 21.1–2: 13–23.

Yang, Dali. 1990. "Patterns of China's Regional Development Strategy," *China Quarterly*, 122: 230–57.

Yang, Xianyi, and Gladys Yang. 1984. *Poetry and Prose of the Tang and Song*. Beijing: Panda Books.

Yazaki, Takeo. 1968. *Social Change and the City in Japan, from Earliest Times Through the Industrial Revolution*. Tokyo: Japan Publications.

Yoon, Hong-Key. 1980. "The Image of Nature in Geomancy," *GeoJournal*, 4.4: 341–48.

Younghusband, Francis. 1984 (1896). *Heart of a Continent*. New York: Oxford University Press.

———. 1971 (1910). *India and Tibet: A History of the Relations Which Have Subsisted Between the Two Countries from the Time of Warren Hastings to 1910, with a Particular Account of the Mission to Lhasa of 1904*. Delhi: Oriental Publishers.

———. 1926. *Peking to Lhasa: The Narrative of the Journeys in the Chinese Empire Made by the Late Brigadier-General George Pereira*. Boston: Houghton Mifflin.

Yuan, Qingli. 1990. "Population Changes in the Xinjiang Uighur Autonomous Region (1949–1984)," *Central Asian Survey*, 9.1: 49–73.

Zelinsky, Wilbur. 1973. *The Cultural Geography of the United States*. Englewood Cliffs, N.J.: Prentice-Hall.

Zhao Songqiao. 1994. *Geography of China*. New York: Wiley.

Zlatkin, I. Ja. 1964. *Istorija Dzhungarskogo Khanstva, 1635–1758*. Moscow: n.p.

Zou Deci. 1986. "A Brief Introduction to the Urban Development and Planning Systems in China," *Chengshi Guihua (Yingwenban)* (China city planning review, English ed.), 2.1: 79–84.

Sources in Chinese and Japanese

Bi Yading. 1986. "Wulumuqi" (Urumqi), *Siluyou*, 1.1: 46–47.

Bian Kui, Tang Peize, Chang Fuxing, and Zhou Wenlin. 1986. *Bianchui gudao* (Ancient road of the fronter): *The Silk Road in the Southwest of China*. Kunming: Yunnan Jiaoyu Chubanshe.

Bo Guangzhang and Re Bi. 1983. *"Gaoyuan gucheng — Lasa"* (Ancient city of the high plateau: Lhasa), *Chengshi Guihua*, 34.1.

Chai Jisen. 1984. "Biancheng yinhang shihua" (The history of banking in a frontier city), *Wulumuqi Wenshi Ciliao*, 7: 99–110.

Changjiang. 1982. Map. Beijing: Zhongguo Ditu Chubanshe.

Chen Jun et al., eds. 1985. *Qinghai fengwuzhi* (Gazetteer of Qinghai scenery). Xining: Qinghai Renmin Chubanshe.

Chen Kangya. 1936. *Xibei shicha ji* (Records of an inspection of the northwest). Hankou: Shanghai Zhongbaoguan.

Chen Meihe. 1986. *Ta'ersi jianzhu* (The architecture of Taer Temple). Beijing: Zhongguo Jianzhu Gongye Chubanshe.

Chen Qiaoyi, ed. 1986. *Zhongguo lishi mingcheng* (China's famous historical cities). Beijing: Zhongguo Qingnian Chubanshe.

Chen Zheng. 1986. "Lanzhou diming kao" (Investigations of place-names in Lanzhou), *Diming Zhishi*, 5: 18–20.

Cheng Guangsu. 1953. *Zhongguo dushi* (Great cities of China). Taibei: Zhongguo Wenhua Chubanshe.

Cheng Taosheng. 1987. *Jincheng manhua* (Comments on "Metal Ramparts" [Lanzhou]). Lanzhou: Gansu Renmin Chubanshe.

Cihai (Word ocean dictionary). 1979. Shanghai: Shanghai Cishu Chubanshe.

Cui Jianwen. 1987. "Jiefangqian lanzhou de yinhangye" (Banking in prerevolutionary Lanzhou), in *Lanzhou fenglai*, listed below, pp. 16–17.

Dai Xueji, ed. 1981. *Huhehaote jianshi* (A short history of Hohhot). Beijing: Zhonghua Shuju.

Dangdai zhongguo de chengshi jianshe (Contemporary Chinese urban development). 1990. Beijing: China Building Industry Press.

Ding Shuiren, ed. 1987. *Chuncheng Kunming* (Kunming, the spring city). Shanghai: Shanghai Jiaoyu Chubanshe.

Du Yuting and Chen Lufan. 1979. *Yunnan Mengguzu jianshi* (A brief history of the Mongols of Yunnan). Kunming: Yunnan Renmin Chubanshe.

Er Chang. 1986. "Jiefangqian de nanmen shichang" (The prevolution south gate market"), *Wulumuqi Wenshi Ciliao*, 12: 73–77.

Fu Chaoching (Fu Zhaojing). 1988. "1977 nian yihou zhongguo dalu jianzhu fazhan gaikuang," 2: "Xiandai jianzhuzhong de diyu juyi quxiang" (A general review of mainland Chinese architecture since 1977, 2: Regionalist approaches in Chinese modern architecture), *Jianzhushi Taibei*, 14.12: 67–77.

Fujian minzhu (Vernacular housing of Fujian). 1987. Beijing: Zhongguo Jianzhu Gongye Chubanshe.

Fukuda Minoru. 1975. *Manshu hoten nihonjin shi* (An account of the Japanese people in Shenyang, Manchuria). Tokyo: Kenkosha.

Gan Xulan. 1987. "Jingsui tielu zaoqi gongren yundongshi zhaxi" (An analysis of the history of the workers' movement of the early period of the Beijing-Suiyuan railway), *Neimenggu Jindaishi Luncong* (Hohhot), 3: 137–58.

Gannan zangzu zizhizhou gaikuang (Basic facts about the Gannan Tibetan Autonomous Prefecture [Gansu Province]). 1987. Lanzhou: Gansu Minzu Chubanshe.

Gansusheng Lanzhoushi chengguanqu diming ziliao huipian (Gansu Province, Lanzhou City, Chengguan District place-names and collected materials). 1983. Lanzhou: Gansusheng Lanzhoushi Chengguanqu Renmin Zhengfu Chubanshe.

Gansu tongzhi (Continued annals of Gansu). 1966. Zhongguo Bianjing Yeshu No. 26. Taibei: Wenhai Chubanshe.

Gao Qinglin. 1987. "Lizu zhuantong—ruiyi chuangxin" (Have a foothold in tradition—determined and dauntless, achieve the new), *Jianzhushi*, 27.1: 30–37.

Gao Yinbiao and Wang Jizhou. 1987. *Qingcheng lansheng* (The origins of the Blue City). Shanxi Xinhua Yinzhichang.

Gong Chang. 1987. "*Lanzhou de huiguan*" (Lanzhou's local associations), in *Lanzhou fenglai*, listed below, pp. 56–57.

Guan Xiaoxian et al., eds. 1987. *Huhehaote gaikuang* (Basic facts about Hohhot). Hohhot: Neimenggu Renmin Chubanshe.

Guisui quanzhi (Complete gazetteer of Guisui). 1910. Reprint Taibei: Huawen Shuju, n.d.

Guisui xianzhi (Gazetteer of Guisui County). 1914. Taibei: Xinxiu Fangzhi Yegan.

Guisui xianzhi (Gazetteer of Guisui County). Ca. 1946. Taibei: Huawen Shuju.

Guo Licheng. 1984. *Zhongguo jindai hangsheng yanjiu* (Studies on Qing dynasty Chinese patron gods and goddesses). Taibei: Zhongguo Minsu Xuehui.

Guo Rirui. 1987. "Minzu fenge yu jiejian zhuantong" (Creating national style and drawing lessons from tradition), *Jianzhushi*, 27.1.

Hagiwara Mori. 1987. "Shindai naimooko kikajo toumeto hata no koobunsho ni tsuite" (In regard to the documents of the Tumud banner of Qing dynasty Guihua, Inner Mongolia). Taikensan Collection, Osaka University, No. 20 (Historical Section).

Han Ji et al. 1982. "Xi'an gucheng baohu guihua" (Conservation of historic monuments in Xi'an), *Chengshi Guihua*, No. 2.

He Yejiu. 1980. "Tang-Song shifang guihua zhidu yanbian tantao" (Evolution of the marketplace and ward-planning system during the Tang and Song dynasties), *Jianzhu Xuebao* (Taiwan), 2: 43–49.

Hohhot city map. 1985. Hohhot: Basic Facts Editorial Committee.

Hu Mingjun, ed. 1984. *Beifang minzu guanxi shilun cong* (Collection of historical essays on northern minority relations). Hohhot: Neimenggu Renmin Chubanshe.

Huhehaote shi (Hohhot city). 1985. Hohhot: Huhehaote Shi Renmin Zhengfu.

Huhehaoteshi dimingzhi (Hohhot gazetteer of place-names). 1985. Hohhot: Huhehaote Shi Renmin Zhengfu.

Imamizu, Seiji. 1988. "Chugoku ni okeru kaimin shoogyoo shihon ni kansuru kenkyuu" (Research on the trade and capital assets of China's Hui people), *Shigaku Ronmura*, No. 1.

Japan, Koka Rikugun. 1939. Maps of the Japanese Military Occupation Army in China.

Ji Nong. 1987. "Gudai Lanzhou de chama jiaochang" (Lanzhou's ancient tea and horse market), in *Lanzhou fenglai*, listed below, p. 38.

Jiangnan tongzhi. (Annals of Jiangnan). 1968. Taibei: Xuesheng Shuju.

Jilin minzhu (Vernacular housing of Jilin). 1985. Beijing: Zhongguo Jianzhu Gongye Chubanshe.

Jilin shiji (Gazetteer of Jilin Province). 1984. Jilin: Jilin Renmin Chubanshe.

Jin Qi. 1987. "Huhehaote zhaomiao, qingzhensi lishi gaishu" (Historical reviews of Hohhot's Lamaist temples and mosques), in *Zhongguo mengushi xuehui lunwen xuangji*. Hohhot: Neimenggu Renmin Chubanshe.

Jin Xuanjiu. 1987. *Yisilanjiao gailun* (Basic facts about Islam). Xining: Qinghai Renmin Chubanshe.

Kunming diqu de mingsheng guji (Famous sites in the Kunming area). 1962. Kunming: Kunming Zhipian Weiyuan Hui.

Kunming minzu minsu he zongjiao diaocha (Investigations of Kunming's minorities' customs and religions). 1985. Kunming: Yunnan Minzu Chubanshe.

Kunming shiqing (About Kunming city). 1987. Kunming: Kunmingshi Renmin Zhengfu Jingji Yanjiu Zhongxin.

Kunming xianzhi (Gazetteer of Kunming county). 1902 (1887). Taibei: Chengwen Chubanshe.

Kunmingshi zhi (Gazetteer of the city of Kunming). 1920s. Kunming: n.p.

La Bingde and Kong Xianglu. 1985. "Mingwen xiaer de Xining Dongguan Qingzhen Dasi" (Xining's renowned Great Mosque), *Qinghai Minzu Xueyuan Xuebao*, 11.2: 57–63.

Lanzhou fenglai (Spirit of Lanzhou). 1987. Lanzhou: Gansu Renmin Chubanshe.

Lanzhou gujin zhu (Lanzhou old and new). 1922 (reprints 1943, 1986). Lanzhou: n.p.

Lanzhou wenshi ciliao xuanji (Compilation of selected materials on Lanzhou's cultural history), vol. 5, 1986; vol. 6, 1987. Lanzhou: Materials on Cultural History Research Committee.

Lanzhoufu zhi (Gazetteer of Lanzhou). 1834. Reprint, Taibei: Chengwen Chubanshe, n.d.

Li Lixin. 1987. "Kashi shimin maoshichang" (Kashgar civic marketplace), *Jianzhu Xuebao*, 11: 66–67.

Li Shengcai, ed. 1985. *Qinghai fengwuzhi* (Gazetteer of Qinghai landscapes). Xining: Qinghai Renmin Chubanshe.

Liu Dunzhen, ed. 1987. *Zhongguo gudai jianzhushi* (History of ancient Chinese architecture). Beijing: Zhongguo Jianzhu Gongye Chubanshe.

Liu Jian. 1987. *Wulumuqi luyou* (Urumqi tourism). Urumqi: Xinjiang Renmin Chubanshe.

Liu Man and Zhao Yun. 1986. "Xining," in Chen Qiaoyi, ed., *Zhongguo lishi mingcheng* (Famous historical cities of China). Beijing: Zhongguo Qingnian Chubanshe, pp. 433–41.

Liu Weidiao. 1988. "Xichui shoufu Wulumuqi" (Urumqi: capital city of the western border region), *Siluyou*, 1.4: 19–20.

Liu Yan. 1988. "Beijing jincheng fenqu baohu zhengzhi guihua—dui jianzhu gaodu he rongji shu'ai de tantao" (Planning for the zoning protection of Beijing), *Jianzhu Xuebao*, 12: 37–41.

Liu Yintong. 1986. "Cong shougongye dao xiandai gongye" (From handicrafts to modern industry), *Wulumuqi Wenshi Ciliao*, 12: 11–22.

Liu Zhi. 1984 (Qing ed.). *Tianfang zhi shengshilu* (Record of the most holy facts of Islam). Beijing: Zhongguo Yisilanjiao Banhui.

Liu Zhiping. 1985. *Zhongguo yisilanjiao jianzhu* (Islamic architecture of China). Urumqi: Xinjiang Renmin Chubanshe.

Liu Zhuxi. 1986. "Cong 'gandaying' xingqi de baihuoye" (From "joining the army" arises the general store), *Wulumuqi Wenshi Ciliao*, 12: 1–5.

Ma Shaoxin. 1985. "Renmin Guangchang—bianjiang jianshe de suoying" (People's Square—the epitome of frontier development), in *Jinri Xinjiang* (Xinjiang today). Beijing: Zhongguo Dianying Chubanshe.

Ma Tong. 1984. *Zhongguo Yisilanjiaopai yu Menhuan zhidu shilu* (History of China's Islamic sects and the Menhuan system). Yinchuan: Ningxia Renmin Chubanshe.

Ma Zhengming. 1984. "Minzu tuanjie de Ningxiawan" (United nationalities of Ningxiawan), *Wulumuqi Wenshi Ciliao*, 8: 149–53.

Meng Mou. 1987. "Xiao chengzhen jianshe dui woguo shaoshu minzu gongtongti de yinxiang" (The influence of the establishment of small cities and towns on China's minority nationality communities), *Minzu Yanjiu*, 1: 1–7.

Menguzu jianshi (Brief history of the Mongols). 1985. Hohhot: Neimenggu Renmin Chubanshe.

Miao Sishu, Li Geng, Qu Youxin, and Luo Faxi, eds. 1987. *Labulangsi gaikuang* (Basic facts about Labrang Monastery). Lanzhou: Gansu Minzu Chubanshe.

Mingcheng shihua (Essays on famous cities). 1984. Beijing: Zhongguo Shuju.

Murata Akifu. 1987. "Kodai chugoku ni okeru jokabe kenchiku—sengoku ki o chuushin ni" (The architecture of walls in ancient China—examples from the centers of the Warring States period), *Shigaku Kenkyu*, 175.

Neimenggu gujianzhu (Ancient architecture of Inner Mongolia). 1959. Beijing: Wenwu Chubanshe.

Neimenggu luyou (Inner Mongolian tourism). 1987. Hohhot: Neimenggu Renmin Chubanshe.

Ogawa Iro. 1988. "Shinkyoo urumuchi chiiki no koogyoo tenkai" (The industrial development of Xinjiang's Urumqi region), *Tasho Daigaku Kyooyobu Kiyo*, 21: 211–16.

Peng Yongan and Li Chongguo. 1985. *Mingcheng Dali: fazhan luyou ji fenqu wenti* (Dali: questions of tourism development and planning). Kunming: Yunnansheng Dili Yanjiusuo.

Qian Li. 1987. "Guanyu Liulichang wenhuajie gaijian de sikao" (On the reconstruction of Liulichang Street), *Jianzhu Xuebao*, No. 11.

Qianjinzhong de zhongguo yisilin (The progress of Chinese Islam). 1957. Beijing: Minzu Chubanshe.

Qiao Xi and Yang Yusheng, eds. 1985a. *Dazhaosi* (Jokhang Temple). Beijing: Zhongguo Jianzhu Gongye Chubanshe.

———. 1985b. *Luobulingka* (Norbulingka Palace). Beijing: Zhongguo Jianzhu Gongye Chubanshe.

Qingguo Shandongsheng (Qing-dynasty Shandong). 1935. Suzhou: Suzhoufu Chubanshe.

Qingguo Shandongsheng. 1936. Cartographic Collection, University of Washington Library, Seattle.

Qinghai fangzhi ciliao leipian (Edited collection of materials from Qinghai's local gazetteers and histories). 1987. Xining: Qinghai Renmin Chubanshe.

Qinghai fengwuzhi (Annals of Qinghai scenery). 1985. Xining: Qinghai Renmin Chubanshe.

Qinghai lishi jiyao (Record of important facts of Qinghai history). 1987. Xining: Qinghai Renmin Chubanshe.

Qinghai sanshiwunian (Qinghai after 35 years). 1985. Xining: Qinghai Renmin Chubanshe.

Qinghai shengqing (The status of Qinghai Province). 1986. Xining: Qinghai Renmin Chubanshe.

Qinghaisheng dili (Geography of Qinghai Province). 1987. Xining: Qinghai Renmin Chubanshe.

Qinghaisheng gaikuang (Basic facts about Qinghai Province). 1984. Xining: Qinghai Renmin Chubanshe.

Qinghua Daxue Jianzhuxi Chengshi Guihua Jiaoyanshi. 1987. "Tunxi laojie lishi diduan de baohu yu bianshiu Guihua" (Renewal and preservation planning for the historical streets of Tunxi city [Anhui Province]), *Chengshi Guihua*, 1: 21–25.

Qiong Zhong. 1987. *Zhongguo xinan bianjiang bianganshi* (History of China's southwestern borderlands). Kunming: Yunnan Jiaoyu Chubanshe.

Quanguo zhongdian wenwu baohu danwei (An introduction to China's important historical preservation units). 1982. Beijing: Wenwu Chubanshe.

Rong Yang. 1979. "Huhehaoteshi yange jiyaogao" (Draft summary of Hohhot's development and evolution). Unpublished manuscript.

Rongxian zhi (Annals of Rong County). 1936. Chongwen Chubanshe No. 208. Taibei.

Ruchengxian zhi (Annals of Rucheng County). 1932. Chongwen Chubanshe No. 312. Taibei.

Suiyuan quanzhi (Gazetteer of Suiyuan Province). 1889. Reprint Taibei: Huawen Shuju, n.d.

Suiyuan xianzhi (Gazetteer of Suiyuan County). 1909. Reprint Taibei: n.p., n.d.

Suiyuansheng fenxian diaocha gaiyao (Suiyuan Province county investigations). 1934. Hohhot: Suiyuansheng Jiaoyu Chubanshe.

Sun Dazhang. 1987. *Zhongguo gudai jianzhu shihua* (Historical narrative of ancient Chinese architecture). Beijing: Zhongguo Jianzhu Gongye Chubanshe.

Ta'ersi (Ta'er Lamasery). 1984. Xining: Qinghai Renmin Chubanshe.

Tian Tanjiang et al. 1984. *Sichou zhilu manji* (Along the ancient silk route). Beijing: Xinhua Chubanshe.

Tuanjie jianshezhong de Neimenggu 1947–1987 (The united development of Inner Mongolia, 1947–1987). 1987. Hohhot: Neimenggu Renmin Chubanshe.

Wang Shiren. 1987a. *Lixing yu langman de jiaozhi: Zhongguo jianzhu meixue lunwenji* (The interweaving of reason and romance: collected essays on aesthetics in Chinese architecture). Beijing: Zhongguo Jianzhu Gongye Chubanshe.

———. 1987b. "Cong shiji chufa jinxing chuangzuo" (Using reality, approach creation—a defense of Chengde's Qingfeng St.), *Jianzhu Xuebao*, 7: 68–70.

Wang Xuepei, Liu Guoquan, Li Xiaoyou, and Li Zhuandong, eds. 1987. *Kunming luyou zhinan* (A tourists' guide to Kunming). Beijing: Zhongguo Luyou Chubanshe.

Wu En, ed. 1987. *Neimenggu fengqing* (Inner Mongolian scene). Beijing: Renmin Ribao Chubanshe.

Wu Jide. 1986. "Yisilanjiao yu dangdai guoji zhengzhi" (Islam and international politics), in *Zongjiao lunqiao*. Kunming: Yunnan Renmin Chubanshe.

Wu Tianzhu. 1987. "Qiantan Chengde shi 'Qingfeng yi tiao jie'" (Comments on the design of Qingfeng Street, Chengde), *Jianzhu Xuebao*, 3: 38–41.

Wu Yue, Wang Huizhao, Wang Mingyong, and Yu Xianjie, eds. 1985. *Gansu fengwuzhi* (Annals of Gansu landscapes). Lanzhou: Gansu Renmin Chubanshe.

Wulumuqi luyou (Urumqi tourism). 1987. Urumqi: Xinjiang Renmin Chubanshe.

Wulumuqi Wenshi Ciliao Liaoshi. 1984. "Shaanxi dasi shigai" (History of the great Shaanxi mosque), *Wulumuqi Wenshi Ciliao*, 8: 146–48.

Xian Xiaowei and Chen Lijun. 1982. *Lanzhou dili* (The geography of Lanzhou). Lanzhou: Lanzhou Xuegan.

Xiao Lianwang. 1987. "Tianjinshi gu wenhuajie Guihua sheji" (Planning for a traditional culture street in Tianjin), *Chengshi Guihua*, 2: 18–22.

Xiningfu xinzhi (The new gazetteer of Xining). 1930s. Xining: Xining City Government.

Xiningfu xuzhi (The continued gazetteer of Xining). 1985 (1937). Xining: Qinghai Renmin Chubanshe.

Xinjiang dilizhi (Gazetteer of Xinjiang geography). 1914. Reprint Taibei: Chengwen Chubanshe, n.d.

Xinjiang weiwuer zizhiqu gaikuang (Basic facts about the Xinjiang Uygur Autonomous Region). 1985. Urumqi: Xinjiang Renmin Chubanshe.

Yamashita Kiyomi. 1988. "Chugoku kansu sho ranshuu no chishi gakuteki koosatsu" (A regional geography of Lanzhou in Gansu Province, China), *Shakai Kagaku*, No. 37.

Yang Bin. 1986. "Shiqu jiaotong de yanbian" (The evolution of city district traffic and transportation [Urumqi]), *Wulumuqi Wenshi Ciliao*, 12: 101–4.

Yang Guangrong. 1987. "Huimin jiqi jingye de xiaochi" (The Hui and their cafes), in *Lanzhou fenglai*, listed above, pp. 181–82.

Ying Ou-yang. 1930. *Zhonghua xilei fenshengtu* (An analytical atlas of China's provinces). Cartographic Collection, University of Washington Library, Seattle.

Yu Jiahua et al. 1986. *Yunnan fengwuzhi* (Gazetteer of Yunnan landscapes). Kunming: Yunnan Renmin Chubanshe.

Yu Weicheng. 1986. *Xinjiang jianzhi yange yu diming yanjiu* (The course of change and development, and place-name research, in Xinjiang). Urumqi: Xinjiang Renmin Chubanshe.

Yu Xixian. 1962. *Kunming diqu de mingsheng guji* (Famous historic sites of the Kunming region). Kunming: Kunming Zhi Pianzuan Weiyuanhui.

———. 1981. *Dianchi diqu lishi dili* (A historical geography of the Lake Dian region). Kunming: Yunnan Renmin Chubanshe.

Yu Xixian and Yu Xiqian. 1982. "Kunmingshi de zhuluo qiyuan chengzhi yanbian chengchu kuozhang jiqi dili yinsu de tantao" (Inquiry into Kunming's settlement origins, site development, district expansion, and geographical factors), *Lishi Dili*, 2: 159–66.

Yu Xueren, ed. 1987. *Qingcheng Kunming* (Spring city Kunming). Shanghai: Shanghai Jiaoyu Chubanshe.

Yun Erfeng. 1985. "Huizu zai Yunnan" (The Hui of Yunnan), *Ningxia Shehui Keshui*, 3: 53–59.

Yun Feng, ed. 1987. *Huhehaote* (Hohhot). Hohhot: Zhonggong Huhehaoteshi Wei Xuanzhuanbu.

Yunnan dizhou shixian gaikuang (Kunmingshi fence) (Basic facts about Yunnan's regions, counties, and cities, Kunming volume). 1987. Kunming: Yunnan Renmin Chubanshe.

Yunnan—keai de difang (Yunnan—a lovable place). 1984. Kunming: Yunnan Renmin Chubanshe.

Yunnan minzhu (Vernacular housing of Yunnan) 1986. Beijing: Zhongguo Jianzhu Gongye Chubanshe.

Yunnanfu zhi (Gazetteer of Kunming). 1967 (Qing ed.). Taibei: Chengwen Chubanshe.

Zan Yulin. 1983. *Wulumuqi shihua* (Essays on the history of Urumqi). Urumqi: Xinjiang Renmin Chubanshe.

———. 1984. "Huiguan manji" (Notes on local associations), *Wulumuqi Wenshi Ciliao*, 8: 80–86.

———. 1986. "Waishang yanghang yu Dihua 'maoyiquan'" (Foreign businesses and Dihua's "trade enclosure"), *Wulumuqi Wenshi Ciliao*, 12: 171–77.

Zhang Qinnan. 1987. "Cong jianzhu chuangzuo de fangxiang tan jianzhu fenge de gongxing yu gexing" (Generality and individuality of architectural style in architecture creation), *Jianzhushi*, 27.1.

Zhang Shangying. 1987. "Jiefangqian Lanzhou de yinjiang pu" (Lanzhou's pre-revolutionary silversmith shops), in *Lanzhou fenglai*, listed above.

Zhang Weiyuan and Zhang Piyu, eds. 1986. *Qinghai minzu tu'anji* (Nationalities patterns of Qinghai). Xining: Qinghai Renmin Chubanshe.

Zhang Yuhuan, ed. 1984. *Zhongguo mingta* (China's famous pagodas). Beijing: Zhongguo Luyou Chubanshe.

Zhao Kai, ed. 1986. *Keai de Qinghai* (Lovable Qinghai). Xining: Qinghai Renmin Chubanshe.

Zhao Shengshen et al. 1985. *Qinghai gudai wenhua* (Qinghai's ancient culture). Xining: Qinghai Renmin Chubanshe.

Zhao Shiqi. 1986. "Lishi wenhua mingcheng de baohu yu fazhan" (Protection and development of historical cities), *Jianzhu Xuebao*, 12: 20–22.

Zhao Shiying. 1987. "Lanzhoushi, qu, xian zhuyao diming gaige" (Important place-name transformations (and information) for Lanzhou), *Lanzhou Wenshi Ciliao Xuanji*, 6: 118–206.

Zhengningxianzhi (Annals of Zhengning County). 1968. Taibei: Taiwan Xuesheng Shuju.

Zhongguo jianzhushi (Architectural history of China). 1986. Beijing: Zhongguo Jianzhu Gongye Chubanshe.

Zhongguo lishi wenhua mingcheng zidian (Encyclopedia of famous cities in Chinese history and culture). 1985. Shanghai: Shanghai Cishu Chubanshe.

Zhongguo mingsheng cidian (A reference to famous sites in China). 1987. Shanghai: Shanghai Cishu Chubanshe.

Zhongguo Yisilin de zongjiao shenghuo (The religious life of Chinese Muslims). 1956. Beijing: Minzu Chubanshe.

Zhongguo Yisilin shenghuo (The life of China's Muslims). 1953. Beijing: Beijing Waiwen Chubanshe.

Zhonghua mingsi gucha (Historical investigations of China's famous temples). 1982. Taibei: Diqiu Chubanshe.

Zhongxiu jingyuanwei zhi (Annals of Zhongxiu Jingyuanwei). 1968. Taibei: Xuesheng Shuju.

Zhou Ganshi. 1987. "Womende xiyue he zhuyuan—shou Xinjiang xianzhushimen" (Our appreciation and best wishes to the architects of Xinjiang), *Jianzhu Xuebao*, 11: 16.

Zhu Maowei. 1986. "Jiucheng gaizao yu fengmao baocun de tantao" (An investigation of the preservation of ancient cityscapes), *Jianzhu Xuebao*, 10: 23–25.

Zhu Xianlu. 1985. *Dongguan Qingzhen Dasi* (Great Mosque of the Eastern Suburb). Xining: Qinghai Renmin Chubanshe.

Zhu Zixuan. 1988. "Jiucheng baohu zhengzhi xin tansu" (New approaches to the preservation and renovation of old cities), *Jianzhu Xuebao*, 3: 2–9.

Index

In this index an "f" after a number indicates a separate reference on the next page, and an "ff" indicates separate references on the next two pages. A continuous discussion over two or more pages is indicated by a span of page numbers, e.g., "57–59." *Passim* is used for a cluster of references in close but not consecutive sequence. City names are followed by the current name of the province or country in which each is or was located.

Library of Congress Cataloging-in-Publication Data

Gaubatz, Piper Rae.
    Beyond the Great Wall : urban form and transformation on the
  Chinese frontiers / Piper Rae Gaubatz.
        p.   cm.
    Includes bibliographical references and index.
    ISBN 0-8047-2399-0 (cloth)
    1. Urbanization—United States—History. 2. Cities and towns—
  China—Growth—History. 3. City planning—China—History.
  4. Urban geography—China—History. I. Title.
  HT384.C6G38   1996
  307.76'0973—dc20   95-2555
                                                                    CIP

⊗This book is printed on acid-free, recycled paper.